P9-AQQ-928

Josefina Figueira-McDonough, PhD
Rosemary C. Sarri, PhD
Editors

Women at the Margins
Neglect, Punishment, and Resistance

Pre-publication
REVIEWS,
COMMENTARIES,
EVALUATIONS . . .

"This is a book that has relevance across disciplines and problem areas. The chapters focus on a range of issues from welfare reform, to substance abuse, to teenage pregnancy, to women in prison, and many others. Within each chapter is a discussion of the intersection of multiple issues across women's lives. For example, the issue of substance abuse cuts across the criminal justice system; the increased emphasis on incarceration of substance abusers has resulted in a dramatic rise in the number of women in prison. It also impacts the child welfare system; mothers in prison are too often denied access to their children and decisions related to their children. It affects the public welfare system; women are denied TANF and food stamps if they have been convicted of a drug penalty. It is also an issue for the mental health system; little is known about the nature, extent, and treatment of women with addiction problems.

Although each chapter in this book stands on its own merits, the reading of the book from beginning to end presents a compelling story of the continuing marginalization of poor women and women in prisons. Chapter after chapter presents empirical evidence of how the welfare and correctional systems victimize women. They also tell the story of the strength and resolve of poor and incarcerated women, and the struggles they have won. There is much to be done, but as the authors of the chapters in the last section of this book aptly identify, resistance can make a difference."

Ann Nichols-Casebolt, PhD, MSSW
Professor and Associate Dean,
School of Social Work,
Virginia Commonwealth University,
Richmond

More pre-publication
REVIEWS, COMMENTARIES, EVALUATIONS . . .

"This book is an inspiration: Figueira-McDonough and Sarri have produced a synthetic analysis of the status of poor women in the United States, and the policies that keep them down. This comprehensive and scholarly collection of research-based essays gives voice to women in prisons and jails. They remind us that we must be dogged in our examination of disadvantage and oppression, or our failures will reduce us all. We are fortunate that they are talking."

Kathleen J. Pottick, PhD
Professor of Social Work,
Rutgers University Institute for Health,
Health Care Policy, and Aging Research,
New Brunswick, NJ

"*Women at the Margins: Neglect, Punishment, and Resistance,* edited by the highly respected scholars, Josefina Figueira-McDonough and Rosemary Sarri, examines the plight of poor women in today's society. The editors present the issues facing marginalized women in the first chapter and end the book with a call for action to address those issues. Throughout the volume, there is a special emphasis on women who have been incarcerated; there are also chapters on poor older women, pregnant teenagers, and children of women in prison. The failure of the welfare system to meet the needs of poor women and the punitive policies placing women in further jeopardy are also given attention. The authors of each chapter are carefully selected experts who have the most current knowledge about the subject matter of their chapters. It is clear, however, that this is more than just a scholarly analysis of issues confronting poor and incarcerated women—the chapters are written by scholars who care passionately about the facts and the issues and what happens to poor women in real life. The authors also utilize the art and literature of the women themselves in a way that enhances understanding of their life experiences and captures the sentiments and the context of their lives. The final section of the book focuses on what action can be taken by professional and poor women together to alleviate some of the problems examined in the preceding chapters.

This excellent book should be read by practitioners and policymakers to learn the discouraging facts about women at the margins and to consider what actions can be taken to improve conditions. I would recommend it to scholars, to practitioners, to students who want to understand how current policies have resulted in devastating life conditions for poor women, and to poor women themselves who will be able to see that there is support for them in a largely unfeeling and uncaring world."

Maeda Galinsky, PhD, MSW
Kenan Professor,
School of Social Work,
University of North Carolina
at Chapel Hill

The Haworth Press®
New York • London • Oxford

Women at the Margins
Neglect, Punishment,
and Resistance

HAWORTH Innovations in Feminist Studies
J. Dianne Garner
Senior Editor

Women at the Margins
Neglect, Punishment, and Resistance

Josefina Figueira-McDonough, PhD
Rosemary C. Sarri, PhD
Editors

The Haworth Press®
New York • London • Oxford

The Haworth Press, Inc., 10 Alice Street, Binghamton, NY 13904-1580.

Cover design by Jennifer M. Gaska.

Library of Congress Cataloging-in-Publication Data

Women at the margins : neglect, punishment, and resistance / Josefina Figueira-McDonough, Rosemary C. Sarri editors.
  p. cm.
  Includes bibliographical references and index.
  ISBN 1-56023-971-9 (alk. paper) — ISBN 1-56023-972-7 (alk. paper)
  1. Women—United States. 2. Women—United States—Social conditions. 3. Women—United States—Economic conditions. 4. Sex discrimination against women—United States. I. Figueira-McDonough, Josefina. II. Sarri, Rosemary C.

HQ1421 .W6528 2002
305.42'0973—dc21

2001051593

We wish to dedicate this book to Peter and the memory of Romilos. They have always been supportive and encouraging of our work and tolerant of the sacrifices that they had to make because of that work. Without their love, good humor, and tolerance we could not have produced the book.

CONTENTS

ABOUT THE EDITORS

Josefina Figueira-McDonough, PhD, is Professor of Justice Studies and Social Work (trained in sociology and social work) at Arizona State University, Tempe. Dr. Figueira-McDonough was trained in social work at the University of Michigan and has held faculty positions at the University of Michigan, Michigan State University, and Vanderbilt University. Her research on social justice, specifically gender, deviance and control, and the ecology of poverty, has been widely published, and her most recent book is *Community Analysis and Praxis: Towards a Grounded Civil Society.*

Rosemary C. Sarri, PhD, is Professor Emerita of Social Work and Faculty Associate for Social Research at the University of Michigan, Ann Arbor. A widely published author on the subjects of child welfare, single-mother families, the impact of social policy on families, and the justice system, she has many years of teaching and research experience in juvenile and adult criminal justice. She has served on several national and international commissions on family well-being and juvenile justice, and is currently engaged in a study of juvenile justice-structured decision-making, a study of programs for high-risk and delinquent female adolescents, and a study of minority overrepresentation in the juvenile justice system.

CONTRIBUTORS

Wendy C. Ascione received a BA from the University of Michigan in 2000, concentrating in Women's Studies (graduating with honors) and in Psychology. Her undergraduate thesis examined the effect of a mother's incarceration on her children and the availability of services and resources to assist children and mothers in coping with the incarceration. She is currently pursuing a master's degree in social work at the University of Michigan.

M. A. Bortner, PhD, is Director of the Center for Urban Inquiry at Arizona State University. Her research focuses on the imprisonment of youths and women, the equitable treatment of minority youths, and the transfer of youths to adult courts. She is the author of *Youth in Prison: We the People of Unit Four,* with Linda M. Williams (Routledge, 1997), *Delinquency and Justice: An Age of Crisis* (McGraw Hill, 1988), and *Inside A Juvenile Court: The Tarnished Ideal of Individualized Justice* (New York University Press, 1982). Professor Bortner holds a PhD in Sociology from Washington University in St. Louis and has taught at Arizona State University for twenty years.

Anna Celeste Burke, PhD, is Associate Professor and Research Officer for the College of Social Work at The Ohio State University. Teaching and research interests include outcome measurement, organizational behavior and performance, employment, substance abuse, and mental health and welfare reform issues. She has written more than forty reports and articles in these areas. Her most recent article, "Outcomes Based Evaluation: Issues of Technology Transfer and Relevance for Social Intervention" appears in *The Journal of Social Work Research and Evaluation.* She currently directs two large studies examining treatment services in substance abuse and mental health settings and has provided outcomes training to thousands of service providers and other community members.

Joyce Dixson received her MSW from the University of Michigan and practiced social work for several years working with juvenile delinquents. She observed that many of these youths had parents in prisons and jails and decided to do something about it. She organized a new agency, SADOI (Sons and Daughters of the Incarcerated) in 1996 and provided innovative services to youths in southeastern Michigan. She continues to work in this area but also has assisted in the development of new programs in many states.

Paula L. Dressel, PhD, is Professor of Sociology and Associate Dean for Graduate Studies and International and Community Partnerships at Georgia

State University in Atlanta. Her research focuses on understanding various dimensions of inequalities; her advocacy and community work seeks to advance policy and practice that promote equity. She is also Senior Fellow at the Annie E. Casey Foundation in Baltimore, the nation's largest foundation with assets devoted exclusively to improving the lives of at-risk children. There she directs research and development activities that inform the Foundation's strategic planning efforts.

Janet L. Finn, PhD, is Associate Professor of Social Work and Anthropology at the University of Michigan. She is the author of *Tracing the Veins: Of Culture, Copper and Community from Butte to Chuquicamata* (Berkeley: University of California Press, 1998), a cultural and political history of two Anaconda Company mining towns. Her current projects include "Women Building Community: Lessons from the Andes to the Rockies," a cross-national participatory study of seven grassroots women's initiatives and "La Victoria/Rescatando La Historia," a participatory documentary about a Chilean community founded in a 1957 land takeover. She is co-authoring with Maxine Jacobson a new social work text entitled *Just Practice: A Social Justice Introduction to Social Work* (Dubuque: E. Bowers, forthcoming 2002). Her article, "The Tracing of Villa Jaraquemada: Building Community in Chile's Transition to Democracy," appeared in *Community Development Journal 36*(3), 2001.

Edith Elisabeth Flynn, PhD, is Professor of Criminal Justice at Northeastern University in Boston. Dr. Flynn specializes in corrections, policy research, personnel management, criminal justice administration, and political crimes. She has testified before the U.S. Congress on corrections policies and has acted in an advisory capacity to past and present U.S. attorney generals. She has also served in leadership positions in the American Society of Criminology, the Society for the Study of Social Problems, and the American Correctional Association. She has conducted a national research project on the management of elderly offender populations in the nation's prisons and jails.

Joel F. Handler is the Richard C. Maxwell Professor of Law at UCLA Law School and Professor of Policy Studies at UCLA School of Public Policy and Social Research. He has written extensively on poverty, social welfare, social movements, and empowerment. His book *Down from Bureaucracy: The Ambiguity of Privatization and Empowerment* was awarded the American Political Science Association 1997 Gladys Kammerer Award for the best political science publication in the field of U.S. national policy. In 1999, he received the ACLU Foundation of Southern California Distinguished Professor Award for Civil Liberties Education.

Nancy J. Harm, PhD, has been Associate Professor at the School of Social Work, University of Arkansas at Little Rock, for ten years. Prior to that she worked in the fields of mental health, corrections, and domestic violence.

Her dissertation was a historical study of social policy toward female prisoners in Illinois. She is active in the domestic violence arena and with community groups working for public education and resources for female prisoners, their children, and their children's caregivers. Her publications and research have primarily focused on issues related to women prisoners.

Deborah LaBelle, JD, is a civil rights attorney whose legal practice over the past decade has focused on addressing the human rights of people in detention. Ms. LaBelle has been lead counsel in over a dozen class actions that have successfully challenged policies affecting and treatment of incarcerated men, women, juveniles, and their families, using innovative legal theories. Outside the courtroom, Ms. LaBelle has been a strong advocate for new discourses on crime and punishment, and instrumental in initiating model projects for change. Ms. LaBelle was the first American to be designated as a Human Rights Monitor by Human Rights Watch for her work on behalf of women prisoners in the United States and was awarded the Champion of Justice award by the State Bar of Michigan, where her practice is located.

Yvonne Luna is a PhD candidate in the School of Justice Studies and Instructor in Women's Studies at Arizona State University. She is a 2000-2001 recipient of a Philanthropic Educational Organization scholar award and Arizona State University Faculty Women's Association Distinguished Achievement Award for Doctoral Candidate. Her research and activism have been in the areas of poverty, inequality, and domestic violence. She is a board member of the Arizona Coalition Against Domestic Violence and is Co-chair of its Women of Color committee.

Harriette Pipes McAdoo, PhD, is Professor in the Department of Family and Child Ecology, Michigan State University at East Lansing. She is the recipient of an MSU Distinguished Faculty Award. She previously was on the faculty at Howard University. Her teaching and research interests center on the social, educational, and parental environment of black children and the psychology of African Americans and black families. Her work documents the social and psychological development and experiences of people of the African diaspora, and she has published widely on this subject, including the nationally acclaimed *Black Families* (Third Edition, Sage Publications, 1997), *Family Ethnicity: Strength in Diversity* (Second Edition, Sage Publications, 1999), and *Black Children: Social, Educational and Parental Environments* (Sage Publications, 1985). She has spent several summers working in AIDS-related programs in Africa.

Elizabeth A. Mulroy, PhD, is Professor at the School of Social Work, University of Maryland–Baltimore, where she teaches courses in Communities and Organizations, Program Management, and Social Planning. She previously held faculty appointments at the University of Hawaii–Manoa. She earned her PhD from the School of Urban and Regional Planning and her MSW at the University of Southern California. Her research interests include women and housing, family-focused community building, and interorganizational collaboration. Her recent (selected) publications include "Starting Small: Strategy and the Evolutions of Structure in an Interorganizational Collaboration" in *The Journal of Community Practice, 8* (4), 2000, and "Building a Neighborhood Network: Interorganizational Collaboration to Prevent Child Abuse and Neglect" (1997) in *Social Work.* She has published two books, *The New Uprooted: Single Mothers In Urban Life* (Auburn House Press, 1995) and *Women as Single Parents: Confronting Institutional Barriers in the Courts, the Workplace, and the Housing Market* (Auburn House Press, 1998), which she edited.

Patricia O'Brien, PhD, MSW, is Assistant Professor at the Jane Addams College of Social Work, University of Illinois at Chicago, teaching social work practice, group work, and practice with women. She is the principal investigator on a National Institute of Justice–funded study of recidivism and reintegration of women exiting prison in Illinois. She is also evaluating a state-funded pilot initiative that supports the integration of services for women affected by both substance abuse and domestic violence. She was a recipient of the 1999 Council of Social Work Education Women's Commission Feminist Scholarship Award for her book, *Making It in the Free World: Women in Transition from Prison* (Albany: State University of New York Press, 2001).

Diana M. Pearce, PhD, is widely recognized for coining the phrase "the feminization of poverty." She received her PhD in Sociology and Social Work from the University of Michigan, and has taught at the University of Illinois, American University, as a Fulbright Professor in Tashkent, Uzbekistan, and currently at the University of Washington. She has testified before the U.S. Congress and the President's Working Group on Welfare Reform, and has helped found and lead several coalitions, such as the Women, Work, and Welfare Coalition. She founded the Women and Poverty Project at Wider Opportunities for Women in Washington, DC, and created the Self-Sufficiency Standard, now calculated for fifteen states/cities.

Sheryl Pimlott is a doctoral candidate in psychology and women's studies at the University of Michigan. She has had extensive experience working as a practitioner with female prisoners, including developing one of the first programs for pregnant women and their children in 1993. She has conducted training in substance abuse education and treatment for the Department of Corrections. She has collaborated on several research projects on juvenile and adult criminal justice, including an evaluation of a program for children of incarcerated mothers. She is currently completing a study of access to welfare for women convicted of a felony drug offense. She has served as a lecturer in social work and women's studies.

Judy Walruff, PhD, is Senior Program Officer with the Flinn Foundation, a Phoenix-based philanthropic endowment. She holds a master's degree in social work from the University of Kansas and a PhD from Arizona State University. Prior to coming to the Foundation, Dr. Walruff was an administrator of public child and family social services in Colorado and Arizona. In the ten years since coming to Foundation, she has been responsible for various program initiatives to address the health and social consequences related to teenage pregnancy and parenting. At present she is overseeing a three-year initiative, Community Partnerships to Reduce Teenage Pregnancy.

Deborah M. Whitley, PhD, is Associate Professor in the School of Social Work at Georgia State University, Atlanta, Georgia. She also is currently Associate Director of Project Healthy Grandparents, a home-based health and social research and services program targeted to grandparents and great-grandparents raising their grandchildren. Most of her professional work centers on social and health care policy issues relative to family functioning. Her most recent publications explore the health and psychological effects of parenting by grandparent caregivers.

Deborah Zinn, PhD, currently lives and works in Pueblo, Colorado, and Melbourne, Australia. Having left the world of working for large corporations in the mid-1990s, she is an artist and sociologist. Zinn graduated with a PhD in sociology and social work from the University of Michigan in 1984. From 1990 to 1995 she was also Adjunct Faculty Member of The Melbourne Business School, The University of Melbourne Australia.

Foreword

When Congress repealed the Aid to Families with Dependent Children program in 1996 and established the punitive and coercive Temporary Assistance to Needy Families Program (TANF) in its place, it set in motion a series of policy changes that degrade poor mothers, punish their families, and undermine their independence. Although welfare "reform" claimed to move poor mothers from welfare to work, it did nothing to move poor mothers out of poverty. Although welfare reform claimed to improve the circumstances of poor children, it actually exposes children to severe economic instability and want and denies them caregiving from their own mothers.

The very structure of TANF, the new welfare policy, assures that families that need welfare will remain poor. In 1999, the median income for employed former TANF recipients was $10,924—considerably below the poverty line of $14,150 for a family of three. The TANF work requirement sends mothers into low-wage jobs in a labor market poisoned by a racialized gender wage gap—usually with little in the way of social supports for their families. Restrictive definitions of "work activities" mean that mothers who seek education and skills training cannot receive it for more than one year. Mothers who cannot forego their caregiving responsibilities unless they can find child care have been stripped of their entitlement to child care under the new welfare law. Many families end up spending 25 percent of their incomes on child care. These same families often lose Medicaid when they move into jobs, even though they remain entitled to receive it, because of bureaucratic decisions; and, in the low-wage sector, they typically are not provided health benefits by employers. Thus, families become medically, as well as economically, indigent.

TANF asserts that working outside the home is more "responsible" and socially legitimate than working inside the home caring for one's own children. Notably, however, TANF imposes this view only on poor women. At the same time that TANF pushes poor mothers into the labor market, White House conferences, scholarly reports, and public debate focus on the significant role of at-home parents in the emotional and intellectual development of children.

Bill Clinton rode his "ending welfare as we know it" slogan into the White House in 1992. Soon, both Republicans and Democrats—and feminists—joined the campaign to "reform" welfare by forcing mothers who need income support into the labor market. This strategy to change welfare policy obscured the causes and circumstances of poverty and generated a law that disregards poor mothers' citizenship guarantees while ensuring their dependence on government rules about how they should conduct their family lives.

In 2002, Congress must revisit TANF to decide whether to reauthorize funding for it. This important volume will advance the reauthorization debate, illuminating the issues that must be confronted by those who value *all* women's liberty and equality.

Patsy Takemoto Mink
Member of Congress
Democrat, Hawaii

Acknowledgments

This book is the fruition of research and work that we have done together for many years because of our commitment to understand and advocate for improved opportunities and well-being for marginalized women and their children. Our special appreciation goes to the women we have known in prison, on welfare, in family violence centers, and to those in many support and advocacy organizations who have worked relentlessly to enhance social policy for poor and disadvantaged women. With the probability that there will be many changes in social policies affecting marginalized women in the years ahead, we encourage advocates and policymakers to consult with the women and families most affected by these social policies.

Special appreciation goes to Judge John Feikens whose efforts to secure equal opportunities in education and legal services for women in prison benefited them enormously. His decisions in the *Glover v. Johnson* case were among the first in the United States to address the tragic plight of thousands of women in prison.

Our very deep appreciation also goes to Mary Fran Draisker who edited and performed myriad tasks involved in producing the final manuscript. We are also grateful to Dean Ann Schneider of the College of Public Programs at Arizona State University for her support and encouragement. The foundation for the book began with a conference held in Tempe in 1999: Cultural Forum on Prison and Welfare Policies: Economic Exclusion, Public Control, and Hidden Apartheid. Thanks also to our hundreds of students who have provided important critiques of policies and programs for marginalized women for many years. In so many ways that they are unaware of, they have helped us tremendously.

We appreciate the contributions of the several authors who were patient about providing us with two to three versions of their chapters. Without their efforts we could not have the range of topics covered in the book and also have careful critiques of policies and problems affecting women at the margins.

Introduction to Art
and Women at the Margins

Deborah Zinn

The category of OTHER is as primordial as consciousness itself. In the most primitive societies, in the most ancient mythologies, one finds the expression of a duality—that of the Self and Other. . . . No group ever sets itself up as the One without at once setting up the Other over against itself.

Simone de Beauvoir
(1974; also cited in Hall and Metcalf, 1994)

Many of the chapters in this book are prefaced by a picture, poem, or text by a female author who has been or is a welfare recipient or a prisoner.

WHY ART?

Art humanizes the creator and the audience.

Art is about beauty, nature, confrontation, thought.

Women prisoners contribute to the debates implicit within this book. On a daily basis, they experience the "politics of control"; they are dehumanized. When they are allowed or encouraged to express themselves through art, they reflect their ideas and concerns in a way that no academic treatise can hope to achieve.

The examples of art prefacing each chapter are the contributions of "women at the margins" to this book. In selecting them, we wish to support this growing body of work and to let the art speak to the readers directly.

Why Prisoner Art?

We have chosen to use prisoner art exclusively because prisoners represent the many roles of marginalized women. Most women prisoners are poor—before, during, and after their time in prison. Many will be mothers before, during, and after. The connection is baldly stated by Jeffrey Reiman (1998): *The Rich Get Richer and the Poor Get Prison.*

In addition, the importance of prisoner art—for the prisoners, the art world, and society—is growing. For prison artists, as for all artists, art provides a way to express, communicate, and empower.

Kathryn Watterson (1996) in *Women in Prison* implicitly reveals the importance of art in developing her 1973 exposé of the prison system. Sadly, in the second edition (twenty-three years after her original work), she decried that the number of women in prison had grown from around 23,000 to more than 108,000.

Watterson quotes Jean Harris (1991), who spent twelve years in Bedford Hills for homicide [and] who wrote in her fine book *Marking Time:*

> In here, God knows, life is not a rose garden. . . . Nothing lovely flourishes here. Little that is good is nourished here. What grows here is hypocrisy, obscenity, illness, illegality, ignorance, confusion, waste, hopelessness. Life in prison is a garden of dross, cultivated by those who never check to see what their crop is. (Watterson, 1996, p. xvi)

How Prisoner Art?

Phyllis Kornfeld's (1997) *Cellblock Visions* provides intriguing insight into the world of prison art, based on her many years as an art teacher in prisons. Her first chapter, "The Penitentiary As Art Studio," captures the challenges that prisoners face. These challenges range from emotional decisions about subject matter to practical challenges, such as medium and materials.

Those of us who have never been inside a prison but who may have had the opportunity to see or purchase prisoner art will immediately understand why prison visual artists employ "unusual" art materials—such as paper scraps, shreds of tobacco, soap, or toilet paper. Traditional materials, such as acrylic paints or watercolors, are also used, but may be too costly, forbidden, or inaccessible.

Kornfeld features brief histories and the work of three women artists: Karen Brown, Lenore Scott, and Crystal Stimpson who paintings preface chapters of this book.

Where to Purchase?

Outsider art, folk art, art, craft

Debates abound about this genre within the art world. Although in some instances art has been perceived to be at odds with commerce, sales figures do attest to the increasing recognition and appreciation of prisoner art.

In reviewing artwork, we have been very impressed by the scope and power of the works, ranging from photographic essays to poetry to textiles to drama to painting and sculpture. If you, too, have been captivated by the possibilities, we encourage you to attend local exhibitions and to experience the power for yourself. We have been able to tantalize only. Check your local newspaper for announcements of galleries, prison gift shops, or shows near you.

Galleries

> Cavin-Morris Gallery, New York City, New York
> Hourglass Gallery, Albuquerque, New Mexico
> Phyllis Kind Gallery, New York City, New York
> Prison Museum Gift Shop, Cañon City, Colorado
> Webb-Parsons Gallery, Burlington, Vermont

On the Web

> Prison Creative Arts Project (PCAP) <http://www.prisonarts.org>
> Phyllis Kind Gallery (New York) <http://www.phylliskindgallery.com>
> Cavin-Morris Gallery (New York) <http://www.artincontext.org/new_york/cavin_morris_gallery/>
> Raw Vision (Magazine) <http://www.rawvision.com/>

Mail Order

Carol Strick has organized several large shows featuring prisoner art and can be contacted via mail for enquiries to purchase. Her address is: Carol Strick, 3516 Whitehall Drive, Apt. 101, Palm Beach, Florida 33401.

Shows

Many of the visual works prefacing these chapters were initially exhibited at "The Annual Exhibition of Art by Michigan Prisoners." This exhibition now features about 135 artists from thirty-five state prisons. Thirty of these artists were women from Michigan's two state women's correctional facilities. Held each year at the University of Michigan in February, the exhibition and related events (including speakers, dialogues, performances, workshops, readings, a panel of artists, and videos) attract approximately 2,000 visitors.

As the exhibition description states:

> The range of artistic experience and skill is wide. . . . The subject matter covers every possibility. . . . [W]e look for originality of vision, for depth, for images that penetrate.
>
> A majority of the artists were not artists before they entered prison. . . . The majority come from very poor backgrounds and school systems and have had meager advantages and opportunities. . . . Exhibiting at the University of Michigan is a powerful breakthrough for them, as many of them testify, and contributes to their crucial processes of growth, increasing self-esteem, achievement, and rehabilitation. (Alexander and Paul, 1999)

REFERENCES

Alexander, Buzz and Janie Paul. 1999. "Description: The Annual Exhibition of Art by Michigan Prisoners." Unpublished.

de Beauvoir, Simone. 1974. *The Second Sex* (trans. and ed. H. M. Parshley). New York: Vintage Books.

Harris, Jean. 1991. *Marking Time: Letters from Jean Harris to Shana Alexander.* New York: Schribner's.

Jones, Hettie (Ed.). 1997. The Writing Workshop, Bedford Hills Correctional Facility. *Aliens at the Border.* New York: Segue Books.

Kornfeld, Phyllis. 1997. *Cellblock Visions.* Princeton, NJ: Princeton University Press.

Reiman, Jeffrey. 1998. *The Rich Get Richer and the Poor Get Prison: Ideology, Class and Criminal Justice* (Fifth Edition). Boston: Allyn & Bacon.

Watterson, Kathryn. 1996. *Women in Prison: Inside the Concrete Womb* (Second Edition). Boston: Northeastern University Press.

(The) Writing Workshop, Bedford Hills Correctional Facility. 1997. *Aliens at the Border* (Hettie Jones, ed.). New York: Segue Books.

Chapter 1

Increasing Inequality: The Ascendancy of Neoconservatism and Institutional Exclusion of Poor Women

Josefina Figueira-McDonough
Rosemary C. Sarri

The poor no longer the creators of wealth
But an expensive nuisance

W. H. Auden

The recession of the early 1980s was handled by cutting welfare and other programs addressing the urgent needs of citizens in poverty, while government decisions greatly benefited affluent groups. A trickle-down rationale justified these policies. The response to the 2001 recession has been molded along the same lines, although the evidence for the trickle-down effect is lacking.

To examine the process of exclusion in the second half of the 1990s when the nation experienced an economic boom, is particularly enlightening. Distributive injustice in times of economic contraction can be blamed on erroneous theories, but hardships imposed on the most vulnerable citizens in a period of affluence require a more complex explanation.

Focusing on the struggles and imprisonment of poor women highlights how welfare and correctional systems have robbed them of their citizenship status and treated them as expendable. These institutions achieve this outcome by constructing a holistic definition of such women as deviant, in fact attributing to them an "other" identity which blocks empathy from the rest of society. Furthermore, the distance and isolation created by stigma and prison walls have the effect of rendering their realities invisible.

The marginality of poor women is not new. Historical evidence on how women in poverty and behind bars have been treated in the United States

5

abounds. While acknowledging the past, the focus of this book is on the present. We need to frame the discussion within the current economic restructuring and the neoconservative ideology shaping policies that affect poor women. Since our purpose is to analyze the constraints imposed on women who are poor and behind bars, the growing economic inequality and the neoconservative ideology that shaped the policies provide a necessary context for discussion.

The oppression of women is embedded in circumstances that oppress others as well. The specific mechanisms that force women toward the margins are located within this broader context.

THE LAISSEZ-FAIRE MYTH, THE NEOCONSERVATIVES, AND THE LIBERAL MODEL OF WELFARE

Economic Restructuring and Inequality

Capitalism brings with it the expectation of inequality. Markets are built on competition—some participants will win; others will lose. Streaks of winning will make future wins easier and result in the accumulation of capital, the engine for further growth. The utilitarian assumption is that, regardless of inequality, the whole will be better off (Kuttner, 1984).

Government regulations, taxation, and income transfers are mechanisms used by capitalist nations to redress some of the inevitable inequality. The United States has never been very efficient with such redistribution. The onset of the welfare state came about relatively late. Transfers to the poor were restricted, residual, and meager, and the taxation policies favored the better off (Marger, 1999). Compared to other capitalist-welfare states, economic inequality in the United States has been greater (Heidenheimer, Heclo, and Adams, 1975), but recently it has risen to levels unknown since the 1920s and far in excess of other advanced societies today (Gray, 1998). For example, the Gini index[1] for the United States in 1998 was .401 as compared to Germany and Canada, respectively .281 and .312 (World Bank, 1999, Table 2.8).

This growth of inequality indicates a decline of working-class income as compared to the higher classes. In 1997, 20 percent of American families with higher incomes received 47 percent of all income, while the lowest 20 percent received 4.2 percent. Comparing such distribution to 1970, the higher income group has increased their share by 6.3 percent while the bottom three quintiles lost the same amount (U.S. Bureau of the Census, 1998, Table F-2). Although productivity increased between 1973 and 1996, the weekly earnings of 80 percent of the rank-and-file workers fell by 18 percent. At the same time, the income of CEOs increased 19 percent (Mishel and Bernstein, 1994). In the past, good times meant the betterment of all classes. Now this link between positive economic cycles and benefits to the whole seems to have been disrupted (Danziger and Gottschalk, 1995).

Explanations for the emergence of a two-tiered society are usually linked to deindustrialization, economic globalization, and technological advances. More precisely, the situation involves the loss of manufacturing jobs due to more effective production processes that have left previously well-paid, low-skilled, blue-collar workers scrambling for lower paid service jobs. Furthermore, some of the low-skilled jobs move to developing countries where production is much cheaper, further depressing the wages at home. Third, demands of world-market competition have created a very well paid technological service workforce (Sassen, 1998). The moral issue of extreme inequality within a democratic regime is thereby erased by the unalienable demands of the market (Gray, 1998).

However, the technological innovations, deindustrialization, and global competition pressures do not impinge only on the United States; therefore, this explanation is incomplete. Inequality levels in other industrialized countries are much lower and have not increased in recent years (Esping-Andersen, 1999).

The Neoconservative Ascendancy and the Fashioning of Exclusion

Kuttner (1984), Phillips (1990), and Gray (1998), among others, agree that the United States has veered away from the democratic equality praised by Tocqueville and the vision of expanding opportunities embodied in the New Deal. They contend that governmental institutions have been high-jacked by neoconservative ideologies. They also agree that this ascendancy gained legitimacy during the Reagan administration, the chief indirect effect of which was to condone wide economic inequality.

A key dimension of this conservative vision was the proposal for a return to a laissez-faire policy that implied a scaling back of regulations and a move toward Lockean restrictions on state interference in the market (Kuttner, 1997). The appeal of this ideology was buttressed by statements linking laissez-faire to the early successes of the young republic and nineteenth-century economic growth. As Goodin and associates (1999) point out, this hands-off role for the state is hardly supported by historical evidence. Examples of early state intervention include the Northwest Ordinance of 1787 and an arsenal of government subsidies that served as a framework for national territorial expansion, the National Road, and the

intercontinental railway. The federal government initiated large-scale public works projects and protectionist tariff policies, a foundation for early
American prosperity. In the backwash of the Civil War, the first war of mass
mobilization, the federal government found itself paying war pensions to a
substantial portion of the northern population (Skocpol, 1992; Goodin et al.,
1999). Gray (1998), in fact, claims that in no other market economy has
state intervention been more invasive of personal liberties than in the United
States during prohibition.

This combination of demanding greater autonomy for the market while
enforcing greater controls on certain citizens on moral grounds is a trade-
mark of the new ideology, reflecting strong class biases. Remolding American society to suit the "imperatives of the market" carried with it an ethos of
rugged individualism, liberal notions of self-help, and puritanical notions of
virtue and punishment.

Through the neoconservative lens, welfare was interpreted on one hand
as contributing to the erosion of American virtues—autonomy, work ethic,
family ethic, and community ethic (Murray, 1984; Mead, 1986)—and, on
the other, as a waste of resources that delayed economic growth by encum-
bering capital with taxation (Greenberg, 1985). The spread of this ideology,
and its eventual effect on social policies, had its onset in the mid-1970s and
culminated in the 1990s.

The Ambivalent Welfare System

Although the American State, as noted previously, was hardly non-
interventionist in the economic development of the country, it remained
indifferent to poverty for a long time. The old poor laws,[2] combined with
private charity, provided the dominant mode of relief for the old and desti-
tute (including orphans and widows) throughout the first third of the twentieth century, fully two or three generations after most other industrialized
countries had enacted public-age pensions.

The Social Security Act of 1935 inaugurated the welfare state in the nation. It provided old age, survivors, and disability insurance to a substantial
number of citizens, doing much to ease the problem of poverty among the
elderly. Nonetheless, enactment was, for a long time, drastically limited in
the portion of the population covered in terms of race and gender (Quadagno, 1994; Gordon, 1994). Also, benefits were quite low (Skocpol, 1995;
Orloff, 1993). This combination left a large residual population relying
upon means-tested public assistance of a traditional poor-law sort.

The United States lacks any universal "family allowance" or "children
benefit" and, in its place until 1996, had only a stringently means-tested pro-

gram, Aid to Families with Dependent Children (AFDC). While the neo-conservative supporters made public assistance the target of reform, especially AFDC, Social Security evaded criticism because it was interpreted in terms of self-help (Goodin et al., 1999). This ideological gloss was almost certainly the result of an awareness of the political power of retirees' organizations. It could not be based on economic considerations because the AFDC program consumed less that one-fifth of the welfare budget (Marger, 1999).

The United States, according to Goodin and associates (1999), is the prototype of the liberal model of welfare. The model argues that the road to citizens' well-being can be achieved primarily through a highly productive economy and participatory insurance and only very secondarily through a residual system of social-welfare transfers. In an economy keeping pregovernment incomes high, pregovernment poverty would by definition be low; therefore, there would be little need for public sector transfers. Transfers should be minimal and exclusively targeted to the "truly" poor (in absolute terms).

A test of the efficiency of this model was carried out by Goodin and associates (1999) using ten-year panel data for three countries considered prototypes of the three welfare models described by Esping-Andersen (1990). The United States represented the liberal model; Germany, the corporatist model; and the Netherlands, the sociodemocratic model. The research sheds some light about the efficiency of each model.

While gross domestic product (GDP) per capita growth in these three countries is quite similar during the ten-year period (1985-1995), the growth in median income was much lower in the United States (50 percent as compared to 63 percent and 75 percent). On the other hand, the amount of pretransfer poverty created by the market in these three countries is equally high (around 20 percent). But the posttransfer poverty level in the United States is considerably higher than in the other two countries at any time in the decade under study. The United States shows a poverty rate of 18 percent as compared to 9 percent in Germany and 4.5 percent in the Netherlands.[3]

The persistence of posttransfer poverty over ten years (e.g., the percentage of people who remained poor during that time) continues to be higher in the United States (13 percent) as compared to Germany (6 percent) and the Netherlands (0.5 percent). Of those in poverty in the liberal system, even after postgovernment transfers, half remain each year in deep poverty (50 percent below the poverty line) and over the ten-year period this percentage was reduced only by 2 percent. While the United States did, in fact, report much higher employment rates than other countries, the data also showed that a large proportion of the employed (10 percent) remain poor (Gray, 1998).

The ineffectiveness of the liberal-welfare system according to its own standards is compounded by the permanence of a large part of the population in deep and persistent poverty. Citizens living in such economic dereliction are also excluded from mediating economic resources (such as education and employment). Using measures of deep and persistent deprivation, such as level and duration of poverty, lack of access to education, health vulnerability, and extent of layoffs, Goodin and associates (1999) built a multideprivation index. They found that in the United States, 5 percent of households with working heads fell in the bottom category. Considering only households with female heads, the percentage was four times higher (20 percent). This calculation is conservative as it does not include homeless and illegal immigrant households or those who are institutionalized.

It was in the context of national economic growth and ineffective welfare performance that the 1996 welfare reform act was passed (Personal Responsibility and Work Opportunity Act). That legislation was especially restrictive for recipients of AFDC, now tellingly relabeled Temporary Assistance to Needy Families (TANF). Beyond the political rhetoric that accompanied it, the shift meant, above all, a retrenchment of the liberal system rather than a reform of an ineffective system. Its base was neoconservative devotion rather than the result of an outcome-and-process evaluation. In the face of the evidence on long-term and deep poverty and the ineffectiveness of the market to improve the situation, residual welfare was tightened and shortened. Most important, the citizenship principle of entitlement was erased. The clock was turned back to pre-New Deal times.

An economic system that creates great wealth and great poverty runs the risk of being contested and possibly creating civil unrest. It needs to show evidence of good performance to preserve legitimacy. Indicators of well-being, such as employment rates, are crucial. The acceptance of such indicators conveniently obscures earnings levels, security and length of employment, and who is and is not counted. An efficient strategy of hiding the true victims of the economic restructure is the use of policies intent on constructing these victims as deviants. Two neoconservative leaders expertly did this: Reagan with his tale of the welfare queen and Bush followed with the scare story of Willie Horton. The stage was set for policies that would demonize the poor.

Women's Marginalization in the Welfare System

The marginalization of women and minorities in the U.S. welfare system has been brought to light most clearly by a group of women (Abramovitz, 1989; Quadagno, 1994; Gordon, 1994; Fraser, 1989) who have historically documented their treatment as second-class citizens. The ADC/AFDC programs were, from the start, less generous than other public assistance programs, and discriminated racially as well as in terms of other moral and character traits. Although some of those barriers fell in the 1960s and 1970s, some resurfaced more subtly in the 1980s. Most important was the fact that since AFDC, unlike other programs (Social Security and SSI), had no system of price indexing, the value of cash benefits was greatly devalued between 1970 and 1994. Adjusting for inflation, the median state paid $792 per month for a mother with three children in 1970. By 1993, that amount had fallen to $435. This has impacted on the criteria of eligibility, so that by 1993 only 61 percent of poor children were in families receiving AFDC (Blank, 1997).

But as Abramovitz (1989), Gordon (1994), and Quadagno (1994) point out, the gendered roots of this biased treatment of women preceded and were perpetuated by welfare policies. Constructions of class, gender, and race intersected in the construction of poor women by the dominant society. These women were always on the brink of being labeled as undeserving, in view of the contradictory expectations set for them and their lived experience. Ideals of the nuclear family, the myth of a family wage, and gender expectations about the division of labor were at odds with the daily experience of women who had to support their families with very low wages and whose family arrangements were essential to their survival (McAdoo, 1999; Reigot and Spina, 1996; Zinn, 1989).

Reinforcing this quasi-deviant perspective was a moral barrage of attribution of all kinds of social evils to mother-headed families (such as increased rates of delinquency, dropout, and teen pregnancy). This breakdown of the family ethic has been a popular explanation for the feminization of poverty in the United States since census data showed that poor, two-parent families were about twice as likely to come apart within two years. However, showing a correlation between family structure and poverty and proving causation is quite different. Class and race differences are more important than family structure in determining poverty (Children's Defense Fund, 1987). For example, female-headed minority families are often the product of a "reshuffling of poverty" from already poor, two-parent families to mother-headed families (Bane, 1986). It is more often the case that poverty creates female-headed families than the reverse (Schram, 1995, pp. 142-161).

Nonetheless, the emergence of welfare for female heads of households was, in fact, a state bargain. It reinforced the duty of mothers to take care of their children in the cheapest possible way. Attributing negative characteristics to the mother made this strategy viable. The controls exercised by the system clearly emphasized an expectation that poor women are not to be trusted because they have not lived up to the family ethic. This construction distorts the public opinion about welfare recipients (Brodkin, 1993; Kluegel and Smith, 1986). It also encouraged withdrawal and passivity on the part of recipients (Schneider and Ingram, 1993; Cloward and Piven, 1974; Wilson, 1996, 180).

Fraser (1989) exposes some of the contradictions of AFDC in the transitional period, which apply as well to the new system:

> [T]his system created a double bind for women raising children without a male breadwinner. By failing to offer day care for their children, job training, and a job that pays a family wage, or some combination of these, it constructs them exclusively as mother. . . . Yet the system does not honor these women [as mothers]. On the contrary instead of offering them a guaranteed income equivalent to a family wage as a matter of right, it stigmatizes, humiliates and harasses them. In effect, it decrees simultaneously that these women must be and yet cannot be normative mothers. (pp. 142, 153)

More recently new norms have emerged that denigrated poor women further. The first was the evolution of the concept of dependence (Fraser and Gordon, 1994) to refer exclusively to economic dependence on the state. The second was the use of the statistical norm of mothers working as a justification for requiring poor mothers to work as a way to achieve self-sufficiency.

New language and policy place additional negative labels on welfare mothers: that they are weak and lazy (Mead, 1986), that they stay on welfare living off generous benefits, and that they have children to increase such benefits. Although such constructions have proven to be false (Berrick, 1995; Blank, 1997; Edin and Lein, 1997), they persist and have come to justify the new draconian regulations.

Blaming female-headed families for growing poverty provides a convenient way to deflect attention from the public deficiencies in redistribution (Males, 1993). The scapegoating of family structure for problems embedded in sexist, racist, and economically exclusionary practices drives popular resistance against public assistance and aggressively silences attempts to articulate a family policy that ensures all families and children might avoid poverty. Attributing poverty to single motherhood implies that women's decisions are the cause of their poverty and that they deserve to be treated punitively. Issues of constrained choices, blockage of equal opportunity, and cumulative barriers against access to resources are ignored.

Public assistance becomes less readily available; more temporary; more contingent on moral and social regulation; more premised on state surveillance of sexual, medical, social, and parental practices; and more attached to work requirements that move recipients from welfare to work irrespective of the lack of improvement in their economic condition. It is also noteworthy that women with felony drug convictions were excluded from all public assistance for life.

Until reproduction is valued as much as production (and also as another form of productive work) and supporting women with children, the work of mothers will not be duly valued. The issue is not which type of family is the best; instead, the question entails the support of mothering as worthwhile work in its own right and an integral part of the well-being of society (Mink, 1998).

There is, however, another dimension about AFDC/TANF policies that addresses the autonomy of women. It is contradictory to laud the dependency of women on men and to denigrate welfare dependency, because, in fact, in applying for welfare women assert their independence and assume their responsibilities in extremely trying conditions. Edin and Lein's (1997) research shows how far welfare mothers will go to respond to the needs of their children. Furthermore, by "enforcing" their project of self-sufficiency the state fails to address conditions of self-sufficiency (decent pay, decent child care, and access to the basic rights of health care, shelter, food, and education).

The popularity of workfare as a means toward self-sufficiency for mothers on welfare was based on statistics which showed that three-fourths of mothers with preschool children (mostly middle class) were working in 1990, and that a higher proportion of these working mothers were single heads of households (Skocpol, 2000; Pear, 2000). The obvious conclusion was that if other mothers were doing it, why not welfare mothers? Neglected in such an inference are the higher earnings of middle-class women, the greater access to programs in the neighborhoods where they reside, and the fact that both their families and the children's father will have more resources to help them. Ignoring different circumstances across socioeconomic strata is a common gimmick in a society that has always denied the existence of classes (Ambert, 1998; Stone, 1988).

A recent report on studies of economists and social scientists about the outcomes and assumptions behind welfare reform sheds new light on both (Bernstein, 2000). First, the prereform concern with the sharp increase from 1990 to 1994 of the welfare rolls (supposedly indicating a chronic problem of dependency) was found to be invalid even beyond its faulty conceptualization of dependence. Much of the change occurred because of policy changes extending eligibility to two-parent families in the fifty states and a rapid rise of cases in which only children received benefits (e.g., children of the crack epidemic and American-born children of undocumented immigrants).

Conversely, reports of the success of TANF, based on reduced welfare rolls taken to represent a shift to self-sufficiency, are grossly inaccurate. Nearly 30 percent of the women who had left have returned to welfare; another third were having trouble meeting the most basic needs; and another 15 percent have been unable to pay utilities and rent. More striking is the finding that the claimed reduction of welfare is due in large part to the greater likelihood that welfare workers will turn applicants away. There is no doubt that some of the mothers who left welfare are working and better off, but that has always happened in booming economies (Bernstein, 2000).

THE AMERICAN GULAG:
EXTENDING THE NET OF CONTROL

The United States has at present the highest rate of incarceration among industrialized nations. After having held more or less stable for decades, the prison population has quadrupled since 1975. Over five million people are in state custody, including prison, jails, probation, and INS (immigration and naturalization service) centers. This growth has disproportionately affected minority racial and ethnic groups (Davis, 1998).

Such extensive and biased imprisonization fosters, among targeted groups, disrespect for and suspicion of authorities and alienates them from the political process. The latest figures for 1996 show that on any given day 30 percent of black men between ages twenty and twenty-nine were under correctional supervision. The African-American rate of imprisonment is ten times higher than that of white men. A young black man aged sixteen in 1996 had a 28 percent chance of spending time in prison during his life (Chaiken, 2000).

What has happened? What is the cause of this epidemic of correctional institutionalization? How to explain that, in the land of the free, more citizens are in prison than elsewhere? Are Americans more crimogenic than other peoples? The rate of imprisonment was never correlated with crime rate, suggesting a disjunction between state control and incidence of deviant behavior (Quinney, 1975). Since reliable statistics have not been collected, the rate of imprisonment for women was never correlated with crime rate. However, at the present the correlation is inverse. Property crime has been declining in this country for the past twenty-five years, so more recently have violent crimes, from 42 percent at the end of the 1970s to 27 percent in the beginnings of the 1990s (Chaiken, 2000).

The "get tough on crime" philosophy as a means of protecting the safety of law-abiding citizens has focused on removing violent criminals from our communities, a commonsensical goal in any society. However, analysis of offenders in prisons reveals that the number convicted for violent crimes constitutes only 17 percent of federal prisoners, 25 percent of jail inmates, and 47 percent of state prisoners. On the whole, 30 percent of the population committed to prison were convicted of violent offenses, while the remaining were convicted for nonviolent offenses and, of all prisoners, 38 percent were first offenders (Tonry, 1995).

Students of deviance have for a long time understood that the more regulations on behavior, the greater the level of deviance (e.g., Quinney, 1975). So, an attempt to examine this astonishing increase of Americans behind bars led analysts to examine connections between policies that emerged in the past decade and the explosion of incarcerated citizens. Three new policies have been linked to the rapid growth of the population in state custody: the War on Drugs, the three-strike federal legislation, and mandated sentences. The first is considered the most important culprit and the most responsible for targeting minorities in poor neighborhoods.

President George Bush's War on Drugs established legislation that indiscriminately punished consumption, possession, small trading, large distribution, and smuggling with preset sentences. Michael Tonry (1995) and Angela Davis (1998) concur that the legislation was designed to commit small traders and users to prison as a symbolic show of success aimed at distracting from a decade of failure at controlling drug production and smuggling (Galbraith, 1992). The intent was not so much to decrease drug availability and use but to punish indiscriminately individuals in the most easily supervised poor urban areas. These communities, as Jargowsky (1997) has found, are overwhelmingly inhabited by minorities.

Reiman's (2001) work indicates that at each level of the justice system, from arrest to conviction to sentence, the probability of the poor being imprisoned for the same offense grows exponentially. Recent data (Butterfield, 2000) show that we are creating a self-perpetuating caste of prisoners. The probability that released prisoners will go back to prison is an important element of the unabated growth in the incarcerated population. In California, for example, four out of five former inmates returned to prison, not for committing new crimes but for technical violations of the terms of their parole.

Two policy decisions account for this. On one hand, states sharply curtailed education, job training, drug treatment programs, earned good time, and other rehabilitation in prisons (compounding the barriers to social integration faced by the released inmate). On the other hand, with the get-tough approach, parole officers were more likely to revoke an inmate's parole. A profile of the released prisoners in California speaks of the entrapment experienced by this population: 85 percent of released prisoners are drug and alcohol abusers, over 70 percent are still jobless after a year, 50 percent are illiterate, and 10 percent are homeless (Butterfield, 2000).

Some cases cited by Butterfield (2000) show how prisoners are becoming permanent outcasts. Steven Buttler was homeless when arrested, found guilty of a drug offense, and sentenced to prison. He did not receive any drug treatment or training during the three years of his sentence. When released, he was given $200 and ordered to contact his parole officer. Having no place to stay and no family, he returned to the skid row where he had lived before. Without a job, he was unable to pay the parole fee[4] and took some drugs. Quickly he was returned to the prison he had left a few weeks before.

The same happened to Ruth Clements. On leaving prison, she regained custody of her sixteen-year-old daughter and both started to reconnect and live as a family. Shortly after, she was arrested in a minor brawl in a bar and sent to prison because the alcohol in her blood indicated inebriation. As she returned to prison, she left behind a troubled and scared adolescent. Even released prisoners who are not rearrested have a hard time reentering society.

Having a prison record is a barrier to employment, but even when ex-prisoners find employment their wages are half of other workers in the same field. Felons in many states are barred from some occupations. When Harriet Davis got out of prison after serving a sentence for having shot her abuser, she was committed to making good. She earned a nursing degree and passed the registered nurse licensing test only to find out that, because she had been found guilty of a felony, she could not practice her profession. She is now a home-care aid.

To a large extent, the discrimination and the human cost of these new policies are dismissed under an interpretation of just desserts, but one would think that the economic costs of this burgeoning institutionalization would disturb taxpayers. Still there is another side to this phenomenon: the prison industrial complex. There are profits to be made from prisonization.

The construction of new prisons has been a bonanza for architects, construction companies, and the construction business in general. The greater the requirements of inmate control (e.g., more isolated areas, computerized locks, and so on) the greater the dividends for businesses in such fields. In addition, the substantial increase in the demand for correctional workers has made this one of the most promising fields for unskilled or semiskilled workers.

Probably the most perplexing contribution to this expansion of the prison population to the "free market" is the emergence of private, for-profit prisons. Between 1987 and 1996 the number of inmates in private prisons jumped from 3,122 to 78,000. Two corporations, the Corrections Corporation of America and the Wackenhut Corrections Corporation, run 114 facilities, raising, in 1997, revenues well over half a billion dollars (Davis, 1998).

Furthermore, what is happening with prison work poses probably the most extreme case of profiteering from incarcerated populations. Although the United States protested vehemently against the unfair practices of China competing in the world market with very cheap products produced by their prisoners, it has fallen prey to the same strategy. For example, Chevron, TWA, and Victoria's Secret use prison labor to do data entry, to book telephone reservations, and to make lingerie at 23 cents an hour. In California alone, goods and services produced by the prison industry in 1997-1998 totaled more that 150 million dollars (Davis, 1998; Lafer, 1999).

A nightmarish vision of ultimate exploitation would suggest that putting the unemployed and poor in prison could eventually prevent the exodus of unskilled jobs abroad. Prisoners' work is equally cheap and businesses would save on the costs of transportation. This calls to mind Jeremy Bentham's prediction of a futurist higher modern society, where the devotion to a free market creates an oligarchic regime reconstructed as an ideal prison (Gray, 1998).

THE ADDED OPPRESSION OF WOMEN BEHIND BARS

Two Control Institutions

The elements of the new control ideology and policy implementation affected women and men. The proportional increase in incarceration, however, was much higher for women than men, in part because the base numbers have been much lower (women constituting at the time of about 7.5 percent of the incarcerated population).

Explanations of this gender difference in incarceration have followed different routes. Some have searched for explanations in the lower criminal rate of women as a function of their nature (e.g., Lombroso, 1920), of their restrictive exposure to the public sphere and, therefore, to public control (Pollack, 1950; Adler, 1975; Simon, 1975; Steffensmeyer, 1978, 1980), or of the greater informal controls imposed on them (Hagan, Gillis, and Simpson, 1985; Hill and Atkinson, 1988).

While pursuing these explanations has led to an understanding of gendered-behavioral differences, the links between gendered-behavioral patterns and the levels of prisonization have offered only a limited understanding. Another avenue explored is the thesis that the judicial system treats women more leniently: the so-called "chivalry hypothesis."

Research reveals instead a gendered justice, not necessarily a more lenient justice. Police react more strongly to "improper" feminine behavior than to the alleged offense (e.g., Visher, 1983; Chesney-Lind, 1978; Steffensmeyer, 1980). In court, women appear to have less access to defense lawyers and plead guilty more often than men (e.g., Figueira-McDonough, 1985). Also, women prisoners receive longer sentences for the same offense than men prisoners. It is as if the seriousness of the offense were defined by ranking criteria following the offense range for each gender. Hypothetically, if larceny were the third most serious offense among women, its level of seriousness would be equated with the third most serious offense among men, robbery (e.g., Figueira-McDonough et al., 1981; Bloom and Chesney-Lind, 2000).

To explore this difference further, we have to ask what the fundamental differences between women and men are, beyond those resulting from socialization, structure, and social construction of gender. This brings us to the century-old division between production and reproduction. While poor women have always worked, only they can be mothers, and the ascription of child care to women is one of the most resilient social norms. The proposal by Newt Gingrich a few years back to remove poor children from the (inept) care of their mothers and put them in asylums—where they would be well-educated and socialized in good values—was quickly withdrawn for two reasons: it infringed on the sacredness of motherhood, and many expressed disgust at the replacement of nurture for efficiency—plus budget specialists showed how tremendously expensive such an alternative would be.

In order to understand the extension of the public control exercised on poor and minority women, we must consider *both* welfare and the justice system as powerful mechanisms impinging on their freedom.

Bad Women and Unfit Mothers

In women's prisons the withdrawal of rehabilitation was, if anything, more extreme than in men's institutions. This absence tended to go unnoticed due to smaller numbers. Yet the disproportionate representation of the poor and minorities in women's prisons is still more blatant than in men's prisons. In 1997 the level of African-American women prisoners was 8.2 times higher, and the rate of Hispanics 3.4 times higher, than that of white women prisoners (Gillard and Beck, 1998). Also, the greatest growth of offenses leading to prison was drugs. While comparison of the consequences of the new approach to corrections had similar consequences for both genders, the results were more accentuated for women.

There are, however, two things that make the experience of the oppression of incarcerated women harsher. The first is as old as criminology itself and was clearly expounded in Lombroso's (1920) work. He saw crime and womanhood as mutually exclusive. While male crime was explained as the dangerous expressions of manly behavior, female crime was defined as abnormal and, therefore, female criminals were monstrous aberrations of nature. A similar line of gender differentiation was taken by Pollack (1950) who attributed to women a manipulative form of behavior consistent with their nature and structural position. Attributing excessive deviance to women criminals evolved later in interpretations to project that these women were not quite responsible agents of their actions, because their crimes reflected deep psychological disturbances (Rock, 1996).

The lingering of this tradition shows up in research that uncovered a gendered implementation of justice; in prison, it has further consequences. The incompatible identities of "criminal" and "woman" have a strong effect on women prisoners and on their treatment by their controllers.

Women prisoners tend to be viewed as failures in their gender roles and, being in prison, this signifies that such women are valueless. To the extent that their identity is eroded, they will be more depressed than men, feel powerless and, hence, less resistant (Human Rights Watch, 1996). Their controllers might perceive them in the same way and be more likely to oppress and abuse them without fear of retaliation. The frequency of sexual abuse in women's correctional institutions in five states, reported by the Human Rights Watch (1996) Women's Rights Project, reflects this. Not only do guards who abuse these women feel that the women have lost their right to privacy and dignity and can be used as they please, but also the women interviewed feel totally powerlessness, while the silence of other guards and wardens proves them right. Millett's (1970) brilliant analysis of the treatment of gay prisoners in male prisons (through the writings of Genet), gives some insight into the consequences of the identity and attribution processes being linked to gender.

Sixty percent of women behind bars are mothers, most with minor children. The view that women criminals are worse than male criminals and, therefore, worthless magnifies distortions regarding their capacity for motherhood. Although their crime might have nothing whatsoever to do with mothering and even often, as related in Edin and Lein (1997), might be a consequence of a motherhood ethic, most correctional policies project a view that these women are bad mothers and, therefore, that distance from their children should be maintained. How those mother-children bridges should be reconstructed once the prisoner returns to the community is of no concern to most correctional departments.

NEGLECT, PUNISHMENT, AND RESISTANCE
OF MARGINALIZED WOMEN

The purpose of this book is to bring to light the oppression of our sisters who live in poverty outside and within prison walls. Because the institutions that control them employ holistic definitions of deviance (dependent, undeserving, or criminal), the women become outsiders and the infractions on their citizen and human rights become invisible to the "deserving" members of society.

In this book we attempt to lift the veil of obscurity that makes these women invisible to the dominant society by examining the processes and outcomes of marginalization of poor women. In an attempt to relate more directly to the lived experience and feelings of women who have been in prison and on welfare, we have borrowed some of their art and reflections which are distributed throughout the book. In her essay, Debbie Zinn argued for the power of art as a form of communication with the potential to transcend social construction and touch the essentially human.

The chapters in the first section of the book critically examine the public systems of control that affect poor women. They describe as well how resistance to oppression, achieved through informal family networks, is distorted by attributing to poor women deviance from the dominant family ethic.

In Chapter 2, Joel Handler argues that the present welfare reform characterizes poor women as undeserving. If women are poor because they do not live up to the prescribed work and family ethic, it becomes the task of welfare policy to enforce work and proper family norms. Since the women are seen as deviant, control takes the form of aversive reinforcement. Punishment prevails not because it has proven effective, but because it lowers the welfare rolls, the true purpose of the legislation. Success in these terms hides the true conditions of low-wage work and ignores women's need for affordable child care, health care, and job training—all conditions for exiting poverty. The costs of punitive policy fall heavily on these mothers, their children, and society in general.

Sheryl Pimlott and Rosemary Sarri give an updated account of women in the correctional system in Chapter 3. They examine the extraordinary growth in the number of women behind bars, making the United States the nation with the highest proportion of female prisoners. They trace this growth to the transfer of juveniles to adult institutions, to sentence increases, and lack of "good time," but more directly to legislation enforced by the War on Drugs.

This body of legislation overlooks the socioeconomic origins of crime and the special circumstances attendant on gender and race. The population of imprisoned females is made up largely of single, minority women with a history of drug abuse. The absence of in-house programs that might prepare the women to cope when they leave prison is further evidence of this disregard.

In Chapter 4, Harriette McAdoo addresses the distortions that afflict African-American women. These distortions are central to the topic of the book. As Handler notes, welfare has become a code word for handling inner-city African-American single mothers. McAdoo emphasizes the double demands put on African-American women: to conform to their own culture and to cope with the dominant white culture. African-American women have to respond simultaneously to race and gender issues. Part of their cultural tradition entails upholding family networks with strong links to the family of origin. Interpreted as deviance from the standard family ethic, narrowly defined as the nuclear family, this commitment has often been misunderstood by the dominant culture. Conventional assessments are insensitive to "aberrant" traditions and to the strength of such families for the survival of populations under siege for centuries.

In the second section of the book, the authors address different forms of entrapment of women in poverty by institutions and policies apparently in place to help them. Deborah Whitley and Paula Dressel (Chapter 5) propose that both institutions (welfare and corrections) are different ways of controlling a consequence of contemporary economic restructuring—namely, surplus labor. The more punitive processes of dealing with poor women either channel them to low-paid and insecure work or remove them altogether from the labor market. Insightfully, they argue that the frontline workers implementing these forms of control are increasingly drawn from the unskilled and semiskilled population and, therefore, are part of the "surplus workforce" as well. These workers are typically deprofessionalized and unskilled. Their work is more closely supervised and geared toestf achieving results through control. Therefore, although both supervisors and those they control may belong to the same class, the economic stability of the latter depends on the former exacting control. This becomes especially dangerous in prisons, where the prisoners are female and black while most of the guards are white and male.

Diana Pearce, in Chapter 6, takes a fresh look at welfare reform and concludes that it is not work requirements and time limits that are the real problem with the new legislation. She rightly points out that we have evidence, starting in the 1970s, that women on welfare have always worked to supplement their meager welfare checks. Also, based on follow-up studies, it is not time limits that account for the dramatic lowering of welfare rolls. The central issue, she argues, is the type of work to which these women have access. Most of them remain in poverty when they leave welfare. Her major point is that the crux of the debate should center on self-sufficiency. She specifies standards of self-sufficiency, based on women's needs and costs of living in different places and what women would need to earn to meet these standards. This procedure makes very clear that, in most cases, women have to be offered opportunities for more education and training in order to achieve the needed wages; or, alternatively, to get support for child care, health care, and housing. The important contribution of this approach is that it operationalizes and builds on the central value of self-sufficiency that has supposedly been the goal of welfare reform.

Concentrating on one of the basic conditions for family self-sufficiency, Elizabeth Mulroy (Chapter 7) discusses in detail the difficulty poor women have in reaching such a goal. Worsening inequality of income, together with the declining availability of low-income housing, has had catastrophic consequences for poor families. This outcome is verified by the very high proportion of income that goes to rent, the constant displacement to underclass neighborhoods, the larger density per residence and, finally, the increase in the number of families (especially female-headed families) that have become homeless.

The repercussions of any of these adaptations on the stability of the family are made worse by the restrictions on public policy assistance brought about by welfare reform and the diversion of housing slots from those most in need as a result of the Housing and Work Responsibility Act of 1998. Mulroy analyzes various policies that could cope with the housing squeeze and finds them insufficient, even if combinations of certain programs have proved successful.

The third section focuses on the vulnerability of poor women with respect to age (the elderly and adolescents) and substance abuse. Anna Celeste Burke addresses the gender gap in research concerning women's addictions and the adequacy of services for them. Contexts that trigger such abuse differ by gender, and the consequences of neglect are also different. Based on biology, socialization, and structural setting, drug abuse among women is more hidden, more disapproved, less tolerated, and more frequently misdiagnosed. Even if this bias applies to all women, it is poor women—more easily controlled by public services—who suffer the brunt of ignorance and punitive attitudes. Addiction is construed as an indicator of lack of moral fiber and, more generally, as the cause of poverty rather than as consequences of tensions derived from the struggle for everyday survival. The implications for women on welfare are extreme. States increasingly check for signs of drug use and this surveillance can result in temporary or permanent cuts in benefits. Furthermore, conviction for a drug offense makes an individual ineligible for welfare for life. Together with the punitive handling of what is universally acknowledged to be a disease, in the poor neighborhoods where these women reside drug rehabilitation programs are for the most part nonexistent and even less so in prisons. The circle of exclusion is closed: desperate situations lead some women to drug addiction; punishments makes their situation still more unbearable. Either the women cure themselves or they fall further into a funnel of despair.

Chapter 9 gives an assessment of older women in terms of their vulnerability to poverty and their unmet special needs when incarcerated. It is common knowledge that the senior population is growing and that women tend to outlive men by a half dozen years. With this in mind, Edith Elisabeth Flynn calls attention to some of the costs of these trends. She points out that although the rate of poverty among the elderly has decreased considerably in the past fifteen years, this development is hardly uniform. Women living alone and minorities have a much higher rate of poverty than white males and couples. Many of these elderly, while not below the poverty line, are concentrated among the near poor. Whether because of biological or lifestyle differences, the greater longevity of women has resulted in many of them being left alone with no one to care for them. Both of these circumstances make women more vulnerable to chronic diseases and more likely to be institutionalized.

Older women in prison are such a minority that their special needs are rarely addressed in an overcrowded system with chronic resource limitations. In view of the very low likelihood of recidivism among the elderly, Flynn considers whether less expensive and more humane forms of control might be appropriate. Even if the numbers of elderly behind bars were minuscule, their number might grow with the lengthening of sentences.

In Chapter 10, Judy Walruff looks at the conditions of adolescent mothers. She discusses the primacy of popular and state concerns with teenage moms in the past twenty years and links this agenda to ideological and pragmatic factors. On one hand, the issue of precocious maternity was a lightning rod for the conservative preoccupation with teenage sex and family values. On the other hand, there was concern about the ability of these young women to attain self-sufficiency, together with the belief that the growth of welfare was due to these young mothers who had forfeited their education and were, therefore, likely to stay on welfare for long periods. Walruff concentrates on the failure of social policy to deal with adolescents. She identifies contradictory policies that either relegate adolescents to a position of dependency or make them totally responsible for their behaviors. She discusses a study researching the relevance of level of maturity on the use of prenatal care by pregnant teenagers. Comparing age, maturity, and family support, she concludes that those variables must be assessed clearly in order to fashion interventions likely to help adolescents confronting serious problems.

Section IV of the book is devoted to the challenges experienced by incarcerated women. M. A. Bortner (in Chapter 11) begins with the statement that the most strongly inculcated social identity for women is that of motherhood. The number of children in poverty in the United States speaks of the continuous concern and frustration felt by their mothers. In prison, where 70 percent of the women have minor children, the anguish of separation is added to previous survival struggles. Male prisoners also have children who are, however, usually in the care of their mothers. Conversely, many women in prison are single mothers who alone were responsible for the children left behind. Bortner calls this a gender tax; beyond punishment for the offense the women committed, this anxiety is a constant burden they have to bear. She describes the general indifference to women's health issues, specifically with those having to do with reproduction. Nothing symbolizes this more accurately than the treatment of women who give birth in jail. Often they remain shackled while delivering a baby, surrounded by guards; the baby is usually taken away immediately.

Wendy Ascione and Joyce Dixson expand on mother-child separation due to incarceration (Chapter 12). Their focus is mostly on the effects that the forced absence of mothers have on children. Again, the fact that most of these mothers are single magnifies the consequences of their absence. This could be called the children tax, because offspring are being punished as well. Traditionally, the criminal justice system has been indifferent to the struggles of these children, and the child welfare system has no program to deal with the trauma of prolonged separation. In fact, few studies have focused on this problem. The research that exists points to disruption in the normal development of the child depending on the age when it occurred, if a relative took the place of the absent mother versus placement in foster care, and the length of separation. A few mostly volunteer programs have developed to help to maintain links between mother and child, and the authors propose various alternatives.

In Chapter 13, Patricia O'Brien and Nancy Harm deal with the process of social integration for women leaving prison. After spending time in prison, women are expected to return to their families, get jobs, and become parts of their communities. Little thought is given to what these apparently normal tasks mean for someone who has been absent in a total institution, who carries an ex-con label, and who has to reconstruct networks that were damaged by imprisonment.

Nonetheless, very few programs exist to help these women. Such programs as do exist tend to lack a theoretical rationale and evaluation guidelines. Both authors use their own experiments, framed in an ecological perspective, that take into account identifying processes in the relationship between personal experiences, supporting relationships, and progress to-

Looking Up and Facing Forward

When both of my sons were less than two years old their father abandoned us. Supporting three of us was difficult because I received no child support when the Court was unable to locate him. Lacking a college degree, the employment that I obtained never paid enough to support us. Eventually these circumstances led me to apply for help from Social Services and to apply for admission to college so that I could have a better income. While working, caring for the boys and my handicapped mother, I graduated with an honors degree in psychology and earned an MSW in social work. I am now employed as a social worker in a juvenile justice agency in a job that is both challenging and fulfilling. Repaying my college loans will take many years, but at least it is now possible.

I learned from personal experience that my freedom of action was severely controlled by those in Social Services who had power over me. I was told outright to quit school and find employment in a fast food or retail industry. My goals and dreams were dismissed as beyond my "lot in life." But those experiences strengthened my resolve to improve not only my circumstances but also that of others. I have learned to be critical of social policies and programs and I am determined to address and alleviate the needs of disadvantaged people. I want to be an advocate for equal access to resources, humane and responsive services, and opportunities. By giving myself to others, I find meaning in my own life.

Francine Farmer

Francine Farmer is a social worker and former welfare mother.

ward self-efficiency. Patterns of failure and success are then identified in their qualitative evaluation.

Although Chapters 2 through 13 identify factors and processes that contribute to the exclusion of poor women on welfare or in prison from mainstream society and, therefore, from many citizenship rights, they also offer evidence of resistance on the part of these women. In the last section of the book, forms of resistance take center stage. In Chapter 14, Yvonne Luna and Josefina Figueira-McDonough first argue that public policy in the United States was always framed as charity, even as the two-tier Social Security Act was signed by Roosevelt in 1935. This, and a puritanical ideology (later secularized into social Darwinism), imprinted on welfare recipients and the poor in general the concept of individual looseness of morals (or limited capacity) making them—not the system—responsible for their poverty. Both dimensions are present in recent welfare reform. The objective of the research reported in this chapter is to assess to what extent single mothers impacted by the 1996 welfare reform accepted the rationale on which the policy was built. Some evidence of acceptance of the reform justification emerged in focus groups; however, as women spoke about their experiences they were able to see the discrepancies between their lives and the negative ascriptions attached to welfare recipients. Some of these women expressed resentment of the reform and were angry about the ignorance of policymakers and the infringement on their rights that the reform represented. This is an example of resistance from below.

Deborah LaBelle introduces the reader to the field of legislative advocacy in Chapter 15. She argues that equity of treatment must take into consideration the inequality of gendered contexts and roles. So, while the majority of women in prison are poor, have little education, and have high rates of substance abuse; they should be entitled to the training and rehabilitation programs available to men from similar backgrounds. Arguments that, given the smaller population of women in prison, such programs are not economically feasible are inconsistent with principles of equal treatment. At the same time, an overwhelming proportion of women in prison are single mothers and, therefore, equity would require that the preservation of contact with their children be assured, as well as the means of representation in decisions of guardianship. LaBelle uses the contradictions between family legislation and its obstructed implementation in prisons to demonstrate how prisoners are barred from their family rights. She examines how constitutional rights and international human rights are not preserved within the prisons. Avenues for redressing such infringements are obstructed by special acts limiting their applicability to prisoners.

Janet Finn, in Chapter 16, engages the reader in a self-examination of the successes and failures of the feminist movement. Failures have included shortfalls in reaching minority, working, and poor women. She argues that the movement has adopted a misguided agenda that assumes a false homogeneity among women. To enhance solidarity among all women, Finn concludes that it is necessary to understand the everyday experiences of poor and minority women, to respect their traditions, and to comprehend the lenses through which they define and activate their gender goals. Hence, rather than impose the dominant women's movement agenda on others, feminists might build bridges in order to give and receive experiences as equals. The effort has been proposed by feminist theory and research, but its activist expression leaves much to be desired. In any event, it is essential to deploy the strength of resistance, based on the solidarity of women, against social injustice.

In the concluding chapter, Rosemary Sarri and Josefina Figueira-McDonough propose steps to ignite resistance into action to integrate the excluded women who have been the topic of this volume. They consider three basic elements for such action. A primary element consists of the women themselves, who know firsthand what their needs are and the obstacles they face. They are the experts to guide action. Second are the more or less organized groups that are devoted to different aspects of social resistance, often working separately. Alliances between these groups working with poor women on problems closer to their needs is indispensable for rallying resources to meet this David-versus-Goliath confrontation. Finally, we need to gather experts who, within their specialties, can alert us to institutional, legal, economic, and political means to enhance the achievement of poor women's goals.

NOTES

1. Gini index is probably the most familiar index of inequality. The smaller the Gini index the more equal the distribution. An index of 1.0 would mean that one individual or one family controlled all the income of a nation; conversely, an index of 0.0 would indicate a society in which everyone would share the same income. The measure can be applied to wealth or income.

2. The American Colonies, later the United States, borrowed their own statutes from the Elizabethan Poor Laws of 1601 (see Abbott, 1940).

3. In the intercountry comparisons, poverty income is established at below 50 percent of the median income (about $23,000 in the United States for a family of three). Deep poverty is defined at half of that amount.

4. Parolees in California have to pay for their supervision.

REFERENCES

Abbott, Edith. 1940. *Public Assistance.* Chicago: Chicago University Press.

Abramovitz, Mimi. 1989. *Regulating the Lives of Women: Social Welfare Policy from Colonial Times to the Present.* Boston: South End.

Adler, Freda. 1975. *Sisters in Crime.* New York: McGraw-Hill.

Ambert, Anne-Marie. 1998. *The Web of Poverty.* Binghamton, NY: The Haworth Press.

Bane, Mary Jo. 1986. Household Composition and Poverty. In Sheldon Danziger and Daniel H. Weinberg (Eds.), *Fighting Poverty: What Works and What Doesn't* (pp. 209-231). Cambridge: Harvard University Press.

Bernstein, Nina. 2000. Studies Dispute Two Assumptions About Welfare Overhaul. *The New York Times,* December 12, p. A14.

Berrick, Jill. 1995. *Faces of Poverty.* New York: Oxford University Press.

Blank, Rebecca M. 1997. *It Takes a Nation: A New Agenda for Fighting Poverty.* Princeton, NJ: Princeton University Press.

Bloom, Barbara and Meda Chesney-Lind. 2000. Women in Prison: Vengeful Equity. In Roslyn Muraskin (Ed.), *It's a Crime: Women and Justice* (pp. 183-204). Upper Saddle River, NJ: Prentice Hall.

Brodkin, Evelyn. 1993. The Making of an Enemy: How Welfare Policies Construct the Poor. *Law and Social Enquiry 18*(3): 647-670.

Butterfield, Fox. 2000. Often Parole Is One Stop on the Way Back to Prison. *The New York Times,* November 11, pp. A1, A28.

Chaiken, Jan. 2000. Crunching Numbers: Crime and Incarceration at the End of the Millennium. *National Institute of Justice Journal,* January (242): 10-27.

Chesney-Lind, Meda. 1978. Chivalry Reexamined: Women and the Criminal Justice System. In Lee Bawker (Ed.), *Women and the Criminal Justice System* (pp. 197-223). Lexington, MA: DC Heath.

Children's Defense Fund. 1987. *Declining Earnings of Young Men: Their Relation to Poverty, Teen Pregnancy and Family Formation.* Washington, DC: Adolescent Pregnancy Prevention Clearing House.

Cloward, Richard and Francis Fox Piven. 1974. The Professional Bureaucracies: Benefit Systems and Influence Systems. In Richard Cloward and Francis Fox Piven (Eds.), *The Politics of Turmoil* (pp. 3-14). New York: Pantheon Books.

Danziger, Sheldon and Peter Gottschalk. 1995. *America Unequal.* Cambridge, MA: Harvard University Press.

Davis, Angela. 1998. What Is the Prison Industrial Complex? Why Does It Matter? *Colorlines,* Fall: 12-17.

Edin, Kathryn and Laura Lein. 1997. *Making Ends Meet: How Single Mothers Survive Welfare and Low Wage Work.* New York: Russell Sage Foundation.

Esping-Andersen, Cøsta. 1990. *The Three Worlds of Welfare Capitalism.* Cambridge, MA: Polity Press.

Esping-Andersen, Cøsta. 1999. *Social Foundations of Post-Industrial Societies.* London: Sage Publications.

Figueira-McDonough, Josefina. 1985. Gender Differences in Informal Processing: Look at Charge Bargaining and Sentence Reduction in Washington, DC. *Journal of Research in Crime and Delinquency 22*(2): 101-33.

Figueira-McDonough, Josefina, Rosemary Sarri, Alfreda Iglehart, and Terri Williams. 1981. *Women in Prison: Michigan 1967-1978.* Ann Arbor, MI: Institute for Social Research.

Fraser, Nancy. 1989. *Unruly Practices: Power, Discourse and Gender in Contemporary Social Theory.* Minneapolis: University of Minnesota Press.

Fraser, Nancy and Linda Gordon. 1994. A Genealogy of Dependency: Tracing a Key Word in the US Welfare State. *Signs 19*(2): 309-336.

Galbraith, John K. 1992. *The Culture of Contentment.* Boston: Houghton Mifflin Co.

Gillard, Darrell K. and Allen J. Beck. 1998. *Prisoners in 1997.* Report No. NCJ 170014. Washington DC: U.S. Department of Justice, Bureau of Justice Statistics (August).

Goodin, Robert E., Bruce Headey, Rudd Muffels, and Dirven Henk-Jan. 1999. *The Real Worlds of Welfare Capitalism.* Cambridge, England: Cambridge University Press.

Gordon, Linda. 1994. *Pitied but Not Entitled: Single Women and the History of Welfare.* New York: Free Press.

Gray, John. 1998. *False Dawn: The Delusions of Global Capitalism.* London: Granta Books.

Greenberg, Edward S. 1985. *Capitalism and the American Political Ideal.* Armonk, NY: M.E. Sharpe, Inc.

Hagan, John A., R. Gillis, and John Simpson. 1985. The Class Structure of Gender and Delinquency: Towards a Power-Control of Common Delinquent Behavior. *American Journal of Sociology* 90(6): 1151-1178.

Heidenheimer, Arnold, Hugh Heclo, and Carolyn T. Adams. (1975). *Comparative Public Policy: The Politics of Social Choice in Europe and America.* London: Macmillan.

Hill, Gary and Maxine P. Atkinson. 1988. Gender, Familial Control and Delinquency. *Criminology* 26(1): 127-147.

Human Rights Watch. 1996. *All Too Familiar: Sexual Abuse of Women in U.S. State Prisons.* New York: Human Rights Watch, Women's Rights Project.

Jargowsky, Paul A. 1997. *Poverty and Place: Ghettos, Barrios and the American City.* New York: Russell Sage Foundation.

Kluegel, James R. and Elliot R. Smith. 1986. *Beliefs about Inequality: American Views About What Is and What Ought to Be.* New York: A. de Gruyer.

Kuttner, Robert. 1984. *The Economic Illusion: False Choices Between Prosperity and Social Justice.* Boston: Houghton Mifflin Co.

Kuttner, Robert. 1997. *Everything for Sale: The Virtues and Limits of the Market.* New York: Alfred A. Knopf.

Lafer, Gordon. 1999. Captive Labor: America's Prisoners As Corporate Work Force. *American Prospect* 46(September): 66-70.

Lombroso, Cesare. 1920. *The Female Offender.* New York: Appleton.

Males, Mike. 1993. Public Policy Infantile Arguments. *In These Times,* August 9: 18-20.

Marger, Martin N. 1999. *Social Inequality: Patterns and Processes.* Mountain View, CA: Mayfield Publishing Co.

McAdoo, Harriette P. (Ed.). 1999. *Family Ethnicity: Strength in Diversity.* Thousand Oaks, CA: Sage Publications.

Mead, Lawrence. 1986. *Beyond Entitlement: The Social Obligations of Citizenship.* New York: Free Press.

Millett, Kate. 1970. *Sexual Politics.* Garden City, NY: Doubleday.

Mink, Gwendlyn. 1998. *Welfare's End.* Ithaca, NY: Cornell University Press.

Mishel, Lawrence and Jared Bernstein. 1994. *The State of Working America.* Washington, DC: Economic Policy Institute.

Murray, Charles. 1984. *Losing Ground: American Social Policy.* New York: Basic Books.

Orloff, Ann S. 1993. Gender and the Social Rights of Citizenship: The Comparative Analysis of Gender Relations and Welfare States. *American Sociological Review* 58(3): 303-28.

Pear, Robert. 2000. Far More Single Mothers Are Taking Jobs. *The New York Times,* November 5, p. 22Y.

Phillips, Kevin. 1990. *The Politics of Rich and Poor: Wealth and the Electorate in the Reagan Aftermath.* New York: Random House.

Pollack, Otto. 1950. *The Criminality of Women.* Philadelphia: University of Pennsylvania Press.

Quadagno, Jill. 1994. *The Color of Welfare: How Racism Undermined the War on Poverty.* New York: Oxford University Press.

Quinney, Richard. 1975. *Criminology, Analysis and Critique of Crime in America.* Boston: Little Brown and Company.

Reigot, Betty P. and Rita K. Spina. 1996. *Beyond the Traditional Family: Voices of Diversity.* New York: Springer Publishing Co.

Reiman, Jeffrey. 2001. *The Rich Get Richer and the Poor Get Prison: Ideology, Class and Criminal Justice.* Boston: Allyn & Bacon.

Rock, Paul. 1996. *Reconstructing a Women's Prison.* Oxford: Clarendon Press.

Sassen, Saskia. 1998. *Globalization and Its Discontents.* New York: New Press.

Schneider, Ann and Ellen Ingram. 1993. Social Construction of Target Populations: Implications for Politics and Policy. *American Political Science Review* 87(2): 334-347.

Schram, Sanford F. 1995. *Words of Welfare: The Poverty of Social Science and the Social Science of Poverty.* Minneapolis: University of Minnesota Press.

Skocpol, Theda. 1992. *Protecting Soldiers and Mothers: The Political Origin of Social Policy in the United States.* Cambridge: Harvard University Press.

Skocpol, Theda. 1995. *Social Policy in the United States: Future Possibilities in Historical Perspective.* Princeton, NJ: Princeton University Press.

Skocpol, Theda. 2000. *The Missing Middle: Working Families and the Future of American Social Policy.* New York: Norton.

Simon, Rita. 1975. *Women and Crime.* Lexington, MA: DC Heath.

Steffensmeyer, Darrel. 1978. Crime and the Contemporary Woman: An Analysis of Female Property Crime, 1960-1975. *Social Forces* 56(2): 566-586.

Steffensmeyer, Darrel. 1980. Assessing the Impact of the Women's Movement on Sex-Based Differences in the Handling of Adult Criminal Defendants. *Crime and Delinquency* 26(3): 344-357.

Stone, Deborah A. 1988. *Policy Paradox and Political Reason.* Boston: Harper Collins.

Tonry, Michael. 1995. *Malign Neglect: Race, Crime, and Punishment in America.* New York: Oxford University Press.

U.S. Bureau of the Census. 1998. *Current Population Survey, March.* Washington, DC: U.S. Bureau of the Census.

Visher, Christy. 1983. Gender, Police Arrest and Notions of Chivalry. *Criminology* 21(3): 5-28.

Wilson, Williams Julius. 1996. *When Work Disappears: The World of the New Urban Poor.* New York: Alfred A. Knopf.

World Bank. 1999. *World Development Indicators.* Washington DC: The World Bank.

Zinn, Maxine Baca. 1989. Family, Race and Politics in the Eighties. *Signs* 14(4): 856-874.

SECTION I:
INCREASING THE DUAL CONTROL
OF WOMEN AND DISTORTING
THEIR STRENGTH

Chapter 2

Welfare Reform:
Tightening the Screws

Joel F. Handler

Aid to Families with Dependent Children (AFDC) has been abolished. The new welfare program created by the Personal Responsibility and Work Opportunity Reconciliation Act of 1996 (PRWORA)—now called Temporary Assistance to Needy Families (TANF)—has stiff work requirements and enforces these requirements with time limits. Not surprisingly, the current welfare reform is being hailed as "new," a fundamental change. Welfare is no longer an entitlement. Instead of a lifetime on welfare, recipients will have to work, and welfare will be available only for relatively short periods of time. In some respects, this is a sharp departure: never before have there been legislatively determined time limits. But in a fundamental sense—the emphasis on work rather than welfare—the current reform is as old as welfare history. The great dividing line in U.S. welfare policy is between the "deserving poor" and "undeserving poor." The former are excused from the paid labor force; the latter are not. From the days of the colonies until post–World War II, most single, poor mothers were not on welfare; thus they were considered part of the paid labor force. It is only since the late 1950s and early 1960s that significant numbers have received welfare, and, as will be discussed shortly, when they finally did receive welfare, they were still subject to work requirements.

After reviewing some of the prior work requirements and the key provisions of the new law, I will discuss the work programs and the assumptions behind these provisions as well as the recent welfare experience. There has been a very dramatic decline in the welfare rolls. Why? Are the welfare-to-work programs succeeding in getting recipients to work? Are families leaving welfare because of sanctions or denied entry? How are the families who have left welfare coping? Finally, I raise questions regarding the future of welfare reform.

WELFARE IN "CRISIS": 1960s-1996

Aid to Dependent Children (ADC)—subsequently changed to Aid to Families with Dependent Children (AFDC)—programs were enacted by the states between about 1910 and 1920; they were popularly known as "mothers' pensions." The programs were for "fit and proper" mothers, which most often meant white widows. Other single mothers—the divorced, deserted, never married, and those of color—were, for the most part, excluded; they were still the "undeserving poor." The programs were small (Bell, 1965). ADC became one of the grants in aid. There were a few federal requirements, but basically the states and local governments had the major responsibility, including financial eligibility and level of support. No other welfare programs were available for single, poor mothers and their children except the very uneven and miserly locally administered general relief.

Dramatic changes came in the late 1950s and 1960s. Over the next three decades, the ADC/AFDC rolls went from 2 million to about 13 million. Expenditures rose from about $500 million to about $23 billion (Handler and Hasenfeld, 1991). In streamed those who had been excluded previously: African Americans, the divorced, separated, deserted, and increasingly never married—in short, the "undeserving poor" (Piven and Cloward, 1977). Welfare was now in "crisis." Eligibility was tightened; benefits were cut. Nevertheless, costs and numbers rose steadily and the program appeared out of control. Political and popular concern focused on the large number of African-American women, out-of-wedlock births, single parents, and generational dependency in the program (Abramovitz, 1988).

The major response by government was a return to first principles. Since AFDC was now supporting the "undeserving poor," they were not excused from work. Although many states had their own work programs, starting in the 1967 the federal government introduced a mandatory work program—the Work Incentive Program (WIN). At first, liberals opposed work requirements; they argued that if nonwelfare mothers were not required to work, it was unfair and punitive to impose work requirements on single poor mothers. Conservatives thought otherwise. Single poor mothers did not shed their historical undeserving status simply because misguided liberals let them into AFDC. They were morally different from mothers who were either dependent on men or self-sufficient. Thus, they should be required to work.

The work requirements never worked to reduce rolls through employment, to set the poor to work, or to impose sanctions for failure to comply. For the most part, the requirements were either too burdensome administratively or too costly. The vast majority of welfare recipients were either declared ineligible for the programs or otherwise excused from the require-

That's the first thing they attack when you come to prison—your sense of identity. They fingerprint you and issue you a number. They put you through your first strip search. Some stranger ruthlessly paws your personal possessions for the first time and tells you what you may keep and what you must send out. They make you take a shower, and they spray you for lice. Usually, they're as intimidating as possible during this process. The message is clear—you're no longer a person. From this point on you're less than an animal.

That's how the struggle for survival begins. It continues through every minute of every hour of every day of every year you spend in prison. From this day forward you will walk the fine line between sanity and insanity. Some survive it better than others, but no one comes out of it whole. The struggle consumes every ounce of your energy constantly. . . .

You watch as different parts of you die against your will. You mourn their passing, but there's little you can do to save them. You don't like what you see yourself becoming, but you know that if you are to survive, you must allow it to happen, even collaborate in it. Before long, you're down to a core self consisting of those traits that are most important to your sense of self. What's left of you is a grossly disfigured resemblance of who you used to be, but it is still you. . . .

Somewhere in the pit of your soul you know that if they get any part of this, there will be no more you. . . . [T]hey will have gotten your very humanity.

That's what they want—your humanity. The prison machine exists solely for the purpose of grinding it out of you. It's the only thing that prisons are efficient at doing.

From "The Visit" by Susan Fair

ments. In the meantime, welfare recipients were condemned for their continued dependency.

Both sides remained unhappy. Conservatives continued to attack the "entitlement state" on the grounds that there are *responsibilities* as well as rights in the social contract. Then, in the late 1980s, the liberals changed. Instead of arguing that it was unfair to require AFDC mothers to work, they now argued that AFDC mothers should be *expected* to work. Two reasons were given. First, social norms concerning female labor had changed. Now, the majority of nonwelfare mothers were in the paid labor force, and therefore, it was reasonable to expect welfare mothers to work. Second, families were better off, both materially and socially, when the adults were gainfully employed rather than continually dependent (Ellwood, 1988; Garfinkel and McLanahan, 1986).

This last point—the claimed rehabilitative benefits from paid labor—illustrates a fundamental characteristic of welfare policy. Although welfare policy is often described in seemingly objective terms—labor markets, wage rates, incentives, earnings, and so forth—these terms are heavily ladened with moral judgments. Who the poor are, why they are poor, whether they should be helped, and under what conditions are social judgments that affirm moral norms of work, family, gender roles, and attitudes toward race and ethnicity. The stigmatization of the "undeserving" poor is much broader than failing to become gainfully employed. AFDC, now TANF (the lightning rod for the current attacks on welfare) uses the term "welfare" as a code word for the inner-city-dwelling, young African-American woman, most likely a substance abuser, having children to stay on welfare and breeding a criminal class. This is the "underclass."

THE PERSONAL RESPONSIBILITY AND WORK OPPORTUNITY RECONCILIATION ACT OF 1996 (PRWORA)

Under TANF, state authority over AFDC—already considerable—has been greatly expanded by converting the federal entitlement into block grants. The block grant is calculated on the basis of the state's AFDC caseload in 1994. Because caseloads have been declining since 1994, states have received excess money under the formula. There are restrictions on the states under the block grants, but whether and how these restrictions apply depends on previously granted state waivers. As discussed in the later section, The Work-First Strategy, over forty states have waivers.[1]

There are two sets of time limits for TANF assistance. There is a cumulative five-year limit on cash assistance (with exceptions for no more than 20 percent of the caseload). In addition, states were required to move an increasing percentage of welfare recipients into the workforce over the next six years, starting with 25 percent of the adults in single-parent families in 1997 and increasing to 50 percent by 2002. States are also required to reduce grant amounts for recipients who refuse to participate in "work or work activities." These welfare-to-work requirements are to be enforced by funding cuts in the block grants.

In addition to the work requirements, there are a variety of provisions dealing with "family values." For example, PRWORA prohibits the use of federal funds for minor parents under eighteen years of age who are not in school or other specified educational activities or living in an adult-supervised setting. States are required to reduce a family's grant by 25 percent if it fails to cooperate (without good cause) with efforts to establish paternity. States may eliminate cash assistance to families altogether or provide any mix of cash or in-kind benefits they choose. They can deny aid to all teenaged parents or other selected groups, deny aid to children born to parents receiving aid, deny aid to legal immigrants, or establish their own or lower time limits for receipt of aid. States can provide new residents with benefits equal to the amount offered in their former state of residence for up to one year.[2] States may choose to deny cash assistance for life to persons convicted of a drug-related felony (which in many states can consist of possession of a small amount of marijuana).

PRWORA also modifies other programs that impact on the well-being and work effort of welfare recipients. For example, while the basic structure of Medicaid remains intact, welfare families are no longer automatically eligible; they must apply separately. Undoubtedly, some percentage will not enroll. States may terminate eligibility for all legal immigrants as of January 1, 1997, again with some exceptions (this provision has since been modified).[3] Furthermore, PRWORA also substantially narrows the supplementary security income (SSI) definition of disability for children. It is estimated that more than 300,000 children could be denied benefits by 2002 (Children's Defense Fund, 1997). A prior law denies eligibility to recipients whose primary disability is alcohol and/or substance abuse. Recipients incarcerated for more than thirty days will be denied eligibility. Most noncitizens (with the same exceptions) will no longer be eligible.[4] PRWORA also affects a variety of other programs, including food stamps, other nutritional programs, child-support enforcement, and child care. Although most attention is concentrated on AFDC, it should be recognized that these other programs often have a critical impact on the employability and well-being of low-income mothers and children.

THE WORK-FIRST STRATEGY

Prior to TANF, over forty states had pending or approved waiver requests which imposed work requirements enforced by some form of time limits. At least twenty states have time limits less than five years; in ten states, it is only two years (DeParle, 1997c). Most states then revoked grants to parents only if they failed to comply with the work requirements; now, in thirty-three states, the whole family loses the entire grant. Some states provide for combinations of welfare and work for a limited period of time. Most states exempt families in which the parent is disabled or incapacitated, in which the parent is caring for a young child, or in which a parent is a minor attending school.

The consensus behind the work provisions (as well as the family values provisions) is that welfare encourages dependency. Recipients, instead of seeking to improve themselves and become self-sufficient, have children to get on welfare and stay on welfare, which then becomes a way of life from generation to generation. Thus, welfare recipients, according to the stereotype, threaten both the two-parent family and the work ethic. Therefore, tough work requirements (enforced by time limits) will not only reduce welfare costs but, more important, replace the entitlement status and permissiveness of the past system with the values of responsibility and self-sufficiency. This will not only benefit the parents, but also provide positive socialization for the children.

The reported experience of these welfare-to-work projects was used to justify the current welfare-to-work approach, known as the "work-first" strategy. The argument for this strategy is:

1. There are plenty of jobs for those who want to work.
2. By taking any job (even an entry-level job) and sticking with that job, a person will move up the employment ladder.
3. Welfare recipients would not otherwise have the motivation nor the incentives to leave welfare and enter the paid labor markets.
4. State programs have shown that recipients can be moved from welfare to work.

The idea is to move not only current recipients but also applicants—before they get on welfare—into the labor market as quickly as possible rather than place them in longer-term training or education programs.

Many states, pursuant to waivers, began implementing their programs between 1993 and 1995. Between 1995 and 1997—the year prior to and the year following the enactment of PRWORA—state reforms began taking effect on a larger scale and the welfare rolls fell sharply (Primus et al., 1999). AFDC/TANF cases, nationwide, declined from their peak of 5 million families in March 1994, to 4.4 million when TANF was enacted, to 2.8 million in December 1998 (Greenberg, 1999, p. 2). To what extent has the decline in the rolls been the result of state programs? Of the federal requirements? Although everyone is claiming "success," it is hard to be precise. The various sources—administrative data, national-longitudinal surveys, and targeted surveys—cover only partially overlapping periods (Cancian et al., 1999, p. 22). Often gaps exist in the data. Then, as discussed later, gathering data on those who have left the rolls but have not engaged in reported employment or who have been "diverted" from the welfare altogether is, at this time, very problematic. What follows, therefore, is based on what information is available.

One of the most noteworthy programs is in Riverside County, operating under the California welfare-work-demonstration program called GAIN (Greater Avenues to Independence). Riverside County is considered the standard bearer for the work-first strategy.[5] The Riverside results are hailed as successful: welfare recipients who work earn more than the controls, welfare payments are reduced, and the program shows a positive cost-benefit ratio. A closer look, however, shows that the Riverside results are indeed modest. Riverside had the best positive results—the highest earnings and the greatest welfare savings. However, participants in the experiment averaged less than twenty dollars per week more than the controls. A variety of research shows that most recipients supplement welfare with work and/or have monthly combined budgets of about $1,000 (Edin and Lein, 1996; Harris, 1993). Therefore, the difference between the Riverside experimentals and the controls (who are working off the books) is about 8.5 percent. Moreover, this difference came about because the experimentals were working longer hours rather than at higher wages. Perhaps even more significant is the fact that despite the great efforts of the Riverside County department, about two-thirds of the experimentals were *not* working at the end of the three-year test period and almost half *never* worked during the entire three-year period. In other words, most recipients did not get jobs, and those who did earned very little more than those who packaged welfare with work on their own. Even with these modest results, replication is, at best, problematical. Florida, for example, has not been able to replicate Riverside's experiment (Handler and Hasenfeld, 1997).

The results from other California welfare-to-work programs are even more disheartening. Smaller percentages of recipients were enrolled, found work, or earned more than the controls. This is also the experience in other states: many programs fail to show positive results, and, of those that do, the results are very modest. Nevertheless, the Riverside work-first strategy has been hailed as a success and has become the standard, both nationally and on the state level (Handler and Hasenfeld, 1997).

Why these modest results? The assumptions behind welfare-to-work programs are totally misconceived as to who welfare recipients are, why they are on welfare, and the characteristics of the low-wage labor market. First, I will consider the characteristics of the low-wage labor market, then the match between the welfare recipients and the jobs. I will conclude by discussing what has been happening to ex-welfare recipients.

The Low-Wage Labor Market

Contrary to one of the basic assumptions behind the welfare-to-work strategy, despite the impressive growth in jobs and the very low unemployment, the big story with the U.S. labor market is the decline in real wages of the less skilled, less educated workers over the past two decades (Danziger and Reed, 1999). Jobs are increasingly contingent or short term and without benefits.[6] In general, the returns from low-wage work are either not improving or just barely beginning to move up (Rivlin, 1999, p. 2). Despite the fact that most Americans are better off, the bottom fifth of the population is *worse* off. The average annual income of this group is $8,800, down from $10,000 in 1997.[7] For a while, the inequality in women's wages narrowed—primarily because of an increase in the hours worked *and* the significant decline in male earnings, rather than an increase in female wages (Mishel, Bernstein, and Schmitt, 1999, pp. 134-135)—but then the gender gap increased during the 1980s (Bernhardt, Morris, and Handcock, 1995, p. 320). The decline in real wages for the less skilled, less educated workers was especially pronounced for adults aged twenty-four to thirty-five with a high school diploma or less. Female dropouts earn only 58 percent of the wages that male dropouts earn. Despite the overall low unemployment figures even before the recession, there was considerable evidence that, at least in this segment of the labor market, there are more job applicants than available positions. Employment mobility is also a myth. Whether or not it was true in the past, increasing evidence today suggests that low-wage workers are not moving up the economic ladder (Mishel, Bernstein, and Schmitt, 1999).

The Work Experience of Welfare Recipients

Contrary to the stereotype, most welfare recipients are adults with small families (1.9 children, on average) and are on welfare for relatively short periods—between two and four years. Long-term dependency (five years or more) is rare—perhaps as low as 15 percent. Furthermore, it turns out—again contrary to myth—that the largest proportion of welfare recipients are connected to the paid labor market. Many package work with welfare, and the most common route away from welfare is via a job. In other words, most welfare recipients have a good work ethic. However, those who leave welfare often have to return. The low-skilled labor market produces a cycling back and forth between work and welfare (Handler and Hasenfeld, 1997).

Thus far, welfare recipients do not fare particularly well in competition for these low-skilled jobs. Employers of low-skilled workers are looking for high school diplomas, work experience, and people or social skills ("soft skills"). They often hire through networks and, in general, prefer workers with similar ethnic backgrounds to their own. African Americans are at the end of the queue. Welfare recipients often lack the characteristics that employers favor, particularly the high school diploma and a steady work experience. Perhaps most significant, welfare recipients are often handicapped by being parents, especially mothers, of small children. Research on women in the low-wage labor market shows that job applicants do not disclose that they have small children. Not only are there the usual child care problems, but children get sick; there may be school or preschool issues; and there is the difficulty of adjusting to shift work and overtime (Handler and White, 1999). Harry Holzer, on the basis of a survey of 900 Michigan employers, found that while employers in general indicated a willingness to hire welfare recipients, only about 6 percent of the jobs would likely be "available to women with few skills, little experience, and poor reading and math skills" (Holzer, 1999, p. 30).

Welfare recipients are in a tough competition for available jobs; the jobs that they get are low paying, usually without benefits, and often short term. This is why most recipients cycle in and out of the labor market. But why welfare? Because in most states, they do not qualify for unemployment insurance. Either they have not worked sufficient hours or they have to quit for family reasons (e.g., lack of day care for shift work), which, in most states, is considered a voluntary quit. In other words, for these women AFDC is the equivalent of unemployment compensation (Williams, 1999).

Turning to the supply side, what barriers do the recipients themselves face? Most welfare recipients are already attached to the labor market— either they are working (often in the underground economy) or have recently worked, or will reenter the labor market on their own relatively shortly. The rapid decline of the welfare rolls with record employment probably means that those still remaining on the rolls are more likely to have more serious barriers to employment than those who have already left (Danziger et al., 1999). Sandra Danziger and her colleagues interviewed 753 welfare mothers (56 percent African American, 44 percent whites) in an urban Michigan county in 1997 and 1998, using fourteen measures that are potentially barriers to employment (such as education, work history, access to a car, skills used on previous employment, attitudes toward common workplace norms, and whether the respondents encountered discrimination, sexual harassment, or domestic violence). They also used standard psychological screening tests, general health, and whether at least one child had physical, emotional, or learning disorders. Only a small percentage (15 percent) had no work barrier; 66 percent had two or more, and 25 percent, four or more. There were few racial differences, although African Americans reported more transportation problems and fewer job skills. Not surprisingly, "the number of barriers that a woman faces is significantly associated with the likelihood that she will work" (Danziger et al., 1999, p. 34). Women who face only one barrier (20 percent) are just as likely to work as women who face none. But thereafter, the likelihood of working steadily declines as the number of barriers increases. The more significant barriers, in addition to education, are few work skills, transportation, poor health, drug dependency, depression, and perceived workplace discrimination (Danziger et al., 1999).

For those recipients who have education, work experience, skills, and fewer and older children, welfare will be relatively short term. For the others, their situation will be very different. Nearly 50 percent of recipients have not completed high school, and "even in today's relatively robust economic climate, high school dropouts face an unemployment rate four times that of college graduates. . . . If states are successful in getting the most disadvantaged recipients into the labor market, these women are likely still to experience long periods without work. . . ." (Pavetti, 1999, p. 18; Loprest, 1999).

Reports are starting to come in about the employment of welfare recipients. In a review of several state studies, the Center on Budget and Policy Priorities reports that employed former recipients and recipients who combine work and welfare typically work a substantial number of hours (usually more than thirty hours per week) but are paid less than eight dollars per hour (and a substantial portion less than six dollars per hour; earnings are higher for those with a high school diploma or GED). Most of the studies that track former recipients find that between half and two-thirds find jobs shortly after leaving welfare. Most of the jobs are in sales, food preparation, clerical support, and other areas of service. Moreover, despite the relatively high number of weekly hours of work, there are substantial periods of unemployment. Thus, the annual incomes range between $8,000 and $10,800, well below the poverty level for a family of three. Most employed recipients do not receive benefits (vacations, sick leave, medical benefits), and many are not covered by the federal Family and Medical Leave Act (Author Sharon Parrott points out that the studies *do not* provide information on families who do *not* apply for assistance or families who are *"diverted"* from welfare [1998].)[8]

Assuming that a welfare recipient does find a job, she also has to compete in the child care market. The crisis in child care—especially for low-wage workers—cannot be overemphasized. Millions of infants, children, and adolescents are at high risk of being compromised both developmentally and in health because of mediocre child care. Yet the current welfare reform requires mothers of young children—in some cases, three-month-old infants—to enter the paid labor force. Child care centers are at capacity, and even if there are vacancies the cost is usually too high for welfare recipients to manage. As of 1998, New York City lacks child care slots for 61 percent of the children whose mothers are supposed to participate in workfare. The state comptroller estimates that New York State will need child care for 61,000 children by the year 2001, but only 27,500 slots are in the budget. Currently 20,000 children are on waiting lists for child care (Children's Defense Fund, 1998). Consequently, most welfare recipients use unregulated relative or family day care. Even in these cases, costs are high and expenses—as well as availability—vary depending on the age of the children and whether it is daytime care or variable due to the mother being on shift work (White, 1999).

How much do families pay for child care? In 1990, the average working-poor family paid thirty-eight dollars per week, which represented a third of their household income. How much does this buy when even mediocre center-based care averaged ninety-five dollars per week per child? The new federal law does provide more funds for child care, but according to the Congressional Budget Office, the amount is $1.4 billion short of what is needed (Clark and Long, 1995). Low child care wages, in turn, often attract workers who lack the skills to face the challenges of higher-wage labor markets. As a result, employees in child care often have low morale, limited training, and high turnover (White, 1999).

Along with child care, the problem of health care cannot be exaggerated. Poor health in either the parent or the children has an impact on the ability to work. Because of poorer health, low-income people need to use more health care services than higher-income people, but they have greater difficulty getting health insurance and health care. AFDC/TANF recipients qualify for Medicaid, and under the new law—as well as under several of the state reforms—Medicaid continues for a period, but for no more than a year after the exit from welfare. Under TANF, welfare recipients are no longer automatically enrolled in Medicaid. There has been a sharp decline in the Medicaid rolls, the reasons for which are not clear. It could be that workers are not advising recipients of their eligibility or are discouraging them from applying, or that ex-recipients mistakenly think that they are ineligible. (The same drop is occurring in food stamps enrollment.) In the meantime, fewer low-wage employers are providing health insurance, especially for family members. Access to health care for low-wage working mothers is becoming increasingly more difficult. The number of Americans without health insurance is now more than 40 million.

Once the life circumstances of welfare recipients are recognized, it is easy to understand why they have such a hard time competing even for low-wage, entry-level jobs. They have low levels of education (half have not completed high school); they have major child care responsibilities, uneven or sparse work experience, and are disproportionately of color.

> Even if they do manage to find and keep jobs, the upper-bound estimate of their earnings should they work full-time year-round . . . is no more than $12,000-$14,000; given their family sizes, this level of earnings will not remove them from poverty. And this assumes full-time work. In fact, most recipients only find temporary jobs paying

less than average wages. Indeed the typical former recipient earns about one-half of this "outer limit" earnings level. (Burtless, 1995, p. 77)

The Decline in the Welfare Rolls

If employment is so uncertain, what, then, accounts for the dramatic decline in the welfare rolls? Politicians—state level as well as national level—are, of course, claiming that welfare reform is "working," despite the fact that rolls were declining significantly before many of the work requirements were enacted (DeParle, 1997b; Brito, 1999; Pear, 1996).[9] Is the work-first strategy succeeding, or are welfare adults getting jobs on their own in a booming economy? As discussed, a variety of evidence shows that most welfare recipients do not live on welfare alone. They often package welfare with other sources of income, such as gifts from family, support from fathers, and off-the-books earnings. Many have significant connections with the low-wage labor market. Because it is so difficult to find out what exactly happens at the street level (and how to interpret what happens) between the worker and the client—is "mere" information about impending time limits a threat and therefore a subsequent work exit is counted as part of the welfare-to-work program?—it is not surprising that various studies estimate the decline in the workers' rolls due to welfare reform to range from "trivial" to about 40 percent (Ziliak et al., 1997; Meyer and Rosenbaum, 1999; Ellwood, 1999; Council of Economic Advisors, 1999).[10]

A significant number of recipients may have lost their benefits for failure to comply with the new rules, which are extensive. Some states require a job search when applicants first approach welfare. Others require prompt participation in job preparation sessions. In some states, recipients who are not successful in finding a job must participate in community service work. The requirements start early; there are forms to fill out and questions to be answered; and it all gets tracked with computers. There are sanctions for failure to comply. Some lose benefits; others are dropped from the rolls.[11] While states vary in terms of the timing and severity of sanctions,[12] the trend is toward more severe sanctioning. Although, again, there is considerable variation among the states,[13] sanction rates between 25 and 30 percent or higher are not unusual.[14] The best estimate is that between October 1996 and June 1997, of those who left the rolls more than a third were the result of sanctions for violating program requirements. The TANF two-year time limit has started to kick in, but some states under the waiver program have already terminated a substantial number of recipients using their own time limits—for example, 5,800 people in Arizona.[15]

How Are Welfare Leavers Doing?

In the most recent study of those leaving welfare, Pamela Loprest of the Urban Institute, found that although leavers are doing as well as nonwelfare low-income mothers, both are concentrated in low-wage, entry-level work; work night hours; often have multiple jobs; and struggle with child care (Loprest, 1999). Most lack health insurance and the median hourly wage of welfare leavers is $6.61. Although this was substantially higher than the minimum wage at that time ($4.75), Loprest (1999) points out that it is in the twentieth percentile of hourly wages for all workers. But these wages are as high or higher than those of low-income mothers (at least 25 percent of low-income mothers earned less than the minimum wage). On an annualized basis, the median earnings of leavers, in 1997, was $13,778, which was roughly the poverty line for a family of three. This does not take into account other sources of income, such as child support or the Earned Income Tax Credit. Substantial numbers of leavers report serious problems providing food and rent (Loprest, 1999, p. 24). The poorest 20 percent of these families lost more in welfare benefits—almost $1,400 per family—than they gained in earnings (Weinstein, 1999).

The National Conference of State Legislators summarized the reports of nine states that tracked leavers.[16] Most leavers (between 50 and 60 percent) are finding jobs. Most of the jobs pay between $5.50 and $7.00 per hour, which still leaves the families in poverty. Child care and transportation remain difficult obstacles to employment. Significant numbers of families experienced hardship and deprivation (e.g., not enough money for food or rent). About 20 percent of the families return to welfare within several months (Tweedie and Reichert, 1998).[17] Work is unstable. In Milwaukee, although 72 percent of leavers worked in the first quarter of 1996, half of those were either unemployed or marginally employed a year later. In New York City, only about 20 to 30 percent of leavers found jobs (Children's Defense Fund, 1998).

Whereas leavers who are working compare favorably with low-income mothers in terms of employment, more than a third of the leavers are not working. Fourteen percent of this group relies on the earnings of a spouse or partner. Of the remaining 25 percent, more than a quarter report that they are disabled, sick, or otherwise unable to work. Others report lack of access or lack of work supports, family responsibilities, transportation problems, and so forth. Of those not working and not disabled, 69 percent say that they are looking for work. As to sources of support for nonworkers, only a small percentage received unemployment benefits and less than half were using food stamps and Medicaid. Almost three-quarters of all former recipients report receiving no private help in the first three months after leaving welfare (Loprest, 1999). Former recipients report more economic struggles than low-income mothers—cutting down or skipping meals because of lack of money (33 percent), worries about lack of money for food (57 percent), running out of food at the end of the month (about 50 percent), inability to pay rent, mortgage, or utility bills (39 percent), and having to move in with others because of lack of money (7 percent).

THE FUTURE

Predictions as to the likely effects of major social legislation are always uncertain. In light of the previous discussion on the state of the low-wage labor market, a significant number of welfare recipients will not be able to permanently leave welfare via work. However, how many will actually be cut off—whether under the two-year or the five-year rule—depends, in part, on the size of the rolls. Whether rolls continue to decline or stabilize or increase depends ultimately on the economy, but even with a good economy those who are left on the rolls are those hard to employ. This group now faces the time limits.

In the meantime, poverty and hardship is increasing for families with potentially very serious impacts on the children. The likelihood of significant impacts on the child-protection system is not far-fetched when one considers how close to the edge many welfare families are living. Today, nationwide, more than a third of the homeless are families, an increase in 10 percent since 1985. Most of these families are headed by women. In addition to poverty and limited employment opportunities, high proportions of these mothers have suffered from physical and sexual abuse. AFDC provided at least some financial stability; families not on AFDC were far more likely to end up homeless than AFDC families (Bussuk, Browne, and Buckner, 1996, p. 62).[18]

Who will bear these costs? The answer is the families as well as the government. It has not come to the point at which mothers and children are turned out of shelters and left to beg and die in the streets. However, shelters, foster families, and group homes must be paid. These are primarily local government costs. Just as the federal government is getting rid of the "welfare problem" by delegating it to the states, so too will state governments delegate the problem to the counties and municipalities. Delegation is a favorite technique of managing conflict in American politics.

If the past is any guide, one would not predict dramatic changes in welfare. Throughout history, welfare policy has been largely symbolic. Myths and stereotypes gain prominence; drastic reforms are enacted; but policy at the field level is usually decoupled from administration. There are many reasons, but usually the policies as enacted are too draconian and, more important, too costly in the end. More often than not, it is states and local governments that bear the increased costs. Serious welfare-to-work programs—including community service jobs—are more expensive than welfare, as are other alternatives such as shelter care and foster care.

Under the present reforms, states have plenty of room to fudge. Welfare rolls are declining, which reduces the number of recipients that states have to place in work programs. In addition, the states can decide what constitutes work or "best effort," and can excuse up to 20 percent of the caseload. Furthermore, even if states do not meet their quotas, serious federal penalties are not likely. Federal government sanctions against states for not meeting quality-control requirements are rarely if ever imposed. States always excuse their failures, and their congressional delegations lobby against federal penalties. Similar considerations may well apply within states. Counties and municipalities will resist state-imposed welfare costs. The usual practice in the face of these conflicting pressures is myth and ceremony. Some recipients will find jobs and leave welfare (whether as a result of the programs is another matter). Others will be sanctioned and everyone will proclaim success—as long as welfare does not remain a salient political "crisis." In many states, compromises are evident. Although some states have very harsh rules, there does not seem to be a race to the bottom, at least in terms of formal rules—yet (DeParle, 1997c).

The present situation, however, looks very different from past welfare reforms. Three kinds of changes have been occurring. One is a continuation of the recent past—the gradual erosion of benefits. Adjusting for inflation, the average welfare grant per recipient in 1970 was $676 per month; in 1996, it was $374—a 45 percent reduction (House Committee on Ways and Means, 1998, p. 402). The second change is one already discussed—the dramatic decline in the caseloads. As previously discussed, most probably between half and two-thirds of the former recipients are working. Although their jobs often pay more than the minimum wage, they are still in poverty, jobs are often temporary, and there is considerable unemployment (Greenberg, 1999).[19] What has happened to the other recipients who have left the rolls? What is happening with families who apply for welfare but are rejected? It is hard to find out.

The third change has been the vast increase in privatization. There is a gold mine to be made by private companies who take over parts or even all public welfare. Thus far, most of the privatization has occurred with specific parts of welfare—for example, work programs, day care, child-support collections, and Medicare. Over thirty states have entered into contracts for various services (Hartung and Washburn, 1998; Cohen, 1998).[20] The states and, increasingly, private contractors are reluctant either to collect or disclose the information. Caseworkers have a great deal of discretion as to how to administer the work requirements. In some states, most applicants must first look for a job before they can enroll (Brito, 2000; DeParle, 1997a).[21] Records on applicants who are deflected may not be kept (Swarns, 1998). With the increase in privatization of welfare, it will become even more difficult to find out what is happening. Private contractors have strong incentives to "cream" (choosing to work only with the most employable) and to fudge the data (Hartung and Washburn, 1998; Cohen, 1998).[22] Furthermore, states can always reduce rolls on the basis of fraud. As we have seen, most families supplement their income by off-the-books earnings and/or gifts from relatives and friends (including some child support). This vital but extra income is not reported; hence, all these families are vulnerable to sanctions for fraud. Under prior law, if a state sanctioned a family, the state would lose the federal cost-sharing contribution. Now, the states make money when clients are dropped from the rolls under the block grant formula. Even though poverty-related costs may show up in another part of the county budget, it would occur at a different time and place.

This low-visibility sanctioning can become increasingly serious as states continue to privatize their welfare systems. Then, state governments and their contractors will be under even more pressure to show a positive cost-benefit ratio. This kind of welfare reform—what Michael Lipsky called "bureaucratic disentitlement" (1984, p. 58)—is particularly insidious because increasingly, the victims have no redress. The poor no longer have legal help. Although technically available, Legal Services was never able to handle the need, and now it is badly crippled.[23]

No one seems to care that when recipients leave welfare via employment, most remain poor and are worse off than when they were on welfare. There is no discussion about poverty. There is no discussion about what is happening to the children. The public discussion is only about work versus welfare. It is assumed that once a family is off welfare, everything is fine.

NOTES

1. For a description on state waivers, see Handler, 1995.

2. Subsequently declared unconstitutional in *Anderson v. Roe* (U.S. Supreme Court, 1999).

3. Immigrants are denied all federally means-tested programs for five years after arrival. There are some exceptions for veterans, military personnel, refugees, political exiles, and immigrants with a ten-year work history in the United States. Medicaid will continue to cover emergency treatment. After five years, many legal

immigrants will be disqualified through the deeming of sponsors' income. See *City of Chicago v. Shalala,* 189 F. 2d 598 (7th Cir., 1999).

4. The Act also reduces food-stamp benefits in a number of ways, including a general tightening of eligibility. Funding will be reduced or eliminated for child nutrition and meals programs, including programs in family day care, the Summer Food Program, the School Breakfast Program, and other meal services. States may deny all federal food assistance, except school lunch and breakfast, to undocumented immigrants. Various child care programs are consolidated into the Child Care and Development Block Grant. Several provisions of PRWORA aim at trying to bolster current child-support enforcement efforts. States are allowed to transfer up to 30 percent of their TANF block grant to the Child Care and Development Block Grant and Title XX Social Services Block Grant, but transferred funds must be used for children and families below 200 percent of the poverty level. In the meantime, funding for the Title XX Block Grant was cut 15 percent.

5. For a discussion of the Riverside program, see Handler and Hasenfeld, 1997.

6. The instability of employment is not confined to the low-wage labor market. A recent survey in California reported that four out of ten workers have been at their jobs for less than three years, and that just one-third fit the conventional mode— working outside of the home at a single, full-time job, year-round as a daytime employee (see Lee, 1999).

7. A discussion of the recently published analysis by the Center on Budget and Policy Priorities.

8. See Parrott, 1998. The federal Family and Medical Leave Act (FMLA) requires employers to provide up to twelve weeks of unpaid leave for employees for certain reasons, including a serious health need or to care for a child with a serious health need. Employees have to have worked for the their current employer at least twenty-five hours a week for at least one year to be eligible for this leave.

9. See Brito, 1999. For example, rolls had declined 26 percent in Maryland, 24 percent in Wisconsin, 21 percent in Indiana, 18 percent in Oklahoma, 15 percent in Louisiana, and 14 percent in Michigan.

10. Ziliak, James, David Figlio, Elizabeth Davis, and Laura Connolly. 1997. "For example, in Wisconsin, the state with the largest caseload reduction from 1993 to 1996, we attribute only 11 percent of the decline to welfare waivers but 53 percent to business-cycle factors. In the twenty-six states experiencing at least a 20 percent decline in per capita AFDC caseloads, we attribute 78 percent of the decline to business-cycle factors and 6 percent to welfare waivers." See Meyer and Rosenbaum, 1999; Ellwood, 1999; Council of Economic Advisors, 1999.

11. States have considerable flexibility in designing sanctions. Generally speaking, there are three types: (1) adult only; (2) full family (either eliminated or reduced); and (3) pay for performance (amount of the penalty corresponds to the amount of hours the recipient fails to work) (Kaplan, 1999). Tonya Brito (2000) summarizes the existing research on sanctions: "Early reports show that in Florida sanctions accounting for more than 25 percent of families whose benefits were terminated between July 1997 to December 1997. In New Jersey over two-thirds of the cases terminated during the first three months of the new state welfare program resulted from sanctions. In Tennessee, at least 35 percent of the 34,000 families who

lost benefits since September 1996 did so as a result of sanctions for non-compli-ance. In Maryland, by contrast, sanctions accounted for only 7 percent of the 2,156 families whose cases were closed between October 1996 and September 1997."

12. Currently, about twenty-one states eliminate the adult share of the grant at the first instance of noncompliance; in fourteen states, the family loses the entire grant (full-family sanction) for the first instance of noncompliance. In twenty states, the minimum time for a sanction is one month even if the recipient starts to comply; in seven states, the minimum time is three months. The length of sanctions increases with subsequent violations. In addition, states can decide whether the sanctioned re-cipient will also receive a reduction in or lose food stamps or Medicaid (but not for children or if the recipient is pregnant). See Brito, 2000.

13. For example, in Delaware, 49 percent of families were sanctioned within the first year of TANF; 31 percent in Montana; 11 percent of average monthly cases were closed in Oklahoma; 3.4 percent in South Carolina (Brito, 2000).

14. Brito, 2000, p. 67.

15. Brito, 2000.

16. Children's Defense Fund, 1997. In Iowa, 49 percent of those sanctioned said that their income had decreased. In South Carolina, 50 percent reported being be-hind in the rent or utilities, as compared to 35 percent on welfare.

17. See Tweedie and Reichert, 1998. The states are: Michigan, Kentucky, Mis-souri, Iowa, New Mexico, Indiana, South Carolina, Maryland, and Tennessee. The studies differ on methodology and are to be treated cautiously.

18. See Bussuk, Browne, and Buckner, 1996. In a study of homeless families in Massachusetts, 91.6 percent of the homeless mothers reported physical or sexual abuse at some point in their lives. Using conservative measures (e.g., excluding spanking, shoving, slapping), almost two-thirds reported violence by parents or caretakers, more than 40 percent reported sexual molestation, and 63 percent re-ported assaults by intimate male partners (including being punched, kicked, burned, choked, beaten, and threatened or attacked with a knife or a gun, but excluded being pushed, shoved, or slapped fewer than six times); and 25 percent reported physical or sexual attacks by nonintimates.

19. See Greenberg, 1999. One study (pre-TANF data) showed that only 40 per-cent of those who entered employment were working six months later, and only one-third worked for 75 percent of the time over a two-year period (Rangarajan, Schochet, and Chu, 1998).

20. See Hartung and Washburn, 1998; Cohen, 1998. The Lockheed bid failed, in part, because of the vigorous campaign of the public employees union, and the re-fusal of the federal government to grant a waiver. A waiver was needed because the law requires the state to handle intake.

21. See Brito, 2000; DeParle, 1997a. A discussion of a wide range of difficulties applicants encounter.

22. See Hartung and Washburn, 1998. In discussing Lockheed's performance managing the child-support operations in San Francisco, the head of the system said, "We'd get slime data, which was incomplete or garbled. The system can't lo-cate people. It can't produce forms."

23. When President Reagan took office, he proposed no funds for Legal Services for seven budgets in a row. The program survived, but funds were sharply cut, forcing significant reductions in staff. Consequently, groups of cases (e.g., bankruptcies, disability benefits) had to be dropped by many offices. The Nixon administration also tried to abolish the program and distribute the funds to the states. When that plan failed, the compromise was to create an independent corporation, the Legal Services Corporation (LSC) (1974) and, for the first time, restrictions on the kinds of cases that Legal Services could handle were imposed—school desegregation, the draft (the Vietnam War), abortion, postconviction civil challenges. The backup centers were eliminated. On the other hand, the corporation's budget was increased dramatically, from $71 million in 1975 to $321.3 million in 1981. In that year, the LSC made annual grants to 323 programs which employed 6,218 lawyers in 1,425 offices providing legal assistance to over 1.2 million matters. Then the cuts started. The 1994 Republican Congress made deep funding cuts (from $400 to $278 million) as part of a three-year plan to abolish Legal Services altogether, and added the most severe restrictions to date: prohibiting all class actions; eliminating the collection of attorneys' fees; prohibiting participation in administrative rulemaking, lobbying, litigation on behalf of prisoners, representing drug-related public housing evictions, and representing certain categories of immigrants; and prohibiting the challenge of state welfare-reform laws under any circumstances—even if such laws violate the U.S. Constitution or federal laws.

The restrictions went into effect in August 1966, and Legal Services had to withdraw from more than 600 class-action lawsuits across the country. In 1997, Legal Service programs employed about 3,500 attorneys. They were assisted by about 59,000 private attorneys, mostly on a pro bono basis. The program closed 1.2 million cases and provided services for 1.9 million clients. In 1998, the budget for Legal Services was actually $21 million less than in 1980. The American Bar Association has estimated that only about 20 percent of the legal needs of the poor are being met. Thus, at a time when there is growing inequality and poverty, when more than 40 million Americans lack health care, and when the poor are facing one of the harshest welfare reforms in recent history, they are also being denied effective legal assistance (Brennan Center for Justice, 2000.) The constitutionality of the restrictions on challenging welfare laws is now pending before the U.S. Supreme Court.

REFERENCES

Abramovitz, Mimi. 1988. *Regulating the Lives of Women: Social Welfare Policy from Colonial Times to the Present.* Boston: South End.

Bell, Winnifred. 1965. *Aid to Dependent Children.* New York: Columbia University Press.

Bernhardt, Annette, Martina Morris, and Mark S. Handcock. 1995. Women's Gains or Men's Losses? A Closer Look at the Shrinking Gender Gap in Earning. *American Journal of Sociology* 101(2): 302-328.

Brennan Center for Justice, 2000. *Restricting Legal Services: How Congress Left the Poor with Only Half a Lawyer.* The Access to Justice Series. New York: New York University School of Law, Brennan Center for Justice.

Brito, Tonya. 1999. The Welfarization of Family Law. Unpublished manuscript.

Brito, Tonya. 2000. The Welfarization of Family Law. *University of Kansas Law Review 48*(2): 229-284.

Burtless, Gary. 1995. Employment Prospects of Welfare Recipients. In Nightingale Demetra and Robert Haveman (Eds.), *The Work Alternative* (p. 77). Washington, DC: The Urban Institute.

Bussuk Ellen, Angela Browne, and John C. Buckner. 1996. Single Mothers and Welfare. *Scientific American 275*(4): 60-67.

Cancian, Maria, Robert Haveman, Thomas Kaplan, Daniel Meyer, and Barbara Wolfe. 1999. Work, Earnings, and Well-Being After Welfare: What Do We Know? *Focus 20*(2): 22-25.

Children's Defense Fund. 1997. Summary of Legislation Affecting Children in 1996 (Public Law 104-193). Available online: <http://www.childrensdefense.org/fairstart_welsum.html> (providing overview of new welfare program). November 17.

Children's Defense Fund. 1998. *Welfare in the States: CDF, New Studies Look at Status of Former Welfare Recipients.* Available online: <http://www.childrensdefense.org/fairstart_status.html>. May 27.

Clark, Sandra and Sharon Long. 1995. *Child Care Prices: A Profile of Six Communities.* Washington, DC: Urban Institute.

Cohen, Adam. 1998. When Wall Street Runs Welfare. *Time 151*(11): 64.

Council of Economic Advisors. 1999. *Technical Report: The Effects of Welfare Policy and the Economic Expansion on Welfare Caseloads: An Update.* Washington, DC: Council of Economic Advisers, August 3.

Danziger, Sandra, Mary Corcoran, Sheldon Danziger, Colleen Heflin, Ariel Kalil, Judith Levine, Daniel Rosen, Kristin Seefeldt, Kristine Siefert, and Richard Tolman. 1999. Barriers to Work Among Welfare Recipients. *Focus 20*(2): 31-35.

Danziger, Sheldon and Deborah Reed. 1999. Winners and Losers. *The Brookings Review 17*(4): 14-17.

DeParle, Jason. 1997a. The Drawer People, Newest Challenge for Welfare: Helping the Hard-Core Jobless. *The New York Times,* November 20, p. A1.

DeParle, Jason. 1997b. Lessons Learned: Welfare Reform's First Months—A Special Report: Success, Frustration, as Welfare Rules Change. *The New York Times,* December 30, p. A1.

DeParle, Jason. 1997c. Success, and Frustration, as Welfare Rules Change. *The New York Times,* December 30, p. A16.

Edin, Kathryn and Laura Lein. 1996. Work, Welfare, and Single Mothers' Economic Survival Strategies. *American Social Review 61:* 253-266.

Ellwood, David T. 1988. *Poor Support: Poverty in the American Family.* New York: Basic Books.

Ellwood, David T. 1999. *The Impact of the Earned Income Tax Credit and the Social Policy Reforms on Work, Marriage, and Living Arrangements.* Memo. Cambridge, MA: Harvard University, Kennedy School of Government.

Garfinkel, Irwin and Sara McLanahan. 1986. *Single Mothers and Their Children: A New American Dilemma.* Washington, DC: The Urban Institute Press.

Greenberg, Mark. 1999. *Beyond Welfare: New Opportunities to Use TANF to Help Low-Income Working Families.* Washington, DC: Center for Law and Social Policy.

Handler, Joel. 1995. *The Poverty of Welfare Reform.* New Haven, CT: Yale University Press.

Handler, Joel and Yeheskel Hasenfeld. 1991. *The Moral Construction of Poverty: Welfare Reform in America.* Newbury Park, CA: Sage Publications.

Handler, Joel and Yesheskel Hasenfeld. 1997. *We the Poor People: Work, Poverty, and Welfare.* New Haven, CT: Yale University Press.

Handler, Joel and Lucie White (Eds.). 1999. *Hard Labor: Women and Work in the Post-Welfare Era.* Armonk, NY: M. E. Sharpe.

Harris, Kathleen. 1993. Work and Welfare among Single Mothers in Poverty. *American Journal of Sociology 99:* 317-352.

Hartung, William and Jennifer Washburn. 1998. Lockheed Martin: From Warfare to Welfare. *The Nation 266*(7): 11-15.

Holzer, Harry. 1999. Will Employers Hire Welfare Recipients? *Focus 20*(2): 26-30.

House Committee on Ways and Means. 1998. *Green Book: Background Material and Data on Programs within the Jurisdiction of the Committee on Ways and Means.* Washington, DC: 103rd Congress, U.S. Government Printing Office.

Kaplan, Jan. 1999. The Use of Sanctions under TANF. Welfare Information Network, Issue Notes, 3, 3. Available online: <http://www.welfareinfo.org/sanctionissue_notes.htm>. April.

Lee, Don. 1999. Nature of Work Has Changed. *Los Angeles Times,* September 6, p. A1.

Lipsky, Michael. 1984. Bureaucratic Disentitlement in Social Welfare Programs. *Social Service Review 3:* 58.

Loprest, Pamela. 1999. Families Who Left Welfare: Who Are They and How Are They Doing? Discussion Paper 99-02. Washington, DC: The Urban Institute.

Meyer, Bruce and Dan Rosenbaum. 1999. *Welfare, the Earned Income Tax Credit, and the Labor Supply of Single Mothers.* Working Paper Series. Washington, DC: National Bureau of Economic Research.

Mishel, Lawrence, Jared Bernstein, and John Schmitt. 1999. *The State of Working America 1998-99.* Washington, DC: Economic Policy Institute.

Parrott, Sharon. 1998. *Welfare Recipients Who Find Jobs: What Do We Know About Their Employment and Earnings?* Washington, DC: Center on Budget and Policy Priorities.

Pavetti, LaDonna. 1999. How Much More Can Welfare Mothers Work? *Focus 20* (2): 16-19.

Pear, Robert. 1996. Most States Find Goals on Welfare Within Easy Reach. *The New York Times,* September 23, p. A1.

Piven, Frances and Richard Cloward. 1977. *Poor People's Movements: Why They Succeed, How They Fail.* New York: Pantheon Books.

Primus, Wendell, Lynette Rawlings, Kathy Larin, and Kathryn Porter. 1999. *The Initial Impacts of Welfare Reform on the Incomes of Single-Mother Families.* Washington, DC: Center on Budget Priorities.

Rangarajan, Anu, Peter Schochet, and Chu. 1998. *Employment Experiences of Welfare Recipients Who Find Jobs: Is Targeting Possible?* Washington, DC: Mathematica Policy Research, Inc.

Rivlin, Alice. 1999. *Sustaining the Good Economic News.* Washington, DC: Brookings Review.

Swarns, Rachel. 1998. Stiff Rules Cut Welfare Rolls at Two Offices. *The New York Times,* June 22, p. A1.

Tweedie, Jack and Dana Reichert. 1998. *Tracking Recipients After They Leave Welfare: Summaries of State Follow-Up Studies.* National Conference of State Legislatures, Welfare Reform Project. Available online: <http://www.ncsl.org/statefed/welfare/followup.htm>. February.

Weinstein, Michael. 1999. Economic Scene: When Work Is Not Enough. Without Training, Success of Welfare Overhaul May Falter. *The New York Times,* August 26, p. C1.

White, Lucie. 1999. Quality Child Care for Low-Income Families: Despair, Impasse, Improvisation. In Joel Handler and Lucie White (Eds.), *Hard Labor: Women and Work in the Post-Welfare Era* (pp. 124-125). Armonk, NY: M. E. Sharpe.

Williams, Lucy. 1999. Unemployment Insurance and Low-Wage Work. In Joel Handler and Lucie White (Eds.), *Hard Labor: Women and Work in the Post-Welfare Era.* Armonk, NY: M. E. Sharpe.

Ziliak, James, David Figlio, Elizabeth Davis, and Laura Connolly. 1997. Accounting for the Decline in AFDC Caseloads: Welfare Reform or Economic Growth? Discussion Papers, DP# 1151-97. Madison: University of Wisconsin, Institute for Research on Poverty.

Chapter 3

The Forgotten Group:
Women in Prisons and Jails

Sheryl Pimlott
Rosemary C. Sarri

The truth about us is that we've been in jail—some of us many times, most only once. We might as well say that first 'cause most of you think that's who we are before anything else. Yes, the truth about us is that some of us sold our bodies, stole money, wrote bad checks, sold drugs, and a few of us have hurt other people in a blackout rage, but mainly we take it out on ourselves. . . . We can tell when you really care. We are survivors. That's the truth about us. (Haven, 2000, p. 9)

INTRODUCTION

Nowhere is the marginalization of women more tragic than in the prisons and jails of the United States where a total of 146,000 women were incarcerated in 1999 (Beck, 2000b). Violence, degradation, abuse, and neglect characterize women's lives in prison today such that only a few women, often with support of the external community of human rights and advocacy groups, are able to resist their denigration and humiliation. We will primarily examine changes that have occurred in the past two decades in the incarceration of women and address issues of classification and assessment, health care, education, employment, family responsibilities, and conditions of incarceration.

With more than two million inmates, prisons and jails in the United States have become institutions for the social control of poor and minority persons. The legislative changes of the 1980s and 1990s in drug laws; lack of adequate legal representation in court; lengthy mandatory sentences for relatively minor property, person, or victimless crimes; lifetime prohibition for receipt of welfare for those convicted of a felony drug violation; lack of at-

55

tention to factors related to minority overrepresentation; and increasing deprivation in the conditions of incarceration all reflect this increased social control (Chesney-Lind, 1997; Pollock, 1995). Billions are spent on law enforcement and punishment, but almost nothing on crime prevention, neighborhood improvement, and income support for poor neighborhoods, or on control of racism in the operation of the justice system. Incarceration is now required for behaviors that previously resulted in diversion or in probation as the most severe sanction (Figueira-McDonough, Sarri, and Iglehart, 1981). Among women at risk for incarceration the majority are poor, minority, and mothers of minor children. Increasingly, income support through public welfare is no longer available to them, and their low-income jobs mean that women with children are almost forced to seek additional alternative employment to survive. Moreover, mental health and drug-treatment services in most communities are unavailable, as is access to vocational training that is required to secure higher income jobs. Instead, prison and law enforcement budgets in the majority of states continue to escalate each year.

BACKGROUND

The population of women in prison rose 709 percent between 1980 and 1999 (12,300 to 87,199), far more than the increase in male imprisonment, although women compose just 6.5 percent of the total prison population (Beck, 2000a). The annual growth rate of 8.5 percent far exceeds the growth in the total U.S. female population or the growth in crime (Beck, 2000a). The numbers of women in jail more than tripled, showing a similar pattern of growth from less than 20,000 in 1980 to 64,000 in 1998 (Greenfield and Snell, 1999; Beck and Mumola, 1999). These growth rates exceed those for male jail inmates, which have risen 294 percent since 1980. Although the population of women in prison is only 6.5 percent of the total, it has increased from 4.1 percent of the total in 1980. The proportion for women in jail also increased; it is somewhat higher at 11.5 percent. This is because it includes many minor misdemeanors handled at that level, along with sentenced offenders who are held locally because of overcrowding or when the state has no separate facility for women. Growth patterns for juvenile females parallel those for adult women, although the increase was not substantial until the late 1990s (Snyder and Sickmund, 1999). The rates of incarceration of women in the United States are more than five times that of Canada, six times that of the United Kingdom, and fourteen times that of Japan (Greenfield and Snell, 1999).

Who Am I???

Who Am I?
    Who Am I?
I was taken, stolen from a land of free,
I've toiled hard, bled, cried, and still no-one knew about me . . .
I was forced to forget a language, that of my people,
I've seen Black bodies piled high, high as church steeples . . .
A great number of my children were feathered and tarred,
Today I can still see where wounds have left their hideous scars . . .
I've been maimed, abused, raped then cast aside,
But through it all I've held pride . . .
I've worked the cornfields, picked cotton too!
And if I show defiance toward white massa, I was lashed a deep shade of blue . . .
I worked from sunup, lots of times till sundown,
Only to return to a shanty where my bed was the ground . . .
I slept with the massa, cuz Miz Cindy was a Lady,
Massa used me, and filled my womb, wid a lil white baby . . .
A baby I couldn't have cuz it wasn't mine,
Just a product to be sold at market, time after time . . .

Who Am I?
Oh I carried kings, princesses and chiefs too!!!
All these babies I made for I am still a part of you . . .
I'm a mother of nations, red, yellow, white and black,
But because of my skin I'm still told to get back.
Yet I walk wid my head in the sky,
You hate me cuz you fear me but you won't telly why . . .

Now you say you is the great one just cuz you man, Who Am I?
I AM THE GREAT ONE CUZ I'M MOTHER OF NATIONS,
    FIRST WOMAN OF THE LAND!!!!!

Gail Yvonne McRaft

Reprinted with permission from *Women in Prison*. J. Figueira-McDonough, R. Sarri, and A. Iglehart. University of Michigan.

Three disturbing trends accelerated female incarceration in the 1990s: increases in the overall placement of juvenile females in both juvenile and adult facilities, national changes in drug-control policies, and longer sentences. First, in all fifty states juveniles may now be tried as adults and, in some states, there are no lower age limits (Torbet and Szymanski, 1998). Legislation that treats juveniles as adults for a large number of offenses— drugs, property, and violent crimes—has resulted in fourteen- to sixteen-year-old females being housed in adult prisons. Because there are few of them, no attempt is made to keep them separated from the general population or to provide for required secondary education. Similarly, more and more young women are being held in local jails, awaiting trial or as sentenced offenders, even though the Juvenile Justice and Delinquency Act (PL96-415) prohibits the holding of juveniles in adult jail facilities. The increasing institutionalization of females for status offenses (truancy, incorrigibility, running away, and so on) is in violation of the Juvenile Justice and Delinquency Act of 1974 that explicitly proscribed such action, but to date there has been no successful legal challenge of these violations.

Secondly, drug-control strategies have significantly impacted both state and federal incarceration rates for women (Mauer, Potler, and Wolf, 1999). "The single most significant change that the Reagan administration made in drug policy was to consider drug abuse almost exclusively a problem of law enforcement" (Falco, 1989, p. 25). The 1988 Drug Control Strategy increased legal sanctions for drug use and lowered the amounts individuals needed to possess for incrimination and confinement. This strategy subsequently impacted budget policies, shifting dollars from treatment to interdiction and reversed court rulings from the 1960s that established it was cruel and unusual punishment to confine an individual in a jail or prison for the "state of being" addicted to drugs or alcohol (*Robinson vs. California,* 1962, 370 US 660). Twenty years later, this action was drastically changed legislatively, reversing trends of civil commitments for drug possession and use and rendering it a criminal act. Mauer and Huling (1995) chronicle the impact of this drug-control policy, better known as the War on Drugs, on minority populations. An analysis of Justice Department data shows that during this period (1989-1994), the number of black, non-Hispanic women in state prisons for drug offenses nationwide increased more than eightfold. In general, the number of women incarcerated in state prisons for a drug offense rose by 888 percent from 1986 to 1996, while nondrug offenses rose 129 percent (Mauer, Potler, and Wolf, 1999).

The third trend is the increasing length of sentences and the lack of any "good time" provisions. Beck (2000b) indicates that the average time served increased from twenty-two months in 1990 to twenty-eight months in 1998.

This trend is likely to continue because new court commitments include even longer sentences to the date of first release.

There are 951,000 adult women under correctional supervision of some type (including probation and parole) in the United States, making us number one in both incarceration and overall correctional control of women in the world. One in every 109 adult women in the United States is under correctional supervision and, if we add the juvenile females, the rate of female correctional supervision increases so that the proportion is about one in about ninety-eight. The increase in the incarcerated African-American female population was pratically significant between 1990 and 1999. The rate increased from 117 to 212 per 100,000, while the increase for white females went from 19 to 34 per 100,000. Whites are underrepresented relative to their proportion in the population, whereas African Americans are significantly overrepresented (Greenfield and Snell, 1999). If one controls for the type of crime, white women are more likely to be placed on probation rather than incarcerated whereas the opposite is true for African-American women. This process of increasing correctional control reflects significant legal changes in state and federal law, often with little regard for constitutional issues or international law, as has been reported by Amnesty International, Human Rights Watch, and other monitoring groups. The incarceration of women is not evenly distributed across the United States. Four states, California, Texas, New York, and Florida have 34 percent of all the females incarcerated in state prisons while Maine, West Virginia, Rhode Island, and Montana have less than .4 percent of the female prisoners. The District of Columbia has the highest rate, 173 per 100,000 population, while the highest state rate is for Oklahoma at 122. The lowest state rates were in Maine and Vermont at 9 per 100,000 (Beck, 2000b).

Accompanying the growth of female incarceration has been a growth in the numbers of prisons and jails for women. However, this increase in facilities has not impacted overcrowding because of the increases in prison sentences, especially for drug offenses.

WOMEN AND CRIME

Explanations for the increased incarceration of women follow two distinct paths: 1) that it reflects an increase of women's criminal activity and 2) that socioeconomic variables are the predominant causal factors. Jonathan Simon (1997) offers a political analysis in the article "Governing Through Crime," in which he suggests that politicians deliberately use crime incidents as mechanisms for gaining influence in decision making.[1] Similarly, Davey (1998) shows that legislators have used "get-tough-on-crime" arguments to promote prison expansion policies and punitive policies, such as those in the area of substance abuse.

In their institutional theory of deviance regulation, Beckett and Western (1999) state that penal and social welfare institutions regulate deviance in ways that change over time and place. They show that where deviance is seen as socially determined, policy is inclusive and offers more social support to people. This is exemplified in more progressive health and welfare policies. In contrast, where crime is attributed to individual characteristics, policy is more likely to be exclusionary, and penalties are greater. States then will operate more punitively in the regulation of deviance, including disproportionate control of minorities. Like Downs (1976) and Sarri (2000), they observe that states with higher proportions of minority populations disproportionately incarcerate more minority persons.

There are also multiple theories about how women offenders should be treated, with some disagreement among theories that illuminates the special characteristics or needs of women versus theories of equity under the law. Some believe that women offenders receive equal treatment by police as well as in sentencing and punishment by the courts; others believe women should be treated differently. The latter argue that women will have more sentencing alternatives because family responsibilities are acknowledged (Belknap, 1996).

Although women make up a much smaller percentage of those convicted and sentenced to incarceration, discrimination arguments or theories have not often been advanced because of historical evidence of "favorable" sentences received by women as compared to men. Explanations of this apparent leniency included judicial chivalry (Pollak, 1950), judicial paternalism (Nagel and Weitzman, 1971), and greater control of sex-role deviance than other illegal behaviors (Simon, 1975; Chesney-Lind, 1997). Daly and Tonry (1997) argue that these theories of leniency may be based on incomplete information. Studies often leave out contextual factors, such as the amount of money embezzled or drugs sold, and instead examine and compare sentences administered based on the charge or conviction. Daly and Bordt (1995) and Steffensmeier and Allan (1996) suggest that gender differences in the social organization of lawbreaking and criminal history contribute to overall shorter sentences. In addition, elements of women's past and present, particularly victimization, make them less blameworthy, more conforming, and better prospects for reform.

Critical race and feminist theorists have begun to question the dominance of the "white/male" point of view that the law represents (Daly and Tonry, 1997; Beckett and Western, 1999) when promoting equity arguments in sanctioning and sentencing. Examples of "white/male" conceptualizations of justice include those who cannot empathize with women's experiences and give support to policies that overcriminalize (e.g., the War on Drugs). This overcriminalization is manifested in the greater use of sentencing guidelines and mandatory minimum sentences (Raeder, 1993), in which current male-based sentencing guidelines are inconsistent with developing sentencing policies for nonviolent female offenders.

Societal expectations and individual perceptions are dependent upon one's race/ethnicity, gender, class, and historical time frame. The complexities of these intersections (Crenshaw, 1991; Fine and Weiss, 1998) are apparent in the analysis of life stories of jailed and imprisoned women (Gilfus, 1992; Jones, 1980; Browne, 1987; Jose-Kampfner, 1995; Richie, 1996). Instead of leniency, these life stories reveal systematic overcriminalization of women's survival strategies from running away from home as a juvenile to avoid abuse, to using drugs as a coping strategy, to killing an abusive partner.

Richie's (1996) study supports a theory of gender entrapment—women, and particularly women of color, trying hard to "fit in" with societal expectations and gendered norms become trapped. In examining women's entry into the criminal justice system, Richie acknowledges and illustrates both the victimization women endure and the choices they make to be good mothers, supportive partners, and survivors. In making these choices with little or no economic support, many women end up with "no good, safe way to avoid the problematic social circumstances that they find themselves in, unable to change their social position and are ultimately blamed" (Richie, 1996, p. 3; Richie and Johnsen, 1996).

BEHAVIOR AND ATTITUDES OF WOMEN IN PRISON

Theories about women and crime usually do not discuss the impact of incarceration on women's subsequent behavior, but these experiences are increasingly recognized as important in women's behavior following incarceration (Kruttschnitt, Gartner, and Miller, 2000). Two models have been recognized as influencing behavior and attitudes of prisoners: functionalism and importation theories. Functionalism refers to the influence of the coercive conditions of incarceration as key factors influencing behavior and attitudes (Sykes, 1958; Goffman, 1961). Others have referred to this model as the deprivational model (Cao, Zhao, and Van Dine, 1997). Situational functionalism focuses particular attention on the ways in which prison conditions affect reactions to incarceration and subsequent behavior. In contrast, the importation model—as described by Heffernan (1972), Ward and Kassebaum (1965), and Irwin (1970)—asserts that women's behavior and attitude prior to incarceration largely explains their behavior in prison. Kruttschnitt,

Gartner, and Miller (2000) suggest that women's behavior in prison is better explained with a model that is a synthesis of functionalism and importation theories. They suggest that the management and control of contemporary prisons, along with their physical structures, have profoundly changed female prisons during the past decade. Prisons are far larger with secure perimeter fencing, elaborate electronic control systems, uniformed inmates and guards, elaborate systems of classification, and housing that permits almost no privacy. The study of two California prisons by Krutschnitt and colleagues highlights the differences between the "old" and the "new" prison to indicate that a synthesis between functionalism and importation is necessary to understand women's behavior. They observed both similarity in the ways in which women "did time" and also behavior which reflected their earlier life experiences. Concern about their children was defined by most women as the hardest part of their prison experience, as was concern about postinstitutional adjustment. However, the ways in which women responded to these concerns reflected differences in their prior experiences, their ages, and their socioeconomic background. The consequences of these experiences have long-term effects on women's subsequent adjustment to their postprison lives.

HISTORY OF THE INCARCERATION OF WOMEN

Although there has been a great increase in incarceration in the past quarter century, the placement of women in jails and prisons is not new (Faith, 1993; Zedner, 1995). Most states established almshouses in the seventeenth century for holding male and female prisoners together, but these facilities also held the mentally ill, the disabled, the developmentally handicapped, and juveniles, as well as the poor and indigent. In other words, they were congregate custodial facilities in which conditions were inhumane and horrible. Only in the nineteenth century, through the sustained work of Dorothea Dix, were the mentally ill removed. Her actions led to a movement of concern about the conditions of confinement for all institutionalized people. During this time, states established central prisons for felons that were large houses in which women were housed in rooms separate from those holding men (Hafter, 1995; Harris, 1998). The large custodial penitentiaries developed later, where women were confined along with men, except in separate rooms or units. In some states, however, the women were held in the same units as men, resulting in frequent abuse of the women (Freedman, 1981). These facilities were established to promote discipline and reformation; instead, punishment and abuse, especially of women, occurred regularly.

The Pennsylvania model of complete isolation of prisoners in cells became the model for several states. Prisoners ate, slept, and worked within the cells with the goal that they would meditate and become penitent about their crimes. An alternate model of the reformatory was developed in the Auburn New York State Prison, opened in 1817. Prisoners worked in shops during the day but lived in enforced silence and isolation at night. Women were confined at Auburn in 1825, in a separate attic above the prison kitchen where they worked. Although women were not as rigidly disciplined as men, they were usually ignored or neglected and assigned to fulfill domestic responsibilities in the prison (Lekkerkerker, 1931). Abuse of women by guards and inmates was a frequent occurrence there as well. In 1835, an incident of pregnancy and beating at Auburn led New York to establish a separate facility for women, the Mount Pleasant Female Prison (Harris, 1998). That facility became so overcrowded that in 1865 it was closed and, because the state did not wish to finance expansion, the women were dispersed to local jails.

Only in the latter part of the nineteenth century were separate institutions established for women, beginning in the Northeast and Midwest. One of the first was the Detroit House of Correction directed by Zebulon Brockway in 1900 (Detroit Municipal Reference Library, Burton Archives, 1930). He initiated features in women's prisons that later were institutionalized: indeterminate sentencing and parole, maternal care by older female staff, emphasis on reformation through religion, acquisition of domestic skills, academic improvement, and the confinement of women guilty of moral offenses (e.g., prostitution) for extended periods. Hafter (1995) describes vividly the Western House of Refuge that opened in New York in 1893, epitomizing efforts of middle- and upper-class women to rescue unfortunate and "fallen" women through religion and work. She observes that they were established to regulate the sexual and vocational work of women. Parole practices also were used to supervise women's sexual behavior. The aim of these programs was to prepare women to be dutiful wives, mothers, and educators of children. The offenses that led to placement of women in reformatories were primarily public-order offenses (such as public intoxication, vagrancy, prostitution, and minor property crimes), none of which required incarceration for public safety. The goal, however, was morality control, punishment, and enforcement of a castelike status for working-class women. It ignored the reality of their lives as poor, stressed, and often single mothers and immigrants in a society in which discrimination toward low-income working women was rampant.

A two-track system for women offenders based on race was created in the twentieth century. African-American women were committed to custodial facilities, while white women were sent to reformatories. The social construct of ideal womanhood was the basis for theories of female criminality, but that applied only to white women (Zedner, 1995). African-American women were viewed as masculine, violent, sexually loose, and more immoral than their white counterparts. In the South, they worked as field hands on prison farms or as servants to families who held a lease on them. They could be ordered to do almost anything, including providing sexual services to male inmates and staff.

In either track, prisons and jails for women were places not only of punishment, but places where women lived under the constant threat of physical and sexual abuse by male staff and inmates (Crites, 1976). All work assigned to women was related to domestic roles, except for the agricultural jobs assigned to African-American women. When women were given manufacturing assignments, they usually made clothes for private contractors. The treatment of female prisoners was a sharp departure from ordinary norms regarding the treatment of women, and those conditions still prevail today in most facilities. The notion of protection of women was and still is nonexistent in most prisons. Much of what women suffer today in prisons has its roots in gender definitions of women offenders, perceptions, and biases that are of very long standing (Harris, 1998; Watterson, 1996; Collins, 1997). During the twentieth century, there was an increase in the number of states with separate facilities for women, but little improvement in educational opportunities or employment-related work. The numbers of women incarcerated were relatively stable at 3 to 4 percent of the male prison population. During the 1970s and 1980s, conditions began to improve as human rights supporters and other advocacy groups publicized the prisons' inadequacies. External programs for education and employment increased in many states (Watterson, 1996). The rapid increase in incarceration during the 1990s, as a consequence of changes in drug laws, slowed and even reversed these improvements (Hirsch, 2000).

CHARACTERISTICS OF FEMALE OFFENDERS

The characteristics of female offenders in different types of correctional programs vary by age, race, marital status, education, and offenses—as the findings in Table 3.1 indicate (Greenfield and Snell, 1999). African-American women are clearly overrepresented in jails and prisons, although the incarceration of Hispanic women is increasing rapidly, especially in the Southwest. Information about the immigrant status of incarcerated women is not documented, but informal reports suggest that it has increased substantially since 1990. The proportions of single mothers among Hispanic-female offenders are high, and their situation may be even more problematic

TABLE 3.1. Characteristics of Adult Women Offenders: 1998

Characteristics of Women	Probation	Local Jails	State Prisons	Federal Prisons
Median age	32	31	33	36
Race				
White	62%	36%	33%	29%
Black	27%	44%	48%	35%
Hispanic	10%	15%	15%	32%
Other	1%	5%	4%	4%
Marital status				
Married	26%	15%	17%	29%
Widowed	2%	4%	6%	6%
Separated	10%	13%	10%	21%
Divorced	20%	20%	20%	10%
Never married	42%	48%	47%	34%
Education				
8th grade or less	5%	12%	7%	8%
Some high school	35%	33%	37%	19%
High school graduate/GED	39%	39%	39%	44%
Some college or more	21%	16%	17%	29%
Offenses				
Violent offenses	9%	12%	28%	7%
Homicide	1%	1%	11%	1%
Property offenses	44%	34%	27%	12%
Larceny	11%	15%	9%	1%
Fraud	26%	12%	10%	10%
Drug offenses	19%	30%	34%	72%
Public-order offenses	27%	24%	11%	8%
Driving while intoxicated	18%	7%	2%	0
Number of women offenders	721,400	27,900	75,200	9,200

Source: Prisons in 1998, Bureau of Justice Statistics, U.S. Department of Justice. Report NCJ 175688. Washington, DC: GPO, August 1999.

Note: The percentages of offenses exceed 100 percent for each column because a single offender can be sentenced for more than one offense.

than those of African-American mothers because of their ambiguous citizenship status. The median age of offenders in federal prisons does not vary substantially across states, although the women are older, a reflection of longer sentences and because three out of four are there for drug violations. If information on admissions were available for each state, it is probable that the median age in state facilities would be lower, in the mid-twenties, because the majority of women spend only one to two years in prison, as compared to those who receive life sentences.

The majority of women under correctional supervision have never been married or are single because of marital disruption, but 70 percent of women have children under the age of eighteen. Women in prison have an average of 2.38 children while those on probation have 2.1 children (Greenfield and Snell, 1999; U.S. Department of Justice, 2000). This suggests that having responsibility for children is not a factor taken into consideration at the time of sentencing (Barry, 1997).[3] Female offenders have more formal education than male offenders, with the majority having at least a high school education or GED. However, educational test scores often indicate that academic performance levels are below that which would be expected of high school graduates. Statements are often made that the lack of education of female offenders reflects the quality of education that they have received, not necessarily the number of years during which they attended school. Women also lack appropriate education for the employment opportunities that will enable them to have an adequate income for themselves and their families.

In 1996, women accounted for 16 percent of all felony convictions, but in the largest courts, 42 percent of female felons had no history of prior conviction, nor had they been charged with a violent offense (Greenfield and Snell, 1999). Among violent offenses, those charged with assault were most often charged with simple assault, including instances of domestic violence. The 1998 female homicide rate was the lowest since 1976 (Greenfield and Snell, 1999). Women incarcerated for homicide or drug violations were in state prisons primarily, while those sentenced for property offenses were more often placed on probation or sentenced to local jails. The numbers sentenced for drug offenses increased in the 1990s to 37 percent of all felonies, but it was nearly double that for women in federal prisons.

Drug use among female offenders is far greater than is represented by the numbers of those who are sentenced for drug offenses. Drug Use Forecasting (DUF) surveys conducted by the National Institute of Justice found that the majority of women (in some cities as high as 75 percent) interviewed at the time of arrest tested positive for illicit drugs, regardless of the charge against them (National Institute of Justice, 1993; Wellisch, Prendergast, and Anglin, 1994). Other studies of incarcerated women demonstrate similar findings. In a survey of over 800 women in a North Carolina correctional facility, over 38 percent of the women had a lifetime prevalence rate of alcohol abuse or dependence and 44.2 percent were drug dependent or drug abusers (Jordan et al., 1996). A recent assessment of the prevalence of substance abuse by women within Michigan prisons revealed that 67 percent were assessed as drug or alcohol dependent (Pimlott, 1998). Figueira-McDonough, Sarri, and Iglehart (1981) and Sarri (1984) documented that a similar relationship between incarcerated women and drug use existed in the 1960s and 1970s. In their review of the female population in prison in Michigan between 1968 and 1979, only 7 percent were incarcerated for drug-related offenses, but 67 percent reported use of illicit drugs. Substance abuse by female offenders, both prior to and during their prison stay, illustrates the synthesis of the functionalism and importation theories of women's behavior in prison, as Kruttschnitt, Gartner, and Miller (2000) observed. The majority of women have abused drugs prior to their admission, but the availability of drugs in prison results either in a continuation or increase in drug abuse. Little attempt is made to treat addicted abusers or to control the spread of drugs (Berkowitz et al., 1996; Inciardi et al., 1997).

Single status, having minor children, being a substance abuser, and having less education than is necessary in today's economy—all of these factors place female offenders in a disadvantaged position when they have to compete with other women for employment (even if the employer does not consider their criminal record). When women are released from prison or jail, they are almost never provided with reintegration services, although their situation is such that social services are urgently needed for them and their children. Typically, custodial responsibility for their children will be returned to them almost immediately, even before they have adequate housing or employment. Female inmates are disproportionately low-income earners or unemployed when they enter prison. Only 40 percent of women report that they were employed full time when they entered prison, and 37 percent had incomes of less than $600 per month at that time. One-third of female inmates reported receiving welfare assistance just prior to the arrest that led them to prison (Greenfield and Snell, 1999). However, given the changes in welfare policy, it is unlikely that any of these women would be eligible for welfare assistance at the time of their release—despite the likelihood that their need will be even greater at that time. Recent welfare-reform legislation, the Personal Responsibility and Work Opportunity Reconciliation Act of 1996 (PRWORA), gave states the option to create a lifetime ban on benefits for those convicted of drug offenses. By November 1997, and still today, thirty-seven states had fully implemented the ban, with several more legislating some form of restriction for those convicted of drug offenses. Only eight states have completely opted out of the legislation, with Vermont being the only state that withheld any decisions pending evaluation of consequences for women and children.

Classification and Assessment

One of the most controversial current issues involves the assessment and classification of female inmates for placement in correctional facilities and programs. Classification is primarily a management tool the purpose of which is to promote rational, consistent, and equitable methods of assessing the needs and risk of each individual and then assigning agency resources accordingly. Most of the current systems for risk, security, or need-based classification are based on the assessments of male offenders and have been found to be inadequate for females. This is because characteristics of female offenders differ substantially from those of male offenders (Robinson and Gilfus, 1991). They point out that female crime is often situational and more reactive than proactive, requiring different assessment and classification. Brennan (1997) points out that the family background, offense patterns, institutional conduct, family responsibilities, health, and education needs of women all require a different approach to classification. Women seldom attempt to escape from prison, nor do they pose serious physical threats to other inmates or staff. Thus, assessment of needs, strengths, and risks becomes a more important factor than security in classification. Classification is important for females in prison because its results govern eligibility and access to programs, housing assignments, selection of cell mates, access to work, as well as general fairness and equity. Glaser (1982) pointed out that sound classification and related programs can reduce recidivism. His recommended programs regarding education, counseling, contact with external groups, and frequent furloughs are almost nonexistent today. Immarigeon (2000) summarizes several recommendations regarding the classification of women:

- Tested and clear female-oriented classification schemes must be utilized.
- Classification needs to occur earlier in the criminal justice process in order to place more women in noninstitutional, community-based programs.
- Only in states with 500 or more women in prison are there opportunities for their placement to be a reflection of the offenders' program needs. In smaller facilities extrainstitutional resources are more commonly utilized. This latter scheme was utilized in the 1970s and early 1980s when women enrolled in vocational and college programs outside the prison and had frequent opportunities for "off-grounds" work placements. Because of current overcrowding in most states, the mere

availability of a bed may be the primary criteria for placement. In a survey of administrators, one respondent said, "Currently the 53 beds for maximum security women are also used for HIV-positive women, for women with mental health problems, and for women on disciplinary detention" (Morash and Robinson, 1998, p. 17).

- Classification at present is disconnected from fiscal resources or the actual programming necessary for effective results. Few decisions are made with respect to the needs and strengths of female offenders; more often they are based only on weakness or risk behavior.

The National Center on Addiction and Substance Abuse estimates that 81 percent of female offenders are substance abusers (National Institute of Justice, 1993). It also indicates that there are gender-specific aspects of women's substance problems that should be considered in the initial assessment. Just identifying substance abuse as a problem is an incomplete form of assessment; there must be careful assessment of both precipitating conditions as well as the needs and strengths of each individual. Correctional administrators report that existing classification instruments are not useful to them in their decision making about placement and programming (Morash and Robinson 1998). Immarigeon (2000) suggests that effective classification schemes for women must assess whether female offenders actually belong in prison and their needs and strengths, monitor the risk for racial or ethnic skewing, relate to available program alternatives, and are a part of ongoing monitoring and evaluation as a basis for classification.

Minority Overrepresentation

The incarceration of both adult and juvenile women greatly overrepresents minority women, and that overrepresentation is not supported by arrest or crime rates where comparisons can be made (Bridges, Crutchfield, and Simpson, 1987). The data presented in Table 3.1 represent the population of women in prison on a given day in 1998. In comparison with males, both juvenile and adult minority females are more overrepresented in correctional facilities. Statistics of prison population on a specific day are necessarily affected by those serving longer sentences (Greenfield and Snell, 1999). Overrepresentation would be even greater if we analyzed the admissions of women during one year, because minority women are incarcerated more frequently for minor property crimes (whereas their white counterparts receive probation, or suspended sentences, or are even dismissed outright).

Minority women are more likely to be single mothers with custodial responsibility for their children. Many are imprisoned for minor property or drug crimes when community supervision would be more than adequate and would not punish the children as well as their mother. Majority women have a lower probability of incarceration for such crimes.

In many states where prisons are located in isolated rural areas, correctional guards are primarily white males who have little or no understanding of the needs and culture of urban minority women. Recent cases regarding sexual assault in prison dramatically illustrate the consequences of such arrangements.[3]

Health and Health Care

Incarcerated women have been identified as being a high-risk group because of their lifestyles, health problems, and related environmental influences (Accoca, 1998; Fogel, 1993; Ingram-Fogel, 1991). The deplorable living conditions of female prisoners have been discussed and numerous negative influences on their physical and mental health have been identified (Ingram-Fogel, 1991; Maeve, 1999). After a recent comprehensive review of the health of incarcerated women, Henderson (1998) concluded that incarcerated women demonstrate an excess of drug abuse, mental health problems, and physical and sexual abuse. "With so many of the prison population from backgrounds of poverty, violence, and drug use, and with limited access to health care in their communities, it is to be expected that women behind bars suffer from a broad range of health problems" (Safyer and Richmond, 1995, p. 316). There is also greater demand for health care by women prisoners, as compared with male offenders, because of more complex reproductive health issues, greater incidence of sexually transmitted diseases, gender-related problems from substance abuse (e.g., prostitution), and pregnancy (Wilsnack and Wilsnack, 1990; Wooldredge and Masters, 1993). In addition, since the median age of prisoners is rising, there is increasing incidence of diabetes, cancer, heart disease, hypertension, asthma, emphysema, and even dementia and Alzheimer's disease. Maeve (1999) points out that many women arrive in prison with numerous health needs, because their health may have been compromised in the community and because they have lacked health insurance. In addition, prison health care systems are not held to the same standards as is the case in the community.

Women in correctional facilities often are not provided with routine physical examinations, even when they are in prison for many years. Gynecological exams are not completed routinely or even at admission. One in four women who enter prison either is pregnant or has recently given birth. These women often receive no prenatal care, no special diets, nor even adequate care at the time of the child's birth (Safyer and Richmond, 1995). Women need continuing health supervision while they are pregnant because past behaviors often result in problematic pregnancies. This is most evident in the case of juveniles, all of which are considered high-risk pregnancies for both the mother and the infant.

The unique health care needs of female prisoners in general, and pregnant prisoners in particular, have created challenges to traditional models of health care provided within prisons. Various studies have explored the effects of incarceration on maternal and infant health. Reports describe the horrors of deliveries without adequate assistance or in shackles, as well as brutal separations of mothers and their infants within minutes of birth (Fogel, 1993). Where prison health care is more available, reports of prenatal care and birth outcomes in jails and prison populations have been more favorable.

Although information is incomplete, 40 to 60 percent of women under correctional supervision report that they were physically or sexually abused at some time during their lives (Greenfield and Snell, 1999). In comparison to the nonoffending population, female offenders have a far greater frequency of both physical and sexual abuse, and frequently that abuse has been severe (Maeve, 1999). Assaults occurred before age eighteen for 69 percent of the female offenders, but for 20 percent the abuse continued after age eighteen (Greenfield and Snell, 1999). Self-medication with drugs is a frequent means by which abused women cope with the impact of the abuse, but seldom is that acknowledged by the court or correctional facilities. Certainly, age of first alcohol use is highly correlated to a traumatic event. In a study of 105 women in treatment for substance abuse, Fullilove, Lown, and Fullilove (1992) found that 32 percent reported childhood physical assault and 42 percent reported experiencing sexual violence as a child. The National Women's Study (Resnick et al., 1993) found a strong relationship between lifetime alcohol dependence and the number of violent assaults, with the dependence level increasing in direct proportion to the number of incidents. Women with post-traumatic stress disorder (PTSD) were 2.48 times as likely as women without PTSD to have alcohol abuse or dependency issues and 4.46 times as likely to have drug abuse and dependency issues. In Teplin, Abram, and McClelland's (1996) study of jailed women (n = 1,272), 33.5 percent had a lifetime prevalence of PTSD and 22.3 percent had a six-month prevalence rate—far exceeding national epidemiological estimates of 10 percent for women (Kessler et al.,1997).

These experiences can lead to lifelong problems such as depression, anxiety and stress disorders, violence, impulsivity, and learning problems. Teplin, Abram, and McClelland's (1997) study also revealed that 80.6 percent of jailed women had a lifetime prevalence of some psychiatric disorder; 17 percent had a severe depressive disorder. In a similar study, Jordan and colleagues (1996) found that 64 percent of imprisoned women (*n* = 805) had some lifetime history of psychiatric disorder, with 13 percent having a major depressive disorder. In addition, treatment for mental illness is lacking in most facilities. Frequent suicide attempts, self-mutilation, and observed depression are only some of the manifestations of mental illness among female prisoners (Jordan et al., 1997; Wexler, Cuadrado, and Stevens, 1998). They also may be overmedicated because of lack of adequate physician supervision.

In recent years the prevalence of sexual assault and harassment by prison and jail guards has received more publicity and attention, as LaBelle reports in Chapter 15. Having been victimized also may affect a woman's ability to parent her children. In addition, some have suggested that having been sexually abused discourages women from obtaining gynecological exams when they are needed (Wooldredge and Masters, 1993).

The National Commission on Correctional Health Care (1994) recommended the following:

1. All correctional institutions should be required to meet recognized community standards for women's health services. Where possible, women should receive services for serious illnesses in the community.
2. Correctional health services and women's advocacy groups should collaborate to provide leadership in developing needed policies and procedures.
3. Correctional institutions should provide for comprehensive exams and testing at admission.
4. Comprehensive services for women's health problems should be provided because of reproductive health needs, high levels of sexual and physical victimization, child custody issues, mental health problems, and substance abuse.

Education

As previously noted in Table 3.1, the majority of female offenders may not appear to be educationally disadvantaged, but many offenders have less than a high school education, and most lack appropriate education for the current employment market. With growing numbers of immigrant women in prisons and jails, the need for basic education also has increased substantially. Thus, both academic and vocational education are needed. Until very recently, however, the education that was provided related to institutional maintenance requirements or to sex-segregated occupations, which have little likelihood of preparing a woman to succeed as a single mother in today's global economy. Even where more relevant educational programs are offered, obstacles exist for women who wish to enroll. Classification status may limit access, library facilities may be very limited, waiting lists may be long, and women may not be allowed to take both academic and vocational courses.

Under the equal protection clause of the Constitution, court decisions in *Glover v. Johnson* found that women lacked educational opportunities equal to those of male prisoners in both academic and vocational areas. The court then ordered that equal opportunities be made available.[4] As a result of sustained judicial action in that case for twenty years, women gained opportunities for vocational education, academic education through college, and some limited vocational counseling and job preparation. However, those opportunities came only after significant efforts by female offenders and their attorneys, because the Department of Corrections strongly resisted any efforts to implement appropriate educational services. College and some vocational programs were offered by local universities. Then, when some success was finally achieved, the department closed educational programs in the men's facilities and stated that women's programs could also be terminated because inequality no long prevailed (Sarri, 2000). Similar situations have existed in many states, even though research has shown that education reduces recidivism substantially (Morash and Robinson, 1998).

Employment

Women seldom have had the opportunity for appropriate employment-related work in most prisons. Instead, most work has been related to institutional maintenance, leaving substantial blocks of "idle" time. The increasing privatization of prisons has not improved this situation; moreover, women are often exploited by corporations who obtain services or products while paying prisoners extremely low wages (Siegal, 1998).

The overwhelming majority of female inmates represent no threat to the community and are seldom escape risks. As a result they could be employed in the community, receiving appropriate compensation for their employment. Where this has been implemented in a few states, prisoners are then expected to pay the costs of their maintenance in prison. Many European countries as well as local jails in the United States have had arrangements whereby prisoners worked in the community during the day and returned to the institution in the evening (Sarri, 2000). There are several new innovations for employment-related reintegration being tested or implemented at the present time. One of these, Women Arise (2000), receives referrals prior to women leaving prison so they are prepared to act immediately upon a woman's release. They provide housing assistance, referral for drug abuse treatment where necessary, educational counseling and referral, as well as job placement. Their program substantiates the need for a comprehensive approach if women are not to recidivate.

Family

When a woman is sent to prison, she has typically been the sole supporter of her children and has a closer relationship with them than her male counterpart. Seventy-five percent of the women in the criminal justice system had legal custody of their minor children before they entered prison, with each woman averaging two children. In addition, when women enter prison, 15 percent are either pregnant or have a child under the age of one year (Fogel, 1993). Nationally, few prisons allow mothers more than a few days to be with their infants after birth (e.g., New York's Bedford Hills or Nebraska for incidence of on-site nurseries). A few other prisons (e.g., Minnesota) have alternative-placement programs for women and children or participate in specialized visitation programs.

The majority of these children will reside with a maternal grandparent or combinations of family members and some with fathers, but many will be under the jurisdiction of the state child welfare department. When children are under the jurisdiction of child welfare, the clock is ticking to complete reunification. Under the Federal Adoption and Safe Families Act of 1997 (PL 105-89), children must have a plan for permanency within twelve months of placement. Some states interpret the law strictly, which makes it more difficult for incarcerated parents to be reunited with their children.

Often women encounter emotional and ethical dilemmas in regards to child placement. For the mothers, placement with the state is a risky venture that may mean never regaining custody because they are unable to meet the conditions set for them. Decisions are frequently made that may look problematic in the short run but offer the best option in the long run. Placing children with family members may place the child at risk or result in their not receiving the welfare and health care benefits to which they are entitled. Women are often reluctant to inform the court about their informal arrangements for fear that their parental rights will be terminated. Most relative placements are with the woman's mother, and that person may become ill or die, upsetting placement arrangements. Women who need to alter custody arrangements encounter much difficulty in doing so. Thus, it is not surprising that problems of child custody and care are the predominant concern of women in prison (Kruttschnitt, Gartner, and Miller, 2000).

Most incarcerated mothers try to stay in contact through phone calls and letters and 85 percent intend to resume custody upon release. Staying in contact is very important in the eyes of child welfare, and mothers need to document all their attempts at communication. Likewise, child welfare agencies have a responsibility to maintain contact with an incarcerated parent, but when the legal parent (and this usually means the mother) is incarcerated, few if any efforts are made by child welfare agencies. Mothers often need help with child custody issues, especially any pending termination of parent rights, but the *Glover v. Johnson* case findings documented that 78 percent of women felt they did not receive adequate custody or reunification services from child welfare agencies (Barry, Ginchild, and Lee, 1995). Often correctional agencies will not permit child welfare workers to have direct contact with prisoners, nor will they even permit these workers to bring children to the prison to visit their mothers, as provisions of PL 96-272 require.

Although women may speak of relationships they are involved in, most have been sole supporters of their children before incarceration. In a recent study conducted with pregnant and postpartum women involved in the criminal justice system, two themes on partners emerged (Stewart, Siefert, and Pimlott, 1999). First, even though at the initial interview the majority of women stated that the father of the child wanted to be involved and supportive, there was rarely a case where the observed behavior matched the women's assertions. Opportunities for visiting, family counseling, and attending the birth were available for partners but only occurred in about 10 percent of the cases. Secondly, the majority of the women depended upon their own families of origin for support rather than the biological father. However, even with help from family of origin factored in, 34 percent of the women stated they had no help with day care or child care, and 30 percent said they would have no one to help with emergency housing (Pimlott, 1998).

Studies of prisoners consistently show that those who maintain strong family and friendship ties during imprisonment and assume responsible marital and parental roles upon release have lower recidivism rates than those who function without family ties, expectation, and obligations. Therefore, communities as stakeholders can expect decreases in recidivism from former prisoners who have maintained family connections and commitments while incarcerated. Likewise, criminal justice systems are concerned with costs, safety, and security. If fewer prisoners circulate through the system due to increased family unity, costs are cut. In addition, family visits enhance the security of the facility, as regular contact relieves the anxiety of the family member behind bars. Family visiting is essentially a free resource for the Departments of Correction as the families bear the burden of travel, food, and lodging needed during visits. Correctional supervision during visits is far less costly than reprocessing.

Contact with family members and loved ones benefits the state, the community, and the individual family members. Several states have maximized the opportunities for family involvement with supportive programs that allow enhanced visitation through special activities for children, overnight visits, and support for families. Only one state has a child welfare worker at each prison facility that works to assist prisoners and their family members with reunification services. Thinking to the future and the importance of relationships in successfully reintegrating the individual will go a long way in supporting families and communities, while maintaining practices that are fiscally responsible by keeping down costs associated with recidivism.

Conditions of Confinement

Recent reports from Human Rights Watch (1999) and Amnesty International (1999) document the inhumane conditions for women in prison or jail in the United States.[5] Moreover, as LaBelle (Chapter 15) notes, the United States has resisted compliance with international law regarding humane conditions for prisoners.

From the moment of incarceration women experience degradation and depersonalization. The prison's use of numbers instead of names, the requirement for uniforms (although there are few escapes by women), deliberate degradation of women in public situations, and the practice of frequent "counts" for which all women must be present in their unit at the exact time required exemplify these practices. Observation of lounges and individual rooms also indicates that living areas are almost devoid of attractive surroundings that women might arrange. In prisons where women live in large dormitories, privacy is almost nonexistent. The humiliation of physical body searches is devastating for many women, especially when male staff members perform them. In many prisons, male unit staff observe the women toileting, showering, and dressing. Frequently, derisive reports accompany their observations. Older women with health limitations are given little or no special accommodations in living situations (Sarri, 2000).

The humiliation of women when family members come to visit is often traumatic for the woman as well as for her children and relatives. Women may be prohibited from holding, hugging, or kissing a child, even one that is very young. Visiting rooms often are extremely crowded. Times and dates for visitation are not convenient for family members, especially for those bringing children to visit when prisons are long distances from where the family resides. Restrictions even exist for who may bring a child to visit a parent.

Control of telephone use is also problematic for women attempting to keep in contact with their family members. All calls must be collect to the person being called; there is a limited list of persons who can be called; and surcharges are added so that one three-minute call might cost as much as twelve dollars in some facilities.

Although not often noted, idleness is a frequent reality in U.S. prisons and jails today. Because of overcrowding there often is insufficient "work detail" for all women, so they are required to remain in their rooms, on their beds, or at least in their units. Prison industries exist for some women, but typically for a selected sample who are permitted to a few hours. Women do not have free access to libraries, nor are they allowed to occupy their time in other constructive activities. They may not even be allowed out into prison yards. For those in jail, confinement and idleness is the usual reality (Bloom, 2000).

The lack of observation and supervision of mentally ill women in living units is unhealthy for the ill person and also for those who live with her, particularly when they may be prohibited from helping her in any way. Women often speak about the difficulties they encounter when trying to help others with either physical or mental illness, especially at night or on weekends when health services are unavailable.

Food is always of importance in any institutional setting, but in prison the food usually is of poor quality, prepared long before it is served, and nutritionally unhealthful for women who are at risk for heart disease, diabetes, and other disorders. As previously noted, pregnant women seldom are provided with the food that they need during pregnancy, thus victimizing the unborn child as well as the mother. In several instances, women have reported to the authors that they were fed spoiled food and had to drink contaminated water.

In many prisons drugs are offered to women by guards in return for sexual or other favors. Sexual assault and harassment are a daily reality in many jails and prisons. Recent publicity by Amnesty International (1999) and Human Rights Watch (1999) has called attention to the seriousness of the problem, but in most states nothing has been done at the time of this writing (2002) to control the situation and to punish guilty staff.

Prisons and jails usually require that inmates purchase their own personal supplies, including toothbrushes and toothpaste, tampons, and some medicines. On top of that, the prices that they have to pay for these supplies are often higher than local retail outlets. Most prisons have prison-benefit funds built up from vending machines provided for visitors, but seldom do in-mates have any decision-making authority over how those funds are used.

Living with all of the confinement conditions illustrated previously is very difficult for the majority of offenders, and many are given various types of penalties for any violation. These penalties then add to the time that they must spend in prison. Many may spend extended periods in solitary segrega-tion, increasing the likelihood of mental as well as physical illness. Al-though none want longer stays in prison, they may not be able to conform to all of the conditions all of the time, as is required by staff. Prison officials have increasingly limited access of the public to prisons; thus, few in the community have actual knowledge of the conditions under which prisoners must live. In addition, the Prison Litigation Reform Act of 1997 (42 USC 1997) prohibits many legal efforts at charging prison officials with main-taining cruel and inhuman conditions in violation of the Eighth Amend-ment.

CONCLUSIONS AND RECOMMENDATIONS

The incarceration of women in prison in 2002 represents a public policy gone awry as the numbers imprisoned continue to increase each year despite the substantial decline in crime during the previous decade. There is some evidence in selected states (e.g., California) that policies are being imple-mented to provide treatment rather than incarceration for substance abusers and to eliminate the arbitrary use of the "three strikes and you're in for life" sentences. Few women need to be incarcerated because of the nature of their crimes or their threat to public safety. Moreover, the inadequate programs and the inhumane conditions of confinement serve only to exacerbate the problems that led to the women's crimes and incarceration. The cost of in-carceration has become prohibitive because of the large numbers of women who are unnecessarily confined. Community supervision has been demon-strated to be at least as effective, if not more effective, in reducing recidi-vism. The overrepresentaton of poor minority women has arisen in large part because these women lack the equal protection of the law that is af-forded to majority women.

Recommendations that appear to be urgently required include:

1. Changes must be made in drug laws and policy so that persons charged with use, possession, or sale of small amounts of drugs are not incarcerated. Instead, the money saved can be used to provide a con-tinuum of treatment programs in the community, as well as to the far smaller number who are incarcerated. Community service and restor-

ative justice alternatives have been found to be far more effective and less costly.[6]

2. Increase scrutiny of the incarceration of women who have minor children to determine whether it is really necessary. If it is necessary, the state should provide for frequent visitation of children, including overnight visits. Also needed are legal services so that women can manage custodial responsibilities.

3. Improved health care needs to be provided, including mental health services, given the frequency of diagnosed depression and other serious mental illnesses in offenders.

4. Open prisons to community residents and groups so that the public has knowledge about prison life and who is held there. Restorative justice programs need to be developed which facilitate reconciliation with community residents. The vast majority of citizens have never visited a jail or prison, nor do they have any understanding of who the inmates are or why they are incarcerated.

5. Strict enforcement of staff violations toward prisoners must be implemented, including sexual harassment or assault, distribution of drugs, degradation of prisoners, and inappropriate application of misconduct penalties.

6. Opportunities and guidance for academic and vocational education will enhance women's access to appropriate employment after incarceration. Wherever possible, women should be treated in the least restrictive programming environment that is appropriate so that access to education is facilitated. The special needs of women, adults, and juveniles alike should be addressed in a female-focused environment that is safe, trusting, and supportive. Cultural awareness and sensitivity should be promoted among the various racial and ethnic groups (Bloom, 2000).

7. Lastly, laws and policies governing imprisoning and jailing of women need to be changed so that upward of 75 percent of the women currently incarcerated remain in the community. The overrepresentation of minority women is the result of discriminatory practices toward them since other women are not imprisoned for similar crimes. These women do not threaten public safety, while the cost to their families and communities far outweighs any benefits from prison penalties. The United States would do well to consider the practices of most Western countries of the world regarding female incarceration.[7]

NOTES

1. The publicity about Willie Horton in the 1992 presidential campaign illustrates one instance, as does the differential sentencing of offenders for "crack" versus "powdered cocaine" use. See also Donzelot (1979).

2. See Chapter 12 for further discussion of children of incarcerated women.

3. See Chapter 15.

4. The *Glover v. Johnson* case spanned more than twenty years in the Federal Court of the Eastern District of Michigan. The following citations apply: *Glover v. Johnson*, 478 F. Supp. 1019 (E.D. Mich. 1979); *Glover v. Johnson*, 721 F. Supp. 808 (E.D. Mich. 1989) aff'd 934 F. 2d 703 (6th Cir. 1991); *Glover v. Johnson*, 75 F. 3rd 262 (6th Cir. 1996).

5. The conditions of confinement described here refer only to women's prisons. Conditions in male prisons differ in many ways because of their size, characteristics of male offenders, and correctional policies toward the handling of males. Most of the observations in this section are based on the observations by both Pimlott and Sarri in women's prisons throughout the United States and in several European countries.

6. See Chapter 8.

7. Sheryl Pimlott and Rosemary Sarri have worked and done research in women's prisons for many years. Many of their personal observations are noted in this chapter, but the names of facilities or persons have not been identified to protect confidentiality.

REFERENCES

Accoca, Leslie. 1998. Defusing the Time Bomb: Understanding and Meeting the Growing Health Care Needs of Incarcerated Women in America. *Crime and Delinquency 44*(3): 46-69.

Amnesty International. 1999. *Rights for All*. New York: Amnesty International.

Barry, Ellen. 1997. Women Prisoners and Health Care. In K. Moss (Ed.), *Man Made Medicine: Women's Health, Public Policy and Reform* (pp. 249-272). Durham, NC: Duke University Press.

Barry, Ellen, R. Ginchild, and D. Lee. 1995. Legal Issues for Prisoners with Children. In K. Gabel and D. Johnston (Eds.), *Children of Incarcerated Parents* (pp. 147-166). New York: Lexington Books.

Beck, Allen. 2000a. *Prison and Jail Inmates at Midyear 1999*. Report No. NCJ 181643. Washington, DC: U.S. Department of Justice, Office of Justice Programs.

Beck, Allen. 2000b. *Prisoners in 1999*. Washington, DC: U.S. Department of Justice, Office of Justice Programs.

Beck, Allen and Christine Mumola. 1999. *Prisoners in 1998*. Report No. NCJ 175687. Washington, D.C.: U.S. Department of Justice, Office of Justice Programs.

Beckett, Katherine and Bernard Western. 1999. The Institutional Sources of Incarceration: Deviance, Regulation and the Transformation of State Policy. Presented at the American Society of Criminology Annual Meeting.

Belknap, Joanne. 1996. *The Invisible Woman: Gender, Crime and Justice.* Belmont, CA: Wadsworth Publishing Co.

Berkowitz, G., Claire Brindis, Z. Clayson, and S. Peterson. 1996. Options for Recovery: Promoting Success Among Women Mandated to Treatment. *Journal of Psychoactive Drugs 28*(1): 31-38.

Bloom, Barbara. 2000. Successful Gender Responsive Programming Must Reflect Women's Lives and Needs. *Women, Girls and Criminal Justice 1*(1-2): 10-12.

Brennan, Timothy. 1997. Institutional Classification of Females: Problems and Some Proposals for Reform. Unpublished paper. Boulder, CO: Institute of Cognitive Science.

Bridges, George S., Richard D. Crutchfield, and Ernest E. Simpson. 1987. Crime, Social Structure and Criminal Punishment: White and Nonwhite Rates of Imprisonment. *Social Forces 34*(3): 345-361.

Browne, Angela. 1987. *When Battered Women Kill.* New York: McMillian/Free Press.

Cao, Lee, Jihong Zhao, and Steve Van Dine. 1997. Prison Disciplinary Tickets: A Test of the Deprivation and Importation Models. *Journal of Criminal Justice 25* (2): 103-113.

Chesney-Lind, Meda. 1997. *The Female Offender: Girls, Women and Crime.* Thousand Oaks, CA: Sage Publications.

Collins, Catherine F. 1997. *The Imprisonment of African-American Women: Causes, Conditions and Future Implications.* London: McFarland.

Crenshaw, Kimberle Williams. 1991. Demarginalizing the Intersection of Race and Sex: A Black Feminist Critique of Antidiscrimination Doctrine, Feminist Theory, and Antiracist Politics. In Katharine T. Bartlett and Rosanne Kennedy (Eds.), *Feminist Legal Theory: Readings in Law and Gender* (pp. 106-116). San Francisco: Westview Press.

Crites, Laura. 1976. *The Female Offender.* Lexington, MA: Lexington Books.

Daly, Kathleen and Rebecca Bordt. 1995. Sex Effects and Sentencing: A Review of the Statistical Literature. *Justice Quarterly 12*(1): 141-176.

Daly, Kathleen and Michael Tonry. 1997. Gender, Race and Sentencing. In Michael Tonry (Ed.), *Crime and Justice: A Review of the Research* (pp. 201-251) (Vol. 22). Chicago: University of Chicago Press.

Davey, Joseph Dillon. 1998. *The Politics of Prison Expansion: Winning Elections by Waging War on Crime.* Westport, CT: Praeger.

Detroit Municipal Reference Library. 1930. Archives of the Women in the Detroit House of Corrections 1861-1900. Detroit Municipal Reference Library, Burton Archives.

Donzelot, Jacques. 1979. *The Policing of Families* (p. vi). Foreword by Gilles Deleuze, trans. Robert Hurley. New York: Pantheon Books.

Downs, George. 1976. *Innovations and Social Policy.* Lexington, MA: Lexington Books.

Faith, Karlene. 1993. *Unruly Women: The Politics of Confinement and Control.* Vancouver: Press Gang Publishers.

Falco, Mathea. 1989. *Towards a National Policy on Drug and Aids Testing.* Washington, DC: Brookings Institute.

Figueira-McDonough, Josefina, Rosemary Sarri, and Alfreda Iglehart. 1981. *Women in Prison in Michigan, 1970-1980.* Ann Arbor: University of Michigan, Institute for Social Research.

Fine, Michelle and Lois Weiss. 1998. Crime Stories: A Critical Look Through Race, Ethnicity and Gender. *Qualitative Stories in Education 3:* 435-459.

Fogel, Catherine I. 1993. Pregnant Inmates: Risk Factors and Pregnancy Outcomes. *JOGNN 24:* 33-49.

Freedman, Estelle. 1981. *Their Sisters' Keepers: Women's Prison Reform in America.* Ann Arbor: University of Michigan Press.

Fullilove, Mindy Thompson, Anne E. Lown, and Robert E. Fullilove. 1992. Crack 'Hos and Skeezers: Traumatic Experiences of Women Crack Users. *The Journal of Sex Research* 29(2): 275-287.

Gilfus, Mary. 1992. From Victims to Survivors to Offenders: Women's Routes of Entry into Street Crime. *Women and Criminal Justice* 4(1): 63-89.

Glaser, Daniel. 1982. Social Science Perspectives on Classification Decisions. In *Classification as a Management Tool: Theories and Models for Decision Makers* (pp. 11-25). College Park, MD: American Correctional Association.

Goffman, Erving. 1961. *Asylums.* New York: Anchor Books.

Greenfield, Lawrence A. and Tracy L. Snell. 1999. Women Offenders. Report No. NCJ 175688. Washington, DC: U.S. Department of Justice, Office of Justice Programs, Bureau of Justice Statistics.

Hafter, Nicole. 1995. *Partial Justice: Women, Prisons and Social Control.* New Brunswick: Transaction Books.

Harris, M. Kay. 1998. A Historical Analysis of Female Offenders Through the Early 20th Century. *Corrections Today* 60(7): 74-80.

Haven, T. 2000. The Truth About Us. *FAAMMGRAM 1:* 9.

Heffernan, Esther. 1972. *Making It in Prison; The Square, the Cool and the Life.* New York: Wiley.

Henderson, Dorothy. 1998. Drug Abuse and Incarcerated Women: A Research Review. *Journal of Substance Abuse Treatment 6:* 579-587.

Hirsch, Anne. 2000. The Impact of Welfare Reform on Women with Drug Convictions. *Women, Girls and Criminal Justice* 49(1): 3, 60-62.

Human Rights Watch. 1999. *No Place to Hide.* New York: Human Rights Watch.

Immarigeon, Russell. 2000. Can Classifying Women Offenders Give Greater Priority to Community Corrections? *Women, Girls and Criminal Justice* 49(1): 3, 60-62.

Inciardi, James, Steven Martin, Clifford Butzin, Robert Hooper, and L. Harrison. 1997. An Effective Model of Prison-Based Treatment for Drug Involved Offenders. *Journal of Drug Issues* 27(2): 261-278.

Ingram-Fogel, Catherine. 1991. Health Problems and Needs of Incarcerated Women. *Journal of Prison and Jail Health* 10(1): 43-57.

Irwin, John. 1970. *The Felon.* Englewood Cliffs, NJ: Prentice-Hall.

Jones, Angela. 1980. *Women Who Kill.* New York: Fawcett Crest.

Jordan, B. Kathleen, William E. Schlenger, Juesta M. Caddell, and John Fairbank. 1997. Etiologic Factors in the Development of BPD in a Sample of Convicted Women Felons in North Carolina. In Mary Zanarini (Ed.), *The Role of Sexual Abuse in the Etiology of Borderline Personality Disorders* (pp. 513-519). Washington, DC: American Psychiatric Press.

Jordan, B. Kathleen, William E. Schlenger, John Fairbank, and Juesta M. Caddell. 1996. Prevalence of Psychiatric Disorders Among Incarcerated Women: II Convicted Felons Entering Prison. *Archives of General Psychiatry 53*(6): 513-519.

Jose-Kampfner, Christina. 1995. Post-Traumatic Stress Reactions in Children of Imprisoned Mothers. In Katherine Gabel and Denise Johnston (Eds.), *Children of Incarcerated Parents* (pp. 89-102). New York: Lexington Books.

Kessler, Ronald, Amanda Sonnega, Evelyn Bromet, Michael Hughes, and Christopher Nelson. 1997. Posttraumatic Stress Disorder in the National Comorbidity Survey. *Archives of General Psychiatry 52:* 1048-1060.

Kruttschnitt, Candace, Rosemary Gartner, and Amy Miller. 2000. Doing Her Own Time? Women's Responses to Prison in the Context of the Old and the New Penology. *Criminology 38*(3): 681-719.

Lekkerkerker, Eugenia. 1931. *Reformatories for Women in the United States.* Groningen, Netherlands: J. B. Wolters.

Maeve, M. Katherine. 1999. Adjudicated Health: Incarcerated Women and the Social Constructions of Health. *Crime, Law and Social Change 31*(1): 49-71.

Mauer, Marc and Tracy Huling. 1995. *Young Black Americans and the Criminal Justice System: Five Years Later.* Washington, DC: The Sentencing Project.

Mauer, Marc, Cathy Potler, and Richard Wolf. 1999. Gender and Justice: Women, Drugs and Sentencing Policy. Washington, DC: The Sentencing Project.

Morash, Merry and Amanda Robinson. 1998. *Correctional Administrators' Perspectives on Family-Related Programming for Women Offenders.* East Lansing, MI: School of Criminal Justice.

Nagel, Stuart and Lenore Weitzman. 1971. Women as Litigants. *Hastings Law Journal 23:* 171-181.

National Commission on Correctional Health Care. 1994. *Standards for Health Care in Prisons and Jails.* Washington, DC: National Commission on Correctional Care.

National Institute of Justice. 1993. *Drug Use Forecasting: 1993 Annual Report.* Washington, DC: U.S. Department of Justice, National Institute of Justice.

Pimlott, Sheryl. 1998. *Results of Substance Abuse Subtle Screening Inventory (SASSI) Pilot.* Lansing: Michigan Department of Corrections.

Pollak, Otto. 1950. *The Criminality of Women.* Philadelphia: University of Pennsylvania Press.

Pollock, Joycelyn. 1995. Gender, Justice and Social Control: A Historical Perspective. In Alida V. Merlo and Joycelyn Pollock (Eds.), *Women, Law and Social Control* (pp. 3-33). Boston, MA: Allyn & Bacon.

Raeder, Michael. 1993. Gender and Sentencing: Single Moms, Battered Women, and Other Sex-based Anomalies in the Gender Free World of the Federal Sentencing Guidelines. *Pepperdine Law Review 20*(3): 905-990.

Resnick, Heidi, Dean Kilpatrick, B. Dansky, Benjamin Saunders, and Connie Best. 1993. Prevalence of Civilian Trauma and Posttraumatic Stress Disorder in a National Sample of Women. *Journal of Consulting and Clinical Psychology 61*(6): 984-991.

Richie, Beth. 1996. *Compelled to Crime: The Gender Entrapment of Black Women.* New York: Routledge.

Richie, Beth E. and Christine Johnsen. 1996. Abuse Histories Among Newly Incarcerated Women in a New York City Jail. *Journal of the American Medical Women's Association 51*(3): 111-117.

Robinson, Robin and Mary Gilfus. 1991. Risk Classification and Needs Assessment of Female Inmates in Idaho Correctional Facilities. Unpublished paper. New Brunswick, NJ: Rutgers University, School of Social Work.

Safyer, Steven M. and Lynn Richmond. 1995. Pregnancy Behind Bars. *Seminars in Perinatology 19*(4): 314-322.

Sarri, Rosemary. 1984. *Changes in Drug Related Behavior of Incarcerated Female Offenders 1968-1979.* Cincinnati, OH: Annual Meeting of the American Criminology Society.

Sarri, Rosemary. 2000. Personal observations of the author while serving as a study consultant for women's prisons in the United States and Europe and as monitor for the Federal Court on the *Glover v. Johnson* Case. Personal observations appear at several points throughout the paper.

Siegal, Nina. 1998. An Interview with Angela Davis and Women in Prison. *MS Magazine* September-October: 48, 68-72.

Simon, Jonathan. 1997. Governing through Crime. In Lawrence M. Friedman and George Fisher (Eds.), *The Crime Conundrum: Essays in Criminal Justice* (pp. 28-64). Boulder, CO: Westview Press.

Simon, Rita. 1975. *Women and Crime.* Lexington, MA: Lexington Books.

Snyder, Howard and Melissa Sickmund. 1999. Juvenile Offenders and Victims: 1999 National Report. Washington, DC: U.S. Department of Justice, Office of Juvenile Justice and Delinquency Prevention.

Steffensmeier, Darrell and Emily Allan. 1996. Gender and Crime: Toward a Gendered Theory of Female Offending. *Annual Review of Sociology 22:* 459-487.

Stewart, Abigail, Kristine Siefert, and Sheryl Pimlott. 1999. *Women and Infants at Risk: An Evaluation of Services to Pregnant, Incarcerated Women.* Detroit, MI: Skillman Foundation.

Sykes, Gresham. 1958. *The Society of Captives.* Princeton, NJ: Princeton University Press.

Teplin, Linda, Karen Abram, and Gary McClelland. 1996. Prevalence of Psychiatric Disorders Among Incarcerated Women: Pretrial Jail Detainees. *Archives of General Psychiatry 53*(6): 505-512.

Teplin, Linda, Karen Abram, and Gary McClelland. 1997. Mentally Disordered Women in Jail: Who Receives Service? *American Journal of Public Health 87* (4): 604-609.

Torbet, Patricia and Linda Szymanski. 1998. *State Legislative Responses to Violent Juvenile Crime: 1996-1997.* Washington, DC: U.S. Department of Justice, Office of Justice Programs, Office of Juvenile Justice and Delinquency Prevention.

U.S. Department of Justice. 2000. *Survey of Inmates in State and Federal Correctional Facilities, 1997.* Bureau of Justice Statistics. Ann Arbor: University of Michigan. Compiled by the U.S. Department of Commerce, Bureau of the Census.

Ward, David and Gene Kassebaum. 1965. *Women's Prison: Sex and Social Structure.* New York: Aldine.

Watterson, Kathryn. 1996. *Women in Prison: Inside the Concrete Womb,* Revised Edition. Boston: Northeastern University Press.

Wellisch, Jean, Michael L. Prendergast, and M. Douglas Anglin. 1994. *Drug-Abusing Women Offenders: Results of a National Survey.* Washington, DC: U.S. Department of Justice, Office of Justice Programs, National Institute of Justice.

Wexler, Henry, Mary Cuadrado, and Sally Stevens. 1998. Residential Treatment for Women: Behavioral and Psychological Outcomes. *Drugs and Society: A Journal of Contemporary Issues 13*(1/2): 213-233.

Wilsnack, Sharon and Richard Wilsnack. 1990. Women and Substance Abuse: Research Directions of the 1990s. *Psychology of Addicted Behaviors 4*(1): 46-49.

Women Arise. 2000. *Project Prove for the Reintegration of Female Prisoners in Michigan.* Detroit: Women Arise.

Wooldredge, John D. and Kimberly Masters. 1993. Confronting Problems Faced by Pregnant Inmates in State Prisons. *Crime and Delinquency 39*(2): 195-203.

Zedner, Lucia. 1995. Wayward Sister: The Prison for Women. In Norval Morris and David J. Rothman (Eds.), *The Oxford History of the Prison: The Practice of Punishment in Western Society* (pp. 329-363). New York: Oxford University Press.

Chapter 4

The Storm Is Passing Over:
Marginalized African-American Women

Harriette Pipes McAdoo

The storm is passing over, the storm is passing over, the storm is passing over, Hallelujah.

Negro spiritual

Many storms have passed over African-American women in the past few hundred years. We have been ignored, put on the front burner and admired, left behind as expendable, used when needed, tossed aside when not needed, and rebuked by most whites and by many blacks, especially the men. This chapter will cover the treatment of women who have been marginalized ever since their appearance in North America and the institutional biases that are held against them. They are as an excluded caste. Their lot has been long quiet acceptance, resistance, and being marginalized by society as a whole. A critical analysis of mainstream theoretical frameworks shows that African-American families, adults, and children can be fully understood only in relation to the interaction of social class, culture, ethnicity, and race (Blackburn and Holbert, 1987). This chapter will examine the developmental processes of marginalized women within family, children, and those who are not in families.

Double jeopardy is the usual assignment given to these women who are black, female, and tossed aside. It does not matter that they may or may not have adequate resources. To the average onlooker they do not have a social class or an education, for they are all given the common label: black and poor. Black women have been more than marginalized, for to be on the margins one must at least be in the game (Johnson, 1998; Huddleston-Mattai, 1995). Black women have been placed outside of the margins and have not been considered even to be in the game. The 1960s and 1970s were times of hope, while the 1980s and 1990s were periods of despair. A few break through into the game, but remaining there is tenuous and subject to missteps, real or imagined.

The social context of African-American women differs from other groups. In contexts there are differences in social status and power, combined with reproductive biology that shapes the experiences of females and males, black and white, and the relationships between the genders (Gilligan, 1982). The voices of African-American women are clearly different. The process of marginalization of African-American women will continue as long as it serves some purpose of those who are in power positions within our society. This process is based on the sociocultural level stereotypes—stereotypes that are consistent with the beliefs of others (Walters, 1999). The use of these stereotypes can be used to oppress black women. The use allows continued marginalization when women do not meet mainline criteria (Walters, 1999).

Members of more advantaged groups within our society can ignore or detach themselves from those who are being marginalized (Snyder and Miene, 1994). Gaines and Reed (1995) felt that the experience of being marginalized is so profound that the nature of identity is different. In addition, the prejudices that are formed differ for groups, depending upon whether the person is or is not part of a marginal group.

Women of color have been placed in special molds. Some of what we are we have been forced to become, and some of it is what we have innately been. Sexism and sexual freedom are contemporary issues for all women in the United States. But African-American women have a special history in America, one that no other group has, in which atrocious acts were committed against them through sexual and reproductive bondage (Johnson, 1998). Their bodies were used for sexual pleasure and for commercial gain, as children were bred as cattle and sold away. On many levels, these memories are still alive today. Exploitation has not been stopped and continues in many forms. For this very reason, it is hard for black and white women to come together to work on common problems. White women do not know or even understand the pain that many of the mothers of present blacks underwent. They feel that slavery happened so long ago that it really is not important today. But there are persons alive today, including the author, whose memories include relatives who were born right after enslavement under the same conditions of enslavement. For those people, these memories are still vivid.

Ethnic socialization occurs for African-American women in differential manners than other race or gender groups. The young girl must learn how to be African American within an African-American culture first; and how to be African American in a white-dominated world. Families exercise primary influence upon their ethnic and gender socialization (Socha and Diggs, 1999). Many African-American parents strongly feel that it is necessary to "racially socialize" their young daughters in order to prepare them for the racial and gender environments that they will face (Ferguson, 1999). It is from families that women learn the behaviors, values, perceptions, and attitudes of their group (Rotheram and Phinney, 1987). They are ascribed to certain positions and then accept themselves as being part of that group. As women have been given these messages, they are at the same time passing these attitudes and values onto the next generation within their own biological families (McAdoo and McWright, 1994).

Double images have been attributed to these women. They have been put forward as strong women who can cope with great stress. They are also seen as women who are less than capable. They are invisible to the average white person in or out of power. Black women are thought of as people with whom one must be cautious and who are untrustworthy. They are followed by store employees, whether they are in luxury department stores or in discount stores, for they are not to be trusted.

Tetrina

Six women argue with their lives
as they write among their dreams
chasing shadows down streets
and reaching for words

like fruit, like stars, words
to save their lives
to snatch them from the streets
defend their dreams

Don't we deserve our dreams
our hard borne words
labor of our lives?
We have taken in our streets

the clash, the color, the broken streets
and shaped them into dreams
and then to words
to change our lives

six lives held by dreams
a world of streets, our luminous words

Workshop Collaboration 1996. (The) Writing Workshop, Bedford Hills Correctional Facility. Hettie Jones (Ed.) 1997. *Aliens at the Border*. New York: Segue Books.

African-American women have put a "face" on when in public and have not allowed their real feelings to show. This is called the "Negro face" and outsiders do not know what is really being felt. Examples are seen in the black mammy in the kitchen in former times and in the business executive in a $300 suit in a downtown office building. They have been put into molds that have placed them in positions that do not allow them to express themselves freely. These women have been put in an inhibited, marginalized caste.

Like many other groups, African-American women find that their gender identity is intertwined with their ethnic identities in an inescapable manner. White women can rail against oppression by their men with justification. But people of color have to align themselves against whites, mostly men, but to some extent women, too. In the past, white women may not have been in positions to make judgments and policies that have oppressed persons of color. They have, however, benefited with white privilege by going along, reaping the benefit of being part of an endowed group, often indifferent to or ineffectual in alleviating the miseries of others. For the most part they have simply gone along with the oppression of persons of color, especially African Americans and, at the same time, their own oppression.

African-American women have to fight against oppression both inside and outside of their racial/ethnic group. At the beginning of the feminist fight, black women were involved, but they became less involved as time went on. Differences in agenda became evident. Some white women were still trying to justify working outside of their home when they had small children. Black women had been required to work for many years, regardless of their family situations. In other groups, the arrogance of whites began to irritate the black participants. Often the white women were not even aware of their grating attitudes, for they were simply treating women of color as they always had in the past. The result is that the women's movement became whiter as time passed.

At the same time, African-American women were facing a battle within their own ethnic group. Often the women had been the leaders in the communities, churches, and homes. Organizational skills, for the most part, resided in the women. This was one area in which the West African traditions had been continued. Women were more active in the communities and were allowed to asume their own level of participation. Within communities, both men and women were always allowed to have roles of leadership.

Evidence suggests that the survival of African-American families has depended in large part on the strength of the women in holding families together, rearing children, preserving and passing on traditions, while at the same time working outside of the home. Women played an active and important role in African societies, and these roles continued in the New World, during slavery, in the antebellum period, and to this day (McAdoo, 1999).

AFRICAN CULTURAL LEGACIES

Many African-American families have a historical past that is substantially different from all of the other immigrant groups that have come to the United States. The American enslavement experience brought dislocation, violent uprootings, and great pain. Brutal experiences have shaped the ideological forces that led to modern-day families, with their strengths and weaknesses (Wilkinson, 1997).

Often writers have approached black families as if slavery did not exist, or if it did, that it was too long ago to have an impact. This is often because writers and scholars do not want to deal with their possible complacent acceptance of such a savage system, or they simply do not know enough about enslavement.

Slavery occurred not that long ago. The writer's own maternal grandfather was born right after slavery ended, on the same plantation where his other nine brothers had been born as slaves. They worked the same plots under the same system as had the slaves for generations before them. So the experiences of slavery are imbedded in my brain by someone special to me whom I knew as a child. The patterns did not change in the years that followed. Schools stopped at the sixth grade for Negro children. Some were fortunate, however, to be able to get higher education in other states. My grandparents and parents worked hard and were able to take advantage of black colleges (Fisk, Tuskegee, Howard, Kentucky State, Atlanta University) and then were able to enter white universities (Michigan, Indiana). As a result, they were able to reach great educational and professional achievements, with the assistance of their wider kin and with tedious work by the individuals themselves. They were not the exceptional persons that many attempt to make them; they simply did what many of the highly motivated Negroes were forced to do across the South at the end of the 1800s and into the middle of the 1900s.

The parenting roles that black women have played, in Africa, during enslavement, and now into contemporary times, show a continuation of the dependence upon the extended consanguineous relationships of the mothers, not the conjugal relationships found within European and American families. There is a "direct nexus" or continuous linkage between Africans and Americans (DuBois, 1969). This points to a major difference between African-American families and mainstream American families (Sudarkasa, 1997).

DEMOGRAPHIC CHANGES

There is a growing diversity within the African-American community. As they increase in proportion of the population, they are also increasing in the types of families.

Another intraethnic component is the role of black males within the wider society and the attempts that women made to compensate for it. Black males were denigrated worse than women were. Stereotypes of the men were rampant. Wider society often did not find that black women were as threatening as the men were perceived to be. Women of color were hired, often before men, for they were seen as pliable and nonthreatening.

Employment of mothers can often mean the difference between economic self-sufficiency and poverty for families (Zill and Nord, 1994). African-American women, in the past and today, earn less than white or black men and white women. Lower status jobs and lower paying jobs have traditionally been reserved for these women, because their labor has been least valued (Allen, 1990; Huddleston-Mattai, 1995). Women have developed many organizational skills from experience. Because men were not able to have positions of esteem in the wider society, places were found for them to shine in more sheltered areas that were under black control. In other organizations, many women made the choice to step back and allow the men to assume power to achieve in certain areas.

This pattern was repeated all over the country, in churches, in social organizations, and in professional organizations. This happened particularly in black churches. This was happening at the same time that white women were organizing to become more experienced within their own groups. Black women were caught in a bind. On one hand, they were oppressed in many ways; on the other, their men were even more oppressed. These women could not remove themselves from the struggle of their men. Both of them were being oppressed by the same people, the white men who were in control. This caused a double bind for the women, who were aware of both sources of oppression, from their own men and from the wider society's empowerment of the male. This was another reason many women of color could not comfortably join women's liberation groups. The antimale thrust found in some groups may have been appreciated but could not be condoned by women of color in light of the positions that many of them took in relation to supporting their male counterparts.

FAMILY STRUCTURE

African continuities have resulted in developing many of the strengths that have facilitated families to cope with adversities (Dodson, 1997; Sudarkasa, 1993, 1997). Among the cultural legacies that are African derived, but which have been transmitted and altered in the United States, are the use of oral traditions, spirituality, rhythmic expression, and sense of community (Boykin, 1997; Jones, 1991). The importance of coresidential extended families and their support systems has been cited as one of the major survival systems of these families (Billingsley, 1999; Hill, 1972; McAdoo, 1997; Hatchett, Cochran, and Jackson, 1991; Sudarkasa, 1997). The importance of maintaining communal family traditions is that it results in more matriarchal family systems (Prince, 1997). There are many similarities in communal family traditions seen in African, Brazilian, West Indian, and American families (Herskovits, 1941).

Women's primary task still is depicted as caretaking of the family and childbearing and child care (Gilbert, Holahan, and Manning, 1981). The active roles within the communities were often misinterpreted by social science writers as being matriarchal (Moynihan, 1965). Families were organized in such a manner that the blood kin of the mothers had usually been of greater primary influence than the family of marriage or procreation (McAdoo, 1997). This meant that children were more a part of the community of the women's relatives, both fictive and actual kin (Stack, 1974). The residential pattern was often neolocal because of cultural patterns and because of poverty. Even when the family had more resources and no longer existed in poverty, these patterns of strong connections with both sides of the families, especially the mother's, continued. If the marital relation was discontinued, the children went along in a manner that was similar to before it ended. The typical family organization was often at odds with the wider white community, which held more to the nuclear family form.

African-American children who are growing up in one-parent homes are finding that the resources from the higher salary level of male employment, child care, and male attention in the home are not as available for them as they would be in homes with two married parents. Bumpass (as quoted in Ingrassia, 1993) has stated that African-American children have only a one-in-five chance of growing up to age sixteen with two parents. Poverty is present in 65 percent of single mother-child units, but only 18 percent of married couples (Ingrassia, 1993).

Having children without the benefit of marriage occurs across all economic levels. Among wealthier women with incomes of over $75,000, 22 percent of black women have children out of wedlock (Ingrassia, 1993).

This is almost ten times the white rate. Black women who are poor have more children without benefit of wedlock at 65 percent, double the number of whites.

Increases in poverty are due to both the greater prevalence of single parenting in black homes and to the reduced employment prospects and earning power of young workers. This is because many have a limited education, which limits skills and earning power (Eggebeen and Lichter, 1991). A large proportion of new families that are established each year may likely live in poverty. Mothers whose risk factors include single parenthood, lack of education, and youth are vulnerable to poverty. Furthermore, when families are dependent upon only one worker, income is often not sufficient to prevent poverty (Zill and Nord, 1994). Yet the Children's Defense Fund data indicated that in reality the majority of babies who are born to unmarried blacks are born to women who are *over* twenty years of age (Edelman, 1997; McAdoo, 1995). These are women who have been previously married and have since divorced or who have never been married. This number now includes a few women of middle-class status who have been unable to find a husband and have decided that they are in a position to raise a child without a husband. This status is now the modal family form.

In the 1990s, two-thirds of babies were born to unmarried mothers (DeParle, 1994). Because it is true that the birth of babies to unmarried teenage mothers is very problematic and laden with predicted challenges, these mothers will need more help in the future. The number of children who are born outside of marriage depends on many factors: the heavy economic and psychological isolation of the African-American male; growing tensions between black men and women in relation to sex-role expectations; and vestiges of the African-derived family organizations that depend upon relatives, rather than upon marriage partners, for assistance.

ROLES OF MALES IN FAMILIES

The roles of men have changed over the past fifteen to twenty years. All of the previously mentioned forces have taken their toll. The inequity in eligible males is overlooked by those who are in positions of formulating national policies and social service programs. Even if all single heterosexual men who were not in jail got married, many women still would be left without mates. The marginalization of males contributes to the stresses that could lead to the high level of divorce in these families. There should be awareness of the situations of women and their children. The most important fact is the growing disparity between black and white incomes that is the result of economic restructuring, discrimination, and consequent impoverishment (Hatchett, Cochran, and Jackson, 1991; McAdoo, 1997).

Black boys are often "shifted out" early in the school process, often as early as elementary school (Baye, 1994). Boys who have a sense of themselves, demanding respect, and those who are assertive or aggressive often get labeled by teachers as being threatening to other students and to the general population. They get punished and suspended more often and, in time, many of these boys give up on education. The downward spiral begins and the prophecy of doom fulfills itself.

The incarceration rate of males is extremely high, with the majority of the males now in prison being men of color. Six percent of the U.S. population is African-American male, but almost half of the men in prison are African American—six times the rate of white men (Mendez, 2000). Three of every ten men face the prospect of going to prison during their lifetimes. Indeed, many of the absent fathers are incarcerated. Many incarcerated African-American men have indicated that they are interested in improving their relationship with their children and that they would be willing to participate in a program that would help them do so (Mendez, 2000).

MARGINALIZATION AND URBAN SPRAWL

To ensure that racial, ethnic, and gender minorities are not marginalized, they must have real access to the opportunity structure of our society (Powell, 1999). The social fragmentation of the urban sprawl that has occurred since the 1950s has made access even more difficult. In 1950, 60 percent of all Americans lived in the central cities, which were the regional hubs for jobs, were good tax bases, and had good schools, decent housing, and retail opportunities. However, by the 1990s, almost 70 percent of the metropolitan population lived in the suburbs. Jobs and the strong tax base of the cities moved out with them. This left a concentration of poor persons and persons of color in the inner cities.

Powell (1999) has referred to this as a racially motivated method of exclusion and marginalization of African Americans, especially women. Policies and regulations of the suburbs, along with redlining and racial steering, made the situations even worse. Women, both single and married, who had to work outside of the home found themselves separated from the jobs in the suburbs. The extra commuting time left their children unsupervised after school. Thus, these women were further marginalized.

There have been efforts to reduce juvenile crime by relocating families from high-poverty neighborhoods to low-poverty ones. Providing this opportunity substantially reduced violent behavior by teens, but moving them into lower-poverty areas (rates under 10 percent) may also cause an increase in property offending in the short term (Duncan, Hirschfield, and Ludwig, 2000). The same group found that moving families into low-income rental subsidies reduced the rates of welfare use by around 15 percent. Most of this reduction appears to be explained by differences in welfare-to-work transitions. But providing families with unrestricted housing vouchers has little effect on economic outcomes beyond the first year (Duncan, Ludwig, and Pinkston, 2000).

THE PASSING STORM

African-American women have been made vulnerable by the lack of opportunity, underemployment, unemployment, and other social realities. This has caused them to make adjustments that have caused them further marginalization.

Having women work instead of getting governmental assistance has recently been put forward as a means of making these women less marginal. But the programs that have been instituted by various states have not provided the benefits that were promised, especially for those women who are poorly educated, have children, and have little job training. As welfare-to-work programs have spread across the country, women continue to be marginalized. Local support for welfare spending increases in step with the percentage of local welfare recipients who belong to one's own racial group (Luttmer, 1999).

Women of different education levels were affected differentially by welfare reform. For lesser-educated women, welfare reform decreased AFDC participation and increased work hours, yet it had no significant effect on earnings, wages, or family income. For better-educated women, welfare reform did lead to an increase in earnings. The goal of working instead of receiving welfare has been only partially successful.

The one positive thing was that working outside of the home has not created a difference in the academic or social behavior or the educational and occupational aspirations of young girls (Bos et al., 1999). Teachers reported that boys behaved better in school and performed better academically when they were in structured care arrangements. As the mothers worked, they did not have to be concerned about negative influences from child care, as long as the care was safe and secure.

Black women have worked outside of their families from enslavement into the present. Black women have not had to go through the mental anguish that many white women did when they first entered the labor market.

Incidentally, the employment of mothers has not had the negative effects that so many have predicted.

The African-American woman has faced storm after storm, and there appears to be no clear skies in the distant future. The urban sprawl will continue. Racial stereotyping will continue, as in the past. Economic inequities will not go away. Financial resources will continue to become more limited. There seems to be nothing on the horizon that will make their plight easier. The storm is not passing over or even ending. It appears to have gotten stuck right over our heads. It seems as if the storm will continue for some time to come.

REFERENCES

Allen, Walter R. 1990. Family Roles, Occupational Statuses, and Achievement Orientation among Black Women in the United States. In Micheline R. Malson, E. Mudimbe-Boyi, Jean F. O'Barr, and Mary Wyer (Eds.), *Black Women in America: Social Science Perspectives* (pp. 79-95). Chicago: University of Chicago Press.

Baye, Betty. 1994. No Wonder Minority Men Fall Behind. *Lansing State Journal,* March 21, p. 6A.

Billingsley, Andrew. 1999. *Mighty Like a River: The Black Church and Social Reform.* New York: Oxford Press.

Blackburn, Robert T. and Betty J. Holbert. 1987. The Careers of Women in Academia. In Josefina Figueira and Rosemary Sarri (Eds.), *The Trapped Woman* (pp. 296-317). Newbury Park, CA: Sage Publications.

Bos, Hans, Aletha Huston, Robert Granger, Greg Duncan, Tom Brock, and Vonnie McLoyd. 1999. Can Anti-Poverty Programs Improve Family Functioning and Enhance Children's Well-Being. *JCPR Policy Briefs.* Chicago: Joint Center for Poverty Research, University of Chicago.

Boykin, A. Wade. 1997. Communalism: Conceptualization and Measurement of an Afrocultural Social Orientation. *Journal of Black Studies 17*(3): 409-418.

DeParle, Jason. 1994. Clinton Target: Teenage Pregnancy. *The New York Times,* March 22, Final Edition, p. 6B.

Dodson, Jualynne E. 1997. Conceptualizations of African American Families. In Harriette P. McAdoo (Ed.), *Black Families,* Third Edition (pp. 67-82). Thousand Oaks, CA: Sage Publications.

DuBois, William E. B. 1969. *The Negro American Family.* New York: Negro Universities Press.

Duncan, Greg, Paul Hirschfield, and Jennis O. Ludwig. 2000. Urban Poverty and Juvenile Crime: Evidence from a Randomized Housing-mobility Experiment. Working paper, Institute for Policy Research, Northwestern University, Chicago.

Duncan, Greg, Jennis O. Ludwig, and Joshua Pinkston. 2000. Neighborhood Effects on Economic Self-sufficiency: Evidence from a Randomized Housing-

Mobility Experiment. Working papers, Institute for Policy Research, Northwestern University, Chicago.

Edelman, Marian W. 1997. An Advocacy Agenda for Black Families and Children. In Harriette P. McAdoo (Ed.), *Black Families* (pp. 323-332). Thousand Oaks, CA: Sage Publications.

Eggebeen, David J. and Daniel T. Lichter. 1991. Race, Family Structure, and Changing Poverty Among American Children. *American Sociological Review* 56(6): 801-817.

Ferguson, Ira. 1999. African-American Parent-Child Communication About Racial Denigration. In Thomas J. Socha and Rhunette C. Diggs (Eds.), *Communication, Race, and Family: Exploring Communication in Black, White, and Biracial Families* (pp. 45-68). London: Lawrence Erlbaum Associates.

Gaines, Stanley O. and Edward S. Reed. 1995. Stereotypes As Consensual Beliefs. In Mark P. Zanna and James M. Olson (Eds.), *The Psychology of Prejudice: The Ontario Symposium* Seventh Edition (pp. 33-35). Hillsdale, NJ: Erlbaum.

Gilbert, Lucia A., Carol K. Holahan, and Linda Manning. 1981. Coping with Conflict Between Professional and Maternal Roles. *Family Relations* 30(3): 419-426.

Gilligan, Carol. 1982. *In a Different Voice: Psychological Theory and Women's Development.* Cambridge: Harvard University Press.

Hatchett, Shirley J., Donna L. Cochran, and James S. Jackson. 1991. Family Life. In James S. Jackson (Ed.), *Life in Black America* (pp. 46-83). Newbury Park, CA: Sage Publications.

Herskovits, Melville J. 1941. *The Myth of the Negro Past.* New York: Harper.

Hill, Robert B. 1972. *The Strength of Black Families.* New York: Emerson Hall.

Huddleston-Mattai, Barbara A. 1995. The Black Female Academician and the "Superwoman Syndrome." *Race, Gender, and Class* 3(1): 49-64.

Ingrassia, Michele. 1993. Endangered Family: Struggling to Save the Black Family. Special report. *Newsweek* 122(9): 16-29.

Johnson, Rachelle. 1998. Unplanned Pregnancies: Stories of Choice. *Black Elegance* 110(May): 42-48.

Jones, James M. 1991. Racism: A Cultural Analysis of the Problem. In Reginald L. Jones (Ed.), *Black Psychology* Third Edition (pp. 609-635). Berkeley, CA: Cobb and Henry.

Luttmer, Erzo. 1999. Group Loyalty and the Taste for Redistribution. *JCPR Policy Briefs.* Chicago: Joint Center for Poverty Research, University of Chicago.

McAdoo, Harriette P. 1995. African-American Families: Strength and Realities. In Hamilton I. McCubbin, Elizabeth A. Thompson, Anne I. Thompson, and Jo A. Futrell (Eds.), *Resiliency in Ethnic Minority Families: African-American Families* (pp. 17-30). Thousand Oaks, CA: Sage Publications.

McAdoo, Harriette P. 1997. *Black Families,* Third Edition. Thousand Oaks, CA: Sage Publications.

McAdoo, Harriette P. 1999. *Family Ethnicity: Strength in Diversity,* Second Edition. Thousand Oaks, CA: Sage Publications.

McAdoo, Harriette P. and Linda McWright. 1994. The Roles of Grandparents: The Use of Proverbs in Value Transmission. *Activities, Adaptation and Aging* 19(2): 27-38.

Mendez, Gary A. Jr. 2000. Incarcerated African-American Men and Their Children: A Case Study. *Annals of the American Academy of Political and Social Science 569*(May): 86-101.

Moynihan, Daniel P. 1965. The Tangle of Pathology. In Robert Staples (1986) (Ed.), *The Black Family: Essays and Studies,* Third Edition (pp. 5-14). Belmont, CA: Wadsworth Publishing Co.

Powell, John. 1999. Achieving Racial Justice: What's Sprawl Got to Do with It? *Poverty and Race 8*(5): 3-5.

Prince, Kevin. 1997. Black Family and Black Liberation. *Psych Discourse 28*(1): 4-7.

Rotheram, Mary J. and Jean S. Phinney (Eds.). 1987. *Children's Ethnic Socialization: Pluralism and Development.* Newbury Park, CA: Sage Publications.

Snyder, Mark and Peter Miene. 1994. On the Functions of Stereotypes and Prejudice. In Mark P. Zanna and James M. Olson (Eds.), *The Psychology of Prejudice: The Ontario Symposium,* Seventh Edition (pp. 33-35). Hillsdale, NJ: Erlbaum.

Socha, Thomas and Ruhnette Diggs. 1999. *Communication, Race, and Family: Exploring Communication in Black, White, and Biracial Families.* London: Lawrence Erlbaum Associates.

Stack, Carol B. 1974. *All Our Kin: Strategies for Survival in a Black Community.* New York: Harper and Row.

Sudarkasa, Niara. 1993. Female-Headed African-American Households: Some Neglected Dimensions. In Harriette P. McAdoo (Ed.), *Family Ethnicity: Strength in Diversity* (pp. 81-89). Newbury Park, CA: Sage Publications.

Sudarkasa, Niara. 1997. African-American Families and Family Values. In Harriette McAdoo (Ed.), *Black Families,* Third Edition (pp. 9-40). Thousand Oaks: Sage Publications.

Walters, Lynda. 1999. Valuing Diversity: Implication for Social Health. *Journal of Family and Consumer Sciences 91*(3): 27-30.

Wilkinson, Doris. 1997. American Families of African Descent. In M. DeGenova (Ed.), *Families in Cultural Context: Strengths and Challenges in Diversity* (pp. 335-360). London: Mayfield Publishing Co.

Zill, Nicholas and Christine W. Nord. 1994. *Running in Place: How American Families Are Faring in a Changing Economy and an Individualistic Society.* Washington, DC: Child Trends, Inc.

SECTION II:
BLOCKAGES TO AUTONOMY

Chapter 5

The Controllers and the Controlled

Deborah M. Whitley
Paula L. Dressel

"Prisoners 'Hired,' So Ex-Welfare Clients Fired." This *Atlanta Journal-Constitution* front-page headline on June 19, 1999, and the story that it introduced are testimony to the utilization of both welfare recipients and prisoners as cheap labor—as well as to the competition between them for work. As the situation was reported, a waste management and recycling plant in a rural Georgia town was experiencing financial difficulty and had to lay off fifty people that it had hired at $5.25 an hour. Thirty-five of the fifty who were laid off had taken the jobs to get off of welfare. In their place, thirty-six inmates from a nearby women's prison spent forty hours a week doing the same work for no pay at all. Instead, the waste-management company pays the state Department of Corrections for the prison guards' salaries and only the inmates' transportation. The chair of the waste management authority board indicated that "the combination of inmate labor and a paid workforce of 130 to 160 people ensures that salaried employees will keep their jobs. The free inmate labor helps put the facility 'a little bit closer to being profitable.'" In short, the displacement of one marginalized group of women by another allowed the plant a cost savings of almost $19,200 per month, or $230,400 annually. These savings were achieved at the expense of the two groups who are the subjects of this book, women on the welfare rolls and women in prison.

This chapter is not about labor exploitation per se or the competition that imprisoned labor creates for even minimum wage workers. Rather, it is about the relationships between the controllers and the controlled: on the one hand, prison guards and welfare workers; on the other hand, prisoners and welfare recipients. But the foregoing vignette gives a vivid glimpse of

The authors thank Shernita Alston (MSW graduate student), Jung Ha Kim, Patricia Bryan, Gary Longstreet, and Meg Price for their assistance on the chapter.

the political-economic function of both women on welfare and women in prison as members of what political economists call the "surplus population." We will turn shortly to explicating this point within a broader political-economic framework, which will be helpful to an understanding of the dynamics between the controllers and the controlled. Notice in this story that the guards were *paid* by the waste-management company to prevent the prisoners' escape from *unpaid* labor and servitude. This distinction indirectly figures into our analysis as well.

The obvious point that we will explore in this chapter is the decidedly different institutional locations in relation to authority of the controllers and the controlled. Although we will use the categorical terminology of "controllers" and "controlled," we are quick to acknowledge Collins' (1998b, p. 931) point that "group 'centres' cannot be constructed in essentialist ways." Indeed, we contend that it would be categorically unwise to think of the controllers and the controlled as wholly different sets of the population. If, as we seek to show below, there is sometimes much in common between the two groups (yet they find themselves performing significantly different roles), the dynamics that are manifested in their interactions are bound to be complex. The previous points move us away from polarizing the two groups into victimizers and victims and instead to problematize their relationships so that even the controllers can be understood to experience their own forms of marginalization. As we maintain later, that experience does much to shape controllers' behaviors toward those over whom they are put in charge.

THE CONTROLLERS AND THE CONTROLLED
IN POLITICAL-ECONOMIC CONTEXT

Elsewhere Dressel and Barnhill (1994) have applied a model of the U.S. political economy to the circumstances of welfare clients and prisoners. In short, it is argued that a capitalist-democratic state has two primary functions. The first is to shape policies and practices that create opportunities for profit making via corporate-friendly tax policies, relaxed immigration enforcement, government subsidies, and the like. These legal frameworks and their implementation practices interact with increasingly technology-intensive workplaces and the immigration of jobs to cheaper sources of labor in ways that displace workers, replace people with machines, and rationalize heretofore complex operations. The predictable result of these dynamics is the creation of a surplus population, or a portion of the population that is under or unemployed regardless of their desire to work and their need for family-supporting wages. Further, the surplus population is disproportionately comprised of persons of color and women across groups, due to the

For Willie Mae

woman spent eleven
pregnant years and
mindfully lives
mindfully is the story
of the fifteen children she
bares to tell of

doctors who don't heal only
to destroy the minds of
seven year old sons with
noses that bleed of

police blue cops that
don't hear
only hear
your words through
the Babylon they maintain of

systems that say
your boy should work
when he's crawling to the
church rolling to God's
hands.

Teller if stories of
consciousness that tells
them to put their trash in
their mouths eat quietly
chewing with an open mouth
is impolite.

Eleven pregnant years of
Stories sixty five non-life giving
Years of stories
Of Real Truth of Mind and Life

Cory Rosenblatt

Cory Rosenblatt is now a graduate social work student at Arizona State University.

ways in which racism and sexism play out in place-based opportunity structures, educational systems, and labor market dynamics.

At the same time that a capitalist-democratic state spawns a surplus jobless population, the state must also function to maintain its legitimacy among that very group and among those who would be concerned about people left behind. The second primary function of the state, then, is legitimation. Legitimation takes two forms: social assistance at levels that will not compete with prevailing minimum wages (which would obviate the other primary state function by raising the price of labor), and police protection and prison systems to constrain the actions of those who would challenge the state or otherwise act out of desperation. One irony of the legitimation function is the creation of jobs—jobs that control the surplus population by one means or another, either through whatever placation comes from subsistence support or through more overt mechanisms of social control via arrest, probation, parole, and confinement. Categorically, women are more likely to obtain jobs within the social assistance arena, while men predominate in carrying out the social control function.

Piven and Cloward (1993) similarly described the role of the state. They postulated that when states establish or expand relief programs, they do so to restore order among disruptive, dependent masses (the bulk of whom are members of the surplus population). However, as they note, any support provided by government cannot compete with the capitalist economy. Expanding beyond Piven and Cloward, we reflect upon the irony that many publicly created jobs are disproportionately filled at the front line with workers whose profiles are not significantly different in one respect or another from the surplus population.

What does this model of the U.S. political economy offer with regard to our interest in the controllers and the controlled? First, the model alerts us to the relationship between the welfare and criminal justice systems. With regard to the state function of legitimation, the latter takes up the work when the former cannot contain political unrest or desperate individuals. Second, the model and data suggest that members of the surplus population are vulnerable to cycling back and forth between the two systems. The poverty of welfare clients creates risks for pursuing illegal means of survival and facing consequent apprehension and confinement. Sixty-four percent of jail inmates in 1996 had incomes of less than $12,000 per year—below the poverty level for a small family—and almost half had less than a high school education (Harlow, 1998). The circumstances of prisoners offer few avenues to self-sufficiency upon release, thus making them vulnerable to a welfare clienthood that is increasingly time limited. This situation is even more detrimental if the parolee is a mother who has been convicted of a drug felony. Federal Temporary Assistance for Needy Families (TANF) policy allows states to prohibit individuals convicted of drug-related felonies from receiving cash assistance and food stamp benefits for life. Third, were it not for frontline employment in either the welfare or the criminal justice systems, those referred to here as the controllers could very well be at risk for membership in the surplus population themselves where they would then become the controlled. Thus, the controllers are located in a contradictory position in that their job is to legitimate the systems in which they work, and thereby the state, even as those same systems express control over people not always strikingly dissimilar from the frontline workers themselves (Dressel, Sweat, and Waters, 1988).

FORMS AND CONTEXT OF CONTROL

The foregoing sections sought to demonstrate the conceptual link between the social welfare and criminal justice systems, the similarities, if not the interchangeability, between controllers and controlled, and the all too frequent interchangeability between both sets of the controlled: welfare recipients and prisoners.

Before turning to the interactional dynamics these claims anticipate, it will be helpful to examine a variety of ways in which control is effected. Collins' (1998a) discussion of the politics of containment of African-American women is conceptually instructive here. Focusing historically and contemporarily, Collins identifies containment as being manifested at different times with varying intensity in the forms of legal or de facto exclusion from citizenship, racial segregation, and various forms of surveillance, all enforced when necessary through patterns of violence. All of these forms of containment impact welfare recipients: recent welfare "reform" laws have eliminated certain entitlements to assistance that had accompanied the expansion of the welfare state since the 1930s; poor women of color are likely to be employed in highly raced and gendered jobs; and recipients' lives are subjected to state oversight and intrusion through "reform" measures enacted on the front line by welfare workers. Prisoners are also subjected to all three forms of containment: imprisoned women may lose voting rights and the custody of their children; they are segregated from the broader society and distributed across prisons differentially (with the bulk of European-American prisoners found in federal rather than state and local prisons); and their lives are under the twenty-four-hour surveillance of prison guards and prison video cameras.

Beyond these forms of containment, Collins describes more sophisticated strategies of control that have emerged since the 1970s. The new politics of containment, she argues, derives from shifting values with regard to public and private arenas of life. Since the 1970s, African-American women have gained public access in two important respects: access to state-entitlement benefits and access to government-sector employment. Collins maintains that these achievements appear to have contributed to European-Americans' abandonment of both arenas insofar as they serve the interests of the poor. Specifically, they have increasingly withdrawn support for welfare-state activities focused on poor women with limited means of self-support and pushed for the privatization of government functions that favor the nonpoor, such as school vouchers. Accompanying whites' selective abandonment of public institutions is the increasing surveillance of public sphere roles, whether the role is that of controller or controlled. Applied to our focus here, this means that welfare workers are increasingly scrutinized for their ability to apply with accuracy the highly complex and frequently shifting rules of policy. The situation of prison guards, who are disproportionately white males, is noticeably different. Prison guards are watched for the tendency to be too friendly with prisoners, but they are not likely to be sanctioned for violent or abusive behavior toward prisoners unless it is extremely egregious and has the potential to become visible to the public—and thus become a public relations problem. In the case of the controlled, the surveillance and containment of both welfare recipients and prisoners, who are disproportionately people of color, through distorted and stereotypical media representations (re)produce a public will inclined toward scapegoating, isolation, and dehumanization in the short term and a protracted invisible genocide over time (Dressel, 1994).

Although the foregoing has delineated varying *forms* of control, it is important to look at the occupational *context* of control before focusing more specifically on policy contexts and interactional dynamics. Within the welfare workplace, the major trends of deprofessionalization and proletarianization have shaped the nature of work and the demographics of workers (Dressel, Sweat, and Waters, 1988). Deprofessionalization is the shift toward reduced education or training requirements for employment; proletarianization is the rationalization and deskilling of work tasks so that complex processes get broken down into discrete and potentially dehumanized and fragmented segments of work. These dynamics have gone hand in hand with periodic policy pushes for the hiring of indigenous workers and governmental job reclassification due to fiscal stress. The consequences of these concurrent changes are at least twofold. First, increased numbers of social workers now resemble recipients more closely in terms of class and ethnic background. The majority of social workers are female, and minority-group members are represented in the occupation beyond their proportion in the population. The numbers by sex and race become even more robust within the paraprofessional classification of welfare service aide. These same workers have narrower functions and less discretion in their interactions with recipients than their predecessors, and they operate within a policy climate that is increasingly punitive toward women in poverty.

The occupational context of control with regard to prisons is framed by the dramatic growth of women's prison facilities in the past decade. In 1990, there were seventy-one state and federal prison facilities for women; by 1995, the number had increased to 104, a 45 percent increase in a five-year period (U.S. Department of Justice, 1997). Concomitant with the increase in correctional facilities is the need for corrections personnel. According to a report on female prisoners by Amnesty International (1999), 70 percent of the guards in U.S. women's prison facilities are men. This growth industry is more likely to provide work, albeit modest wage work, for men in rural areas where prisons may be one of the few sources of newly available jobs.

These men are likely to be limited in educational background and thus paid very modest wages. Within the Federal Bureau of Prisons, 45 percent of guards have only a high school diploma, and only 16 percent have a college degree (U.S. Department of Justice, 1999). Average entry level wages for work as a state prison guard hover around $20,000 annually (Corrections Compendium, 1999). Although prisoner demographics reflect a disproportionate representation of women of color, European-American men predominate within the population of prison guards (Stephan, 1997). Thus, while the typical male guard fares marginally better than female prisoners in terms of education and income, he has decided status advantage over the typical female prisoner by virtue of his race and sex, as well as his occupational location. Furthermore, he is likely to reside in the rural community or small town in which the prison is located, whereas the woman is likely to be considerably distant from her family and her community of support and residence (which is typically urban). Thus, she is not only vulnerable to guard misbehavior within prison confines, but she also cannot count on support for her well-being from the surrounding community. These features of the occupational and relational contexts operate within a policy climate that is intended to focus on punishment rather than rehabilitation.

The recent conservative political agenda has left distinguishable marks on public welfare and criminal justice policies and practices. Such conservatism has particularly impacted those women who are dependent on the public welfare system for economic support and those who are incarcerated. Because the social policies that emanate from this conservative agenda provide the context for the interactional dynamics that occur between the controllers and the controlled, limited descriptions of the policy frameworks, which inform the control of welfare recipients on the one hand and prisoners on the other are offered.

POLICY FRAMEWORK OF CONTROL:
PERSONAL RESPONSIBILITY AND TANF

The Personal Responsibility and Work Opportunity Reconciliation Act of 1996 (PL 104–193) replaced the former cash assistance program, Aid to Families with Dependent Children (AFDC), with Temporary Assistance for Needy Families (TANF). TANF's primary goal is to reduce the number of mothers on welfare by requiring individual responsibility and economic self-sufficiency, while supposedly protecting the children of these mothers from severe poverty. At the same time, TANF is designed to reduce federal government spending for income-tested public assistance programs (Gueron, 1996). Individual responsibility and economic self-sufficiency are inferred by several components in the federal law, including the elimination of federal entitlements, family cap provisions, time limitations for benefits, and strict work requirements. TANF has been viewed as punitive rather than rehabilitative because it erroneously emphasizes the recipient's presumably immoral behavior rather than the numerous structural factors that produce dependency (e.g., unequal distribution of employment opportunities in metropolitan areas, poor educational resources in urban/rural schools, racism, sexism, and urban divestment by local businesses).

Such a policy came about within a conservative policy climate that reflects a combination of contentious attitudes about federal and state government spending on social welfare programs and an inferred lack of individual responsibility and motivation on the part of young mothers to obtain work and care for their own children. Critics of the previous welfare system argued that work incentives were lacking in former programs, and thus laziness, poor motivation, and lack of initiative in recipients were tolerated (Bartle, 1998). Conservative arguments generally maintained that those who are dependent on welfare have some personal responsibility for their current status, dismissing the relevance of social structural and economic fault lines (Withorn, 1996). Irresponsibility, poor judgment, and promiscuous behavior are cited as primary characteristics of individuals who must turn to welfare instead of achieving gainful employment. Even liberal analysts agreed that the former welfare system was plagued with problems that discouraged self-sufficiency among recipients. Positing some ideas similar to those of conservatives, liberals argued that the old welfare system failed because it increased the federal budget deficit, devalued middle-class notions of family and work, and promoted illegitimacy and dependency (Withorn, 1996). In a study of state legislators' perceptions about poverty, Beck, Whitley, and Wolk (1999) found that even liberal legislators believe the poor exhibit behaviors that, if not the cause of poverty, certainly perpetuate it. Consequently, persons dependent on the welfare system are viewed as being marginalized through their own accord from mainstream society.

An additional criticism fueling welfare reform, which was offered by both liberal and conservative camps, was that the federal government's control over welfare programming denied the states autonomy to conduct programs as they deemed appropriate for their constituencies. This view caught on more broadly. Elected officials were quick to cite opinion-poll data that suggest the public's support for states to have greater authority in designing and implementing welfare programs because "states know what works best in their communities." Thus, attacking both the victim (dependent women) and the welfare system served to justify new welfare reform legislation (Bartle, 1998).

Implicit in the TANF policy is the notion that women on welfare lack the initiative to work. The new policy forces women to develop the initiative for work in the shortest time possible, if they do not already have it. As such, their responsibility is to participate in some work activity (e.g., performing paid employment, actively seeking employment, attending educational/ training programs) as soon as the state determines they are ready for work participation or two years after beginning to receive assistance, whichever comes first (Hagen, 1999). In general, the number of hours mothers must engage in work activities is twenty hours per week, which increased to thirty hours per week in the year 2000. Mothers who fail to comply with any aspect of the work activity requirements may be sanctioned by the state by having their already meager welfare benefits reduced. To be certain that states enforce the work requirements on recipients, TANF ties state block-grant funding to work expectations. First, states have to meet overall work participation rates for recipients beginning at 25 percent in 1997 and reaching a high of 50 percent by the year 2002 (Hagen, 1999), with higher expectations for two-parent families. Second, states must require all recipients who have received assistance for two years to be involved in some work activity. If states fail to meet the established work expectations, they are at risk of losing portions of their grant funding. Since state-funding levels are preset based on 1994 enrollment figures, which have been declining steadily since then, states stand to lose a considerable amount of money. According to a recent Urban Institute study, about 30 percent of parents who left welfare between 1995 and 1997 returned and were again receiving benefits when the study was conducted in 1997 (Loprest, 1999). Thus, a sizable number of families who are unable to survive without support from welfare benefits may become an increasing problem for states. This suggests that the decline in welfare rolls will level off in the near future, ultimately impacting states' federal funding levels. As noted later, such an occurrence would have dramatic consequences for the controllers as well as for the controlled.

Unlike former welfare policies, TANF shows less emphasis on determining eligibility for family funds, a function generally regarded as a clerical task, and a greater emphasis on providing social and job-ready services that prepare mothers for the workplace. As such, employees in welfare offices are shifting their focus to making women more "job worthy." In practice this means that welfare workers must communicate to recipients the reality of the time limits, inform them about their options for education and training, help them to become informed consumers about child care resources in their local communities, and educate them about the process for appealing agency decisions (Hagen, 1999). Long-term case management, while necessary in many cases, is not going to be available to most women due to the time limits embedded within the TANF policy. Only the most severe cases will be afforded ongoing case management services. Instead, the norm is likely to be case monitoring to ensure that clients are adhering to the prescribed activities in order to maintain benefit eligibility (Hagen, 1999). In short, the federal government has put pressure on states to produce certain rather unrealistic outcomes; states pressure workers to undertake their assignments in ways presumed to produce the expected dramatic outcomes; and workers pressure recipients to conform to the numerical results necessary for demonstrating policy responsiveness.

The results of the TANF legislation are not encouraging. Those leaving welfare are moving into jobs that do not put them above the poverty line; rather, the numbers of near-poor and low-income families are increasing. There is little indication that many will move beyond their current economic status. Even with the financial support of other public benefits (food stamps, Medicaid, Social Security, and child support), many of these former recipients are struggling to make ends meet, and others are falling out of sight. About 20 percent of all former welfare recipients reported that they were not working, had no partner working, and were not receiving government disability benefits (Loprest, 1999).

PRACTICE FRAMEWORK OF CONTROL:
WELFARE WORKERS AND WELFARE RECIPIENTS

The forgoing expectations set by federal policy put pressure on states to remove women and their children from the welfare rolls as quickly as possible to avoid federal sanctions. How will these policy expectations affect the dynamics between clients and workers? Hansenfeld (1987) stated that the effectiveness of social welfare practice is partially dependent on the relationship between the client (controlled) and the worker (controller). Generally, the worker has considerable power over the client (e.g., power of expertise, referent power, legitimate power) as dictated by the organizational and policy contexts in which their relationship operates. TANF serves as the authoritative policy for structuring the relationship between welfare workers and their clients. Any decisions on monetary assistance made by the welfare worker on behalf of the recipient are controlled by the standards set within TANF itself.

One consequence of TANF as compared to former welfare policies is that it limits worker flexibility and autonomy in addressing individual family needs. Disallowing worker flexibility and autonomy in case-managing clients potentially weakens the working relationship between workers and clients. Workers have few options by which to provide supports necessary for clients to move into the workforce, thereby enhancing the likelihood of tension and frustration between workers and recipients. In contrast to policy under AFDC, TANF implementers cannot offer clients many educational options, even though the efficacy of these is well documented (Sheak and Haydon, 1996; Brooks and Buckner, 1996; Marcenko and Fagan, 1996) because the types of accepted educational activities are severely restricted; post high school educational choices are even more limited. Furthermore, recipients have a short period of time in which they can participate in educational activities, usually six months to one year.

To compensate for the lack of formal educational resources and limited job opportunities, workfare programs have been instituted for recipients who cannot find a job and thus must earn their grants through public service jobs. Some states are placing welfare recipients into government-sponsored work programs that consume workers' time but do not provide substantive work experience, making it difficult to look for substantive work or to engage in a training program to increase work skills (Whitman, 1998). The frustration felt by women who are confined to this kind of work is evident. One workfare parent in New York who spends twenty hours a week picking up city trash remarked, "What can you really learn cleaning up? I'm out in the streets now picking up garbage. But picking up garbage is what I do every day at home" (Whitman, 1998, p. 3). Besides the frustration of having to comply with restrictive work programs, there are concerns about the extent to which welfare-to-work programs comply with federal regulations affording participants the same labor law protections as other employees (e.g., antidiscrimination and sexual harassment protections). Since they are often regarded as trainees, strict adherence to these requirements is not clearly documented.

Another source of client-worker tension resulting from TANF is the pressure on welfare workers to reduce their caseloads. Successful job performance is partly predicated on how quickly workers can close their cases to meet state and federal requirements. As welfare workers feel the pressure to reduce cases, workers may put pressure on parents to find any job as quickly as possible. The result could lead them either to withdraw from welfare altogether because of their inability to conform to workers' demands, or to be forced into jobs that are unsuitable for their educational experience, family needs, or long-term well-being.

The premises of TANF also put welfare workers in a tenuous employment position. According to policies, they must reduce their welfare rolls, but as the welfare rolls decline, the need for welfare workers presumably will also decline. The potential decline in frontline worker positions could increase local demand for other employment opportunities, social supports, and other resources for moderately skilled workers. It is not yet clear how former welfare workers might be absorbed into the labor market. As noted earlier, Collins (1998a) asserts that public institutions have become the least-valued institutions in our society, especially as more women of color have assumed positions of status in them. If this assertion is valid, as public institutions such as welfare offices suffer devaluation, workers needing to move to private institutions or other sectors for employment may have difficulty doing so. Former welfare system employees may come to be imbued by the public with many of the same negative attributes that currently plague their clients.

If states are not able to adhere to federal expectations regarding roll reductions, they will lose money and the jobs of frontline workers may still be in jeopardy. Either way, then, frontline welfare workers could be facing a difficult employment situation. Considering that the qualifications for frontline income maintenance and case management positions in welfare offices do not require advanced formal educational training or skills, these workers could find themselves in direct competition for the same jobs with the clients that they have served. Moreover, they themselves may require the very state assistance that they once controlled.

POLICY FRAMEWORK OF CONTROL: THE GET-TOUGH POLICY

Although there is no singular authoritative policy like TANF for defining the relationship between prison workers and prisoners, there is a similarity in the conservatism that sets the stage for behaviors by prison authorities within criminal justice systems. Urged by strong public opinion to "get tough" with those who participate in criminal activity, federal, state, and local authorities since the early 1980s have moved to a decidedly punitive stance in sentencing with the passage of such policies as the Comprehensive Crime Control Act of 1984. Kaplan and Sasser note that the goal of the conservative movement is to create a less tolerant criminal justice system, one that is viewed as a system of crime control, "including executions and mandated long periods of incarceration" (1996, p. 44). Crime-control practices derived from the perspective of general deterrence theory focus on increasing the risk of punishment and the severity of the punishment in order to deter future criminal activity (Zedlewski, 1997).

The conservative viewpoint on crime control in principle affords little regard for unique differences between male and female prisoners and the crimes they commit. The tendency is to lock them up, regardless of the circumstances, and with limited regard for individual rights. This outlook epitomizes Collins' notion of the politics of containment. Practices that serve to control individuals by limiting their private rights and public access ultimately contain them in designated positions within the social hierarchy. The ability to move within the social, economic, and political structures of society is by definition truncated by imprisonment and is negatively impacted upon release because of the experience of imprisonment.

The criminal justice system's "get-tough" policy, primarily resulting from the War on Drugs campaign, has meant that more women are being confined. According to Snell and Morton (1994), the majority of incarcerated women are serving time for nonviolent offenses (e.g., fraud, drug possession, and drug sales) as opposed to violent offenses. Between 1980 and 1994 there was a 386 percent increase in the number of women incarcerated in federal/state prisons and local jails. The number of women in state and federal prisons is growing at a faster rate than for men. During 1998, the number of female prisoners rose by 6.5 percent while the rate of increase for men was 4.7 percent (Beck and Mumola, 1999). Women also have been receiving longer sentences, up 40 percent between 1985 and 1990 (Gordon, 1994). The majority of women who are imprisoned are from racial minority groups. The proportion of incarcerated African-American women is eight times higher than for European-American women, while for Hispanic women the rate is four times higher (Amnesty International, 1999). Furthermore, the rate at which Hispanic women are being incarcerated has well surpassed that of Hispanic males. Between 1990 and 1997, the Hispanic female incarceration rate increased 55 percent, while the Hispanic male rate rose 25 percent (Reaves and Goldberg, 1999).

The 1990s witnessed the emergence of an overcrowded penal system practicing punitive law enforcement against women. This same system offers fewer rehabilitative resources for women than it does for men; thus, resources for health and education/training, which are necessary for successful transition to mainstream society, are routinely inadequate where they exist at all (Kaplan and Sasser, 1996). Despite the increasing numbers of women entering penal institutions, appropriate rehabilitative services are not sufficient for successful outcomes. Research has cited inadequacies in the areas of medical services, education, vocational training, prison industries, law libraries, and parenting programs, as well as a lack of objective knowledge about what works for female prisoners (Rafter, 1990).

The recognition that women prisoners need targeted services has been slow. It was not until 1986 that federal correctional facilities began instituting parenting programs in their facilities, and only in 1995 did parenting programs become a requirement for all Bureau of Prison facilities (U.S. Department of Justice, 1998a). Their availability remains spotty in other systems. The inconsistent availability of parenting programs across correctional facilities is imprudent considering that approximately seven in ten women under correctional sanction have a child under the age of eighteen; 70 percent in local jails, 65 percent in state prisons, and 59 percent in federal prisons have young children (Greenfeld and Snell, 1999). Without such programs, mothers may be released from prison with an inability to assume appropriate parental roles and responsibilities, given that they had little opportunity for such while in prison (Young and Smith, 2000).

According to Koons et al. (1997), programs structured for women inmates are often "watered-down" versions of male programs, with little consideration as to their appropriateness for women. Even in essential services such as health care, correctional facilities seem to be ill equipped to address the needs of female inmates. As late as 1990, 35 percent of the county jails in New York had no health care services for women, particularly obstetrics and gynecology. In 1992 and 1993, the National Institute of Justice conducted surveys of drug treatment programs for female offenders. They found that women's programs were similar to those for men in that group counseling, psychotherapy, drug education, and twelve-step programs were readily available; however, programs were limited for women who were pregnant, mentally ill, and/or violent offenders. There were also insufficient services for women inmates with multiple needs such as parenting, educational instruction, vocational training, and transitional services (Wellisch, Prendergast, and Anglin, 1994).

Similarly, vocational programs for incarcerated women emphasize stereotypical work roles. Programming in women's facilities focuses on clerical work, domestic service, and cosmetology, with little opportunity for women to be trained in the more lucrative work roles which are available to male inmates, such as maintenance and repair, forestry, or farming. At the same time, however, Schram (1998) found that female inmates (along with correctional officers) have negative stereotypes about nontraditional vocational programming for women. These perceptions can be viewed as forms of social control and self-limitation if they actually inhibit program participation.

These programmatic inadequacies are especially troubling in light of data that show strong need for such resources. According to Koons et al. (1997), many incarcerated women have experienced prior sexual and/or physical abuse; others have mental health and drug-related problems that are linked to their experiences of prior abuse (e.g., women in prison used more drugs and used those drugs more frequently than men); and a large number of female inmates are charged with other drug-related offenses (ranging from possession to the manufacture and sale of drugs). In light of these issues, most female inmates report histories of prolonged periods of unemployment, which are exacerbated by their lack of educational credentials or competitive work skills.

The incarceration of women with children has an impact well beyond the criminal justice system. Snell and Morton (1994) found that 10 percent of children whose mothers were incarcerated went into foster care, making the termination of parental rights a possibility. The majority of children whose mothers are imprisoned live with a grandparent (Dowdell, 1995; Dressel and Barnhill, 1994; Gaudin and Sutphen, 1993). However, as grandparents assume parenting roles for extended periods of time, many experience severe psychological stress stemming from financial pressures, inadequate housing, social isolation, failing physical health, and the everyday pressures of raising children. To address some of their needs, grandparents find they must learn to maneuver the welfare, child welfare, health care, criminal justice, and school systems simultaneously (Kelley et al., 1999). The policies and practices of these public institutions are not always sensitive to families that have been disrupted by imprisonment.

As women are being confined for longer periods of time within systems oriented to punishment rather than rehabilitation, they have little hope of being released with marketable skills that would make them valuable in the labor force, practically insuring their immediate return to welfare rolls (if their time limits have not been exceeded or they have not committed a drug felony which would prohibit them permanently from receiving public assistance) and to the prison system at some future time. As Conley (1998) notes, women ex-prisoners must simultaneously comply with conditions of probation or parole, achieve financial stability, access health care, locate housing, and commence the process of reuniting with their children. Without strong support in the community to help them negotiate the rules and regulations of innumerable public agencies as well as readjust to life outside prison, women may spiral back into a life of substance abuse, prostitution, and related crimes.

PRACTICE FRAMEWORK OF CONTROL:
RELATIONS BETWEEN GUARDS AND PRISONERS

One effect of the increase in women prisoners is the rising need for women's correctional facilities and staff. As we noted earlier, these staff members are overwhelmingly male, unlike in some countries, such as Canada, where the employment of women guards is the norm. International human rights standards specifically state that female prisoners should be guarded by female officials. But the United States has not fully adopted such human rights standards and, therefore, male guards commonly watch over women prisoners, even when the women are dressing and showering. They may also do body searches of female prisoners when looking for contraband (Amnesty International, 1999).

Collins' conceptualization of containment becomes total when considering the relationship between women prisoners and male prison guards, especially when those guards are white and the prisoners come from racial or ethnic minority groups. The specific behaviors that male corrections officers execute in controlling female inmates ensure their absolute authority and dominance over prisoners. The various forms of male dominance and racialized privilege that exist outside of prison have a greater likelihood of being exhibited in a setting where the women have no power or allies. Sexism and racism are constant themes in these relationships. Too often violence is used as an enforcement mechanism for containment and for the maintenance of power relations based on race and gender; violence in the service of enforcing power structures is legitimated (Collins, 1998b). Corrections officers are in a position to define and conceptualize what types of violence are and are not sanctioned. Further, women prisoners, by virtue of carrying the stigma of being prisoners, are not often viewed as victims by prison officials.

Female prisoners report sexual misconduct, sexual assault, and verbal and physical abuse from guards as common complaints. In 1999 the U.S. General Accounting Office investigated sexual misconduct in four correctional systems—the Federal Bureau of Prisons, the California Department of Corrections, the Texas Department of Criminal Justice, and the District of Columbia's correctional system. Despite efforts to institute policies to ban sexual assault by staff, between 1995 and 1998 a total of 506 allegations of staff sexual misconduct were made; ninety-two of them were sustained, generally resulting in staff firings or resignations. But, according to the U.S. General Accounting Office (1999), understanding the full extent of the problem is difficult because all institutions do not systematically maintain data on all types of allegations, including the number of allegations, their nature, or their outcomes. In most cases, allegations of sexual misconduct are dismissed due to lack of evidence. Fear of retaliation by prison officials stops many women from coming forward to report abuses. Only a minimal number of institutions have confidential reporting systems that would allow female inmates to report acts of abuse by corrections officers in confidence.

Besides exposure to violence and abuse from prison guards, women prisoners are contained by virtually every rule and regulation of prison life: what they wear and eat, when they sleep and work, where they can go on the grounds, whom they can see or talk to, and how they can act. These are the routine rules and regulations that structure everyday interaction between guards and prisoners, with the former paid to contain the latter. As noted earlier, the lack of rehabilitative supports virtually ensures that confinement will not prepare inmates for self-sufficiency upon their release.

PROSPECTS FOR THE FUTURE

The political-economic framework we laid out in the beginning of the chapter with regard to the creation of a surplus population implies certain kinds of broad changes that are needed in order to alter the situations this chapter has described. These changes include greater emphasis on the creation of jobs that pay living wages and commitment to the development of human capital in order for peoples' skills to match living-wage jobs. Indeed, it would not be outside of the framework to suggest that the political economy could maintain a reasonable equilibrium even in the face of less profit taking by small numbers of elite in order to create such jobs and provide such training. Further, direct and indirect approaches to the reduction of sexism and racism in their many permutations across economic and political arenas and social assistance and social control functions could at least alter vulnerabilities so that they become more randomized than group targeted.

Smaller changes could be undertaken on larger scale. Certain labor-intensive welfare-to-work programs have proven successful when both employers and potential employees make a commitment to alter the arrangements and behaviors that discourage hiring and retention. Spearheaded by the Clinton administration, businesses of varying sizes are providing access to employment for welfare recipients. The National Alliance of Business (NAB) has received support from the private sector to facilitate a process for bringing welfare recipients into the private labor market. NAB's efforts include providing information and assistance to companies to develop a mixture of services and work programs (e.g., education, training, mentor programs, life skills workshops, and counseling) that would support welfare recipients in the work environment. Examples of businesses that have built internal structures to support welfare-to-work initiatives include Marriott International, United Parcel Service of America, Inc., Coors Brewing Company, and Cessna. The federal government, particularly the Departments of Agriculture and Defense, has also taken a leadership role in developing the internal structures to hire and retain welfare recipients. Other companies collaborating with community partners to employ welfare workers include American Airlines, Pacific Bell, Walgreen Company, and Xerox Business Services.

With regard to prisoners, one area for further development is support services that can produce inmate self-sufficiency. Morash, Haarr, and Rucker (1994) recommend that female prisoners be afforded work and vocational training opportunities and resources similar to male prisoners. A recent National Institutes of Justice (U.S. Department of Justice, 1998b) survey of state-level correctional administrators, prison and jail administrators, and program administrators about the needs of female inmates cited classification and screening for familial, health, and mental health needs and the use of alternatives to incarceration for more women, in addition to work release. The work of formerly incarcerated women and their advocates and allies around these issues, as well as support for parenting, represents an important voice on the outside for improved conditions and prospects for prisoners. Certainly the standards on human rights established by Amnesty International need to be adopted within the U.S. prison system to provide women prisoners protection from male assault. Federal and state criminal codes have little effect if women are afraid to lodge complaints against an abusive staff member.

At the heart of the ability to address these issues lies the fundamental matters of equity, collective responsibility, and a political will that recognizes the shortsightedness of practices of containment. One promising sign is some states' recognition that skyrocketing prison-focused expenditures cannot be sustained. The challenge is to bring to this recognition an analysis that moves away from the politics of containment and to the broad array of issues impacting both the controlled and those hired to control them.

REFERENCES

Amnesty International. 1999. *United States of America: Not Part of My Sentence, Violations of the Human Rights of Women in Custody.* New York: Amnesty International.

Bartle, Elizabeth. 1998. Exposing and Reframing Welfare Dependency. *Journal of Sociology and Social Welfare* 25(2): 23-41.

Beck, Allen and Christopher J. Mumola. 1999. *Prisoners in 1998.* Washington, DC: U.S. Department of Justice, Office of Justice Programs, Bureau of Justice Statistics.

Beck, E., Deborah M. Whitley, and J. Wolk. 1999. Perceptions About Poverty: Views from the Georgia General Assembly. *Journal of Sociology and Social Welfare* 26(2): 87-104.

Brooks, M.G. and Buckner, J.C. (1996). Work and Welfare: Job Histories, Barriers to Empowerment, and Predictors of Work Among Low-Income Single Mothers. *American Journal of Orthopsychiatry* 66(4): 526-537.

Collins, Patricia Hill. 1998a. The More Things Change, the More They Stay the Same: African-American Women and the New Politics of Containment. In Patricia Hill Collins (Ed.), *Fighting Words: Black Women and the Search for Justice* (pp. 11-43). Minneapolis: University of Minnesota Press.

Collins, Patricia Hill. 1998b. The Tie That Binds: Race, Gender and U.S. Violence. *Ethnic and Racial Studies* 21(5): 917-938.

Conley, Catherine H. 1998. *The Women's Prison Association: Supporting Women Offenders and Their Families*. Washington, DC: U.S. Department of Justice, Office of Justice Programs, National Institute of Justice.

Corrections Compendium. 1999. *Correctional Employee Wages Corrections Budget and Compensation*. March. College Park: MD: American Correctional Association.

Dowdell, E. 1995. Caregiver Burden: Grandmothers Raising Their High-Risk Grandchildren. *Journal of Psychological Nursing* 33(3): 27-30.

Dressel, Paula L. 1994. . . . And We Keep on Building Prisons: Racism, Poverty, and Challenges to the Welfare State. *Journal of Sociology and Social Welfare* 21(3-4): 7-30.

Dressel, Paula L. and Sandra K. Barnhill. 1994. Reframing Gerontological Thought and Practice: The Case of Grandmothers with Daughters in Prison. *The Gerontologist* 34(3-4): 685-691.

Dressel, Paula, M. Sweat, and M. Waters. 1988. Welfare Workers As Surplus Population: A Useful Model? *Journal of Sociology and Social Welfare* 15(1): 87-104.

Gaudin, James M. Jr. and Richard Sutphen. 1993. Foster Care vs. Extended Family Care for Children of Incarcerated Mothers. *Journal of Offender Rehabilitation* 19(3-4): 129-147.

Gordon, Diana R. 1994. *The Return of the Dangerous Classes: Drug Prohibition and Policy Politics*. New York: W. W. Norton.

Greenfeld, Lawrence A. and Tracy L. Snell. 1999. *Women Offenders*. Special Report. Washington, DC: U.S. Department of Justice, Office of Justice Programs, Bureau of Justice Statistics.

Gueron, Judith M. 1996. A Research Context for Welfare Reform. *Journal of Policy Analysis and Management* 15(4): 547-561.

Hagen, Jan L. 1999. Public Welfare and Human Services: New Directions Under TANF? *Families in Society* 80(1): 78-90.

Hansenfeld, Yeheskel. 1987. Power in Social Work Practice. *Social Service Review* 61: 469-483.

Harlow, Caroline Wolf. 1998. *Profile of Jail Inmates, 1996*. Washington, DC: U.S. Department of Justice, Office of Justice Programs, Bureau of Justice Statistics.

Kaplan, Mark S. and Jennifer E. Sasser. 1996. Women Behind Bars: Trends and Policy Issues. *Journal of Sociology and Social Welfare* 23(4): 43-56.

Kelley, Susan J., Deborah Whitley, T. Sipe, and Beatrice C. Yorker. 1999. Psychological Distress in Grandmother Kinship Care Providers: The Role of Resources, Social Support and Physical Health. *Child Abuse and Neglect 24*(3): 311-321.

Koons, Barbara A., John D. Burrow, M. Morash, and Tim Bynum. 1997. Expert and Offender Perceptions of Program Elements Linked to Successful Outcomes for Incarcerated Women. *Crime and Delinquency 43*(4): 512-532.

Loprest, Pamela. 1999. How Families That Left Welfare Are Doing: A National Picture. Series B, No. b-1. August. Washington, DC: Urban Institute.

Marcenko, Maureen and Jay Fagan. 1996. Welfare to Work: What Are the Obstacles? *Journal of Sociology and Social Welfare 23*(3): 113-131.

Morash, Merry, Robin Haarr, and L. Rucker. 1994. A Comparison of Programming for Women and Men in U.S. Prisons in the 1980s. *Crime and Delinquency 40*(2): 197-221.

Piven, Frances F. and Richard Cloward. 1993. *Regulating the Poor: The Functions of Public Welfare*, Revised Edition. New York: Vintage Books.

Rafter, Nicole Hahn. 1990. *Partial Justice: Women, Prisons, and Social Control*, Second Edition. New Brunswick, NJ: Transaction Publishers.

Reaves, Brian A. and Andrew L. Goldberg. 1999. *Law Enforcement Management and Administrative Statistics, 1997: Data for Individual State and Local Law Enforcement Agencies with 100 or More Officers*. Washington, DC: U.S. Department of Justice, Office of Justice Programs, Bureau of Justice Statistics.

Schram, Pamela J. 1998. Stereotypes About Vocational Programming for Female Inmates. *The Prison Journal 78*(3): 244-270.

Sheak, Robert J. and Warren Haydon. 1996. Real Welfare Reform Requires Jobs: Lessons from a Progressive Welfare Agency. *Journal of Sociology and Social Welfare 23*(3): 89-111.

Snell, Tracy L. and Danielle C. Morton. 1994. *Women in Prison: Survey of State Prison Inmates, 1991*. Washington, DC: U.S. Department of Justice, Department of Justice Programs, Bureau of Justice Statistics.

Stephan, James J. 1997. *Census of State and Federal Correctional Facilities, 1995*. Washington, DC: U.S. Department of Justice, Bureau of Justice Statistics.

U.S. Department of Justice. 1997. *Census of State and Federal Correctional Facilities, 1995*. Washington, DC: U.S. Department of Justice, Office of Justice Programs, Bureau of Justice Statistics.

U.S. Department of Justice. 1998a. *A Profile of Female Offenders*. Washington, DC: U.S. Department of Justice, Federal Bureau of Prisons.

U.S. Department of Justice. 1998b. *Women Offenders: Programming Needs and Promising Approaches*. Washington, DC: U.S. Department of Justice, Office of Justice Programs, National Institute of Justice.

U.S. Department of Justice. 1999. *Table 1.68: Characteristics of Federal Bureau of Prisons Correctional Officers, 1998. Sourcebook of Criminal Justice Statistics*, Twenty-Sixth Edition. Washington, DC: U.S. Department of Justice, Office of Justice Programs, Bureau of Justice Statistics.

U.S. General Accounting Office. 1999. *Women in Prison: Sexual Misconduct by Correction Officers*. Washington, DC: U.S. General Accounting Office.

Wellisch, Jean, Michael L. Prendergast, and M. Douglas Anglin. 1994. *Drug-Abusing Women Offenders: Results of a National Survey*. Research in Brief. Washington, DC: U.S. Department of Justice, National Institute of Justice.

Whitman, David. 1998. Maddening Statistics of Welfare Jobs. *U.S. News* Online, January 12, pp. 1-4. Available online: <http://www.usnews.com/usnews/issue/980112/12work.htm>.

Withorn, Ann. 1996. Why Do They Hate Me So Much?: A History of Welfare and Its Abandonment in the United States. *American Journal of Orthopsychiatry 66* (4): 496-509.

Young, Diane S. and Carrie J. Smith. 2000. When Mothers Are Incarcerated: The Needs of Children, Mothers, and Caregivers. *Families in Society 81*(2): 130-141.

Zedlewski, Edwin W. 1997. Why Prison Matters: A Utilitarian Review. *Corrections Management Quarterly 1*(2): 15-24.

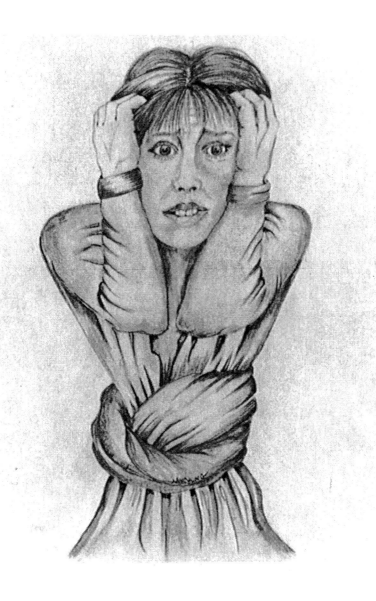

Stressed, Nancy Jean King
Exhibited at the Fourth Annual Exhibition of Art by Michigan Prisoners, February
9-25, 1999, University of Michigan, Rackham Galleries.

Chapter 6

Welfare Reform Now That We Know It: Enforcing Women's Poverty and Preventing Self-Sufficiency

Diana M. Pearce

The welfare system engages in economic violence against poor women, trapping them in poverty. This is true not only because it provides so little support, nor because it forces more women into the workforce than ever before. Most important, the welfare system is "economically violent" because it reinforces and, indeed, creates economic dependence and exploitation both inside and outside the labor market. Sometimes this connects with, and translates into, physical violence.

THE CENTRALITY OF MOTHERHOOD AND FAMILY PRESERVATION

I have put mothers and motherhood at the center of this discussion. It is important to remember that it is women, specifically mothers, who are the subjects of the welfare system and the objects of welfare reform. That is, it makes a difference that it is *women*—and not men—who head the low-income families subject to welfare reform and that it is *mothers*—and not fathers—trying to survive in the low-wage labor market. Why is gender so important to this story? There are two reasons: the vulnerability/strengths of motherhood and the gendered nature of the labor market.

Ultimately, mothers do what they feel they must to keep their children and to keep their family intact. Most women do not willingly go on welfare; it is too little money and too much hassle. Most women do not willingly take lousy jobs; it is too little money and too much hassle. However, single mothers do both of these things for one simple reason: to keep their families together. Ultimately, indeed, many women are in prison for the same reason:

they have stolen or cheated or lied to get money to meet their families' needs. Mahdevi Varma, the Indian feminist, said:

> Woman is never more vulnerable in any other state than when she has a child clinging to her bosom; in no other situation is she so violently aggressive as at the time of defending and protecting her offspring. (1941, p. 1)

Many mothers want to work to support their families and turn to welfare only because they see *no other way to keep their children.* Whether these mothers have been deserted or are fleeing a violent and abusive partner or do not have a job or cannot work, they turn to welfare as the last resort after exhausting every other option. Especially now, given that it is so stigmatized, many avoid public assistance if at all possible. In addition, some might end up in prison as they try to survive in the underground economy.

MOTHERS, WORK, AND WELFARE:
NOT A NEW COMBINATION

Historically, the central intention of both public and private welfare programs—from mothers' pensions/mothers' aid to AFDC to TANF—was *not* to keep mothers in or out of the labor force, but rather to allow mothers to raise their own children. This was not because poor mothers were thought to be good mothers or even comparatively better at raising their children than institutions, such as the orphanage or later foster parents (Vandepol, 1982). Rather than a ringing endorsement of the fine job that poor mothers do, this policy was the result of a combination of financial and pragmatic reasons having to do with increasingly negative evaluations of orphanages and out-of-home care for children (Katz, 1986).

Financially, it was (and continues to be) considerably more expensive to care for children in an institution or a foster family than to support the mother so she could take care of them herself. Pragmatically, evaluations of the orphanages had found that the lack of nurturing meant that very young children died at very high rates from "failure to thrive" syndrome, while older children became "street children," petty criminals, or what came to be called "juvenile delinquents." But because it was not in fact based on an affirmation of poor mothers' abilities and, indeed, involved a great deal of skepticism both about their parenting and the causes of their poverty, the support provided was meager. So meager, in fact, that women then and now have been forced to supplement the aid they received through earnings, however that could be managed (Skocpol, 1992).

In the nineteenth century, opportunities for women in the workforce were very limited and the wages were low even for the better paying jobs in factories. Many of the "nurseries" that provided child care were so bad that it was considered a kind of neglect to use them (Gordon, 1988). Some mothers were forced to use orphanages to "board" their children during the week (seeing them only on Sunday afternoons) if they lacked in-home child care from relatives and if they could not bring their children to work with them. Not surprisingly, orphanages were full of "half-orphans"—children of single parents—but putting children in orphanages was risky, for it could mean losing the children, as they could be farmed out to frontier families in the Midwest or put up for adoption (Costin, 1994).

Faced with these dilemmas, women sometimes turned to churches, charities, or the city for help (with food, fuel, and so forth), so that they would not be forced to place their children in orphanages. This help was risky: as Gordon (1988) documents, sometimes "social workers" would aid mothers' efforts to keep their families together and sometimes they would pass judgments on the quality of parenting, refuse to provide economic support, and remove the children. Given the denial of the reality of domestic violence and child abuse by men, many women were forced to choose between enduring violence/abuse in the family or risking the loss of their children if they left (or kicked out) a violent spouse (Gordon, 1988).

In the early twentieth century, a new state-level program was devised: mothers' aid or mothers' pensions. These programs provided single mothers with sufficient income to avoid working long hours in a factory to support their children and also helped them avoid putting their children in orphanages. Poor women were never provided enough support to avoid work altogether, rather the intention was to supplement the meager earnings received from the kind of work that could be combined with caring for children—laundry, piecework, taking in boarders. Even under AFDC, which "federalized" the mothers' pensions program, a certain amount of informal work was expected. In the South, families were routinely kicked off of these programs seasonally when there was agricultural work to be done (Piven and Cloward, 1972).

At no time in the nineteenth or twentieth century did this work provide substantial income, benefits, or future prospects. This informal "system" that required work to supplement inadequate benefits—but work that was on the margins of the labor market—has been most recently documented by Edin and Lein (1997). They found that many low-income families "make ends meet" by packaging welfare with a variety of other sources of income—including gifts ("in kind" or cash) and various jobs in the gray and black economy that provide income which is not officially reported.

Edin and Lein's (1997) study has added detail of the kinds of work women do to supplement low benefits, but it has long been known that women have done this kind of "packaging" of income to meet their families' needs. One of the earliest of these studies is that of Rein and Rainwater (1978). Based on 1970s' data, they found that families were able to make ends meet by combining a variety of sources of income—including welfare, wages, and other transfer income (such as a grandmother's Social Security, disability, and SSI). Most interestingly, Rein and Rainwater (1978) found that the longer the family is on welfare the less likely they are to be wholly or primarily dependent on welfare alone for income and, thus, the more likely they are to combine work and other sources of income with welfare. That is, seemingly paradoxically, the longer a family was on welfare, the less dependent the family was on welfare for its income. It was, however, only one piece of the package.

Likewise, the work of Spalter-Roth et al. (1995) has documented that many families in the 1980s and early 1990s also combined work and welfare over a two-year period—either concurrently or alternating between work and welfare and between short-term jobs and short spells on welfare. Families who did not combine these sources of income, moreover, were generally worse off, a finding also documented by Edin and Lein (1997).

Perhaps most disturbing about these studies is that families that are most careful to follow the rules, reporting all other sources of income and not engaging in any gray market activities (such as buying stolen goods or working under the table), were clearly less well off in terms of level of consumption—so much so, in fact, that in one instance other mothers considered a certain mother's strict adherence to "the rules" a form of neglect—her little girl lacked all but the bare minimum of food and clothing and did not have any of the necessities (such as brand name shoes or the clothes in current fashion rather than those from the thrift store) to be accepted by her peers (Edin and Lein, 1997). Thus families are faced with a no-win choice: either live legally and by the book but at a level of deprivation that amounts to neglect on the one hand, or meet one's needs however one can—which necessitates a certain amount of cheating, lying, and deception on the other. This not only puts the family at risk of an encounter with the justice system, but also forces the adults to model a way of life for their children that is constantly skirting or violating norms of honesty. It is fraught with instances of lying, cheating, buying stolen goods, or supporting/condoning these activities by others. It should be noted that many times this involves what we would ordinarily laud as generosity, such as opening one's home (or couch) to homeless families—but not reporting the extra occupants to the landlord.

Even for the families who do combine wages and welfare, this still leaves the families with insufficient income. The most generous of assumptions do not suggest that we are talking about large sums of money. Work and other sources of income (such as under-the-table child support) add perhaps up to 40 to 60 percent to the value of the welfare benefit—maybe a few hundred dollars a month (Jencks and Edin, 1990). Furthermore, it is likely that this is somewhat of an overestimate as their findings are not based on a random sample, but rather on people known to agencies who are more likely to be adept at garnering these additional resources.

THE IMPACT OF THE 1996 WELFARE REFORM: WORK REQUIREMENTS AND TIME LIMITS

First, it is important to be clear about what the 1996 welfare reform legislation did *not* do. In brief, it did not force women into the workforce for the first time, nor has it cut women off directly because of the time limits. This does not deny that welfare reform has had profound effects on the economic status of women, particularly single parents.

As we have described previously, most single mothers have worked before, either concurrently with welfare or alternating between spells of welfare and spells of employment. Thus, it did not force most female welfare recipients into the workforce for the first time. Of course, it did force more women into the labor force more quickly than before, and also into a narrower range of jobs. These are differences that have important implications and to which we will return later. Put another way, welfare reform did not so much impose work on poor mothers as make the work that they already did no longer as effective in meeting their families' income.

Second, time limits have not been the prime cause of people leaving welfare. Although the number of people on welfare is about half what it was at the time of the passage of the legislation in 1996, most left for other reasons. (Loprest [1999] finds that only about 1 percent self-report leaving because of time limits.) First and most obviously, most have not reached their time limit. The federal legislation imposed a lifetime limit of five years (for those whose assistance is federally funded). Though thirty-five states adopted that limit, with the "clock" starting when they implemented the legislation— usually during 1997—it does not expire until at least 2002. Thus in most states families have not reached a time limit. Even in the few states with very short state-imposed time limits—or time limits begun under waivers at an earlier point—there have been relatively few families who have actually lost their benefits because of the time limits. That is because these states often have either provided extensions (if families are complying with work and other requirements, as in Connecticut), or provided exemptions (for disability or age, for example), or have put such families on state-only monies not governed by the federal rules (as in Illinois, for single parents who are employed, for whom officials "stop the clock" using state funds). Finally, as families have begun to reach their final year of eligibility, some states have begun to develop various programs that will provide support, though often in the form of vouchers rather than cash assistance, with labels such as TimeOut or Time Beyond, that provide post-time limit support using state-only funds.[1]

If time limits have not been the cause of the dramatic decline in the numbers of families on the welfare rolls, what does account for this trend? There are at least three factors: the economic boom of the late 1990s, the increase in sanctions, and the effect of employment on eligibility. The booming economy has provided people with an alternative to welfare that, even if it is not very remunerative, is preferable for other reasons (such as fewer hassles). Indeed, the numbers leaving welfare began to rise with the beginning of the economic upturn in 1993, not in 1996 when the legislation was passed (Danziger, 1999). At the same time, the labor force participation rate of unmarried mothers has increased, so that by 1998 it equaled that of married mothers (Burtless, 1998).

The increase in sanctions results from the general pressure on families across the board to enter work quickly ("work first"), coupled with new requirements and rules that are applied much more broadly than previous work requirements (Tweedie, Reichert, and O'Connor, 1999; U.S. GAO, 2000). Because some families cannot or will not comply with these new rules—including work hours requirements, mandatory meetings with caseworkers, filling out job applications, attending motivational classes, accepting jobs or child care, and a variety of other requirements—they are sanctioned, losing part or all of their benefits (U.S. GAO, 1998). As a result, the number of families who have been sanctioned for noncompliance with rules and work requirements has increased, and this does not count those who have left welfare "voluntarily" or been "diverted" from pursuing an application. Thus time limits (along with sanctions) act more as "signals" (that welfare is not available indefinitely or even for long) than as a direct and specific cause of leaving welfare. Indeed, substantial proportions of recipients, while aware of the time limits generally, are quite wrong on the specific rules, exceptions, and requirements that apply in their own state or community (Moffitt and Roff, 2000; Cherlin et al., 2000).

Finally, there is a very high "tax" on earnings, so that the welfare client who works loses about one dollar in benefits for each two dollars earned. In many states, a full-time minimum-wage job, or even thirty hours per week at minimum wage, results in total loss of benefits and leaving welfare. In short, people are leaving welfare for many reasons, the least of which is reaching the time limit.

The focus on these two issues of "forced work" and "time limits" has been problematic because they have distracted and distorted the impact of welfare reform, diverting attention from the fundamental changes that have occurred which are having profound effects on the economic status and long-term viability of low-income families maintained by women alone. The changes wrought by the 1996 welfare reform are not forcing women into the workforce—they were, by and large, already there—nor cutting them off because of time limits—they were, by and large, already leaving welfare, but for other reasons. Rather, this welfare reform is drastically restricting the ability of single mothers to provide sufficient income for their families to meet their basic needs and survive as families. Indeed, if we waved a magic wand and got rid of time limits, not much would change. Likewise, it is not work itself that is new, but the new restrictions that make it difficult for families to use work in combination with other resources to make ends meet.

Welfare reform has increased poverty among affected families in three major ways:

1. Welfare reform has made it virtually impossible for families to use welfare to supplement low and uneven earnings—as had been done for a century and a half.
2. Welfare reform has drastically reduced the ability of women to obtain education or training (beyond high school) which would lead to higher-waged employment.
3. Rather than overcome the gender disadvantage women experience in the labor force, welfare reform has deepened and reinforced that disadvantage.

Enforcing Women's Poverty #1: Ending Welfare As a Backup/Supplement for Insufficient Wages

The patterns of welfare use already described and documented by researchers over the past three decades (Rein and Rainwater, 1978; Spalter-Roth et al., 1995; Edin and Lein, 1997) are quickly disappearing. Ending entitlement to welfare removes the right to it as a backup or supplement. When there is an entitlement, the basic criterion is need: if there is no other income, or if earnings are insufficient, the family has a right to assistance. Of course, this assistance was not substantial and never even brought the family up to official poverty levels, but it helped.

Though important, ending entitlement is not the prime mover in and of itself that increases women's poverty by ending the role of welfare as a backup/supplement to low and uneven earnings. This effect is happening aside from the loss of the entitlement, due to the interaction of three factors: the push to work first, low benefits/income disregard rules, and time limits.

Because the level of cash benefits is so low, in many states almost any job—even part time and at minimum wage—results in enough income to disqualify the family from receiving any cash assistance. This is in part due to the declining value of cash benefits. That is, the value of cash benefits has been eaten away by inflation, especially in the late 1970s and 1980s.

This happens in spite of the fact that many states have adopted more generous "earned-income disregard" rules, which allow parents to keep more of their earnings than under the federal rules that governed the previous welfare program, AFDC.[2] For example, under the most common rule, welfare disregards 50 percent of earnings in calculating the family's benefit; the benefit reaches zero when one is earning double the benefit. For example, if we use the median monthly benefit for a family of three (a single parent with two children) of $377, under this rule a single parent in a family of three could earn up to double that amount, or $754, before her benefits declined to zero. Of course, $754 is still quite a bit less than working full time at the federal minimum wage ($5.15 per hour), which would be $906 per month. Further, even minimum-wage earnings of $900 per month in many places would barely cover the rent, much less food, clothing, transportation, taxes, health insurance, and so forth. In addition, there are some states, such as Wisconsin, in which paid work of any amount results in a total loss of benefits. In short, pushing welfare recipients, and even applicants, quickly into the workforce, even at very low wages, results in many losing their cash assistance.

In addition, many lose Medicaid, food stamps, and/or child care, even though they continue to be eligible for these benefits (Schumacher and Greenberg, 1999; U.S. GAO, 1999a,b).

As for alternating welfare and work as circumstances dictate, imposing lifetime limits on the amount of time one can receive benefits (a maximum total of five years, which states can reduce but not increase) has effectively removed welfare as a backup or supplement. One reason this is true is that there is a strong fear of "running down the clock." Thus it is not uncommon for welfare advocates to ask a recipient, or recipients to ask themselves, "Do we really need this now? If not, can we get by somehow? Maybe we should do without, and 'save' our time on welfare for when we might *really* need it" (Coleman, November 1999, personal communication). In a sense, recipients are choosing (or are being urged) to "bank" their benefits against a "rainy day" when they might need them even more desperately (for example, if the mother or one of her children becomes ill or she loses her job).

Thus the impact of time limits at this point is not in the numbers who are forced off by them, for most recipients in most states have not reached their time limits. Rather, the effect is immediate, subtle, pervasive, yet difficult to document as to whether those in need receive the help they need. The bottom line is that fewer mothers are able to use welfare as a backup/supplement to uneven and inadequate earnings from paid employment.

Enforcing Women's Poverty #2:
Eliminating Education and Training

The flip side of putting welfare recipients and applicants to work immediately is that it affords little opportunity for women to obtain the education or training they need to earn decent wages (or that would gain them entry to the kind of jobs that provide the experience and/or on-the-job training and opportunities to move up in terms of earnings). Although a few women who were already in college at the time PRWORA was enacted were allowed to finish their education, those who have come into the program since 1996 have in some states been prevented from obtaining a college education. The result has been a dramatic drop in the number of welfare recipients participating in welfare-to-work activities who are obtaining college or other postsecondary education: for example, the proportion in Wisconsin dropped from 60 percent to 12 percent; in Connecticut, from 85 percent to 32 percent; and, in Texas, from 75 percent to 36 percent (U.S. GAO, 1998). Although college education or other postsecondary education is not specifically prohibited by federal or state legislation, the structure of TANF programs makes it a de facto prohibition. The barriers to pursuing education or training beyond high school are substantial:

- Although federal law allows recipients to participate in activities other than work the first two years, most states have chosen to require work first—in part because under federal law states face financial penalties unless a certain proportion of the caseload is "working" or preparing for work (this proportion rises each year), of which no more than 30 percent may be in education or training. Moreover, starting in 2000, teen parents completing high school are included in that 30 percent, further limiting the number of adults who can participate in education and training without threatening the ability of the state to meet its work participation requirements (Strawn, 1998).
- Most states require that recipients must work at least twenty hours per week, so that any education and training must be in addition to this work. Thus single mothers who do pursue education or training must

combine work (twenty hours or more), part- or full-time studies or training, and being a single parent—which is a triple burden few can pull off, let alone do all three roles well.

- Of forty-two states for which data have been verified, only eight states allow education alone to count toward the state work requirement (Illinois, Iowa, Kentucky, Maine, Missouri, Rhode Island, Utah, and Wyoming) and if they do so, it is for a maximum of two years. Only three states, Hawaii, Georgia, and Michigan, allow further education beyond twenty-four months, and only if the participant is also working at least thirty hours per week (Greenberg, Strawn, and Plimpton, 1999). This effectively prevents welfare clients from pursuing or completing four-year degrees, unless they have already completed two or more years of coursework.

- Most states will not provide subsidized child care for the hours recipients are in class.

- Welfare staff in many states have been given liberal discretion to help or hinder recipients in their efforts to further their education. Many simply do not inform recipients of options available to them or do not provide or help recipients obtain the assistance required if they are to be successful as higher education students.

Because it remains true that a woman must have a four-year college degree before she can expect to earn what a man can earn with only a high school diploma, preventing women from obtaining education beyond high school virtually sentences them to poverty. The average weekly wage of women with only a high school education who work full time is $396 (Bowler, 1999). This is about 71 percent of the earnings of men who work full time and have a high school diploma (this gender gap is larger than at any other educational level).

The impact on women has been substantial, as the number of female welfare recipients who were in college programs or postsecondary training (including technical, two-year associate, and certificate programs, as well as four-year college) plummeted.[3] For example, the number of students in college programs in New York City fell from about 27,000 to 17,000 in three years. Baltimore City College lost 29 percent of its welfare-client enrollees, and Massachusetts' community colleges lost 50 percent of their welfare students (Schmidt, 1998). In Illinois, the number of welfare recipients in college fell from about 5,800 in 1995 to less than 2,000 in 1998—of which only fifty-eight recipients were pursuing four-year degrees (Gruber, 1998). Instead of welfare helping women make the transition to self-supporting single parent, by using this time to further their education, women are instead pushed willy-nilly into the first job that comes along. Without the opportunity to obtain education or training, there is little prospect that women will be able to parlay that first job into a better job—because of the nature of women's labor force position, the topic discussed next.

Enforcing Women's Poverty #3: Reinforcing the Disadvantaged Position of Women in the Labor Market

It is well known that women earn less than men, about 76 cents for each dollar that a man earns (Bowler, 1999). But that is only part of the picture of women's labor force disadvantage. That wage ratio is based upon a comparison of earnings of men and women who work full-time and year-round. Yet only about half of working women are employed full-time and year-round (compared to more than two-thirds of men). Among those leaving the welfare rolls, two-thirds are employed during the year, but only about one-sixth to one-fourth—depending on the state and the year—are employed full-time, year-round (Danziger, 1999). Women who work only part-time or part year experience lower wages, not only because of fewer hours of work but also because the gender gap in wages is likely to be even larger. This is because women's seasonal and part-time work tends to be in low-paid occupations (such as production factories and holiday or seasonal retail) while much of men's seasonal work is relatively highly paid (for example, construction and road work). Moreover, equal pay laws often do not cover part-time or seasonal work.

In addition to part-time and/or part-year work, female workers' wages are lower because of occupational segregation and gender-based discrimination (including pay inequity and sexual harassment). This is hardly news. However, of interest here is the fact that even though an obvious and multi-faceted connection exists between the disadvantaged position of women in the labor market, women's wages, and the poverty of the families they support, knowledge of this linkage has failed to inform the welfare system or welfare reform.

Under the TANF program, nothing is done to counter these gender-based, labor-market sources of income disparities that lead to poverty for women and their families. Indeed, by pushing women into the first available job, often in the expanding sectors such as the service sector—with many occupations such as waitress that have been traditional female ghettoes, and low wage—the program reinforces occupational segregation, resulting in increased women's poverty. By requiring women to work a minimum number of hours but not seeking out full-time work and jobs with benefits, the welfare system reinforces the disadvantage experienced by part-time temporary workers in terms of wages and benefits. By not steering women to the higher-paying nontraditional jobs, the welfare system—by default—perpetuates occupational segregation and wage inequities that directly contribute to women's poverty.

Indeed, there has *never* been a welfare reform that even acknowledged, much less addressed, gender (or for that matter race, national origin, sexual orientation, or disability either) as a source of women's poverty. The fact that the jobs women are forced to take have consistently and sometimes considerably lower wages than those held by men with similar education and experience *just because they are women* simply is not recognized in any programmatic way. Rather, the approach used by current welfare officials that treats all jobs and, by extension, all wages as "equal" no matter how inadequate the compensation may be, not only fails to bring single mothers out of poverty but actually reinforces that poverty.

Understanding the Impact of Welfare "Reform" on Women's Poverty

Although all of the preceding may be true in theory, how do we know that in fact this welfare "reform" is actually reinforcing and creating women's poverty? This actually is two questions. The first asks what is happening, and the second has to do with what is meant today by "poverty."

Unfortunately, by and large, very little is known about the outcomes of welfare reform beyond a very narrow range of information. Almost every official "evaluation" or assessment looks only at two indicators: (1) the number of people who have left welfare and/or (2) the number of current and former welfare recipients who have entered paid employment. Some studies go slightly farther and look at wages or, even more rarely, occupations. Whether those mothers who have left welfare, working or not, have enough resources to take care of their children adequately is simply and largely unknown because officials are not asking those questions.

A century ago, the fact that the numbers of children in orphanages increased was a clear indication that public programs or private charity had failed to provide single mothers with sufficient support. In fact, this happened quite dramatically once: in Brooklyn, in 1882, a campaign to "end outdoor relief" (aid to families in their own homes) resulted in the number of children in Brooklyn's orphanages doubling in a few short years (Katz, 1986).

Today such obvious indicators do not exist. A number of indicators, however, point to a very troubling picture for a substantial number of families. A comprehensive review of census and other studies by analysts at the

Children's Defense Fund (Sherman et al., 1998) found a number of indicators that families leaving welfare were experiencing severe hardships, sometimes threatening the ability of families to remain together. The most dramatic outcome was the substantial number of families with incomes, even with earnings, that were not only below poverty, but were below half the poverty line. Other indicators were high levels of unstable employment and periods of unemployment, substantial numbers of families becoming homeless or living in temporary housing (also as a direct result of benefit cuts), and access to health care, adequate food, and other necessities decreased. Perhaps most troubling, several studies reviewed by the Children's Defense Fund—which compared families before and after receiving welfare or similar families receiving welfare and no longer receiving welfare—found that even with earnings, the families on welfare were frequently "better off" (more income relative to expenses) than those not on welfare (Sherman et al., 1998).

One study reviewed in the Children's Defense Fund analysis was conducted in the state of Washington (Washington Welfare Reform Coalition, 1999), which has had a phenomenal reduction in welfare caseloads. Even among those working full-time, whose salaries averaged over $7 per hour, there were many troubling impacts:

1. Thirty percent had their phone cut off.
2. Eighteen percent had their heat or electricity cut off.
3. Twenty percent went without food for a day or more.
4. Twenty-two percent became homeless.

Moreover, those surveyed more recently have had more problems, with those going without food for a day or more increasing to 43 percent. Clearly, substantial numbers of families leaving welfare have lacked enough resources to meet even their most basic needs for food and shelter. By any definition, these families are experiencing not only poverty, but severe deprivation. Yet official state reports do not even examine these issues. Others, of course, may make this connection: in Wisconsin, which has experienced one of the most dramatic decreases in its welfare caseload (almost 90 percent have left welfare), there has not been a corresponding drop in the number of families with incomes below the official poverty level. This suggests that many families that have left welfare, including many with employed adults, still have insufficient resources (Moore and Selkowe, 1999).

Reports such as those cited are largely being made by advocacy groups and lack the authority of official or representative studies. Although such data were mandated in earlier experiments and policy-changing welfare

(such as under the Welfare Incentive Program (WIN)-demonstration projects in the 1970s, implementation of Omnibus Budget Reconciliation Act (OBRA) in the 1980s, and the 1,115 waivers in the 1990s), the much more extensive changes brought about by PRWORA in 1996 do not have any required evaluation that would allow one to assess, for example, what families' incomes are postwelfare or how many remain in poverty. In fact, by leaving the numbers, such as those previously cited, standing alone, without contextualizing them in terms of income and expenses in these families' budgets, there is the implication that for some families at least, the shortages of food or rent money reflect some fault of theirs—such as lack of budgeting skills, failure to anticipate needs, and so on.

One of the most severe consequences of the loss of adequate income— through very low benefits, inadequate earnings, or both—is homelessness. In spite of the economic boom of the 1990s, the use of soup kitchens, food pantries, and shelters has increased substantially since welfare reform in 1996 (Miller, 1998). Again and again, studies point to the lack of adequate income to meet rising housing costs as the primary cause of homelessness (rather than psychiatric causes) (Shinn, 1997). Yet families experiencing homelessness are treated not as indicators of the failure of welfare reform, but as individual failures. That is, because not providing one's children with food and shelter can be interpreted as neglect, homeless families may lose their children to foster care. How does one count, as "increased family poverty," families broken up because the family lacked the income to secure housing? Equally difficult is the task of counting homeless families who are still intact: many homeless families with children go to great lengths to remain unseen, driven by the fear that the children will, in fact, be taken away and put into foster care. Even if known, they are not included in the annual official count of the poor (which is based on a household survey that excludes shelters), thus making invisible one of the most severe effects of welfare reform on women's poverty.

EVALUATING THE ECONOMIC RESOURCES
OF FAMILIES POSTWELFARE

Although it does not cover all the consequences, a measure of well-being that assesses whether a family's resources are sufficient to meet their basic needs would go a long way toward providing a comprehensive measure of the impact of welfare reform on women's poverty and the families' ability to survive intact. The Self-Sufficiency Standard, which measures how much is needed for a family to meet its basic needs in the marketplace (that is, with-

out public or private subsidies), is such a measure. Although it is similar to the official poverty measure, it differs from it in several important ways:

1. The Self-Sufficiency Standard assumes that all adults work full-time, so it allows for transportation to and from work, taxes, and child care if there are young children.
2. It is varied by where the family lives—by city or by county. It varies by the age as well as the number of children for costs such as child care, health care, and food.
3. It includes the net effect of taxes and tax credits.
4. It is calculated based on the costs of *each* of the basic needs, which are updated annually, thus allowing costs to rise at different rates and, thus, is generally higher and more varied (by family type and place) than is the poverty standard.

Table 6.1 shows the constituent costs and the Self-Sufficiency Wages for four different family types living in Indianapolis, Indiana. It can be seen from the figures in this table that the expenses faced by different family types living in the same place are quite different, depending upon the number and age of the children. Thus a single parent has almost double the expenses of a single person. Although the levels of the Self-Sufficiency Standard may seem high, the level of costs allowed is only adequate, not luxurious—thus the food budget does not allow for any restaurant or takeout food, not even a pizza! Housing is set at the level of the fair market rent—what those getting housing assistance are allowed to spend, which is pegged at the fortieth percentile of the rental housing market.

Table 6.2 shows the Self-Sufficiency Wage for a number of places, and for different family types. It is clear from this table that in many places single mothers must command substantial wages, even if they have only one young child, to pay for their basic needs fully. Obviously, many single mothers, including many who are leaving welfare for employment, will not be able to obtain wages at the levels shown in this table—even those for less expensive areas, particularly in their first jobs.

For many such mothers, subsidies are crucial to their being able to survive and meet their needs at an adequate level. That is, by reducing the costs of various needs, subsidies lower—often substantially—the wages a single parent needs to meet her family's needs adequately and, thereby, secure for them adequate nutrition, decent housing, dependable child care, and so forth.

Typically, single parents leaving welfare receive three subsidies: child care, Medicaid (for at least one year, sometimes more, depending upon the state), and food stamps. Table 6.3 shows the effects of various subsidies on

Monthly Expenses	One Adult		One Parent, One Infant		One Parent, One Infant, One School-Age		Two Parents, One Infant, One School-Age	
	Costs	% of Total	Costs	% of Total	Costs	% of Total	Costs	% of Total
Housing	445	39	535	28	535	22	535	19
Child Care	0	0	418	22	700	28	700	24
Food	163	14	239	13	361	15	499	17
Transportation	147	13	147	8	147	6	290	10
Health Care	90	8	188	10	208	8	261	9
Miscellaneous	85	7	153	8	195	8	228	8
Taxes	206	18	344	18	469	19	521	18
Earned-Income Tax Credit (–)	0	0	(50)	(3)	(10)	(0)	0	0
Child Care Tax Credit (–)	0	0	(46)	(2)	(80)	(3)	(80)	(3)
Child Tax Credit (–)	0	0	(33)	(2)	(67)	(3)	(67)	(2)
Self-Sufficiency Wage								
Monthly	$1,136.00	100	$1,895.00	100	$2,458.00	100	$2,887.00	100
Hourly (per adult)	$6.46		$10.77		$13.96		$8.20	

Source: The Self-Sufficiency Standard for Indiana, Wider Opportunities for Women, Washington, DC.
Note: Column total may differ slightly due to rounding.

TABLE 6.2. The Self-Sufficiency Standard for Selected Family Types in One Urban and One Rural County, by State and Year of Data, for Eleven States

State	Single Adult	Parent + Infant	Parent + Preschool	Parent + Infant + Preschool	Parent + Preschool + Schoolage	Parent + Schoolage + Teenage	2 Parents + Infant + Preschool
Iowa (1994)							
Des Moines	$5.82	$11.60	$10.06	$15.59	$13.05	$9.47	$8.90 per adult
Boone County	$4.74	$9.69	$8.16	$13.97	$10.88	$7.48	$8.51 per adult
California (1994)							
Los Angeles—Long Beach	$7.61	$12.23	$13.06	$16.23	$13.00	$22.21	$9.51 per adult
Alpine County	$5.62	$8.74	$8.41	$11.99	$8.16	$16.79	$7.68 per adult
North Carolina (1996)							
Raleigh-Durham-Chapel Hill	$6.70	$10.74	$11.01	$14.64	$10.23	$18.94	$8.35 per adult
Warren County	$5.05	$7.30	$7.55	$10.09	$7.35	$14.39	$6.59 per adult
Texas (1996)							
Houston	$5.74	$9.70	$9.84	$13.52	$11.06	$19.06	$7.78 per adult
Kerr County	$4.96	$7.76	$7.85	$10.78	$7.47	$15.11	$6.83 per adult
Pennsylvania (1996)							
Philadelphia	$6.64	$11.99	$12.27	$16.38		$11.16	$9.13 per adult
Warren County	$4.97	$8.22	$7.82	$11.43		$8.38	$7.01 per adult
Illinois (1996)							
Chicago	$7.15	$12.31	$12.19	$16.21	$14.48	$11.08	$9.11 per adult
Williamson County	$4.63	$7.19	$7.31	$10.05	$9.84	$7.73	$6.58 per adult
Massachusetts (1997)							
Boston	$7.52		$15.28	$22.37	$18.54	$13.73	$11.99 per adult
Berkshire County	$6.16		$11.68	$16.61	$13.98	$8.86	$9.40 per adult

TABLE 6.2 (continued)

Pennsylvania (1998)							
Philadelphia	$7.10	$12.39	$12.70	$16.61	$15.35	$11.23	$9.22 per adult
Warren County	$5.50	$8.27	$8.26	$11.76	$11.43	$8.66	$7.34 per adult
Indiana (1998)							
Indianapolis	$6.45	$10.74	$11.01	$15.04	$14.20	$10.22	$8.76 per adult
Pike County	$5.30	$7.77	$7.66	$10.22	$9.38	$7.76	$6.64 per adult
Washington, DC (1998)							
District of Columbia	$7.99	$13.52	$16.06	$20.16	$22.69	$17.10	$11.23 per adult
Montgomery County, MD	$9.20	$16.38	$15.73	$21.67	$21.10	$16.86	$12.06 per adult
Prince George's County, MD	$7.94	$13.81	$12.95	$17.82	$17.14	$14.18	$10.13 per adult
Alexandria, VA	$8.66	$14.92	$15.16	$20.18	$20.46	$16.28	$11.34 per adult
Arlington County, VA	$9.19	$15.97	$16.52	$21.96	$22.86	$17.94	$12.23 per adult
Fairfax County, VA	$8.60	$15.56	$15.63	$21.36	$21.36	$16.63	$11.93 per adult
New Jersey (1999)							
Northern Bergen County	$8.03	$16.71	$15.56	$22.93	$18.03	$12.09	$12.33 per adult
Atlantic County [Cape May]	$7.28	$12.41	$13.91	$17.28	$16.28	$11.66	$9.91 per adult

Source: The Self-Sufficiency Standard Reports for Iowa, California, North Carolina, Texas, Pennsylvania, Illinois, Massachusetts, Pennsylvania, Indiana, Washington, DC Metro Area, New Jersey, published by Wider Opportunities for Women, Washington, DC.

TABLE 6.3. The Impact of Subsidies on the Self-Sufficiency Wage for a Single Parent with a Preschooler and an Infant in Washington, DC, 1998, in Dollars

Monthly Costs	#1 Self-Sufficiency Standard	#2 Child Support	#5 Child Care, Medicaid, and Food Stamps
Housing	807	807	807
Child Care	1,178	1,178	62
Food	318	318	109
Transportation	94	94	94
Health Care	189	189	0
Miscellaneous	259	259	259
Taxes	876	757	113
Earned-Income Tax Credit (−)	0	0	0
Child Care Tax Credit (−)	(106)	(106)	(21)
Child Tax Credit (−)	(67)	(67)	(20)
Child Support	0	(250)	0
Monthly Self-Sufficiency Wage	3,548.00	3,179.00	1,403.00
Hourly Self-Sufficiency Wage	20.16	18.07	7.97

Source: Table 7, *The Self-Sufficiency Standard for the Washington, DC Metro Area,* by Diana Pearce and Jennifer Brooks, Wider Opportunities for Women, Washington, DC, 1999.

the required wage for a single-parent family in Washington, DC. In this table, it can be seen that child support (we have chosen the figure of $250 because it is the average amount of child support per family nationally for those receiving any child support) reduces the wage required to meet her needs by about two dollars an hour, to just over $18.00 per hour—still a very high wage. In contrast, the three subsidies which she would typically receive after leaving welfare reduce the wage she needs to earn to less than $8.00 per hour, assuming she is working full-time. Note that this effect is the result of the direct reduction in costs which result from the provision of subsidies as well as the indirect effect of reducing taxes. Thus, for example, her child care costs are reduced from the full cost of $1178 per month to just her income-contingent (sliding scale) fee of $62, and her taxes from $876 to $113 per month.

With this standard, we can evaluate welfare and subsidy policies by state and even by county, taking into account the two essential factors that determine the adequacy of a given wage: (1) the costs of living in a given county/state, and (2) the specific policies and subsidy programs available in that county/state.

Not only do costs of living vary substantially from one state to another but subsidies as well. That is, one of the effects of the devolution approach to welfare reform is that single parents confront not only very different costs of living, as can be seen in Table 6.2, but also very different subsidy policies, depending upon in which state and sometimes in which county they live. For example, in the Washington, DC, metropolitan area, a single parent with two children, earning $8.00 per hour and working full-time, is expected to pay $70 toward her child care in the Virginia suburb of Alexandria, $120 in the District of Columbia, and $344 in suburban Montgomery County, Maryland. Thus a wage in the same metropolitan area, with the support of substantial subsidies in Washington, DC, or Alexandria, Virginia, goes much further in meeting a family's basic needs than the same wage in the Maryland suburbs—particularly in Montgomery County. This is true despite the fact that the latter place has substantially higher income, on the average, and substantially more public resources from that tax base.

When Wages Are Not Enough

With the help of a measure of income adequacy such as the Self-Sufficiency Standard, we can determine what are not only self-sufficiency level wages (given place and family type), but also what are adequate wages (a concept which takes into account available subsidies, as in Table 6.3). But sometimes wages do not even reach the level of adequacy, much less self-sufficiency. The Self-Sufficiency Standard, by defining what is enough objectively, facilitates a focus on what happens when there is not enough—from wages and/or subsidies, singly or in combination. Clearly, parents then have to make choices as to which needs they will meet and how they will meet them, and these choices have consequences such as:

1. *Finding private subsidies:* The first consequence of not having adequate resources is to do without—parents may choose to share housing or seek child care by relatives. While these may sometimes be ideal situations for all concerned, when not chosen freely but instead for economic reasons, some of the possible results are:
   - Relative care, though often preferred, is the least dependable. This can lead to lost work hours, job loss—or harm to children poorly cared for.
   - Shared housing is often in dwelling units not meant for the larger number of people. It is well documented that such housing results in more abuse and is often quite unstable, leading to frequent moves and higher rates of homelessness (Bassuk, 1990).

2. *Doing without:* A second consequence of not having adequate resources is to do without—parents go without meals, leave children alone or with an older sibling, or choose to live in housing that is inadequate or unsafe.

3. *Seeking resources elsewhere:* Parents turn or return to a source of resources that bring other problems; hence, many women turned away or turned out of a domestic violence shelter return to their abusers (because they have nowhere else to go and economically they cannot make it on their own). Likewise, inadequate incomes force women into relationships or back into relationships for economic reasons that have negative emotional/psychological consequences, with future economic ramifications (Edin and Lein, 1997).

All three of these alternatives involve hidden subsidies with often undesirable costs and consequences. With an objective Self-Sufficiency Standard, the case can be made that it is not from bad choices or inadequate budgeting that families are unable to meet their needs, but rather that they lack adequate income—or even income plus subsidies—which results in consequences such as those listed previously (see Edin and Lein, 1997, for more detailed descriptions of strategies used by families to make ends meet). This then becomes the basis for framing the issue as how best to raise incomes or lower costs so that parents are able to meet their families' needs without resorting to these often problematic strategies. The question then becomes how women might gain access to jobs with adequate wages, whether it is necessary to adopt a living-wage ordinance, or what kinds of education and training should be provided to raise women's earning power.

A New Perspective on Evaluating Welfare

Ending the economic inequities experienced by women in the hands of both the welfare system and the labor market is no easy task. A first step is to refocus attention away from the numbers game of how many have left welfare, or how many are employed, to the question of how many have adequate resources from employment alone or in combination with public subsidies/supports—that is, resources sufficient to meet their families' needs without compromising nutrition, the adequacy of child care, or security of housing. After all, if families are not able to survive and thrive, statistics for those off welfare or employed are ultimately meaningless.

Of course, this does not solve all problems or answer all important questions. Women seeking to become economically self-sufficient find, in this violence-prone society, that such moves are threatening to some partners.

Often such efforts are thwarted in subtle and not-so-subtle ways through increased violence against the woman and her children. However, the economic inequities and physical violence against women will never end unless barriers faced by women as women—in the labor market and as single parents—are addressed. Until welfare reform explicitly seeks to overcome the barriers women face as workers—unequal pay, sexual harassment, occupational segregation, mommy tracks, and glass ceilings—economic independence for women will not be truly possible. Without economic self-sufficiency and adequate wages, women will not be truly free from poverty.

NOTES

1. States may impose additional, more restrictive time limits—such as the twenty-one-month limit imposed by Connecticut—or they may set limits such as no more than twenty-four months of assistance in any one sixty-month period. Alternatively, they may not impose any time limit at all—as is true of Michigan and Vermont. For details of each state plan, see the State Policy Documentation Project at <http://www.clasp.org/spdp.htm>.

2. Rather than decrease the cash benefit one dollar for each dollar of earnings, benefits under these rules would be reduced less, typically 50 cents for each dollar.

3. The discussion of postsecondary education postwelfare reform in this paper draws heavily on the analysis by Nina Dunning in her independent studies paper, "Post-Secondary Education and TANF," 1998.

REFERENCES

Bassuk, Ellen L. 1990. Who Are the Homeless Families: Characteristics of Sheltered Mothers and Children. *Community Mental Health Journal 26*(5): 425-434.

Bowler, Mary. 1999. Women's Earnings: An Overview. Monthly Labor Review 122(12): 13-21.

Burtless, Gary. 1998. *Can the Labor Market Absorb Three Million Welfare Recipients?* Madison: University of Wisconsin-Madison, Institute for Research on Poverty.

Cherlin, Andrew, Pamela Winston, Ronald Angel, Linda Purton, P. Lindsay Chase-Lansdale, Robert Moffitt, William Julius Wilson, Rebekah Levine Coley, and James Quane. 2000. What Welfare Recipients Know About the New Rules and What They Have to Say About Them. Policy brief (00-1), *Welfare, Children and Families: A Three-City Study*. Baltimore, MD: John Hopkins University. Available online: <www.jhu.edu/~welfare/>. Date of access: October 18.

Costin, Lela B. 1994. The Orphan Trains: Placing Out in America. *Social Service Review, 68*(4): 605-606.

Danziger, Sheldon. 1999. Introduction: What Are the Early Lessons? In Sheldon Danziger (Ed.), *Economic Conditions and Welfare Reform,* (pp. 1-10). Kalamazoo, MI: W. E. Upjohn Institute for Employment Research.

Dunning, Nina. 1998. Post-Secondary Education and TANF. Unpublished independent studies paper. University of Washington.

Edin, Kathryn and Laura Lein. 1997. *Making Ends Meet: How Single Mothers Survive Welfare and Low-Wage Work.* New York: Russell Sage Foundation.

Gordon, Linda. 1988. *Heroes of Their Own Lives: The Politics and History of Family Violence, 1880-1960.* New York: Viking.

Greenberg, Mark, Julie Strawn, and Lisa Plimpton. 1999. *State Opportunities to Provide Access to Post-Secondary Education Under TANF.* Washington, DC: Center for Law and Social Policy.

Gruber, Andrew S. 1998. Promoting Long-Term Self-Sufficiency for Welfare Recipients: Post-Secondary Education and the Welfare Work Requirement. *Northwestern University Law Review 93* (1): 247-300.

Jencks, Christopher and Kathryn Edin. 1990. The Real Welfare Problem. *American Prospect 1*(1/spring): 31-50.

Katz, Michael B. 1986. *In the Shadow of the Poorhouse: A Social History of Welfare in America.* New York: Basic Books.

Loprest, Pamela. 1999. Families Who Left Welfare: Who Are They and How Are They Doing? Urban Institute Discussion Paper (99-00). Washington, DC: The Urban Institute. Available online: <http://newfederalism.urban.org/pdf/discussion99-02.pdf>. Date of access: October 18, 2000.

Miller, Paul. 1998. *Hunger, Welfare Reform, and Non-Profits: Food Banks and Churches.* Missoula: University of Montana.

Moffitt, Robert and Jennifer Roff. 2000. The Diversity of Welfare Leavers. Policy brief (00-2). *Welfare, Children and Families: A Three City Study.* Baltimore, MD: John Hopkins University. Available online: <www/jhu.edu/~welfare/>. Date of access: October 18, 2000.

Moore, Thomas S. and Vicky Selkowe. 1999. *The Growing Crisis Among Wisconsin's Poorest Families: A Comparison of Welfare Caseload Declines and Trends in the State's Poverty Population, 1986-1997.* Milwaukee: Institute for Wisconsin's Future.

Piven, Frances Fox and Richard C. Cloward. 1972. *Regulating the Poor: The Functions of Public Welfare.* New York: Vintage Books.

Rein, Martin and Lee Rainwater. 1978. Patterns of Welfare Use. *Social Service Review 52*(4): 511-534.

Schmidt, Peter. 1998. States Discourage Welfare Recipients from Pursuing a Higher Education. *The Chronicle of Higher Education 44*(20): A34.

Schumacher, Rachel and Mark Greenberg. 1999. *Child Care After Leaving Welfare: Early Evidence from State Studies.* Washington, DC: Center for Law and Social Policy.

Sherman, Arloc, Cheryl Amey, Barbara Duffield, Nancy Ebb, and Deborah Weinstein. 1998. *Welfare to What: Early Findings on Family Hardship and Well-Being.* Washington, DC: Children's Defense Fund.

Shinn, Marybeth. 1997. Family Homelessness: State or Trait? *American Journal of Community Psychology 25*(6): 755-769.

Skocpol, Theda. 1992. *Protecting Soldiers and Mothers: The Political Origins of Social Policy in the United States.* Cambridge, MA: Belknap Press of Harvard University Press.

Spalter-Roth, Roberta, Beverly Burr, Heidi Hartmann, and Lois Shaw, with Jill Braunstein and Robin Dennis. 1995. *Welfare That Works: The Working Lives of AFDC Recipients.* Washington, DC: Institute for Women's Policy Research.

Strawn, Julie. 1998. *Senate Amendment to Welfare Law Allows States to Train Hardest-to-Employ Adults, Helps Others Find Better Jobs.* Washington, DC: Center for Law and Social Policy.

Tweedie, Jack, Diana Reichert, and Matt O'Connor. 1999. *Tracking Recipients After They Leave Welfare: Summaries of New State Follow-Up Studies.* Washington, DC: National Conference of State Legislatures. Available online: <www.ncsl.org/statefed/welfare/leavers.htm>. Date of access: October 18, 2000.

U.S. General Accounting Office (GAO). 1998. *Welfare Reform: States Are Restructuring Programs to Reduce Welfare Dependence.* Washington, DC: U.S. General Accounting Office.

U.S. General Accounting Office. 1999a. *Food Stamp Program: Various Factors Have Led to Declining Participation* (GAO/RCED-99-185). Washington, DC: U.S. General Accounting Office.

U.S. General Accounting Office. 1999b. *Medicaid Enrollment: Amid Declines, State Efforts to Ensure Coverage After Welfare Reform Vary* (GAO/HEHS-99-163). Washington, DC: U.S. General Accounting Office.

U.S. General Accounting Office. 2000. *Welfare Reform: State Sanction Policies and Number of Families Affected* (GAO/HEHS-00-44). Washington, DC: U.S. General Accounting Office.

Vandepol, Ann. 1982. Dependent Children, Child Custody, and the Mothers' Pensions: The Transformation of State-Family Relations in the Early Twentieth Century. *Social Problems* 29(3): 221-235.

Varma, Mahdevi. 1941. Ateet Ke Chalchitra [Moving pictures from the past]. Unpublished paper translated by Neera Sohoni, 1994, Stanford University.

Washington Welfare Reform Coalition. 1999. *Reality Check.* Seattle: Washington Welfare Reform Coalition.

Prison Life by Lenora Scott
Reprinted with permission from Kornfeld, Phyllis. 1997. *Cellblock Visions.*
Princeton, NJ: Princeton University Press.

Chapter 7

Low-Income Women and Housing: Where Will They Live?

Elizabeth A. Mulroy

The economic boom of the mid and late 1990s showered riches on many households who were able to purchase luxury homes and vacation retreats. There remained, however, thousands of households that could not afford *any* permanent place to live, and these households were largely headed by women with very low incomes. They do not seek to trade up one home they own for another. They own no home and have acute housing needs. These women seek apartments located in safe neighborhoods, but they cannot afford to pay the prevailing rents in these areas.

The U.S. Department of Housing and Urban Development (HUD), the federal agency responsible for implementing federal housing policy across the United States, has defined acute, worst-case housing needs as follows: renter households who do not receive federal housing assistance, have incomes below 50 percent of the median family income in their area (as established by HUD), and pay more than one-half of their income for rent and utilities or live in severely substandard housing. HUD defines "affordable" rent as 30 percent of a household's monthly income.

Janice Brown and Maria Hernandez (all names have been changed) have acute housing needs. Janice Brown is a nineteen-year-old black single mother of two (ages three years and six months) who lives with her children in a city in the Northeast. Her income from public welfare is only 14 percent of the area median income. She rents a one-bedroom apartment in the private rental market (that is, unsubsidized unit) and pays 83 percent of her monthly income for rent. She remarks:

> I never realized being on my own would be so hard. . . . My radiator's broke; it went down in March. I haven't had hot water in two months. It's rat infested in my ceiling and floor panels. It's a disaster. . . . The

street I live on is okay, but drugs are a very serious problem on the weekends. . . . You can see the piles of beer cans and little empty bottles of drugs in front of the houses.

Janice's landlord filed eviction proceedings against her because she was behind in rent payment. She searched for more affordable housing and also applied to nine different city housing authorities for both public and assisted housing, but they had no vacancies. She remains on the waiting list at all nine housing authorities where she was told the wait could be from two to four years. In the meantime, Janice sought help from the Legal Aid Society to represent her in landlord/tenant negotiations in an effort to stave off eviction and potential homelessness.

Maria Hernandez is a Hispanic eighteen-year-old single mother with a two-year-old daughter. They lived in a small apartment in the private rental market in another city. Her only source of income was public assistance. Maria was hurt in an accident, incurred medical bills, and fell behind on paying utility bills and rent. Her $446.00 in monthly welfare benefits was too little to cover her expenses. Stressed from the accident, raising a two-year-old alone, losing her boyfriend, and being chased by collection agency hounds proved to be more than she could bear. Coping became very difficult, and Maria and her daughter ended up homeless.

The central role that housing plays in family well-being has long been understood and appreciated (Mulroy, 1995b; Birch, 1985; Polikoff, 1978). Housing cost, quality, location, safety, unit density, and maintenance are central factors in community life that can enhance or impair family functioning. Because affordable housing is a basic need that has been documented to impact many areas of life—access to safe neighborhoods, quality public education and recreation activities, transportation systems, employment opportunities, and asset accumulation (Mulroy, 1995a, 1988)—the current housing crisis portends very serious problems for women at the margins, especially women of color. Consider these recent statistics:

- Of those households with the most acute housing needs, 57 percent are headed by women and 46 percent are headed by persons of color.
- Of households with acute housing needs that are families with children, 63 percent are headed by women and nearly two-thirds of these are women of color.
- Households experiencing housing problems are headed by both very low-income women and very low-income men—their spouses, partners, and potential mates (U.S. Department of Housing and Urban Development, 1998).

This chapter will begin by analyzing the structural underpinnings of the housing crisis and the implications of recent housing policy decisions. Then it will identify the impacts of a housing-affordability squeeze on women at the margins. Finally, it will conclude with a discussion of why, in the new millennium, housing must be understood as a women's issue and made a priority on the feminist agenda.

ROOTS OF THE CRISIS: STRUCTURAL AND PERSONAL FACTORS

We are currently experiencing a policy paradox in America. The purpose of welfare reform and housing reform is to force recipients, who are mostly female heads of households, off of public welfare and simultaneously out of public and assisted housing. These dual policies have the goal—or guise—of personal economic "self-sufficiency" at a time when rising economic marginality and vanishing affordable housing markets have converged to create a population of potentially homeless people (Wolch and Dear, 1993; Mulroy, 1995b). How will women at the margins, even with personal motivation and newly acquired job skills and training, achieve a modicum of self-sufficiency when jobs go global? Entry-level jobs pay a low hourly wage with few if any benefits. In addition, there are fewer affordable apartments to rent, particularly in the suburbs where higher-paying jobs are located. The safety net has been intentionally unraveled by welfare reform, and the business boom has left them behind. The impacts of the widening gap between Americans getting rich and richer and those who toil at $12,000 to $20,000 a year are widely acknowledged. Even *Business Week* reported that "Most Americans feel that the business boom has left them out" (Conlin, 1999, p. 52). Until the policy paradox is untangled and this national direction in social policy is reversed, the outcome will not be economic self-sufficiency for women at the margins, but rather economic disaster that will bury them even deeper in environments of despair.

Impacts of the Political Economy

Factors underlying the crisis in rental housing include economic globalization and shifts in the nation's economy (both of which increased income gaps between rich and poor people); skyrocketing housing costs; and the mismatch between a shrinking supply of affordable housing as demand for it is increasing. Between 1980 and 2000, there was minimal construction of low-income housing, which further aggravated the situation. The shortage of housing was also exacerbated by the closure and destruction of some large urban housing blocks where crime, drugs, and general deterioration made living in such situations unsafe and/or nearly impossible. In some cities, such as Chicago, urban low-income housing was also destroyed to make way for urban development and middle- or high-income housing. To alleviate the situation, HUD increased the provision of Section 8 housing vouchers. These vouchers can aid low-income earners, but there must be housing to which these subsidies apply. When combined with restructuring the welfare state, the number of female renters with acute housing needs continues to rise.

Conventional wisdom assumes that when people move it is a personal preference to improve housing conditions, living arrangements, or to take a better job—all choices made in a pattern of upward mobility. Housing choices for women with acute housing needs are constrained by actions outside their personal sphere of control and by forces in the political economy. External forces may include landlords who raise rents and evict; banks that "redline" (the systematic divestment by mortgage lending institutions in targeted urban areas); urban and suburban communities that prohibit construction of low-income housing in the "NIMBY" (not in my back yard) tradition; elected officials who slash affordable housing appropriations; and absentee landlords who abandon or neglect properties rather than repair them.

Displacement

The confluence of external factors combined with personal factors puts very low-income women (such as Janice Brown and Maria Hernandez) at risk of displacement—a forced move. A pattern of frequent residential mobility may be set in motion. If frequent mobility is not stopped by locating a stable housing situation, the low-income family cycles downward toward homelessness, the worst-case scenario of housing displacement (Mulroy and Lane, 1992). Faced with such conditions, women at the margins seek affordable, stable housing solutions thought to be available through public and assisted-housing programs. However, this supply has been shrinking due to a movement in U.S. Congress to get government out of the housing business.

Shrinking Supply of Affordable Rental Housing

The dilemma for women at the margins is that the supply of both affordable, private market rental housing stock and publicly funded, affordable rental housing have not kept pace with increased demand. There are fewer and fewer rental units available to low-income households. Between 1993 and 1995, the number of private market rental units affordable to very low-income households (those with incomes at 50 percent of the area median) dropped by almost 900,000. However, the largest losses were for units affordable to even poorer families with incomes below 30 percent of median: these units dropped from 1.8 million in 1993 to 1.5 million in 1996, a 16 percent loss in two years (U.S. HUD, 1998). The availability of these rental units in the private market is important not only because it is where most poor people live but also because it is the basis of the government-subsidized Section 8 program that expands the supply of affordable rental housing to very poor households. Without available private market units, the Section 8 program cannot work.

Historic Reversal of Federal Housing Policy

Congressional action to restructure the welfare state with cuts to public assistance, the Food Stamp Program, the Special Supplemental Food Program for Women, Infants, and Children, Medicaid, and Medicare—in combination with cuts in affordable housing and community development—was intended to unravel the safety net for poor people. It began more than a decade ago as a purposeful conservative redirection of public policy. The philosophical underpinning assumed that through the workings of supply and demand, the housing market generally functions well to meet the country's housing needs. Problems of affordability could be attributed to divorce, low-income, or other personal factors not meriting government intervention (Gilderbloom and Applebaum, 1988). Based on this ideology, existing government affordable housing programs were vulnerable to severe cutbacks in appropriations, restrictions in eligibility criteria, restructuring of program intent, and elimination.

Federal housing policy to provide low-income renters with decent quality, affordable housing has been in place since after the Great Depression in the 1930s. Until recently, the United States has experienced uninterrupted growth in government support of construction, rehabilitation, and rental-assistance programs. This trend ended abruptly in 1996 when, for the first time, the number of renters receiving federal housing assistance dropped (see Figure 7.1).

Figure 7.1 shows that the late 1970s' housing-production programs to construct and rehabilitate units affordable to poor people were completed and occupied by the 1980s, and that the number of eligible households also grew because of annual increases in congressional appropriations for Section 8 rental assistance during the same period. Moreover, in the face of the

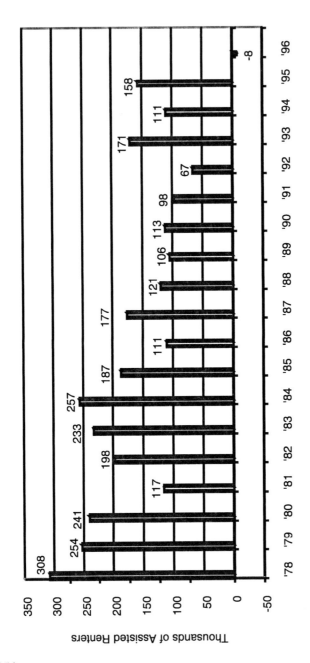

FIGURE 7.1. Annual Increase in Number of Households with Public and Assisted Housing, 1978-1996 (*Source:* Congressional Budget Office; based on data provided by the Department of Housing and Urban Development and the Farmers Home Administration. U.S. Department of Housing and Urban Development. Office of Policy Development and Research, 1998.)

robust economic boom of the 1990s, the fastest growth in acute housing needs was among working families. Structural factors were responsible for lags in wages for the lowest paid workers, who then faced a diminishing supply of housing at rents they could afford. People with stronger incomes put upward pressure on rents and rent levels escalated. Then, in 1995, Congress operationalized its conservative "Contract with America" in the housing area by denying Clinton administration requests and providing no funding for new rental assistance to serve those with acute housing needs.

Another serious problem is that housing assistance has never been available to all those who have qualified for it and needed it. It is not an entitlement. Even when congressional appropriations for affordable rental housing were at their most generous, waiting lists were still long—from two to eight years in some cities. Its rationing now is a critical problem facing low income women.

AFFORDABLE HOUSING PROGRAMS

Knowledge of existing types of housing programs is important for three reasons. First, it helps to understand the baseline of federal housing options slated for reduction and elimination. Second, it informs how political tinkering with housing policy and programs can generate structures of inequality with profound effects on women. Third, the programs described are viewed by housing advocates as resources to be preserved and expanded. When funding from multiple housing programs is packaged together, it can provide opportunities to develop many types of housing (including supportive, service-enriched housing for populations in need, especially for women at the margins). Examples include but are not limited to transitional shelters for the homeless, mentally ill, or teenage mothers; special-needs housing for persons with HIV/AIDS; housing with supportive services for the frail elderly, the homeless, and single mothers with substance abuse problems; victims of domestic violence; and women exiting prison.

There are three basic types of federal housing programs: public housing, project-based housing, and tenant-based assistance, better known as the Section 8 or voucher program.

Public Housing

Established by the Housing Act of 1937, these units are owned by local public housing authorities (PHAs). Today, there are 1.2 million occupied units of public housing. Although the large, older, high-rise projects that became centers of concentrated poverty may have a blighted history (Meehan,

1979), small-scale, scattered site projects have more recently been built in desirable locations, adding to the diversity of public housing stock.

Project-Based Assisted Housing

Popular in the 1970s and 1980s, project-based assisted housing offered deep subsidies to nonprofit and for-profit developers for the construction and rehabilitation of apartments. The subsidies allowed monthly rents to be established at amounts affordable to eligible low-income households. These programs added 1.4 million rental units for low-income people but, distributed throughout the country, its impact on the need for low-cost rental housing was very limited.

Tenant-Based Assisted Housing

These programs, of which the Section 8 and voucher programs are the most widely known, began in 1974 and provided rental assistance directly to eligible households to help them find their own housing in the open, private housing market. Since inception, this has been a program for women—nearly three-quarters of those participating nationwide were female heads of household (Mulroy, 1988). Unlike the project-based subsidy that is tied to the unit, tenant-based subsidies are tied to the household. That is, the subsidy is "portable" and can move with the family when it needs or wants to relocate. But there are institutional and bureaucratic constraints. Affordability is insured as long as each landlord agrees to participate in the Section 8 program. Studies show that women who are single parents, for example, have had difficulty using tenant-based programs based largely on discrimination against them and their children by landlords, but also by federal lease requirements and rent levels that serve as disincentives for landlord participation (Mulroy, 1995b, 1988).

HOME and Low-Income Housing Tax Credit Programs

There are a number of other federal housing programs, both old and new, that work in combination with existing programs to help make rental housing more affordable. Two examples include the HOME Investment Partnerships Program and the Low-Income Housing Tax Credit (LIHTC) program. The HOME program is a formula grant to states that targets low income homeowners and renters with incomes at or below 65 percent of area median income, while the LIHTC program subsidizes the capital costs of rental units to make them affordable to people with incomes at or below 60 percent of area median income. The tax credit has produced more than 600,000 units since its enactment in 1986.

The main difference between HOME, the LIHTC, and the three traditional housing programs just discussed is that rental projects developed under HOME and the tax credit programs have a formula-driven flat rent. That means that residents all pay the same rent regardless of their actual incomes. Thus, these rental projects may be occupied by families with a range of incomes, including extremely low incomes, making these developments truly "mixed income." Income mixing is a popular goal in urban policy because it can be a means to deconcentrate poverty (Mulroy, 1991).

Housing Trust Funds: Innovative Local Responses

Not all housing resources are federal. More than 100 Rental Housing Trust Funds (RHTFs), for example, have been created by cities, counties, and state governments across the country during the past fifteen years in direct response to the striking reduction in federal spending for affordable rental housing. RHTF has these characteristics: (1) it has a secured, dedicated source of ongoing revenue, usually through legislation or ordinance; (2) it is committed to the production and preservation of housing affordable to low-income households, including the homeless; and (3) it represents funds that would not otherwise be used to address housing needs (Brooks, 1997). These are local ways of finding creative solutions to increase the amount of money available to house a community's low-income residents. In a study of RHTFs nationwide, Brooks (1997) found that their outputs were quite diverse, depending on which populations or needs housing advocates or developers in each local community chose to address.

Who Is Eligible for Housing Assistance?

Rental assistance programs serve different income and demographic groups. How do women at the margins qualify for the limited stock of affordable housing? First, they need to meet program-specific income eligibility requirements. The three basic affordable housing programs and other federal housing programs described previously restrict eligibility to households whose incomes do not exceed a specific percentage of the median family income for the area in which the applicant household lives. HUD defines the median income for each metropolitan area and nonmetropolitan county (called area median income) and sets income limits for federal program participation. Therefore classifications of eligibility are determined on a location-specific basis (see Table 7.1).

TABLE 7.1. Extremely Low, Very Low, and Low Income: Examples of 1997 Income Limits for Four-Person Households, in Dollars

	Extremely Low Income (30 percent of median)	Very Low Income (50 precent of median)	Low Income (80 percent of median)*	Area Median
Los Angeles	15,400	25,650	41,050	47,800
New York	14,700	24,500	39,200	47,300
Chicago	16,750	27,900	43,500	55,800
Philadelphia	15,400	25,650	41,050	51,300
Detroit	16,000	26,650	42,650	53,330
Washington, DC	21,100	35,150	43,500	70,300
Boston	17,900	29,800	43,500	59,600
Houston	14,750	24,550	39,300	49,100
Atlanta	15,950	26,550	42,500	53,100

Source: HUD Section 8 Income Limits, Fiscal Year 1997. *Rental Housing Assistance —The Crisis Continues.* U.S. Department of Housing and Urban Development and Research, 1998.

Note: In 1997, the average poverty threshold of a family of four was $16,400.
*The "80 percent of median" limits for each area cannot exceed the national median of $43,500.

Income limits for four-person households, for example, are categorized as Low Income (80 percent of area median); Very Low Income (50 percent of area median); and Extremely Low Income (30 percent of area median). However, despite what former President John F. Kennedy had dreamed, the rising tide did not lift all boats. As area median incomes have risen, the incomes of the poor did not keep pace. HUD has had to reclassify the "Low-Income" category further into very low- and extremely low-income groupings to capture the increasing disparity between the rich and the poor in America. Programs such as traditional public housing and Section 8 were established to target low-income families with incomes at 30 percent of area median. Rental assistance through public housing subsidies were intentionally targeted to assist those who had no other option in the private housing rental market. Public housing became the housing of last resort. But the stunning reality across America in the new millennium is that the housing of last resort has a very long waiting list because of the great need of so many working families.

People who qualify as Extremely Low Income—with maximum incomes of $14,750 in Houston; $16,000 in Detroit; $17,900 in Boston; and $21,100 in Washington, DC—are likely working. Data show that the working poor who live in the private housing market (not in public or assisted housing) have jobs and still cannot afford to pay their rents. In 1995 more than 95 percent of very low-income renters paid more than one-half of their reported income for housing. Of these households, half of the families with children and three-quarters of households without children (nonelderly and no disability) reported that earnings were their main source of income (U.S. HUD, 1998).

Nonetheless, current conservative ideology in the U.S. Congress is steeped in old myths that the very poor are stereotypical, lazy "welfare queens" not attached to the labor market, or those with ties to the underground economies of illicit drugs. Residents of many large, troubled public housing projects would not deny, and in fact decry, the presence of illegal drugs, guns, and gang activity that blights and destroys their communities. Activities to change and empower such communities through tenant management, on-site family support services, and community-building initiatives have helped to make these communities safer and have improved residents' lives (Naparstek and Dooley, 1997). The community organizing and leadership needed to achieve this level of change has often been generated directly by the women residents themselves without support from the politically entrenched, usually male-dominated public housing authority boards (Blundo et al., 1999).

Who Benefits?

Over the past two decades, the public housing and Section 8 programs have targeted and served the poorest families. Female heads of household and minorities have been key beneficiaries. Three-quarters of all tenant-based Section 8 program beneficiaries, 70 percent of project-based Section 8 beneficiaries, and three-quarters of public-housing residents have incomes of 30 percent or less of their area median income (U.S. HUD, 1998). In reality, families who live in public and assisted housing have incomes that are far lower; they are very poor. In 1995, a family receiving the maximum Aid to Families with Dependent Children (AFDC) grant for a family of three would have an income of only 16 percent of the area median income in New York City, 10 percent in Chicago, 5.5 percent in Houston, and 16 percent in Los Angeles. Therefore cutbacks in and elimination of funding for these specific housing programs severely impact affordable housing resources for women at the margins and their children.

THE HOUSING AFFORDABILITY SQUEEZE

Of all the measures of housing quality established by HUD—physical adequacy, overcrowding, excessive costs (paying more than 30 percent of income for rent)—the major problem now is excessive cost. The actual physical condition of the nation's housing stock has greatly improved in the past fifty years. The key problem is the affordability squeeze between incomes, on one hand, and housing costs, on the other.

Women at the margins experience this squeeze to an extraordinary degree because of their disproportionately low incomes. A woman's economic marginality may be caused by separation and divorce, low wages, non-receipt of child support, incarceration, amount of public assistance benefits, or a combination of these, as reported in other chapters of this book. Faced with the affordability squeeze, women attempt to locate in new places with less expensive living arrangements. The consequence is often frequent mobility, a situation that contributes to destabilization and insecurity. The reduced supply of affordable rental housing in desirable communities near jobs that pay a family wage—as exists in the burgeoning suburbs—has restricted low-income women's freedom to move. One consequence, particularly for women of color, is the concentration of poor families in urban neighborhoods where lower-cost rental housing has traditionally been more available, but also where there may be higher crime rates, unsafe streets, and gang violence.

Women experience the squeeze in different ways depending on their source and amount of income, life-cycle stage, condition of their physical and mental health, coping abilities, economic and social support networks, and range of available housing options and resources. Those with the most options fare better than those with the fewest. Two populations are of increasing concern. They include very low-income women who live alone, especially those with disabilities, and families headed by very low-income single mothers on public welfare. Women coming out of prison are represented in both groups.

Women Alone

HUD data show that of the 5.3 million households with severe, acute housing needs, 20 percent are headed by an elderly person, 40 percent are families with children, and a surprising 40 percent comprise a category called "other"—but they are all extremely poor. "Others" are nonelderly, working-aged single women and men or childless couples, and it is estimated that over half of these households include adults with disabilities (HUD, 1998). Eighty-eight percent of those who are disabled and receive Supplemental Security Income (SSI) live alone, and half of these are women. Moreover, women comprise nearly half of all the working-aged single adults with severe housing needs who do not receive SSI—an invisible population that has received very little attention in the housing literature. These are women who work in low-wage jobs yet are still extremely poor, and they usually are living alone. Data on both women and men in this category show that 86 percent completed a high school education; three-quarters report earnings as their main source of income; yet nearly 70 percent have incomes that are less than 30 percent of area median. Considering the wage gap between women and men generally, it is likely that women in this subpopulation of worst-case renters are even worse off than the men in terms of their rent burdens.

When public assistance is the only source of income in an expensive urban-housing market, the amount is generally insufficient to cover monthly rent and utilities. Apartments will cost, on average, far more than a woman's entire monthly income. But these recent findings suggest that the housing affordability squeeze extends widely to also include the working poor—both singles and families with children. The impact of the affordability squeeze can be observed in the quality of the units women can afford. Even though women living alone report severe rent burdens in the private rental market, single mothers report not only severe rent burdens but multiple other housing problems as well.

Women and Children on Public Welfare

Women with children on public assistance experience the affordability squeeze to a profound degree, but teenage mothers are especially vulnerable. When teenage mothers venture out on their own in the private rental market, they are severely disadvantaged not only by their low level of income, but also by their youth, lack of resources needed to conduct a housing search, and inexperience. They have little or no knowledge of how to go about conducting a search, such as locating vacancies, contacting landlords, or getting selected for tenancy. They must compete for scarce units with people who are older and more sophisticated, have more education, more income, and better negotiating skills.

For young women on welfare, this lack of familiarity with the rental market may be compounded by limited access to key resources (such as telephones). Some women make all contacts with landlords on pay phones or on telephones belonging to family or friends (Mulroy, 1988). One woman reported:

> I had no car and no phone, so I had to go to friends' homes to make and receive phone calls to landlords. Then I had to ask relatives and friends to drive me around. The search was extremely complicated from beginning to end. It was frustrating and hostile.

In addition, good writing skills are needed to complete complex rental application forms, and significant amounts of cash are required up front to cover the first and last month's rent plus security deposit. If a real estate firm was used to help find the unit and complete the transaction between landlord and tenant (a common practice used by the poor in some cities), an additional commission is levied on the renter household. The sum of these costs far exceeds a woman on welfare's ability to pay.

If women on welfare seek public housing, they will likely sit on waiting lists for years (as Janice Brown is doing). If they are very lucky, they might get a unit in public housing, but in inner cities it may not be located in a neighborhood of their choice.

Adolescent Mothers

Teenage mothers share the same aspirations as those held by older women: providing for family, adequate housing, and a good job. They are even less likely, however, to achieve their housing aspirations using the Section 8 program than are older mothers (Mulroy, 1995b, 1988). This situation is particularly serious for adolescent mothers of color. Some single mothers of color, irrespective of age, were unable to find even one landlord willing to rent to them under the Section 8 program. At the end of an arduous search in which they tried hard to move, they still remained trapped in inner-city poverty—unlike white single mothers, who were more likely to find landlords willing to rent to them in a range of communities and even some in the safe suburbs. One young black woman explains how landlords screen out applicants:

> Newspaper ads for apartments have phone numbers to call. When I called, there was this recorded message asking you to leave your name, address, and phone number, the number of children you have, how you are going to pay for the apartment, and your place of employment. So you say, I'm Jane Doe of Shawmut Ave., Roxbury, I have four children, I'm using Section 8, and I'm not employed. Landlords don't call you back.

Women Leaving Prison

Institutional barriers to housing or for the use of rental assistance programs were greatest for women exiting prison. In addition to all of the barriers described previously, landlords may consider them punished for their deviant behavior but not rehabilitated and, therefore, very poor housing risks. Three out of four women in prison have custody of minor children when they enter prison, and those children are usually returned to them immediately upon their leaving prison. Often this occurs before the woman has been able to obtain housing. She has no resources for rental deposits, household furnishings, and supplies. If she was ever convicted of a felony drug crime, she will be excluded from all types of welfare assistance in thirty-seven states. If the woman has been in prison for several years, she will have limited knowledge of the housing market or rental assistance programs or even about community agencies that could help her. Thus, this group needs special attention with respect to their overall reintegration into the community.

Unsafe Neighborhoods

The advantage of public housing is the consistently affordable rent, but the disadvantage can be its location in unsafe environments. A safe location near jobs facilitates employment and social mobility; a physically isolated, unsafe location does not. Long before welfare reform mandated it, many mothers traveled long distances by public transportation to finish high school through general education diploma (GED) programs, to attend job-training classes, or to work. These activities required them to come and go at various hours of the day and evening. Unsafe environments in older projects served as barriers because young mothers barricaded themselves inside their apartments at dusk.

According to twenty-two-year-old Patsy Young, resident of a public housing project considered one of the most dangerous in her city, she is afraid to walk alone from the bus stop to her apartment building after dark. She does not know any of her neighbors, although tenants are, like her, mostly single-parent families of color. Patsy comments:

> It's a terrible, unsafe neighborhood. I'm worried about stray bullets crashing through the window. Once I come home from school, I don't come back out for nothing. I don't talk to no one. One night I got home late and was too scared to go into my own building.

She continues to work on her GED although, given her personal situation, Patsy and her counselor expect it will still take a few years more to complete.

Discrimination and Subsidized Housing Programs

Possession of a Section 8 certificate does not necessarily lead women to subsidized housing in a safe neighborhood or in any neighborhood because of multiple discriminatory barriers in the private rental market. For many women, the program is very hard to use. The multiplicity of barriers can create a "search hassle" that prevents program participation. In a study of fifty-six single mothers looking for affordable housing with the Section 8 certificate, more than three-quarters (44) reported that the major barrier to program use was that landlords refused outright to participate in the program, though it is illegal to do so (Mulroy, 1988). Even though many women were employed, both white women and those of color reported that possession of the Section 8 certificate itself seemed to stereotype them automatically to landlords as a class of poverty-stricken women to whom undesirable tenant characteristics were ascribed. Many landlords reported that the fair market rents the government would pay were too low. But 57 percent of women reported being rejected by landlords who refused to rent to families with children, while nearly half experienced rejection because of their public-assistance status. Nearly one-third of the searchers also experienced bias against them because of their single-parent status, while 20 percent felt discriminated against because of their race (Mulroy, 1988).

Despite the difficulties of using the tenant-based subsidies (such as the Section 8 program just described), it remains the key to affordability for extremely poor households who rent in units built with project-based subsidies. In their efforts to find safer, more livable environments for their families, women on public welfare often apply for tenancy in new, privately developed projects advertised as "affordable." These projects are built by nonprofit community-development corporations or private developers using project-based subsidies provided to the developer through multiple public sources, as described in an earlier section. These funding sources also determine each project's targeted tenant population, income eligibility requirements, and rent levels, as the following example suggests.

In a study of affordable housing in Hawaii, a state with high rents and severe affordability problems for low-income families, one development that utilized multiple project-based subsidy programs still had renter households with severe affordability problems—these were women on public welfare (Mulroy et al., 1997). This newly constructed housing development was the first phase in a large, multiphased planned project built on rural land previously zoned for agriculture. The long-term goal was to provide mixed-income housing for workers expected to fill service-sector jobs in the coastal-tourism industry. This first phase of development consisted of thirty-three three-bedroom homes targeted to low-income families with incomes at or below 60 percent of area median as required by the sources of public funding: the HOME, the LIHTC, and the state RHTF programs. The median income for the project's census tract was $41,805 and the HUD-established income limit for a four-person family was $29,100, but income limits varied by household size. All tenants would pay the same rent of $548, irrespective of income, per funding guidelines.

An analysis of project rent rolls showed that tenants did help to integrate the neighborhood economically, as their annual incomes ranged from $6,840 to $38,310, with the lowest income tenants having only 16 percent of the area median income. Those with higher incomes were male-headed families and thus they had lowest rent burdens (the ratio of rent to income), while those with lowest incomes were female-headed families who had the highest rent burdens.

One family with a total monthly income of $570 from public assistance paid the full rent, leaving it with only $22 a month to spend for all other basic needs. Only those few AFDC recipients who were able to secure a hard-to-get Section 8 rent subsidy could bring down their share of rent to the affordable 30 percent level. The Section 8 program rent structure superseded the other programs for Section 8 participants, and the rent was reduced to

$150—a far better rent burden. The developer did not lose money by partici-
pating in the Section 8 program since the federal government pays the difference between the asking rent and the tenant's share. In this case, the
owner still got the full $548 per month because the tenant paid $150 and the
government paid the balance of $398 directly to the developer. For the ten-
ant, however, this still left only $420 a month to meet all the family's basic
needs for food, clothing, transportation, children's school-related expenses,
insurance, and myriad other expenses.

A recent national study of the LIHTC program by the U.S. General Accounting Office (White, 1997) confirmed the Hawaii findings concerning
the importance of tenant-based rent subsidies to very low-income households. It found that 39 percent of households occupying tax-credit units also
received rental assistance (such as from the Section 8 program) to make
their housing affordable. The average income of the families with rental assistance was only 25 percent of the area median, compared with 45 percent
of area median for renters of tax-credit units that did not also receive a rental
subsidy (U.S. HUD, 1998). In sum, "affordability" is a relative term, and
achieving it is like putting together a complex puzzle. What is clear, however, is that for women at the margins, use of a tenant-based subsidy is one
key piece of that puzzle.

HOUSING IS A WOMEN'S ISSUE

This chapter has attempted to demonstrate that housing must be understood as a women's issue. While other chapters in this book make convincing arguments that, in the new millennium, the public welfare and justice
systems have jeopardized the human rights of poor women, this chapter has
extended the argument to the housing market. Housing reinforces and perpetuates economic and social divisions that exist within society as a whole,
and the outcome is housing segregation and inequality (Gilderbloom and
Applebaum, 1988). The legacy of federal housing policy suggests that solutions to housing problems for low-income women are complex because the
production of housing in America is a function of the private sector (through
the activities of real estate developers and banking interests). The role of
government has been a supportive one to private sector interests (Mulroy,
1995a). In this context, it is not surprising that attention to the housing needs
of poor women, as a societal issue, have remained outside the housing policy debate. Nonetheless, for millions of women and children, federal rental
assistance has met their basic housing needs, ended the affordability squeeze,
and provided a safe and stable living arrangement. In addition, despite barri-

ers to use, it has served as the way out of abusive domestic relationships for many and a means to independent living.

Feminists should be vigilant in monitoring several profound changes in federal housing policy that will further limit the supply of affordable housing for women at the margins. One of these changes is that Congress loosened income targeting of rental assistance, thus diverting current slots of rental assistance to higher-income households with less serious housing needs. The analysis provided in this chapter suggests that this policy direction is misguided. The implications of the current housing crisis for women at the margins are these:

- *New housing assistance:* Continue to expand rental assistance for all those with worst-case housing needs. Federal tenant-based subsidy programs, despite the institutional barriers to use, serve as a cornerstone for housing stability and should be increased. Women participating in welfare-to-work programs and those already working at very low wages require states and localities to address this issue also, not only in central cities but also regionally and in suburban communities where employment networks are located.
- *Expanded use of multiple subsidies:* Increase new housing-production programs for those with worst-case housing needs through HOME, LIHTC, RHTF, and tenant-based rental assistance. Without the addition of tenant-based rental assistance, women at the margins will not be able to afford the housing created by the production programs.
- *Balanced housing goals—Mixed-income and equity:* Deconcentrate urban poverty through mixed-income housing. Although this is a desirable goal, it must be balanced with continued housing assistance for those with worst-case housing needs at a level of support that meets those needs. These goals are not mutually exclusive. Income targeting can and must support both goals.
- *Women-run housing development corporations:* Increase housing and community development corporations that target the production of housing designated for women with worst-case housing needs. Women with capital and access to capital can successfully develop local organizations to serve their sisters in need.

It is ironic that the conservative-driven devolution of decision making from federal level to states and localities gives feminists the clearest window of opportunity to become agents of change. Local communities control each zoning decision that determines whether a permit for a specific use will be approved or denied. Community resistance to land uses that benefit women at the margins—transitional shelters, residential group homes with treatment facilities, residential group homes for women on prison work-release programs, and scattered-site public housing—will remain intransigent until communities elect local planning board and city council members who understand the power of zoning as an equity tool and affordable, designated housing as a community-building and stabilizing strategy. That is, family strengthening for the most vulnerable is enhanced when the families are surrounded by nurturing, supportive networks of neighborhood organizations and institutions (Mulroy, 1997). Local access to all forms of affordable and service-enriched housing will increase women's opportunities for family stabilization, integration into the community, and long-term well-being for the children.

When committing to unravel the policy paradox for women at the margins, housing must be a substantive topic on the feminist agenda. Then solutions can be crafted and implemented on multiple levels of intervention: locally through grassroots-community organization specific to local neighborhood issues; citywide and regionally as part of multisector, comprehensive, community-building initiatives; and statewide and federally through empirical scholarly research and policy analysis. Without a strong feminist commitment to affordable housing for the United States' most vulnerable women, the structures of misery will soon unleash a tidal wave of homeless people, and they will be women at the margins and their children.

REFERENCES

Birch, Eugenie. 1985. *The Unsheltered Woman: Women and Housing in the 1980s.* New Brunswick, NJ: Center for Urban Policy Research.

Blundo, Robert, Christopher Mele, Rhonda Hairston, and Josephine Watson. 1999. The Internet and Demystifying Power Differentials: A Few Women Online and the Housing Authority. *Journal of Community Practice* 6(2): 11-26.

Brooks, Mary. 1997. *A Status Report on Housing Trust Funds in the United States.* Frazier Park, CA. Housing Trust Fund Project of the Center for Community Change.

Conlin, Michelle. 1999. Hey, What About Us? *Business Week* (December 27), 52.

Gilderbloom, John I. and Richard P. Applebaum. 1988. *Rethinking Rental Housing.* Philadelphia: Temple University Press.

Meehan, Eugene. 1979. *The Quality of Federal Policy Making: Programmed Failure in Public Housing.* Columbia: University of Missouri Press.

Mulroy, Elizabeth. 1988. The Search for Affordable Housing. In Elizabeth A. Mulroy (Ed.), *Women As Single Parents: Confronting Institutional Barriers in the Courts, the Workplace, and the Housing Market* (pp. 123-163). Dover, MA: Auburn House Publishing Co.

Mulroy, Elizabeth. May 1991. Mixed-Income Housing in Action. *Urban Land* 50(5): 2-7.

Mulroy, Elizabeth E. 1995a. Housing Policy. In R. Edwards (Ed.), *Encyclopedia of Social Work,* Nineteenth Edition, Vol. 2, (pp. 1377-1384). Washington, DC: NASW Press.

Mulroy, Elizabeth. 1995b. *The New Uprooted: Single Mothers in Urban Life.* Westport, CT: Auburn House.

Mulroy, Elizabeth. 1997. Building a Neighborhood Network: Interorganizational Collaboration to Prevent Child Abuse and Neglect. *Social Work 42*(3): 255-264.

Mulroy, Elizabeth, Katheryn Dyjak, Susan Bollig, Scotty Ruis, and Cynthia Teramoto. 1997. Expanding the Supply of Affordable Rental Housing in Hawaii: Who Benefits? Unpublished report. Honolulu: Hawaii Rental Housing Trust Fund.

Mulroy, Elizabeth and Terry Lane. 1992. Housing Affordability, Stress, and Single Mothers: Pathway to Homelessness. *Journal of Sociology and Social Welfare 19* (3): 51-64.

Naparstek, Arthur and Denis Dooley. 1997. *Community Building in Public Housing: Ties That Bind People and Their Communities.* Washington, DC: The Urban Institute for the Department of Housing and Urban Development.

Polikoff, Arthur. 1978. *Housing the Poor: The Case for Heroism.* Cambridge, MA: Ballinger.

U.S. Department of Housing and Urban Development. 1998. *Rental Housing Assistance—The Crisis Continues.* The 1997 Report to Congress on Worst Case Housing Needs. Washington, DC: U.S. Department of Housing and Urban Development, Office of Policy Development and Research.

White, James R. 1997. Tax Credits Opportunities to Improve Oversight of the Low-Income Housing Program: Statement of James R. White, Associate Director, Tax Policy & Administration Issues, General Government Division, before the Subcommittee on Oversight, Committee on Ways and Means, House of Representatives. GAO/T_GGD/RCED_97_149, Report 97-55, March. Washington, DC: U.S. General Accounting Office.

Wolch, Jennifer and Michael Dear. 1993. *Malign Neglect: Homelessness in an American City.* San Francisco: Jossey-Bass Inc.

SECTION III:
GENDER, AGE, AND HEALTH INTERACTIONS

Chapter 8

Triple Jeopardy: Women Marginalized by Substance Abuse, Poverty, and Incarceration

Anna Celeste Burke

INTRODUCTION

There can be no doubt that the lives of many women in the United States are profoundly affected by the use of alcohol and other drugs (AOD). Evidence also suggests that the addiction careers of women emerge and develop differently than do those of men, and that they are deeply influenced by the social context of a life embedded in family relationships and gender socialization (Henderson, 1998). Women with AOD problems are greatly disadvantaged, however, by the fact that little is yet known about the causes and consequences of substance use among women. Existing evidence suggests that women are often placed at risk by elements of their gender status and experiences as women which increase their likelihood of developing AOD problems while reducing their capacity to deal with those problems effectively. This is especially true for poor women with substance abuse problems, facing new risks with increased sanctions and diminished benefits in the wake of welfare reform. Women have also been placed at increased risk by societal responses to substance use and abuse that, in the 1980s and 1990s, moved from neglect to punishment with expanded reliance on incarceration of women with substance abuse problems. As a result, the past decade has witnessed a dramatic increase in the number of women placed in double and even triple jeopardy by substance abuse, poverty, and incarceration for drug-related offenses.

In the following pages, existing evidence from epidemiological and etiological studies will be examined to provide the best available account about the nature and extent of AOD use and abuse among women. Evidence will also be presented from studies exploring differences between men and women in the onset, context, and course of substance use and abuse. Differences by women in their access to and utilization of prevention and treatment services will also be examined. These studies elucidate how more fundamental forces of gender socialization and the subordination of women interact with their use of substances to influence the course and outcome of the AOD-related problems they experience. In conclusion, a number of recommendations will be made regarding ways to improve circumstances and outcomes for women with AOD-related problems.

VICIOUS CYCLES AND DOWNWARD SPIRALS

When taken together, evidence about substance use and abuse among women suggests that the onset, course, and outcome of AOD-related problems among many women is rooted in a vicious cycle that begins with their initial victimization, typically in childhood. This specific victimization of women—which encompasses personal experiences of sexual abuse and physical violence—may be reinforced and even amplified by exposure to more general forms of violence and victimization directed at women as a category of persons. The categorical victimization of women includes media portrayals of violence against women, cavalier attitudes by law enforcement toward the prevention of violence against women, and cultural or institutional legitimations that subordinate women by, for example, holding them responsible for their own victimization.

Women who abuse substances are further disadvantaged by the stigma placed on women who use or abuse substances (Finkelstein, 1994). Stigmatization of women with substance abuse problems reflects notions that such behavior is not only counternormative but fundamentally incompatible with the female role, especially for women with young children (Finkelstein, 1994). At the same time, women with AOD-related problems, because they are bound by constraints imposed upon them by their gender role and family ties, are often discouraged from seeking treatment (Beckman and Amaro, 1986). They are further disadvantaged and discriminated against in seeking treatment through lack of access to resources to pay for treatment, and through the lack of availability of women-centered treatment. Women in conventional treatment may be vulnerable to further victimization, given reports of sexual harassment of female clients in these settings (Nelson-Zlupko et al., 1996). Vicious cycles of victimization, stigmatization, disadvantage, and discrimination are further perpetuated through policies of punishment and neglect directed at women who abuse substances—resulting in effect in their revictimization. These punitive policies are most apparent in the increasing use of sanctions against poor women on welfare who abuse

Why?
because I could not live
in the world as it was
because I did not want to be
what I was born for
because I careened between
hope and despair
because my eyes saw what others denied
and were blind to what was
right in front of me
because I felt a terrible only
and wanted to burst open into my molecules
among everyone else's molecules
because I wanted to be invisible
because I wanted to be known
because I wanted to crawl
like a snake, out of my skin
and into another's, at least
for one lifetime
because I felt weak and afraid
and wanted to dare courage into me

Judith Clark

Reprinted with permission from (The) Writing Workshop, Bedford Hills Correctional Facility. Hettie Jones (Ed.) 1997. *Aliens at the Border.* New York: Segue Books.

substances and the dramatic escalation in the number of women imprisoned for drug offenses.

Too often cycles of victimization and revictimization produce a downward spiral in personal well-being and social functioning with pernicious and even deadly consequences for women. Women who abuse substances have higher rates of morbidity and mortality than women in the general population or men with similar problems (Blumenthal, 1998; Hill, 1982).

SUBSTANCE USE AND ABUSE AMONG WOMEN: CLOSING THE GENDER GAP

According to Joseph Califano, former secretary of Health, Education and Welfare and current president of the National Center on Addiction and Substance Abuse (CASA) at Columbia University, knowledge about the nature and extent of women's AOD-related problems has been masked by national denial and inexcusable neglect (Center on Addiction and Substance Abuse

[CASA], 1996). It is only recently that attention has been paid to "alarming inequities in women's health research including: the failure to include women in clinical trials; inadequate attention to sex differences in biomedical, behavioral, and health services research and insufficient funding for research on women's health concerns" (Blumenthal, 1998, p. 15; U.S. General Accounting Office, 1990). Much of the addiction research that has been done simply has not included women and, when it has, such studies have too often "centered on the impact of women's addiction on children and family life, particularly the effect on the fetus. These concerns have reflected the traditional view of women in terms of their reproductive capacity" (Blumenthal, 1998, p. 19).

In part, this neglect reflects the fact that for most of this century in the United States, AOD-related problems have been portrayed as problems associated with men (Blumenthal, 1998). Until recently, epidemiological studies have consistently provided evidence for a "gender gap" between men and women in their use of tobacco, alcohol, and illicit drugs. Since the early 1960s, men typically reported using these substances at higher rates than women and were more likely than women to be heavy users of such substances and to report symptoms indicative of alcohol and drug abuse or dependence disorders (U.S. General Accounting Office, 1991).

Historically, this has not always been the case. Before the Civil War, for example, 60 to 75 percent of opium-morphine addicts were women (Courtwright, 1982). Moreover, while current rates of substance use and abuse for women are still lower than for men, their numbers are large and growing, thus the gap between men and women is narrowing (Substance Abuse and Mental Health Services Administration [SAMHSA], 1996; Almog, Anglin, and Fisher, 1993; Boyd and Mieczkowski, 1990; Zimmer-Hofler and Dobler-Mikola, 1992). Recent studies reveal that 21.5 million women smoke (CASA, 1996). Alcohol consumption among women has become the rule rather than the exception, with half the women of childbearing age (fifteen to forty-four years old) indicating that they are "current" consumers of alcohol, meaning that they had consumed alcohol in the past month (Centers for Disease Control and Prevention, 1997a). In 1995, nearly as many women (45 percent) in this same age group reported they had used an illicit drug at least once in their lives (SAMHSA, 1996). Overall, one in three women report lifetime use of at least one illicit drug, a rate similar to that for the general population in the United States aged twelve and over (SAMHSA, 1996).

Perhaps more important is recent evidence that, for teenagers, the gender gap has disappeared (CASA, 1996; SAMHSA, 1996). Teenage girls and boys (ages twelve through seventeen) are equally likely to smoke, and female college students are more likely than their male colleagues to smoke.

Girls in the teenage group are also more likely than boys to report using prescription drugs such as tranquilizers, sedatives, and stimulants for nonmedical purposes (SAMHSA, 1996). The percentages of adolescent girls and boys who drink or use illicit drugs are also similar. Approximately one in four twelfth graders and one in eight eighth graders is a "current" drug user (Johnston, 1997). About half (49.6 percent) of high school seniors report having used marijuana, the most commonly used illicit drug, at least once in their lives (Johnston, 1997).

Studies conducted during the periods between 1961 and 1965 and 1986 and 1990 indicated that girls typically initiated alcohol use at later ages than did boys. Between 1991 and 1995, however, evidence reveals gender differences in the age of first use of alcohol disappeared. Both males and females reported that they began drinking at fifteen years of age and began smoking at an even younger age (thirteen years old). In 1996, about one in five youths aged twelve through seventeen indicated they were "current users" of alcohol or cigarettes, reporting that they had used alcohol or smoked cigarettes in the past month (SAMHSA, 1997). Nearly one-third (31 percent) of high school seniors reported binge drinking, defined as having consumed five or more drinks in a row, and one-fourth reported daily cigarette smoking (Johnston, 1997).

Over the past three decades the changes in use behavior among girls in the ten-to-fourteen-year-old age group have been particularly startling. Data from the 1960s revealed that, among girls, about 7 percent of new users of alcohol were in the ten-through-fourteen-year-old age group. By comparison, in the early 1990s, nearly one-third (31 percent) of girls identified as new users of alcohol were in this age group. Rates of first-time marijuana use among girls have demonstrated a similar trajectory, increasing from 5 percent of ten-to-fourteen-year-olds in the early 1960s to 25 percent in the early 1990s (SAMHSA, 1996).

Although prevalence rates for substance abuse disorders are difficult to determine, estimates are that 11.3 percent of the U.S. population abuses or is dependent on alcohol or other drugs based on epidemiological studies using the DSM III-R criteria for these disorders (Kessler et al., 1994; Rouse, 1995).

> Alcohol abuse is manifested by recurrent alcohol use despite significant adverse consequences of drinking, such as problems with work, law, health or family life. The diagnosis of alcohol dependence is based on the compulsion to drink. The dependent drinker devotes substantial time to obtaining alcohol, drinking and recovering, and continues to drink despite adverse social, psychologic, or medical conse-

quences. A physiologic dependence on alcohol, marked by tolerance or withdrawal symptoms, may or may not be present. (Burge and Schneider, 1999, p. 3)

About 5 percent (4.7 percent) of the U.S. general population qualifies for a "current" (within the past year) diagnosis of alcohol abuse and fewer (3.8 percent) qualify for a diagnosis of current alcohol dependence (Grant, 1994). Prevalence rates for alcohol abuse and dependence tend to be higher than rates for abuse and dependence of other drugs (Regier et al., 1990; Anthony, Arria, and Johnson, 1995).

In sum, then, epidemiological data suggest that AOD use is commonplace among women, especially among teens. Although too little data yet exist about the impact of substance use on women, some evidence suggests that women are more susceptible to negative consequences of use. For example, while research indicates that men may derive health benefits from regularly consuming small quantities of alcohol, women may be placed at risk by adopting the same pattern of consumption. Thus, "moderate drinking" for women is less than one drink per day compared to no more than two drinks per day for men (National Heart, Lung, and Blood Institute, 1996). Women are also more likely than men to become addicted to cigarette smoking and may find it more difficult to quit (National Cancer Institute, 1996; National Institute on Drug Abuse, 1999). There is also evidence suggesting that women may be biologically predisposed to develop dependence on particular illicit substances more rapidly than do men (NIDA, 1999). Of course, more research is needed to provide conclusive support for these findings and to better understand the risks facing women who use various substances.

The impact of substance use on women also appears to change with age, with indications that women over age fifty-nine are particularly vulnerable to alcohol abuse and the addictive properties of psychoactive prescription medications (CASA, 1998b). Women sixty and older are far more likely than their male counterparts to be prescribed psychoactive medications, such as sedatives or antidepressants. This is consistent with findings that older women are typically prescribed more medications of all types than are older men (Abrams and Alexopoulos, 1987). The common misperception that AOD-related problems are men's problems may increase the risk to women that these problems go unrecognized and untreated. Primary care physicians are prone to misdiagnose symptoms of alcohol abuse among women as depression, prescribing medications that are potentially lethal when mixed with alcohol (CASA, 1998b).

DIFFERENCES IN THE "ADDICTION CAREERS" OF MEN AND WOMEN

Despite the paucity of research regarding the etiology of substance use and abuse in women, evidence exists that men and women acquire and exhibit alcohol and drug abuse problems differently, and that they present distinct characteristics and experiences that may be implicated at the onset and through the course of AOD-related disorders and recovery. Women with substance abuse problems are more likely than men to be unemployed, tend to be less educated, and have fewer marketable skills, fewer work experiences, and fewer resources available to them (Beckman and Amaro, 1986; Marsh and Miller, 1985; Reed, 1985). While men often tend to externalize their AOD problems by driving drunk, fighting, or displaying anger or aggression in some way, women's symptoms tend to be more "inner directed" (CASA, 1996). For example, women with substance abuse disorders are more likely than men to use drugs in isolation (Marsh and Miller, 1985). Women are also more likely than men to express symptoms indicative of a coexisting disorder such as depression, anxiety, panic disorder, personality disorder, eating disorders, or post-traumatic-stress disorder (PTSD) (SAMHSA, 1996; Blume, 1990; NIDA, 1999).

Perhaps one of the most striking features evident from studies of women with AOD-related problems is the large percentage who have been physically or sexually abused as children, or who have been victims of violence as adults (Fullilove et al., 1993; Fullilove, Lown, and Fullilove, 1992; Wyatt, 1985; Wallen, 1992; Boyd, Blow, and Orgain, 1993; NIDA, 1994, 1999; Nurco et al., 1995; Thompson and Kingree, 1998). Estimates for a history of sexual abuse vary greatly, ranging from 30 to 75 percent among women with substance abuse problems. Such variation in rates can be attributed to a number of issues—including differences in the characteristics of the samples being surveyed, the definitions of abuse used by researchers, and the level of trust established between clients and those gathering information about sexual abuse.

Even the lowest figures in this range suggest, however, that sexual abuse and related trauma are key factors contributing to women's drug abuse (Chiavaroli, 1992; Davis, 1990; Root, 1989; Thompson and Kingree, 1998; NIDA, 1999). In one study, women with histories of sexual assault were more than twice as likely to have alcohol or drug abuse or dependence disorders than a matched sample of women who had not been victimized (Burnam et al., 1988), suggesting that substance abuse problems among women may represent efforts to cope with trauma (Boyd, 1993). Unfortunately, women who abuse substances are often at increased risk of assault, raising the possibility that efforts to cope with previous violence through the use of substances will result in subsequent abuse. This is particularly true for women who engage in drug trafficking and/or prostitution, two illegal activities commonly associated with both substance abuse and violence (Fullilove, Lown, and Fullilove, 1992).

Evidence also suggests that given the social context of women's lives "family relationships are more salient in the addiction careers of women than men" (Henderson, 1998, p. 581). Interpersonal relationships with family, friends, and significant others may have greater influence on women's substance use, abuse, recovery, and relapse than on men's. Evidence indicates that women are more influenced than men by their parents' substance abuse (Wilsnack and Wilsnack, 1990; Boyd et al., 1994), and that their own use closely resembles that of their parents, especially their mothers (Boyd, Blow, and Orgain, 1993). Partners, friends, and family members may also have a great deal of influence over the initial decision by women to use substances (Hser, Anglin, and McGlothlin, 1987; Rosenbaum, 1981a,b; Eldred and Washington, 1975; Henderson and Boyd, 1992; Henderson, Boyd, and Mieczkowski, 1994). Women with substance abuse problems are more likely to live with a spouse who abuses alcohol than are men (Marsh and Miller, 1985). Relationships with significant others also often have a negative impact on women's decisions to enter or to stay in treatment (Beckman and Amaro, 1986; Copeland et al., 1993). More specifically, many women, when faced with opposition from partners and spouses, may decline to seek or remain in treatment for substance abuse problems (Beckman and Amaro, 1986).

Differential Access and Utilization of Substance Abuse Services by Men and Women

Given lower reported rates of substance use and abuse among women in the 1960s, 1970s, and 1980s, it is not surprising that women have comprised much smaller percentages of those in treatment than men. In part, the smaller number of women in treatment has reflected the traditional gender gap in patterns of substance use and abuse. It also reflects a gender gap in access and utilization of substance abuse treatment services by women. Women are underrepresented in substance abuse treatment settings in proportion to the occurrence of disorders among them. Although women are more likely than men to use health care services, they are less likely than their male counterparts to seek treatment for substance abuse problems (Blume, 1990; Finklestein, 1994; Weisner and Schmidt, 1992; Wells and Jackson, 1992). Evidence suggests that "the greater social sanctions and stigma that drug-using women face compared with men, including concerns regarding the loss of custody of their children, have made women less willing to seek help and treatment of addictive disorders" (Blumenthal, 1998, p. 21).

The representation of substance abuse as a man's problem is not only a reflection of traditional differences in patterns of abuse but is also indicative of the "gendering" of symptoms and behaviors associated with such disorders. The assignment of substance abuse problems to the male realm enlarges the chasm that women must traverse in admitting to themselves and others that they are experiencing such problems. Moreover, substance abuse by pregnant or parenting women is often viewed as more deviant than drug or alcohol abuse by those not responsible for small children (Finkelstein, 1994). It is not surprising, then, that once labeled as addict or alcoholic, a woman's status as mother is called into question.

Gender differences in seeking help for AOD-related problems may also reflect women's unwillingness to participate in treatment that fails to recognize and address their special needs. Such difficulties are compounded for female adolescents who are similarly disadvantaged by lack of availability of treatment that is both gender specific and sensitive to developmental issues associated with substance use and abuse among adolescents.

Women in need of substance abuse treatment are also often disadvantaged by the fact that they earn less money than men, even when performing the same or comparable work. Women are more likely than men to occupy part-time or seasonal positions, or to work in low-wage jobs that do not provide workers with insurance coverage or sufficient income to pay out-of-pocket expenses for behavioral health care treatment (Blumenthal, 1998). Women who are financially dependent on spouses or partners may also be especially disadvantaged in pursuing recovery by partners who undermine their efforts to seek and complete treatment (Beckman and Amaro, 1986).

Many women with AOD-related problems are primary caregivers for minor children, and lack of affordable child care may be a barrier to entering or remaining in treatment (Reed, 1987). Lack of transportation or safe housing and sexual harassment in male-dominated treatment settings also pose barriers to women's participation in substance abuse treatment (Nelson-Zlupko et al., 1996; NIDA, 1999).

POLICIES OF NEGLECT AND PUNISHMENT TOWARD WOMEN WITH SUBSTANCE ABUSE PROBLEMS

Lack of access by women to substance abuse treatment, in particular women-centered treatment, is part of a long-standing pattern of neglect toward women with AOD-related problems. Estimates are that 200,000 women in the United States die of substance abuse-related illnesses each year. "The growing morbidity and mortality rates from the addictive disorders in women are preventable tragedies demanding greater attention in research, service delivery, public policy, and education" (Blumenthal, 1998, p. 1). Increasing evidence suggests that women may be inherently predisposed to experience more negative consequences from their use of substances. For example, death rates among female alcoholics are 50 to 100 percent higher than they are for male alcoholics; in addition, female alcoholics are more likely than their male counterparts to die from suicide, alcohol-related accidents, circulatory disorders, and cirrhosis of the liver (Hill, 1982).

Welfare Reform and the Poverty Penalty

For many women the response to their use and abuse of substances exceeds neglect to encompass a variety of negative sanctions aimed at punishment. This punishment has been most strongly directed at poor women. Debate surrounding Clinton's promise to "end welfare as we know it" took shape amid increasingly negative characterizations of poverty (as a condition produced by an underclass of undeserving women who eschewed traditional values of marriage, work, and family). Representations about what is blameworthy among the poor have varied over time. They include attributions of moral failure, portraying the poor as weak-willed—choosing to live a life of sloth or debauchery, especially if alcohol or drug use is involved (Katz, 1989). The poor may also be characterized as lacking ability, desire, motivation, or—in the most recent variation on this theme—as belonging to a culture of poverty that limits their imagination and thwarts their will to achieve (Murray, 1984; Mead, 1986). In the process of vilifying poor women, "policymakers have increasingly attributed key problems of the welfare system, such as welfare dependency and the poor job prospects of recipients, to alcohol and drug addiction" (Schmidt, Weisner, and Wiley, 1998, p. 1616).

Welfare reform, culminating in passage of the 1996 Personal Responsibility and Work Opportunity Reconciliation Act (PRWORA), transformed Aid to Families with Dependent Children (AFDC) from an entitlement program into the time-limited program of Temporary Assistance to Needy Families (TANF). The full repercussions of this legislation have not yet been realized as millions of U.S. residents, most of them women and their children, are just reaching the limits of their lifetime eligibility for use of TANF subsidies and face termination from the welfare roles.

Although this legislation places large groups of the poor at risk, women who have substance abuse problems are especially vulnerable to welfare reform legislation on several counts, as are their children. First, key provisions of PRWORA direct states to deny assistance to recipients with felony convictions for drug offenses, making them ineligible for TANF or food stamps for life. Second, PRWORA provides states with the option to test recipients for illegal drugs and to impose sanctions on those who test positive. Recipients of public assistance may also be sanctioned for failure to comply with mandates that they participate in assessment and treatment for alcohol and other drug problems. Similar efforts have been undertaken by county providers of general assistance to mandate receipt of substance abuse treatment for persons with substance abuse disorders (Schmidt, Weisner, and Wiley, 1998).

Much of this increasingly punitive approach toward poor women with AOD-related problems stems from "a weak base of data and research regarding the overall burden of alcohol and drug problems on the welfare system" (Schmidt, Weisner, and Wiley, 1998, p. 1616). Studies to date have demonstrated widely varied prevalence rates among welfare recipients in federal programs (Salomon, Bassuk, and Brooks, 1996; CASA, 1994). In one study conducted by CASA (1994), researchers asserted that one-fourth (27 percent) of women receiving Aid to Families with Dependent Children were addicted to alcohol and drugs, compared to 9 percent of women not receiving welfare. Among eighteen-to-twenty-four-year-old women on welfare, they estimated that the proportion was even greater, with one in three reporting alcohol or drug abuse or dependence.

More recently, however, researchers examining data from the National Longitudinal Alcohol Epidemiologic Survey (NLAES) reported that rates of alcohol and drug use and abuse among welfare recipients were relatively low and comparable to rates in the general population and to U.S. citizens not receiving assistance (Grant and Dawson, 1996). Longitudinal data obtained from representative samples of AFDC and general-assistance recipient groups over a six-year period in California revealed that, among AFDC recipients, rates of problem drinking were comparable to those obtained for the general population. Rates of heavy drug use and alcohol or drug dependence were somewhat higher, however. General-assistance recipients, on the other hand, were far more likely than the general population or AFDC recipients to report such problems (Schmidt, Weisner, and Wiley, 1998). This study also demonstrated that, for AFDC recipients, there was no relationship between substance abuse and length of stay on welfare, repeated use of welfare, or the total amount of time recipients remained on welfare during the six-year study period. Substance abuse was, however, associated with repeat use of welfare for general-assistance recipients.

Existing studies suggest that substance abuse, at least among federal welfare recipients, is not as widespread as indicated by popular portrayals—nor does it appear to cause welfare dependency for the vast majority of AFDC or TANF recipients. Poverty has long been associated with increased risk for both substance abuse and mental health problems, however, and the relationship between poverty and behavioral health problems seems more complex than can be captured by any simple, unilinear model of cause and effect.

To be sure, welfare recipients who have substance abuse problems are doubly disadvantaged by the combination of poverty and substance abuse. This is especially true for poor, single mothers struggling to make the most of limited personal and material resources to meet the challenges of work and family. Substance abuse can be a major impediment to job readiness and can undermine the capacity of welfare recipients to establish and maintain a stable living situation (CASA, 1994; Schmidt, Weisner, and Wiley, 1998). As caseloads shrink, TANF recipients facing health and behavioral-health problems—in addition to limitations imposed by lack of education, transportation, and child care—are likely to be left behind. These women, and their children, are increasingly vulnerable if they exhaust lifetime eligibility limits for receipt of TANF before addressing the complex array of problems that inhibit their ability to move into the labor market. As indicated previously, poor women who have substance abuse problems are also at risk for loss of eligibility if they are caught using substances while receiving assistance or if they are convicted of a drug-related felony. Evidence suggests that these women may not understand their rights of due process and review when sanctioned, and many are not aware of benefits and supports available to their children even when they are under sanction or otherwise ineligible for services (Lukens and Pokempner, 2000). TANF recipients are not likely to receive appropriate assistance from service providers in an environment of service delivery marked by increasingly complex eligibility rules—rules that vary at both the state and local levels and change over time. Too often states and providers have contributed to the confusion by providing too few procedural safeguards, by maintaining insufficient standards and inadequate oversight of program staff, and by permitting caseworkers to disseminate too little or even incorrect information to TANF recipients (Lukens and Pokempner, 2000; Welfare Law Center, 2000; Fernandez et al., 2000).

The circumstances of poor women with substance abuse problems are made worse by the fact that they have fewer options for support from other federal and state sources. For example, in 1997 federal legislation placed restrictions on eligibility for Supplemental Security Income (SSI) and Social Security Disability Insurance (SSDI) by persons with disabilities exclusively due to substance abuse. In addition, although welfare reform has resulted in increased use of screening and referral to substance abuse treatment, it is not clear that the existing service system is prepared to respond to this increased demand—particularly when it comes to providing free treatment services or services that are truly women centered.

The Prison Solution

The increased association between substance abuse and welfare dependence has coincided with a decade-long escalation in prohibitionist sentiment in the United States. This latest wave of antidrug sentiment was marked by a shift away from policies emphasizing a view of substance abuse as an illness, for which persons are entitled to receive treatment, to policies of punishment and control (Burke, 1992). During the 1960s and 1970s in the United States, an effort was made to increase the availability of publicly funded treatment for substance abuse, to decriminalize public drunkenness and addiction, and to divert persons with substance abuse problems from jails and prisons to community treatment settings. By the early 1980s, however, the War on Drugs had reinvigorated a moralistic view of substance use and abuse as intentionally irresponsible and malicious behavior. Campaigns urging communities to practice "zero tolerance" and admonishing citizens to "just say no" to drug use sparked what has become a national preoccupation with law enforcement as a means to control substance use.

As a result, the number of women incarcerated for drug-related problems has increased dramatically. Estimates are that between 1980 and 1996 the U.S. prison population tripled from 500,000 to 1.7 million. By 1997 one in 155 U.S. residents was incarcerated (Gilliard and Beck, 1998). Convictions for drug-law violations accounted for nearly three-fourths of the increase in the federal prison population between 1985 and 1995, and during the same period of time the number of inmates incarcerated for drug violations in state prisons increased by nearly 500 percent (Office of National Drug Control Policy, 1998). By the end of 1996, women accounted for 6.3 percent of this burgeoning population of federal and state inmates (U.S. Department of Justice, 1997). The number of women arrested for drug offenses increased by 89 percent from 1982 to 1991 (Federal Bureau of Investigation, 1992). While the number of men in federal, state, and local prisons increased by 229 percent between 1980 and 1996, the number of women increased by 439 percent from 24,180 to 130,430 (CASA, 1998a).

The typical female inmate is young, poor, a woman of color, and a single mother (Henderson, 1998). In 1991, most women in state prisons were thirty-one years of age or younger; about two-thirds (64 percent) were women of color, had never been married (43 percent); or were separated or divorced (32 percent); and more than half (53 percent) were unemployed prior to their incarceration (U.S. Department of Justice, 1994). Incarcerated women are more likely than women in the general population to have a history of mental illness, substance abuse, and physical or sexual abuse (Jordan et al., 1996; Teplin, Abram, and McLelland, 1996; Ladwig and Anderson, 1989; Sargent, Marcus-Mendoza, and Ho Yu, 1993). Incarcerated women are five to twenty-five times more likely than women in the general population to have a substance abuse disorder, depending on the type of disorder examined (Jordan et al., 1996). Estimates are that between 36 and 80 percent of incarcerated women have substance abuse problems (National Institute of Justice, 1992; Schilling et al., 1994; Singer et al., 1995). As with estimates for rates of childhood victimization among women with substance abuse problems, these ranges are wide. Such wide-ranging estimates make it difficult to calculate unmet need, to plan for treatment, and to estimate the costs associated with meeting the needs of women with substance abuse problems in the prison system. Nevertheless, even the lowest estimates point to the need to screen for alcohol and other drug problems routinely and to expand the availability of substance abuse treatment for incarcerated women. Treatment is also important for incarcerated women because alcohol- and drug-related problems are major factors associated with violations of parole and the commitment of subsequent offenses (CASA, 1998a; Henderson, 1998).

Despite these figures indicating that alcohol and other drug abuse is widespread among female offenders, little assistance is provided to them. Only 20 percent of the $17 billion federal drug control budget is spent on drug and alcohol treatment (ONDCP, 1998). Although the number of prisoners who need treatment for alcohol and drug abuse has continued to grow, the proportion of prisoners who actually receive treatment has declined. In 1997 only 18 percent of offenders who used drugs at the time of their offense were receiving treatment compared to 40 percent in 1991 (CASA, 1998a). In 1996, only 13 percent of state inmates were in any sort of treatment, and evidence indicates that the number who received treatment actually declined between 1995 and 1996 (CASA, 1998a).

Even in prison women cannot escape added penalties for being female. Since the early 1980s concerns have been raised about a gender gap in the prison system revealing that "women in correctional institutions are not provided with comparable services, educational programs, or facilities as male prisoners" (U.S. General Accounting Office, 1980, p. 7). Perhaps even more alarming is the increased recognition that women in prisons who have substance abuse problems are also vulnerable to sexual harassment and assault by prison guards, and they may fall prey to guards who supply inmates with drugs in exchange for sex. Amnesty International and other human rights groups have called attention to the plight of inmates who become victims of sexual assault in prisons. Between 1991 and 1998 the number of states with legislation prohibiting sexual contact between inmates and correctional officers increased from seven to thirty-eight (Governor's Commission on Women, 2000). In addition, in 1998 the Bureau of Prisons began training corrections facility staff regarding new policies and procedures to recognize, prevent, and report sexual abuse of inmates (Federal Bureau of Prisons, 1999).

BRINGING AN END TO VICIOUS CYCLES AND DOWNWARD SPIRALS

Making Up the Distance in Research

It is important to note how little definitive research yet exists to indicate clearly the prevalence of various substance abuse disorders among subgroups of women, such as those on welfare or in prison. Nor is it clear how exposure to poverty, violence, and other forms of discrimination and victimization interact to increase risk for substance abuse problems. Further research on the etiology and course of substance abuse among women seems likely given recent federal initiatives aimed at increasing research on women's health and well-being. Such initiatives hold out some hope of redressing ignorance and misunderstanding resulting from long-standing apathy and neglect toward research on the etiology and course of AOD problems among women.

Clearly more information is needed about the biological and psychosocial risk factors associated with substance abuse among women. In particular, effort is needed to better understand the role played by violence and abuse in the etiology of their substance abuse disorders. In addition, "given the high level of trauma among substance-abusing women, research is particularly needed regarding the role of trauma in their treatment outcomes" (Thompson and Kingree, 1998, p. 258). Future research on the etiology and course of AOD-related problems among women must make a concerted effort to focus more attention on various subgroups of women including women of color, older women, poor women, and incarcerated women.

Drug-Policy Reform to Decriminalize Use and Expand Treatment

Probably no single strategy would have a more positive impact on women with substance abuse problems than a return to a drug policy aimed at decriminalizing use and redirecting the huge sums of money required to arrest, convict, and imprison women toward increasing the availability of treatment. Although the current mass incarceration of men and women is typical of the "history of criminal justice decision making in the United States [which] has often been described as a chronicle of missed opportunities, failed experiments, and arbitrary and misguided judgments" (Inciardi, 1998, p. 2), no rational argument can be made for the use of law enforcement as a means for reducing or eliminating drug use and abuse among women. Imprisonment provides no guarantee that an individual will abstain from the use of licit or illicit substances since many incarcerated individuals continue to use substances even while imprisoned. In the absence of treatment it is unlikely that persons prevented from using substances while imprisoned will maintain their sobriety upon release. Moreover, a good deal of evidence indicates that treatment is not only more effective than incarceration for reducing or eliminating substance abuse problems, but also it can do so at a much lower cost (SAMHSA, 1998).

Women-Centered Approaches to Prevention and Treatment

Although drug-policy reform aimed at expanding treatment is an important part of the effort to limit the harm to women caused by AOD use and abuse, more is needed. In order to be more effective, prevention and treatment programs for girls and women must be appropriate to their gender status, paying more attention to the social and economic circumstances that confront women. Women-centered prevention and treatment efforts must also address the context and conditions associated with AOD-related problems for women over the life course.

Evidence suggests that existing campaigns aimed at preventing the use of alcohol, tobacco, and other drugs do not appear to be targeting young women effectively, since young women (twelve through seventeen years old) are not showing the same rate of decrease in substance abuse as other segments of the population. Their use of alcohol and drugs has, in fact, increased slightly in recent years, eliminating the gender gap in substance use between teenage males and females (SAMHSA, 1992; National Center for Health Statistics, 1996). Lack of attention to prevention and the ways that diseases manifest in women also account for the fact that women are the fastest growing group infected with HIV (Karon et al., 1996). Teenage girls are closing the HIV infection gender gap with teenage males at an alarming rate (Maternal and Child Health Bureau, 1996). Nearly two-thirds of all female AIDS cases have occurred in women who were either injection drug users or were exposed to HIV through sexual contact with an injection drug user (CDC, 1997b). Given the apparent impact of social relationships on use and recovery among women, more attention to strategies that focus on the promotion of positive peer-group associations and interpersonal skills would seem to be especially valuable to women.

Prevention campaigns aimed at young women must be tailored to their concerns and vulnerabilities (CASA, 1996). More specifically, women-centered prevention programming must address the links between smoking, the use of other drugs by young women, and their concerns about body image and thinness directly (CASA, 1996). To be effective, such efforts must focus on how to provide girls with "greater support and a more empowered view of their future during their vulnerable teen years" (Chavez, 1997, p. 1). This means not just educating young women about the dangers associated with women's use of substances and enhancing their ability to resist pressure from media and peers to use then, but also creating safer, more supportive, and resourceful environments for them.

Older women may also stand to benefit from women-centered prevention messages that more clearly communicate that lung cancer, heart disease, and stroke are not only men's problems. Among older women, rates of lung cancer and chronic pulmonary diseases continue to climb, whereas they have begun to decline for men (National Cancer Institute, 1996). Moreover, older women can benefit from better information about changes in their ability to use substances as they age and potential interactions among alcohol, over-the-counter, and prescription drugs.

Advocating on behalf of women's rights and forging links to violence-prevention efforts can reduce economic dependence and abuse among women, perhaps preventing the victimization of women and associated substance abuse problems. Continuing efforts aimed at changing community norms and police response to domestic violence, incest, and rape can prevent both the primary and secondary or categorical victimization of women by challenging their subordinate status as victims directly. Increasing opportunities for educational attainment and occupational mobility are essential to securing economic independence and self-sufficiency for women. Greater economic opportunity for women can reduce vulnerability rooted in dependence on social and interpersonal bonds that limit their ability to make choices about substance use and to afford treatment when they need it. Thus, prevention efforts for women must take a more comprehensive approach, addressing a broader range of issues including "primary health care, violence, HIV/AIDS and other social and economic issues that impact the quality of lives of women" (Chavez, 1997, p. 2).

Evidence also indicates that the substance abuse treatment system must change.

> Little awareness exists among health care professionals regarding sex-based differences in physiology and cultural environment that may place women at risk of substance abuse: physical and sexual abuse, poverty, anxiety and depression resulting from multiple roles as care-givers and wage earners, issues of poor self-esteem and dead-end employment (or no employment at all), low educational attainment, and specific life stresses such as single parenthood, divorce and loneliness. (Blumenthal, 1998, p. 22)

Women-centered services must begin with a comprehensive assessment that takes into account the full range of circumstances surrounding women's substance use. This information can then be used to assist in treatment planning and matching of female clients to the most appropriate level of care and treatment approach (Inciardi, 1998). Assessment and treatment planning must focus on gathering information needed to establish a better understanding of factors that can affect addicted women's recoveries including inherent predispositions, concerns related to gender role and relationships with family members, and peers and significant others who may inhibit or promote their recovery (Henderson, 1998). For example, smoking cessation efforts may be less successful among women than men "given fears of weight gain, reduced social support for smoking cessation, greater impact of advertising on women, increased addictive properties of nicotine on women" (see Blumenthal, 1998, p. 20). Moreover, assessment and treatment planning must address child care concerns which are among the most important factors impinging on women's entry and retention in treatment (Nelson-Zlupko et al., 1996).

Despite increasing evidence for the prevalence of sexual abuse and domestic violence experiences among women with substance abuse disorders, too little effort is yet made by most treatment settings to assess or address these issues. Moreover, symptoms of PTSD may be a "hidden factor that hinders treatment response or increases the likelihood of relapse" (Hien and Levin, 1994, p. 421). Similarly, women-centered-treatment settings must pay attention to the possibility that women with substance abuse problems may have other coexisting conditions such as depression, anxiety, or an eating disorder. Improved services to women will inevitably require better training of existing health care and service professionals so they are more knowledgeable about women's vulnerability to substance use and can more easily recognize and respond to their needs.

Targeting Especially Disadvantaged Women

Women who are already deeply disadvantaged by the combination of substance abuse problems with poverty and/or incarceration are likely to need even more assistance if they are to curtail the vicious cycles of victimization and revictimization associated with their substance abuse problems. For example, policies that sanction women for using substances by withdrawing assistance through TANF and other social service programs are counterproductive. Such actions undermine efforts aimed at creating greater stability in the lives of poor women, supporting their recovery from substance abuse, and encouraging progress toward self-sufficiency (Schmidt, Weisner, and Wiley, 1998). Sanctions against women with substance abuse problems may reflect a fundamental lack of understanding about the chronic and relapsing nature of substance abuse disorders. Even with periodic relapses, treatment can improve the well-being and circumstances of women with AOD problems and, in the long run, can improve their odds of sustaining recovery.

Until policy change brings about the return of incarcerated women with substance abuse problems to their communities, an effort must be made to close the gap in state and federal prisons "between available substance abuse treatment—and inmate participation—and the need for such treatment" which is "enormous and widening" (CASA, 1998a, p. 10). This means providing women with more appropriate services that deal with gender-specific issues and that also more fully address the circumstances associated with their incarceration. Learning more about the drug practices of women during incarceration and during their transition back into the community can aid in the development of better strategies for treating women within the institution and can allow for better coordination of care during the transition back into the community (Henderson, 1998).

FINDING THE WILL TO CHANGE WOMEN'S LIVES

In the current political climate, little apparent concern exists for the fate of poor women, especially those who develop problems with substance abuse or the legal system. Historically, social welfare policy in the United States has demonstrated a long-standing tradition of providing differential assistance to those deemed "deserving" and "undeserving." It is difficult to identify another era in U.S. history, however, where so few have been deemed deserving of so little, or where those regarded as undeserving have been so thoroughly characterized as without value. Under such circumstances, what impetus for change is there that can benefit marginalized women, particularly those in triple jeopardy from a past marked by poverty, substance abuse, and incarceration?

Although poor women have been written off by many as unworthy of further investment, particularly when they have failed to heed the directive that they "just say no" to drugs and have developed substance abuse problems, there are advocates at large who remember that these women are often mothers. Nationally, a number of child advocacy groups have taken steps to defend the rights of poor children. These groups have sponsored initiatives aimed at refocusing the debate about welfare on the large proportion of welfare recipients who are children and, through no fault of their own, are endangered not only by poverty but by welfare reform initiatives that sanction their parents. This child-centered approach to poverty policy and intervention has the potential to rekindle awareness for the central importance of welfare as a means for targeting children to limit the harm associated with poverty. Such a strategy may also renew appreciation for the value of parent-child bonds and family ties, particularly in the context of an approach that emphasizes family resilience and strengths (cf. Knitzer, 2000). Singly and in combination, advocacy groups (such as the National Center for Children in Poverty, the Children's Defense Fund, the Urban Institute, and the National Child Welfare League) have intensified efforts to influence federal and state policy on behalf of poor children and their mothers. Some state and local welfare authorities have shown a willingness and ability to approach welfare reform with flexibility, introducing innovations and allocating additional funds to improve outcomes for poor families (such as expanded benefits through state Earned-Income Tax Credits).

In addition, the substance abuse treatment system, including leadership within the national institutes, has stepped up efforts to document the effectiveness of treatment as an alternative to incarceration for drug-related problems. They have also become increasingly aware of the need to develop a more solid research base of evidence regarding the effective treatment for various subgroups including women and adolescents, as well as members of diverse ethnic groups and inmates. Along with increased emphasis on making sure that research and evaluation studies encompass greater diversity, they have also recognized the need to get away from a "one-size-fits-all" view of alcohol and drug treatment and to redress the lack of attention paid to women's issues by the substance abuse treatment delivery system (Blumenthal, 1998).

With a strong tradition of consumer participation, the substance abuse treatment system also provides avenues for women to advocate on their own behalf through a variety of mutual assistance and self-help initiatives. Such self-help efforts could be particularly effective if combined with other grassroots activities focused on community and workforce development, advocating for the homeless, organizing workers in low-wage jobs, and protecting the human rights of current and former inmates. In the current political context, with the devolution of policymaking to state and local authorities, such advocacy efforts will have to be directed at a much larger number of targets in order to achieve meaningful change. In the wake of welfare reform and drug policy dominated by law-enforcement approaches, advocates for poor women and female inmates have turned to the court systems to address grievances and violations of rights. As the numbers of incarcerated persons has grown, federal and state courts have been called upon to step in and take actions aimed at protecting the rights of prisoners from overcrowding, from sexual assault, and other forms of victimization. Court orders have mandated greater attention to screening and treatment for sex offenders and inmates with learning disabilities and other behavioral health disorders. Further elucidation by the courts regarding protections provided to persons with substance abuse problems by the Americans with Disabilities Act may also provide new avenues for assistance to women with alcohol and other drug problems in welfare and correctional systems. Courts are increasingly being called upon to test the validity of procedures used to determine eligibility for welfare benefits or to mete out sanctions (cf. Welfare Law Center, 2000).

Needless to say, changes brought about for the members of the diverse groups identified here are likely to be hard won. For the short term at least, successful social action on behalf of women marginalized by substance abuse, poverty, and incarceration seem more likely to be achieved through dozens or even hundreds of small, incremental changes, rather than sweeping national reform. Moreover, in the fragmented, new federalist political economy of the early twenty-first century one of the greatest challenges for those who are able to achieve positive changes for marginalized women will be to consolidate gains and disseminate information about success in an effort to counter what has become a "crazy quilt" of differential outcomes and opportunities for marginalized women.

REFERENCES

Abrams, Robert C. and George S. Alexopoulos. 1987. Substance Abuse in the Elderly: Alcohol and Prescription Drugs. *Hospital and Community Psychiatry 38* (12): 1285-1287.

Almog, Yishai J., M. Douglas Anglin, and Dennis G. Fisher. 1993. Alcohol and Heroin Use Patterns of Narcotics Addicts: Gender and Ethnic Differences. *American Journal of Drug Alcohol Abuse 19*(2): 219-238.

Anthony, James G., Amelia M. Arria, and Eric O. Johnson. 1995. Epidemiology and Public Health Issues for Tobacco, Alcohol and Other Drugs. In John M.

Oldham and Michelle B. Riba (Eds.), *Review of Psychiatry* Vol. 14 (pp. 15-46). Washington, DC: American Psychiatric Press.

Beckman, Linda J. and Hortensia Amaro. 1986. Personal and Social Difficulties Faced by Women and Men Entering Alcoholism Treatment. *Journal of Studies on Alcohol 47*(2): 134-145.

Blume, Sheila. 1990. Chemical Dependency in Women: Important Issues. *American Journal of Drug Alcohol Abuse 16:* 297-307.

Blumenthal, Susan J. 1998. Women and Substance Abuse: A New National Focus. In Cora Lee Wetherington and Adele B. Roman (Eds.), *Drug Addiction Research and the Health of Women* (pp. 13-33). Rockville, MD: National Institute on Drug Abuse. Available online: <http://www.nida.nih.gov>.

Boyd, Carol J. 1993. The Antecedents of Women's Crack Cocaine Abuse: Family Substance Abuse, Sexual Abuse, Depression and Illicit Drug Use. *Journal of Substance Abuse Treatment 10*(5): 433-438.

Boyd, Carol J., Frederic Blow, and Linda Orgain. 1993. Gender Differences Among African-American Substance Abusers. *Journal of Psychoactive Drugs 25*(4): 301-305.

Boyd, Carol J., Barbara Guthrie, Joanne Pohl, Jason Whitmarsh, and Dorothy Henderson. 1994. African-American Women Who Smoke Crack: Sexual Trauma and the Mother-Daughter Relationship. *Journal of Psychoactive Drugs 26*(3): 243-247.

Boyd, Carol J. and Thomas Mieczkowski. 1990. Drug Use, Health, Family and Social Support in "Crack" Cocaine Users. *Addictive Behaviors 15*(4): 481-485.

Burge, Sandra K. and F. David Schneider. 1999. Alcohol-Related Problems: Recognition and Intervention. *American Family Physician* January 15. Available online: <http://www.aafp.org/afp/990115ap/361.html>.

Burke, Anna C. 1992. Between Entitlement and Control: Dimensions of U.S. Drug Policy. *Social Service Review 66*(4): 571-581.

Burnam, M. Audrey, Judith A. Stein, Jacqueline M. Golding, Judith M. Siegel, Susan, B. Sorenson, Alan B. Forsythe, and Cynthia A. Telles. 1988. Sexual Assault and Mental Disorders in a Community Population. *Journal of Consulting and Clinical Psychology 56*(6): 843-850.

Center on Addiction and Substance Abuse (CASA). 1994. *Substance Abuse and Women on Welfare.* New York: Columbia University, Center on Addiction and Substance Abuse.

Center on Addiction and Substance Abuse (CASA). 1996. *Substance Abuse and the American Woman.* New York: Columbia University, Center on Addiction and Substance Abuse.

Center on Addiction and Substance Abuse (CASA). 1998a. *Behind Bars: Substance Abuse and America's Prison Population.* New York: Columbia University, Center on Addiction and Substance Abuse.

Center on Addiction and Substance Abuse (CASA). 1998b. *Under the Rug: Substance Abuse and the Mature Woman.* New York: Columbia University, Center on Addiction and Substance Abuse.

Centers for Disease Control and Prevention. 1997a. Alcohol Consumption among Pregnant and Childbearing-Age Women—United States, 1994. *MMWR Morbidity Mortality Weekly Report 46*(16): 346-350.

Centers for Disease Control and Prevention. 1997b. Update: Trends in AIDS Incidence, Deaths, and Prevalence—United States, 1996. *MMWR Morbidity Mortality Weekly Report 46*(8): 165-173.

Chavez, Nelba. 1997. New National Study on Substance Use Among Women in the United States Released: Press Release. September 22. Rockville, MD: Substance Abuse and Mental Health Services Administration. Available online: <www.hhs.gov/news/press/1997pres/970922.html>.

Chiavaroli, Tonya. 1992. Rehabilitation from Substance Abuse in Individuals with a History of Sexual Abuse. *Journal of Substance Abuse Treatment 9*(4): 349-354.

Copeland, Jan, Wayne Hall, Peter Didcott, and Vicki Biggs. 1993. A Comparison of Specialist Women's Alcohol and Other Drug Treatment Service with Two Traditional Mixed-Sex Services: Client Characteristics and Treatment Outcome. *Drug and Alcohol Dependence 32*(1): 81-92.

Courtwright, David. T. 1982. *Dark Paradise: Opiate Addiction in America Before 1940*. Cambridge, MA: Harvard University Press.

Davis, Shoni. 1990. Chemical Dependency in Women: A Prescription of Its Effects and Outcome on Adequate Parenting. *Journal of Substance Abuse Treatment 7*(3): 225-232.

Eldred, Carolyn A. and Mabel N. Washington. 1975. Female Heroin Addicts in a City Treatment Program: The Forgotten Minority. *Psychiatry 38*(1): 75-85.

Federal Bureau of Investigation. 1992. Crime in the United States, 1991. Research Monograph Services No. 98 (pp. 136-155). Washington, DC: United States Government Printing Office.

Federal Bureau of Prisons. 1999. Bureau of Prisons Statement Addressing Amnesty International Report on Female Inmates. Press release, Office of Public Affairs. March. Washington, DC: U.S. Department of Justice, Federal Bureau of Prisons. Available online: <http://www.bop.gov/>.

Fernandez, Hilder, Suzy Harrington, Dale Lowery, and Bob Erlenbusch. 2000. Welfare to Worse: The Effect of Welfare Reform in Los Angeles County 1998-2000. Report from the Welfare Reform Monitoring Project. Los Angeles, CA: The Los Angeles Coalition to End Hunger and Homelessness. Available online: <http://www.peoplesguide.org/lacehh/article1/article.html>.

Finkelstein, Norma. 1994. Treatment Issues for Alcohol and Drug Dependent Pregnant and Parenting Women. *Health and Social Work 19*(1): 7-15.

Fullilove, Mindy Thompson, Robert E. Fullilove, Michael Smith, Karen Winkler, Calvin Michael, Paula G. Panzer, and Rodrick Wallace. 1993. Violence, Trauma and Post Traumatic Stress Disorder Among Women Drug Users. *Journal of Traumatic Stress 6*(4): 533-543.

Fullilove, Mindy Thompson, Anne E. Lown, and Robert E. Fullilove. 1992. Crack 'Hos and Skeezers: Traumatic Experiences of Women Crack Users. *The Journal of Sex Research 29*(2): 275-287.

Gilliard, Darrell K. and Allen J. Beck. 1998. *Prison and Jail Inmates at Midyear 1997.* Washington, DC: U.S. Department of Justice, Bureau of Justice Statistics.

Governor's Commission on Women. 2000. *Sexual Assault of Inmates.* Brief report regarding Vermont bill H.312. Montpelier, VT: Governor's Commission on Women. Available online: <http://www.state.vt.us/wom/assault.html>.

Grant, Bridget F. 1994. Alcohol Consumption, Alcohol Abuse and Alcohol Dependence. The United States as an Example. *Addictions 89*(11): 1357-1365.

Grant, Bridget F. and Deborah A. Dawson. 1996. Alcohol and Drug Use, Abuse, and Dependence Among Welfare Recipients. *American Journal of Public Health 86*(10): 1450-1454.

Henderson, Dorothy J. 1998. Drug Abuse and Incarcerated Women: A Research Review. *Journal of Substance Abuse Treatment 15*(6): 579-587.

Henderson, Dorothy J. and Carol Boyd. 1992. Women and Illicit Drugs: Sexuality and Crack Cocaine. *Health Care for Women International 16*(2): 113-124.

Henderson, Dorothy J., Carol Boyd, and Thomas Mieczkowski. 1994. Gender, Relationships and Crack Cocaine. *Research in Nursing and Health 17*(4): 265-272.

Hien, Denise A. and Frances R. Levin. 1994. Trauma and Trauma-Related Disorders for Women on Methadone: Prevalence and Treatment Considerations. *Journal of Psychoactive Drugs 26*(4): 421-429.

Hill, Shirley Y. 1982. Biological Consequences of Alcoholism and Alcohol-Related Problems Among Women. Special Populations Issues. Department of Health and Human Services Publication No. (ADM) 82-1193. Rockville, MD: National Institute on Alcohol Abuse and Alcoholism.

Hser, Yih-Ing, M. Douglas Anglin, and William McGlothlin. 1987. Sex Differences in Addict Careers: 1. Initiation of Use. *American Journal of Drug Alcohol Abuse 13*(1 and 2): 33-57.

Inciardi, James A. 1998. Classification, Assessment, and Treatment Planning for Alcohol and Drug-Involved Offenders. *TIE Communique: A Memo to the Field from CSAT's Treatment Improvement Exchange.* Rockville, MD: Center for Substance Abuse Treatment. Available online: <http://www.treatment.org/communique/comm93/inciardi.html>.

Johnston, Lloyd. 1997. *Preliminary Results on Illicit Drug and Alcohol Use from Monitoring the Future 1997.* Ann Arbor: University of Michigan.

Jordan, B. Kathleen, William E. Schlenger, John A. Fairbank, and Juesta M. Cadell. 1996. Prevalence of Psychiatric Disorders Among Incarcerated Women: II Convicted Felons Entering Prison. *Archives of General Psychiatry 53*(6): 513-519.

Karon, John M., Philip S. Rosenberg, Geraldine McQuillan, Meena Khare, Marta Gwinn, and Lyle R. Petersen 1996. Prevalence of HIV Infection in the United States, 1984-1992. *JAMA 276*(2): 126-131.

Katz, Michael B. 1989. *The Undeserving Poor: From the War on Poverty to the War on Welfare.* New York: Pantheon.

Kessler, Ronald C., Katherine A. McGonagle, Shanyang Zhao, Christopher B. Nelson, Michael Hughes, Suzann Eshleman, Hans-Ulrich Wittchen, and Kenneth S. Kendler. 1994. Lifetime and 12-month Prevalence of DSM-III-R Psychiatric Disorders in the United States: Results from the National Comorbidity Survey. *Archives of General Psychiatry 51*(1): 8-19.

Knitzer, Jane. 2000. *Promoting Resilience: Helping Young Children and Parents Affected by Substance Abuse, Domestic Violence, and Depression in the Context of Welfare Reform.* New York: National Center for Children in Poverty.

Ladwig, Gail and Marcia D. Anderson. 1989. Substance Abuse in Women: Relationship Between Chemical Dependency of Women and Past Reports of Physical and/or Sexual Abuse. *International Journal of the Addictions* 24(8): 739-754.

Lukens, Robert J. and Jennifer K. Pokempner. 2000. Pennsylvania Must Provide Additional Procedural Safeguards to Present Economic Sanctions. Report included in *Sight Highlights.* New York: Welfare Law Center. Available online: <http//:www.welfarelaw.org/penn.html>.

Marsh, Jeanne C. and Nancy A. Miller. 1985. Female Clients in Substance Abuse Treatment. *International Journal of Addictions* 20(6/7): 995-1019.

Maternal and Child Health Bureau. 1996. *Child Health USA, '95.* Rockville, MD: Health Resources and Services Administration.

Mead, Lawrence. 1986. *Beyond Entitlement: The Social Obligations of Citizenship.* New York: Free Press.

Murray, Charles. 1984. *Losing Ground: American Social Policy 1950-1980.* New York: Basic Books.

National Cancer Institute. 1996. Cancer Death Rate Declined for the First Time Ever in the 1990s. NIH News Release. Bethesda, MD: National Cancer Institute.

National Center for Health Statistics. 1996. *Health, United States, 1995.* Hyattsville, MD: U.S. Public Health Service.

National Heart, Lung, and Blood Institute. 1996. *Facts About Heart Disease and Women: So You Have Heart Disease.* National Institute of Health Publication No. 96-2645. Bethesda, MD: National Heart, Lung, and Blood Institute.

National Institute of Justice. 1992. *Drug Use Forecasting.* Washington, DC: U.S. Department of Justice, National Institute of Justice.

National Institute on Drug Abuse (NIDA). 1994. *Women and Drug Abuse.* National Institute of Health Publication No. 92-3457. Rockville, MD: National Institute on Drug Abuse.

National Institute on Drug Abuse (NIDA). 1999. *Drug Abuse and Addiction Research: 25 Years of Discovery to Advance Health of the Public.* The sixth triennial report to Congress from the Secretary of Health and Human Services. Rockville, MD: National Institute on Drug Abuse. Available online: <http://165.112.78.61/STRC/report.pdf>.

Nelson-Zlupko, Lani, Martha Morrison Dore, Eda Kauffman, and Karol Kaltenbach. 1996. Women in Recovery: Their Perceptions of Treatment Effectiveness. *Journal of Substance Abuse Treatment* 13(1): 51-59.

Nurco, David N., Thomas E. Hanlon, Richard W. Bateman, and Timothy W. Kinlock. 1995. Drug Abuse Treatment in the Context of Correctional Surveillance. *Journal of Substance Abuse Treatment* 12(1): 19-27.

Office of National Drug Control Policy. 1998. *The National Drug Control Strategy, 1998: A Ten-Year Plan.* Washington, DC: Office of National Drug Control Policy.

Reed, Beth G. 1985. Drug Misuse in Women. *International Journal of Addictions* 20(1): 63-97.

Reed, Beth G. 1987. Developing Women-Sensitive Drug Dependence Treatment Services: Why So Difficult? *Journal of Psychoactive Drugs* 19(2): 151-164.

Regier, Darrel A., Mary E. Farmer, Donald S. Rae, Ben Z. Locke, Samuel J. Keith, Lewis L. Judd, and Frederick K. Goodwin. 1990. Comorbidity of Mental Disorders with Alcohol and Other Drug Abuse: Results from the Epidemiologic Catchment Area (ECA) Study. *Journal of the American Medical Association* 264(19): 2511-2518.

Root, Maria P. 1989. Treatment Failures: The Role of Sexual Victimization in Women's Addictive Behavior. *American Journal of Orthopsychiatry* 59(4): 542-549.

Rosenbaum, Marsha. 1981a. Sex Roles Among Deviants: The Woman Addict. *The International Journal of the Addictions* 16(5): 859-877.

Rosenbaum, Marsha. 1981b. When Drugs Come into the Picture, Love Flies out the Window: Women Addict's Love Relationships. *The International Journal of Addictions* 16(7): 1197-1206.

Rouse, Beatrice A. (Ed.) 1995. *Substance Abuse and Mental Health: Statistics Sourcebook.* Department of Health and Human Services Publication No. SMA 95-3064. Rockville, MD: Department of Health and Human Services.

Salomon, Amy, Shari S. Bassuk, and Margaret G. Brooks. 1996. Patterns of Welfare Use Among Poor and Homeless Women. *American Journal of Orthopsychiatry* 66(4): 510-525.

Sargent, Elizabeth, Susan Marcus-Mendoza, and Chong Ho Yu. 1993. Abuse and the Woman Prisoner. In Beverly R. Fletcher, Lynda D. Shaver, and Dreama G. Moon (Eds.), *Women Prisoners: A Forgotten Population* (pp. 55-65). Westport, CT: Praeger.

Schilling, Robert, Nabila El-Bassel, Andre Ivanoff, Louisa Gilbert, Kuo-Hsien Su, and Steven M. Safyer. 1994. Sexual Risk Behavior of Incarcerated, Drug-Using Women, 1992. *Public Health Reports* 109(4): 539-547.

Schmidt, Laura, Constance Weisner, and James Wiley. 1998. Substance Abuse and the Course of Welfare Dependency. *American Journal of Public Health* 88(11): 1616-1622.

Singer, Mark, Janet Bussey, Li-Yu Song, and Lisa Lunghofer. 1995. The Psychosocial Issues of Women Serving Time in Jail. *Social Work* 40(1): 103-113.

Substance Abuse and Mental Health Services Administration (SAMHSA). 1992. *National Household Survey on Drug Abuse: Population Estimates 1992.* Rockville, MD: U.S. Public Health Service, Substance Abuse and Mental Health Services Administration.

Substance Abuse and Mental Health Services Administration (SAMHSA). 1996. *Preliminary Estimates from the 1995 Household Survey on Drug Abuse.* Rockville, MD: U.S. Public Health Service, Substance Abuse and Mental Health Services Administration, Office of Applied Studies.

Substance Abuse and Mental Health Services Administration (SAMHSA). 1997. *Preliminary Estimates from the 1996 Household Survey on Drug Abuse.*

Rockville, MD: U.S. Public Health Service, Substance Abuse and Mental Health Services Administration, Office of Applied Studies.

Substance Abuse and Mental Health Services Administration (SAMHSA). 1998. *Services Research Outcomes Study (SROS): Outcomes Five Years After Drug Abuse Treatment.* Rockville, MD: U.S. Public Health Service, Substance Abuse and Mental Health Services Administration.

Teplin, Linda A., Karen M. Abram, and Gary M. McLelland. 1996. Prevalence of Psychiatric Disorders Among Incarcerated Women. I. Pretrial Jail Detainees. *Archives of General Psychiatry 53*(6): 505-512.

Thompson, Martie P. and J. B. Kingree. 1998. The Frequency and Impact of Violent Trauma Among Pregnant Substance Abusers. *Addictive Behaviors 23*(2): 257-262.

U.S. Department of Justice. 1994. *Special Report: Women in Prison.* Washington, DC: U.S. Department of Justice, Bureau of Justice Statistics.

U.S. Department of Justice. 1997. *Bureau of Justice Statistics.* Washington, DC: U.S. Department of Justice.

U.S. General Accounting Office. 1980. *Women in Prison: Inequitable Treatment Requires Action.* Washington, DC: U.S. General Accounting Office.

U.S. General Accounting Office. 1990. *National Institutes of Health: Problems Implementing the Policy on Women in Study Populations.* Washington, DC: U.S. General Accounting Office.

U.S. General Accounting Office. 1991. The Crack Cocaine Epidemic: Health Consequences and Treatment Fact Sheet for the Chairman, Select Committee on Narcotics Abuse and Control, House of Representatives. No. GAO/HRD-91-55FS. Washington, DC: U.S. General Accounting Office.

Wallen, Jacqueline. 1992. A Comparison of Male and Female Clients in Substance Abuse Treatment. *Journal of Substance Abuse Treatment 9*(3): 243-248.

Weisner, Constance and Laura Schmidt. 1992. Gender Disparities in Treatment for Alcohol Problems. *Journal of the American Medical Association 268*(14): 1872-1876.

Welfare Law Center. 2000. *Sight Highlights.* New York: Welfare Law Center. Available online: <http://www.welfarelaw.org/>.

Wells, Deborah V. B. and Joyce F. Jackson. 1992. HIV and Chemically Dependent Women: Recommendations for Appropriate Health Care and Drug Treatment Services. *International Journal of the Addictions 27*(5): 571-585.

Wilsnack, Sharon and Richard Wilsnack. 1990. Women and Substance Abuse: Research Directions for the 1990s. *Psychology of Addictive Behaviors 4*(1): 46-49.

Wyatt, Gail E. 1985. The Sexual Abuse of Afro-American and White American Women in Childhood. *Child Abuse and Neglect 9*(4): 507-519.

Zimmer-Hofler, Dagmar and Anja Dobler-Mikola. 1992. Swiss Heroin-Addicted Females: Career and Social Adjustment. *Journal of Substance Abuse Treatment 9*(2): 159-170.

Reflections of My Heart, Penny Flannery
Exhibited at the Fourth Annual Exhibition of Art by Michigan Prisoners. February 9-25, 1999, University of Michigan, Rackham Galleries.

Chapter 9

Life at the Margins:
Older Women Living in Poverty

Edith Elisabeth Flynn

America's elderly population, defined here as those aged sixty-five and older, is the fastest-growing age group in the population (U.S. Bureau of the Census, 1998b). In 1998, more than one out of every ten residents (34 million), or 12.7 percent of the total population, were sixty-five years old or over. This represents a dramatic increase from the beginning of the 1900s when those sixty-five or older numbered just 4 percent of the population. U.S. Census Bureau projections forecast a continued rapid growth of the older population in the twenty-first century (1998b). During the next three decades, the population aged sixty-five and over will more than double, while the number of elders over the age of eighty-five is expected to triple. Figure 9.1 shows the actual and projected growth of the older population from the base year of 1900 through 2040 and reflects the extraordinary rise of this segment of the population. The net effects of this trend are changing the way America lives, looks, and works.

The public discourse and media portrayals of the elderly are full of misleading stereotypes. They depict older persons as a frail, frequently senile, and static population group. Nothing could be further from the truth. If there is one distinguishing characteristic of America's elders, it is their heterogeneity (Quinn, 1987). There is also much confusion about the definition of the term *old age.* First, there is no commonly accepted cutoff age on the basis of which Americans are officially or legally considered old. Second, such terms as *elderly, seniors,* or *senior citizens,* are used interchangeably in the literature and may span as many as three or four decades of a referent's life. Nationwide, the retirement age of sixty-five set by Congress under the provisions of the Social Security Act is the most commonly accepted benchmark for defining the critical passage from middle age to old age. For the purpose of this chapter, old age is formally defined as sixty-five and over—

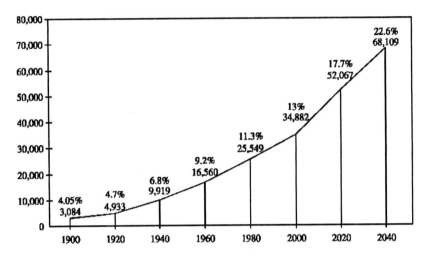

FIGURE 9.1. The Graying of America—Actual and Projected Growth of the Older Population: Persons Age Sixty-Five and Over, 1900-2040. (*Source:* Adapted from A. J. Darnay, Ed. *Statistical Record of Older Americans,* pp. 10-11. Detroit: Gale Research Inc. 1994.)

in view of the fact that pertinent census data and a majority of related data-bases continue to utilize this benchmark (Cheal, 1996).

Recent studies of the aging population clearly document that the majority of older Americans are women (U.S. Bureau of the Census, 1998b). As women grow older, they bear disproportionate health, economic, and social burdens when compared with men (Holtz-Eakin and Smeeding, 1994). This chapter has two purposes: (1) to examine the prevailing demographic trends for the aging female population and to discuss the gender of poverty in America's aging population, and (2) to examine the special conditions of older women in prison. Utilizing available aggregate and individual-level databases, this chapter will show that there is much diversity in the poverty rates among older women. Among this country's older women, we find some of the poorest of the poor, and disproportionate numbers are members of minorities and those who live out their lives in loneliness or in nursing homes. Compared with males, these women spend higher proportions of their lives physically or mentally disabled. This segment is truly a forgotten portion of the aging population—left out of the protections of society's social safety net—and clearly lives at society's margins. The final segment of the chapter examines the issues of older women prisoners and the problems of aging in prison.

DEMOGRAPHIC TRENDS FOR THE AGING
FEMALE POPULATION

Recent demographic data clearly show that the majority of older Americans are women. Table 9.1 charts the U.S. population aged sixty-five and over by age group and sex from 1980 to 1997. Comparing females aged sixty-five and over with their male counterparts in every age category reveals significantly more women than men. This holds true for every year charted from 1980 through the year 2000. Among the reasons for the plurality of women in U.S. society is female longevity, based on physiological and gender differences in health and mortality (Manton, 1997). Today, the average life expectancy at birth is 79.7 years for women and 73 years for men. Looking at differential life expectancies by race only accentuates the disparities. In the new millennium, white females have a life expectancy at birth of 80.5 years; white males, 74.2 years; black females can expect to live 74.7 years; while black males are at the low end of the spectrum with 64.6 years (U.S. Bureau of the Census, 1998b).

A recent analysis of mortality and disability data from national longitudinal surveys of the health and functional status of elderly men and women noted that physiological changes associated with age differ considerably for older men and women (Manton, 1997). Female life expectancy was found to be higher not only at birth, but also at age sixty-five when compared with men. By the same token, gender-specific mortality rates, initially deemed stagnant during the first half of the twentieth century, began to favor the female population during the second half of the century (Fogel, 1994; National Center for Health Statistics, 1964, 1966). Theoretically, the "gender gap" in favor of women has been related to chromosomal, hormonal, and lifestyle differences (Timiras, 1994). Also, there is the generally recognized effect of estrogens that protect women against cardiovascular disease (primarily before menopause). Furthermore, lifestyle differences include a higher propensity among men to ingest alcohol, consume tobacco, use guns, and generally take more risks compared with women.

Historically, the vast majority of medical studies on the effects of aging on health have focused almost exclusively on men. As a result, Manton (1997) is correct when he notes that little is known about "the physiological and behavioral bases of gender differences in health and mortality at late ages" (p. 99). Nonetheless, a number of serious and chronic illnesses appear to be age, gender, and race related. In the case of breast cancer, studies suggest that age, fertility, hormonal exposure, and family history are likely to be related to the incidence of this disease (Berrino et al., 1996; Colditz, Rosner, and Speizer, 1996). Manton identifies a number of chronic illnesses

TABLE 9.1. U.S. Population Sixty-Five Years Old and Over, by Age Group and Sex, 1980-2000

Age Group and Sex	1980	1990	1997	2000
Persons 65 years and over	25,549	31,082	34,076	34,709
65-69 years old	8,782	10,067	9,762	9,410
70-74 years old	6,798	7,980	8,736	8,726
75-79 years old	4,794	6,103	7,063	7,415
80-84 years old	2,935	3,909	4,642	4,900
85 years old and over	2,240	3,022	3,871	4,259
Males 65 years and over	10,305	12,494	14,010	14,346
65-69 years old	3,903	4,508	4,461	4,321
70-74 years old	2,854	3,400	3,807	3,859
75-79 years old	1,848	2,389	2,915	3,092
80-84 years old	1,019	1,356	1,713	1,846
85 years old and over	682	841	1,112	1,228
Females, 65 years and over	15,245	18,587	20,066	20,364
65-69 years old	4,880	5,559	5,301	5,089
70-74 years old	3,945	4,581	4,929	4,867
75-79 years old	2,946	3,714	4,148	4,323
80-84 years old	1,916	2,553	2,929	3,055
85 years old and over	1,559	2,180	2,759	3,031

Source: U.S. Bureau of the Census. *Statistical Abstract of the United States: 1998.* Washington, DC: U.S. Government Printing Office.

as carrying gender and racial risk differentials. They range from diabetes, hypertension, Alzheimer's disease, osteoporosis, heart disease, and stroke, to a number of autoimmune diseases, such as lupus erythematosus, rheumatoid arthritis, and multiple sclerosis (1997).

There is some speculation (in the empirical and theoretical literature on aging) on whether the existing differences in longevity, mortality, and quality of health between males and females will decrease with the passage of time (Bayo and Faber, 1983; Colditz, Rosner, and Speizer, 1996). This is, in essence, what the Social Security Administration (SSA) (1996) predicted when it estimated that the current life-expectancy gender gap would decline due to the differential impact of a variety of "environmental hazards" and other kinds of "social pressures" on women. That year, the SSA noted that the longevity gender gap would decrease from 7.6 years in 1980 to 5.7 years by 2030. (There is an understandable need for keeping predictions of this nature accurate, if Social Security is to remain solvent for future generations.) However, Manton, utilizing data from the National Long-Term Care Surveys (NLTCS 1982, 1984, and 1989) casts serious doubts on any future "age convergence" between the sexes (Manton, 1997; Manton, Corder, and Stallard, 1997).

Comparing male and female differentials in survival and disability from age sixty-five to ninety-five years and over, Manton's study produced a number of interesting results. First, women's life expectancy will remain greater at all ages past age sixty-five when compared with men (Manton, 1997). Second, when the proportion of total life expectancy spent in a functional or nondisabled state is considered, the data favor men in all age categories. This is because men live with their disabilities for shorter periods than women do. Controlling for age, Manton observed that the number of years expected to be spent in a disabled state is higher for women when compared to men.[1] According to Manton's findings, women at all ages can expect to spend more time in institutions compared with men (1997). Table 9.2 shows important gender differentials of life expectancies for certain ages, the percent of total life expectancy by gender, and the proportion of life expectancy that will be spent in institutions by gender.

TABLE 9.2. Estimates of Life Expectancy Post Attainment of Ages Listed; Percentage of Total Life Expectancy and Percentage of Life Expectancy Spent in Institutions, 1997

Age	Life Expectancy After Age X	% of Total Life Expectancy Lived in an Active, Nonimpaired State	% of Life Institutionalized
65 Men	15.7	92.1	2.2
Women	21.9	85.5	5.9
75 Men	10.1	87.3	4.3
Women	14.0	78.0	9.7
85 Men	5.8	79.2	7.9
Women	8.2	65.9	17.2
95 Men	3.1	70.5	11.3
Women	4.7	57.2	25.3

Source: Adapted from K. G. Manton, 1997. "Demographic Trends for the Aging Female Population," *Journal of the American Medical Women's Association,* *52*(3).

The fact that greater proportions of older women are institutionalized when compared with men in the same age categories can be verified by examining nursing home statistics. Although only 5 percent of the U.S. population sixty-five years old and over live in nursing homes,[2] women comprise 75.3 percent of all nursing home residents in that age group. According to the U.S. National Center for Health Statistics (as cited in the U.S. Bureau of the Census, 1999), nursing homes held a total of 1,385,000 male and female residents sixty-five years old and over. Males sixty-five years old and over had an institutionalization rate of 247.7 per 1,000, while females aged sixty-five and over had an institutionalization rate of 753.1 per 1,000. Epidemiologists searching for the reasons behind the sex differences in chronic disabilities and institutionalization have yet to find any satisfactory explanations. At best, it can be conjectured that females are at greater risk for a number of serious, chronic degenerative diseases compared with men (Timiras, 1994). Since women are more likely than men to live alone during their advanced years, no informal caregivers are available to provide assistance when they become disabled. The ratio of older women to men who experience chronic disabilities and impairments seems destined to increase. It needs to be understood, however, that the health and disability status of the elderly will continue to vary widely in the population because it is affected by many individual characteristics, such as genetics, socioeconomic status, educational attainment, race, and ethnicity.

THE GENDER OF POVERTY
IN AMERICA'S AGING POPULATION

Aggregate statistics indicate that poverty has decreased for the nation's older population during the past three decades (Cheal, 1996). However, a more detailed analysis of the socioeconomic status of older residents reveals much diversity in the poverty experience across subgroups of elderly (Carr, Pemmarazu, and Rice, 1996). For example, in 1992, poverty rates ranged from a low of 5.3 percent for married males aged sixty-five and over, to a high of 21.4 percent for widowed females (Holtz-Eakin and Smeeding, 1994). That same year, the poverty rate for African Americans and Hispanic elders in the same age bracket was even more pronounced: 39.5 percent for black females and 24.5 percent for Hispanic females (U.S. Bureau of the Census, 1992).

Elders were also more likely than nonelders to have incomes just above the poverty threshold. The latter is defined by a set of income thresholds that varies by family size and composition.[3] According to the U.S. Bureau of the Census, the poverty threshold for persons under sixty-five years of age was

$8,350; for those sixty-five years and over, it was $7,698. By comparison, the average threshold for a family of four people in 1997 was $16,400 (U.S. Bureau of the Census, 1998a). If a family's total income is less than that family's threshold, it (and every person in it) is considered poor.

Table 9.3 shows the ratio of family income to the poverty level by age, race, and family status.[4] In 1997, 14.6 million persons (or 5.4 percent of the U.S. population) were classified as "severely poor." This means that persons in that category had a total family income less than one-half of their poverty threshold.[5] Another 36 million (or 13.3 percent of the U.S. population), were living in the "near poor" category, with income at least equal to their poverty threshold but below 125 percent of that threshold (U.S. Bureau of the Census, 1998a).

Comparatively speaking, the percentage of older males and females (sixty-five or older) living in severe poverty appears low, 2.2 percent versus 5.4 percent of all of persons living in poverty. However, the percentage of all elders with family incomes at 125 percent of poverty rises to a substantial 17 percent. Again, the ratio of family income to the poverty level rate for African Americans of all ages (12.2 percent) and Hispanics (10.9 percent) is significantly greater when compared with whites. Even though the poverty rates declined for all minorities in recent years, their poverty rates remain much higher than those for any other racial or ethnic group (U.S. Bureau of the Census, 1998a).

Looking at the Family Status data, Table 9.3 reflects the relative advantages of living with other family members when compared with living alone. The Cenus Bureau defines "unrelated individuals" as people living alone or with nonrelatives only. Persons living in the latter category are twice as likely to live in severe poverty, compared with those living with other relatives. Data from the 1998 population survey show that over 30 percent of single female householders are below the poverty level. Even though the data do not focus directly on gender, age, and poverty, it is reasonable to assume that poverty after age sixty-five is heavily concentrated among women. In fact, a recent analysis of age and poverty by Barrow (1996) noted that women comprise more than 70 percent of the older poor. Although poverty rates have been falling over the past two decades, they have declined more slowly among older women living alone, compared to poverty rates for older men or for older married couples.

Among older women living alone, three in five are of African-American heritage and two in five are Latinas (Administration on Aging, 1999). The literature on the gender of poverty identifies a number of conditions that put women at greater risk of poverty, compared with men (Holz-Eakin and Smeeding, 1994). Among those risks, living alone is a major factor leading to poverty. This is true for both sexes, but it is a particularly strong risk fac-

TABLE 9.3. Ratio of Family Income to the Poverty Level by Age, Race, and Family Status, 1997 (Numbers in Thousands)

	Total	Under 0.50		Under 1.00		Under 1.25	
		Number	% of Total	Number	% of Total	Number	% of Total
People Total	268,480	14,594	5.4	35,574	13.3	47,853	17.8
Age 60-64	10,065	366	3.6	1,127	11.2	1,554	15.4
65 and over	32,082	713	2.2	3,376	10.5	5,440	17.0
Race White	221,200	9,427	4.3	24,396	11.0	33,612	15.2
White, not Hispanic	191,859	6,316	3.3	16,491	8.6	23,100	12.0
Black	34,458	4,189	12.2	9,116	26.5	11,646	33.8
Other races	12,822	977	7.6	2,062	16.1	2,595	20.2
Asian and Pacific Islander	10,482	664	6.3	1,468	14.0	1,795	17.1
Hispanic origin*	30,637	3,329	10.9	8,308	27.1	11,003	35.9
Family status In families	225,369	10,615	4.7	26,217	11.6	35,460	15.7
Householder	70,884	2,957	4.2	7,324	10.3	10,032	14.2
Related children under 18	69,844	5,907	8.5	13,422	19.2	17,144	24.5
Related children under 6	23,363	2,356	10.1	5,049	21.6	6,472	27.7
Unrelated individual	41,672	3,602	8.6	8,687	20.8	11,581	27.8
Male	19,804	1,586	8.0	3,447	17.4	4,588	23.2
Female	21,868	2,016	9.2	5,240	24.0	6,992	32.0

Source: Adapted from U.S. Bureau of the Census, 1998, *Current Population Survey*, Table C, p. xi.
*Persons of Hispanic origin may be of any race.

tor for older women. Other risk factors include longevity, gender-linked discrimination, historically limited educational and employment opportunities, gender-differentiated life-cycle events, and failed public policy and social programs. Together, these factors lend considerable support to the feminization-of-poverty thesis, which focuses on the reasons for the historical and continuing economic and social disparities between the sexes. A brief examination of each of these factors is instructive.

Longevity, as previously discussed in the section on the demographics of aging, constitutes a major risk factor leading to the poverty of many older women. Longer life spans dictate that women must stretch the financial resources they have over longer time periods than men.

Gender-linked discriminations are the direct result of traditionally gendered family structures, including historical patterns of women's economic dependence on men. To the degree that women will continue to carry disproportionate (and often exclusive) child care and family responsibilities, gender-linked discriminations will be a fact well into the future (Abramovitz, 1988; Goldberg and Kremen, 1990; Hardy and Hazelrigg, 1993). Correlated interrupted work patterns, and sporadic and typically low-wage or marginal-employment histories have predictable economic consequences on earned retirement income (such as Social Security) and related public and private pension plans (Cheal, 1996; Leira, 1992). Since the education and employment picture is improving for many women with each passing generation, this pervasive gender disparity affects mostly the older generation (Lewis, 1997).

The combined effects of historically limited educational and occupational opportunities of women are clearly visible in the employment levels of older women. In 1997, a vast majority (16.4 million women sixty-five and over) did not work at all that year (U.S. Bureau of the Census, 1998a). Of this group, 2.4 million (14.4 percent) were living below the poverty level. Another 1.6 million (4.3 percent) held part-time jobs, with 69,000 (4.3 percent) of that group living below the poverty level. Only a small number of older women (618,000) worked full-time in 1997. Yet even with working full-time 3,000 older women (0.5 percent) were living below the poverty level (U.S. Bureau of the Census, 1998a). Comparative data of the work experience for women between the ages of eighteen and sixty-four years are just as devastating, if not more so. About 20.1 million women between the ages of eighteen and sixty-four did not work at all in 1997. Of these, 5.9 million (29.6 percent of the total) lived below the poverty level. Another 26.6 million in this age category worked part-time. Of these, 15.4 percent lived below the poverty level. About 37 million of women between eighteen to sixty-four worked full-time. Of these, 2.6 percent were living below the poverty level. Together, these data clearly reflect the heritage of sporadic, frequently low-wage, or nonexistent employment histories of women, which in turn are related to their culturally attributed roles as primary caregivers.

Examining the income sources of elderly males and female, Social Security—otherwise known as the Old-Age and Survivors Insurance Program (OASI)—constitutes the primary source of income for 95 percent of all poor couples (Cutler, 1996). It is important to remember that when Social Security was first designed under the Roosevelt administration, it was premised on a family structure consisting of a working husband and a stay-at-home wife. Although OASI continues to work relatively well for married couples, its benefits are greatly reduced upon the death of the spouse. Specific reductions are based on a combination of the principal beneficiary's past earnings and retirement age. They range between 33 percent and 50 percent. Given the importance of OASI as a primary income source, particularly for low-income females, the reduction in OASI can mean a descent into poverty (Holtz-Eakin and Smeeding, 1994). Of course, widowhood is not the only cause of poverty in older women. Many more elders are affected by other kinds of marital or household disruption, ranging from divorce to separation to abandonment. The majority of older women experiencing disruptions in their relationships, however they are defined, are left to face myriad financial problems (Cheal, 1996).

Gender-differentiated life-cycle events may also trigger a slide into poverty for a group of women not usually associated with destitution. They are an aggregation of women who have lived relatively secure, middle-class lives who may find themselves literally being "cycled" into poverty after divorce, desertion, or the death of their spouse. Compared with women who have been poor all of their lives, this group may first experience poverty, or near poverty, only after they have reached old age (Lewis, 1997). The risk of poverty in this group of older women is particularly great, if their financial resources have been depleted during any long and costly illnesses of their spouses. This is because Medicare[6] provides neither long-term care nor the cost of medications outside a hospital stay. While Medicaid[7] does provide extended care for the "medically needy" elderly and others, the recipients and their spouses are required legally to "spend down" their life savings and related assets before assistance is granted. Since the implementation of the Medicare and Medicaid programs, the cost of medical services has risen each year. As a result, elders are now spending a greater proportion of their income on health care. As such, acute health care expenses often exceed 20 percent of the meager income of the elderly poor (Kane and Friedman, 1996).

The persistence and growth of poverty among some older women, and particularly older women of color, suggest that current policies and programs are not working. The base income for the aged in this country consists of a combination of OASI, Supplementary Security Income (SSI),[8] and food stamps. The current system is more patchwork than comprehensive. Although notable success has been achieved in decreasing poverty among the elderly in the aggregate, the programs have failed to address the blight of poverty among a growing segment of the older female population. As has been shown, gender differences in poverty rates are attributable not only to longevity, but also to widowhood, divorce, or abandonment. Never having been married also increases the poverty risk of older women. Social Security policies, health insurance, and retirement pensions do not compensate for the very real effects of gender-linked discriminations that occur, either during the life course or at the end stage of the life cycle. The reasons behind this socioeconomic vulnerability is not deliberate neglect by government and policymakers, but a lack of awareness of the subtleties of the poverty experience across the different subgroups of older women. These women are simply overlooked in the totality of the nation's antipoverty efforts. Unrecognized, neglected, and without political clout, they live out their lives in privation and destitution.

Older women have a significant stake in the ongoing debates on Social Security and health care programs (Lewis, 1997). A recent analysis of gender, age, and Social Security income by the American Federation of Labor—Congress of Industrial Organizations (AFL-CIO, 1999) notes the following: More than half of all women aged sixty-five and over are unmarried due to widowhood, divorce, or never having been married. On average, these older women depend on Social Security for 72 percent of their income, compared with 66 percent for unmarried men in similar circumstances. One in four older women relies on Social Security for all her income. If it were not for Social Security, 45 percent of unmarried older women would be in poverty. Predictably, the situation is worse for women of color. On average, older, unmarried African-American women depend on Social Security for 79 percent of their income, while older Hispanic women depend on it for 77 percent of their income.

Given this significant dependency, care must be taken that any reduction of Social Security payments—or the raising of eligibility requirements or the reduction of benefit levels—does not harm a population segment that is least able to defend itself. For example, given the previously discussed fact that older women are more likely than men to experience chronic illnesses, they are more likely to be affected negatively by the rise in retirement age for Social Security. The increase in retirement age began in 2000 and will gradually rise from sixty-five to sixty-seven. This change affects people born in 1938 or later. Yet even short delays in eligibility age are likely to have more negative effects on older women than on men of comparable age.

For instance, arthritis, osteoporosis, and related joint pain may turn such jobs as waitress, cashier, or custodian into serious hardships for those experiencing such chronic illnesses.

The solvency of Social Security, Medicare, and Medicaid programs is critical for all ages. But these programs are particularly important for older women, given their longevity and propensity for institutionalization. Curtailed cost-of-living increases, increases in Medicare exclusions, and related program cuts would fall more heavily on older women. For example, cost-of-living adjustments (COLAs) to Social Security occur automatically when there is an increase in the Consumer Price Index (CPI) in the first quarter of the year—in comparison with the same period of the previous year. In the face of the impending retirement of the "baby boomers," there is much speculation that Social Security's funds will begin breaking down unless serious steps are taken to cut expenditures. Typical suggestions include freezing COLAs. Others recommend a recalculation of the CPI to reflect more realistic (meaning lower) cost-of-living expenditures.

Medicare exclusions fall disproportionately more heavily onto women, including elders. This is because Medicare Part A (the hospital insurance fund for elders) and Part B (which pays for outpatient doctor's services) focus principally on acute care and hospitalization. As such, Medicare does not pay for outpatient drugs, nor does it pay for long-term care in nursing homes. Given these exclusions, it is clear that Medicare does not address the chronic health needs of older women, many of whom require an assortment of drugs for chronic ailments and disability-related long-term institutionalization.

Finally, related Medicare cuts have already negatively affected older women. This is because, as previously discussed, the majority of older women (compared with one-third of older men) require either nursing home care or extensive home care. Since Medicare pays less than 5 percent of such costs, older persons of both sexes spend an average of 12 percent of their total annual income on such care, compared with 3.7 percent for younger persons (Lewis, 1997).

To compensate for the historical effects of gender-linked discriminations, various proposals are being discussed that would remedy the existing gender-equity problems of Social Security and the national health care programs. Some of these are budget neutral, while others would increase public expenditures (and hence carry a measure of political risk). For example, current spousal benefits could be reduced and shifted to increase survivor benefits (Burkhauser and Smeeding, 1994). Under this proposal, there are advantages as well as disadvantages. Wives who have never worked would receive less income during their spouses' lifetimes, but they would receive more money when widowed. Another option involves "earnings sharing," in which a marriage is considered to be an economic partnership. The income of both spouses would be equally divided and credited to each partner's work history (Lewis, 1997). Earning sharing would be particularly advantageous to divorced spouses. Still another plan first surfaced at the 1995 White House Conference on Aging (O'Grady-LeShane, 1995). It would recognize the labors of currently unpaid family caregivers by attributing to them a base amount for each year spent on child care (age seven and under), or for the care of severely disabled spouses or parents. This plan comes closest to offsetting the legacy of gendered-family structures. The final option would treat all women entitled to spousal and survivor benefits as equals, whether they have participated in the labor market or not (Lewis, 1997). This option would give Social Security credits to currently unpaid family caregivers. By the same token, this option would bring no advantage to the working wife whose wages are so low that her spousal benefits are larger than her own. The last two options are not budget neutral. Proposals along these lines might well produce a backlash against this marginalized group of older women. This is because older women do not represent a particularly powerful constituency. Any increases in budgetary outlays on behalf of elders is likely to be opposed by more powerful interest groups, such as businesses, corporations, and the taxpaying public. But then it is a function of government to provide leadership and set income-support policies that are equitable for all of its people.

Older women are less likely than men to have private pensions. Although the gender gap in pension coverage is narrowing, women's pension income is on average only 59 percent of pensions drawn by men (Arber, 1996). With the passage of the Employer Retirement Income Security Act (ERISA) of 1974, Congress made widows (and widowers) eligible for survivor benefits from their spouses pensions. ERISA mandates that private pensions offer survivor benefits by default, with survivors receiving at least 50 percent of their spouse's retirement benefits after death. In her discussion of possible improvements for women in the private-pension system, Lewis recommends wider coverage, retirement-fund solvency, portability, improved enforcement of existing pension legislation, and shorter vestment periods (1997). Cost-of-living increases and increases in the percentage of survivor benefits (beyond 50 percent) would also be desirable. Since these improvements to the private-pension system would benefit widows only, other provisions would have to be developed for those who are divorced or separated from their spouses. For example, pension benefits could be patterned after the current Social Security provision that divorced women can collect half of their former husband's benefits, provided they had been married for ten years (or more) and have not remarried. As desirable as these changes would be from the perspective of women, they would clearly increase the costs of pension plans to employers. Given that, resistance from business and corporate America is likely to be fierce.

Since more older women than men are beneficiaries of Medicare and Medicaid, this population subgroup has a very large stake in the future of these programs. With passage of the Balanced Budget Act of 1997, Congress extended the life of the Medicare Trust Fund for ten years, expanded health plan choices, and added coverage of preventive benefits (White House, 1998). The Act also established the National Bipartisan Commission on the future of Medicare. Its recommendations will be critical to equity issues affecting older women. Also, rising health costs are spurring a host of government efforts to reduce spending in this area. Efforts range from reductions in payments to hospitals and health care providers to coaxing more elders into joining health maintenance organizations (HMOs). It is also likely that Congress will raise Medicare and Medicaid payroll taxes (and increase current premium levels for both programs) to offset the mounting cost of these appropriations (Butler, 1996).

AGING IN PRISON:
FOCUS ON THE OLDER FEMALE PRISONER

In general, the nation's prison population is older than in previous years. Using 1997 data, about 30 percent of male and female state and federal prison inmates were between the ages of thirty-five and forty-four, compared with 23 percent in 1991 (U.S. Department of Justice, 1999a). This increase was offset by a decline in the percentage of inmates aged eighteen to thirty-four. The percentage of inmates fifty-five years old and over remained about the same between 1991 and 1997. Women inmates in state and federal prisons are older than their counterparts in local jails. While about one in five women in local jails are under the age of twenty-five, one in eight state prisoners and one in eleven federal prisoners are in this age group. Nearly 25 percent of federal prison inmates are at least forty-five years old. Table 9.4 reflects the latest available age distribution of women prisoners in local jails, state prisons, and the federal prison system on a given day.[9] It shows that the majority of incarcerated women fall into the age category of twenty-five through thirty-four. The next highest group is between the ages of thirty-five and forty-four. Looking at the age category of fifty-five and over, there are very few women prisoners. Specifically, only 1 percent of female inmates in probation and local jails are fifty-five years old and over. The percentage of incarcerated women fifty-five and over is 2 percent for state prisons, and 6 percent for the federal prison system.

TABLE 9.4. Women Offenders

Age	Probation	Jails	State	Federal
24 or less	20%	21%	12%	9%
25-34	39%	46%	43%	35%
35-44	30%	27%	34%	32%
45-54	10%	5%	9%	18%
55 or more	1%	1%	2%	6%
Median Age	32 years	31 years	33 years	35 years

Source: U.S. Bureau of Justice Statistics, *Women Offenders,* December 1999, NCJ 175688.

A recent national study of elder offenders (Flynn, 1997) noted that half of the fifty-plus state corrections systems (including the Federal Bureau of Prisons and Puerto Rico) in the country had no specific age designation for their older inmates. Only nine state systems have adopted the recommendation of the National Institute of Corrections that age fifty be considered as the chronological starting point for defining older offenders. Another twelve systems have adopted age fifty-five as their designation for older offenders. Three systems use age sixty, and five systems use age sixty-five as their designations for older offenders. In a similar vein, there is a lack of uniformity in age definitions and age brackets among the basic sources for statistics describing women offenders. Worse, national data focusing specifically on older women prisoners are almost nonexistent. For example, one of the better sources for annual criminal justice statistics, the *Sourcebook of Criminal Justice Statistics,* published by the U.S. Department of Justice (1999b), fails to break down the gender of inmates in its age categorizations. Thus, it is instructive to look at a recent publication of the American Correctional Association (2000) featuring adult inmate populations by age and gender for each state correction system and the federal prison system. Table 9.5 depicts germane highlights from this report.

Given the small number of older women prisoners in local, state, and federal institutions, it is understandable (albeit not equitable) that little attention is paid to this particular segment of the inmate population. Today's corrections institutions are experiencing severe crowding, with most facilities operating well above their rated capacities. Largely the result of a host of legislative measures (including preventive detention, longer prison sen-

TABLE 9.5. Older Inmate Populations by State and the Federal System, Midyear 1998

State	Age Category Ages 55-75		Age Category Age 75 and over	
	Male	**Female**	**Male**	**Female**
Alabama	696	30	20	0
Alaska	141	8	5	0
Arizona	956	35	24	0
Arkansas	305	23	9	0
California*	4,165	220	0	0
Colorado	N/A	N/A	N/A	N/A
Connecticut	278	10	0	0
Delaware	N/A	N/A	N/A	N/A
Florida	2,214	88	91	3
Georgia	1,195	63	40	0
Hawaii	136	6	5	0
Idaho	189	6	18	0
Illinois	799	34	35	0
Indiana	517	34	19	2
Iowa	N/A	N/A	N/A	N/A
Kansas	285	9	8	0
Kentucky	599	25	24	0
Louisiana	673	30	10	0
Maine	N/A	N/A	N/A	N/A
Maryland	N/A	N/A	N/A	N/A
Massachusetts	408	9	8	0
Michigan	N/A	N/A	N/A	N/A
Minnesota	153	3	4	0
Mississippi	409	30	11	1
Missouri	635	36	71	2
Montana	N/A	N/A	N/A	N/A
Nebraska	93	2	4	0
Nevada	N/A	N/A	N/A	N/A
New Hampshire	N/A	N/A	N/A	N/A
New Jersey	691	20	0	0
New Mexico	139	4	7	0
New York	1,834	79	50	0
North Carolina	818	36	28	2
North Dakota	19	0	0	0
Ohio	1,710	84	73	4
Oklahoma	695	37	30	2

State	Age Category Ages 55-75		Age Category Age 75 and over	
	Male	Female	Male	Female
Oregon	N/A	N/A	N/A	N/A
Pennsylvania	1,444	53	46	2
Rhode Island	90	1	3	0
South Carolina	492	27	23	0
South Dakota	N/A	N/A	N/A	N/A
Tennessee	574	22	22	0
Texas	6,056	268	2,048	64
Utah	N/A	N/A	N/A	N/A
Vermont	71	2	0	0
Virginia	850	22	38	0
Washington	525	23	24	0
West Virginia	N/A	N/A	N/A	N/A
Wisconsin	450	14	26	0
Wyoming	63	7	2	0
Total	**31,367**	**1,400**	**2,826**	**82**
Federal Bureau of Prisons	6,671	461	106	6

Source: Adapted from *Vital Statistics in Corrections, 2000,* Lanham, MD: American Correctional Association. *Ages 55-70

tences, career-offender statutes, and mandatory minimum sentencing provisions—such as "three-strikes" laws), most correctional administrators are hard-pressed to keep their institutions on an even keel. Most of their efforts are spent in trying to meet the basic needs of their fast-growing inmate populations, many of whom are young and violent.

A recent analysis of the extraordinary growth in the state-prison population between 1990 and 1997 identifies a number of key factors (U.S. Department of Justice, 1999a). First, an increasing number of parole violators are being returned to prison. Second, the inmate release rate has declined. Third, the average time served in prison is increasing significantly; growing numbers of inmates will serve twenty or more years in prison, some of whom will never be released.

Older female inmates are anything but monolithic. At least three general types of older female offenders are recognized: first-time offenders, career or habitual offenders, and women who have grown old in prison (Aday, 1994; Flynn, 1993). Each group adjusts differently to prison life and has different prospects on release in terms of recidivism. Many first-time, older female offenders commit crimes rather late in life. They are serving long sentences for serious crimes, such as premeditated homicide and manslaughter. More often than not, these crimes are the result of domestic violence. Women kill due to anger, frustration, and fear. Some kill with premeditation; others do so accidentally. Many kill in self-defense and some kill under the influence of drugs or alcohol. An interesting study of 235 women serving time for murder and manslaughter in Georgia found that 44 percent had killed a husband or significant other. Most of these murders were classified as domestic killings. Almost half of these women claimed that their partners beat them regularly. Most had repeatedly reported domestic violence to police with no action being taken (Hansen, 1992). The study findings fit the general offense patterns of female-violent crime, in which approximately 62 percent of women had a prior relationship with their victim either as an intimate, a relative, or an acquaintance (U.S. Department of Justice, 1999c).

Looking at homicide statistics, which are generally recognized as the most reliable data, given the nature of the crime, the majority of murders are committed by females under the age of sixty-four. Between 1976 and 1997, white women aged fifty and over were responsible for only 11 percent of all murders. The applicable percentage for African-American women aged fifty and over was 7.7 percent. But because homicide and other serious, violent crime generally draw long prison sentences, women convicted of these crimes tend to enter old age in the prison systems. Because these newcomers have little knowledge of prison life, members of this group tend to have adjustment problems. To some extent, institutions respond to the needs of these women, and their prospects for successful reintegration upon return to the community are favorable, especially in the absence of prior records (Goetting, 1984).

Career or habitual female offenders have long histories of crime and a record of successive imprisonments. Offenders in this category often have serious substance abuse problems. Many are alcoholics or have other chronic difficulties that make coping with life outside of prison problematic. Some of these offenders have committed violent crimes (such as rape, robbery, and aggravated assault). Others have engaged in successive nonviolent crimes (such as burglary, larceny, fraud, motor vehicle offenses— including driving under the influence—and drug offenses). This group adjusts relatively well to institutional life and presents few management problems, but the nature of their difficulties and their lack of necessary life, social, and coping skills lead to high recidivism upon return to society. Weak community ties and limited employment experience make successful reintegration even less likely. Members of this group are also most likely to join the ranks of geriatric inmates (Morton, 1992; Vitiello, 1997). Unless drug treatment is provided, this pattern will continue.

The third and final group are female inmates who committed very serious crimes while they were young. Upon sentencing, these individuals wil grow old in prison due to the inordinate length of their prison terms (Walsh, 1990). Included here are females who have been waived from juvenile court. Keeping them active for the duration through work and programs is a major challenge for prison administrators. Predictably, the few who return to the community face serious roadblocks due to absent community ties and a lack of appropriate coping and work experiences (Flynn, 1993).

SPECIAL NEEDS OF THE OLDER FEMALE PRISONER

Because they are so few in number, the older female prisoner virtually disappears inside the prison and jail environment. For the most part, their lives are characterized by loneliness, lack of activity, monotony, and by social and psychological isolation (Flynn, 1997). The majority suffer from chronic health problems, such as hypertension, diabetes, arthritis, peripheral-circulatory problems, stroke, cancer, and senile dementia (including Alzheimer's disease). At least one-third of older inmates suffer from significant functional disabilities. Due to a weakening of their immune system, older inmates are more prone to illness and are at greater risk of contracting contagious diseases such as tuberculosis (Morton, 1992).

Given the seriously limited resources of most corrections systems, few have the luxury of addressing the needs of this subpopulation group. Even fewer are able either to hire specially trained staff or to train existing staff in providing needed services, ranging from differentiating between normal aging and serious illnesses to providing age-appropriate programming.

A recent assessment of corrections systems housing practices (Flynn, 1997) identified four basic options for housing the older female inmate: (1) mainstreaming, as long as the woman is free from disease and is mobile; (2) clustering older inmates in the main population; (3) providing housing within designated units, and (4) accommodating physically and mentally impaired older inmates in medical units. Very few systems provide specialized programs for this population, such as life skills training or individualized recreation activities that meet the needs of the older and physically challenged inmate. In general, mainstreaming of healthy elders is desirable and in line with the spirit and requirements of the Americans with Disabilities Act of 1990. Strong arguments have been made, however, for placing the older female inmate in special housing, which would enable administrators to focus scarce resources and specialized staff on this group. Research evidence also suggests that most elders prefer housing that affords more privacy (Flynn, 1997), as well as safety, structure, and emotional feedback, compared with younger inmates (McCarthy and Langworthy, 1988; Walsh, 1990).

Few existing programs are suitable for the older female inmate. Most are discouraged from participating in counseling, educational programs, and vocational training, which are generally viewed as more suitable for the younger female inmate. The absence of appropriate activities leads to idleness and isolation and tends to hasten the older inmate's mental and physical decline.

Prison administrators must increase their awareness of the impact of aging on inmates. Any efforts that encourage the older female inmate to remain functional and mobile will pay off in terms of lower costs for health care. Keeping active is of critical importance and consistently tied to improved mental and physical health. Of course, programs and activities must be appropriately gauged to individual inmates' functional abilities. Since most inmates—even elders—are eventually released, they too must be prepared for reentry into society. Wellness programs, preventive medicine, activity, and even work, to the extent that it is possible, will prove to be the best options in the long run (Morton, 1992; Neely, Addison, and Craig-Moreland, 1997).

THE OLDER FEMALE OFFENDER AND RECIDIVISM

It is a well-established fact in criminology that arrest rates decline after age thirty. From age fifty on, arrest rates become marginal (1.3 percent and below). This decrease in criminal activity with increasing age is known as maturational reform or the "aging-out effect" (Flynn, 1996). Since recidivism declines rapidly with increases in age, the long-term incarceration of offenders who grow old in prison invests scarce resources where they will do the least good. The older female offender, and especially those who have committed capital crimes, are even less likely than their male counterparts to experience recidivism. Most who have studied the special problems and needs of the older female offender have long agreed that more humane sanctioning alternatives could often achieve the same crime-reduction benefits as does lifelong incarceration (Chesney-Lind, 1997; Dobash, Dobash, and Gutteride, 1986). For example, programs such as intensive supervision, early release, compassionate release, or other special parole could easily target the older inmate who no longer poses a threat to society. Given the low risk presented by these offenders, it would be the civilized thing to do.

CONCLUSION

The majority of older Americans are women since, on average, they live longer than men. As a result, they experience greater health and socio-economic challenges than any other age group, except young children living in single-parent families. As a whole, older women are very diverse. A small segment is even relatively secure economically. However, the combined effects of differences in genetics, ethnic and cultural backgrounds, educational attainment, employment opportunities, life-course events, and gendered income-support programs are putting some older women at great risk of poverty. Older women are twice as likely as men to live in poverty. Spousal death, divorce, separation, and other relationship disruptions cycle many women into poverty before they reach old age. Older women are also more likely to spend a larger proportion of their lives disabled and institutionalized than are men. Over three-quarters of older women have incomes below or near the national poverty level. The majority relies on Social Security for most if not all of its income. Women of color are particularly dependent on government-subsidized income. Gendered family structures, including persistent unequal caregiving responsibilities, place disproportionate financial pressures on a large segment of older women. Few receive private pensions compared to men, and those who do have much smaller pensions than men. Finally, unless the current policies governing private pensions and public income-support (including health maintenance) programs are changed to reflect the realities of longevity and gender-linked discrimination, subgroups of older women will continue to bear the negative consequences of these policies.

This chapter has also focused on the older female offender incarcerated in the nation's correctional institutions. Largely because there are so few older women inmates in jails and prisons, this subgroup of prisoners is by far the most neglected and underattended in corrections. Criminal justice data on this population are sparse, as research on this topic is almost nonexistent. Since older female inmates comprise only a small portion of a sizeable special-needs population in corrections, it is unlikely that any resources of consequence are spent on this group. Nonetheless, equity and fairness—the marks of a civilized justice system—require that the needs of these inmates be addressed to the degree that it is possible. These needs include staff awareness of the problems of the aging female offender, staff training, improved assessment techniques, and special programming. Special care must be provided in terms of housing, wellness programs, and preventive medicine with programs and services appropriate for their age being developed. The goals of these programs include keeping the older inmates physically active and mentally engaged, and preparing even these inmates for their eventual return to society.

Given that most older inmates present few, if any, risks to society, the pursuit of more appropriate sentencing procedures and early-release programs would not only be appropriate but also more humane.

NOTES

1. The NLTCS measures chronic disabilities by counting impairments of daily living, or ADLs, and instrumental activities of daily living, or IADLs (Katz and Apkom, 1976; Lawton and Brody, 1969). ADL dimensions describe a person's ability to perform basic self-care activities, such as eating, bathing, dressing, and so on, while IADLs measure independence in activities requiring persons to adapt to their environments (such as cooking, shopping, money management, and so on).

2. The U.S. National Center for Health Statistics defines nursing and related care homes in the coterminous United States as having three or more beds, being staffed for use by residents, and routinely provide nursing and personal care services (U.S. Bureau of the Census, 1997, Advance Data, Washington, DC: USNCHS, No. 289, July 2).

3. The official definition of poverty is based on the work of Orshansky, who first computed the "needs" of the population by utilizing a food multiplier technique (1965).

4. The official poverty definition counts money income before taxes and does not include capital gains or noncash benefits such as public housing, Medicaid, and food stamps.

5. Poverty thresholds are updated annually and adjusted for inflation in accordance with the Consumer Price Index. The thresholds do not vary geographically, even though there are significant differences in the cost of living across the United States (U.S. Bureau of the Census, 1998a).

6. Medicare is a federal entitlement program that provides universal entitlement to basic acute health care insurance coverage to all persons sixty-five and over, and a small group of those with permanent disabilities (Kane and Friedman, 1996, p. 635).

7. Medicaid is a cooperative federal-state program designed to provide health insurance coverage to persons based on their state of poverty (Kane and Friedman, 1996, p. 635).

8. Supplementary Security Income (SSI) is a federal program designed to help guarantee a minimum income for the aged (Holz-Eakin and Smeeding, 1994).

9. Longitudinal data would be more sensitive to the movement of prisoners. Cross-sectional data will necessarily reflect more prisoners with longer sentences and, therefore, tend to inflate age.

REFERENCES

Abramovitz, Mimi. 1988. *Regulating the Lives of Women: Social Welfare Policy from Colonial Times to the Present.* Boston: South End Press.

Aday, Ronald H. 1994. Aging in Prison: A Case Study of New Elderly Offenders. *International Journal of Offender Therapy and Comparative Criminology* 38(1): 79-91.

Administration on Aging. 1999. *Older Women: A Diverse and Growing Population*. Washington, DC: U.S. Department of Health and Human Services, National Aging Information Center.

American Correctional Association. 2000. *Vital Statistics in Corrections*. Lanham, MD: American Correctional Association.

American Federation of Labor-Congress of Industrial Organizations (AFL-CIO). 1999. Working Women: Equal Pay—Equal Pay and Retirement. Available online: <http://www.paywatch.org/women/retirement.htm>. Date of access: February 14, 2000.

Americans with Disabilities Act of 1990. July 26. Public Law 101-336.

Arber, Sara. 1996. Gender Roles. In James E. Birren (Ed.), *Encyclopedia of Gerontology*, Vol. 1 (p. 555). San Diego, CA: Academic Press.

Barrow, Georgia M. 1996. *Aging, the Individual, and Society*. Minneapolis, MN: West Publishing Co.

Bayo, Francisco R. and Joseph F. Faber. 1983. Mortality Experience Around Age One Hundred. *Transaction of the Society of Actuaries 35*: 37-59.

Berrino, F., P. Muti, A. Micheli, G. Bolelli, V. Krogh, R. Sciajno, P. Pisani, S. Panico, and G. Secreto. 1996. Serum Sex Hormone Levels After Menopause and Subsequent Breast Cancer. *Journal of the National Cancer Institute* 88(5): 291-296.

Burkhauser, Richard and Timothy M. Smeeding. 1994. *Social Security Reform: A Budget Neutral Approach to Reducing Older Women's Disproportionate Risk of Poverty*. Syracuse, NY: Center for Policy Research.

Butler, Robert. 1996. On Behalf of Older Women. *New England Journal of Medicine 334*(12): 794-796.

Carr, Deborah Ann, Ann Pemmarazu, and Dorothy P. Rice (Eds.). 1996. *Improving Data on America's Aging Population*. Committee on National Statistics. Washington, DC: National Academy Press.

Cheal, David. 1996. *New Poverty, Families in Postmodern Society*. Westport, CT: Praeger.

Chesney-Lind, Meda. 1997. *The Female Offender: Girls, Women and Crime*. Thousand Oaks, CA: Sage Publications.

Colditz, Graham A., Bernard A. Rosner, and F. E. Speizer. 1996. Risk Factors for Breast Cancer According to Family History of Breast Cancer. *The Journal of the National Cancer Institute 88*(6): 365-371.

Cutler, Neil E. 1996. Pensions. In James E. Birren (Ed.), *Encyclopedia of Gerontology*, Vol. 2 (pp. 261-269). San Diego, CA: Academic Press.

Dobash, Russell P., R. Emerson Dobash, and Sue Gutteride. 1986. *The Imprisonment of Women*. Oxford, England: Basil Blackwell, Inc.

Flynn, Edith E. 1993. The Graying of America's Prison Population. *The Prison Journal 72*(1/2): 77-98.

Flynn, Edith E. 1996. Crime and Age. In James E. Birren (Ed.), *Encyclopedia of Gerontology* (pp. 353-359). San Diego, CA: Academic Press.

Flynn, Edith E. 1997. Managing Elderly Offenders: A National Assessment. Un-published report to the National Institute of Justice. Boston: Northeastern University.

Fogel, Robert W. 1994. Economic Growth, Population Theory, and Physiology: The Bearing of Long-Term Processes on the Making of Economic Policy. *American Economic Review 84*(3): 369-395.

Goetting, Ann. 1984. The Elderly in Prison: A Profile. *Criminal Justice Review 9*(2): 14-24.

Goldberg, Gertrude S. and Eleanor Kremen. 1990. *The Feminization of Poverty*. New York: Praeger.

Hansen, Jane O. 1992. Is Justice Taking a Beating? *The Atlanta Constitution*, April 26, p. A1.

Hardy, Melissa A. and Lawrence E. Hazelrigg. 1993. The Gender of Poverty in an Aging Population. *Research on Aging 15*(3): 243-278.

Holtz-Eakin, Douglas and Timothy M. Smeeding. 1994. Income, Wealth, and Intergenerational Economic Relations of the Aged. In Linda G. Martin and Samuel H. Preston (Eds.), *Demography of Aging* (pp. 102-145). Washington, DC: National Academy Press.

Kane, Robert L. and Bruce Friedman. 1996. Health Care and Services. In James E. Birren (Ed.), *Encyclopedia of Gerontology* (pp. 635-641). San Diego, CA: Academic Press.

Katz, S. and C. A. Apkom. 1976. A Measure of Primary Sociobiological Functions. *International Journal of Health Services 6*(4): 493-508.

Lawton, M. Powell and Elaine M. Brody. 1969. Assessment of Older People: Self-Maintaining and Instrumental Activities of Daily Living. *Gerontologist 9*(2): 179-186.

Leira, Arnlaug. 1992. *Welfare States and Working Mothers: The Scandinavian Experience*. Cambridge: Cambridge University Press.

Lewis, Myrna I. 1997. An Economic Profile of American Older Women. *Journal of the American Medical Women's Association 52*(3): 107-112.

Manton, Kenneth G. 1997. Demographic Trends for the Aging Female Population. *Journal of the American Medical Women's Association 52*(3): 99-105.

Manton, Kenneth G., L.S. Corder, and E. Stallard. 1997. Estimates of Change in Chronic Disability and Institutional Incidence and Prevalence Rates in the U.S. Elderly Population from the 1982, 1984, and 1989 National Long-Term Care Survey. *Journal of Gerontology 47*: S153-S166.

McCarthy, Belinda and Robert Langworthy. 1988. *Older Offenders: Perspectives in Criminology and Criminal Justice*. New York: Praeger.

Morton, Joan B. 1992. *Administrative Overview of the Older Inmate*. Washington, DC: U.S. Department of Justice, National Institute of Corrections.

National Center for Health Statistics. 1964. *The Change in Mortality Trends in the United States*. Washington, DC: Public Health Service.

National Center for Health Statistics. 1966. *Mortality Trends in the United States*. Washington, DC: Public Health Service.

Neely, Connie L., Laura Addison, and Delores Craig-Moreland. 1997. Addressing the Needs of Elderly Offenders: Medical Care, Physical Environment Are of Special Concern. *Corrections Today 59*(5): 120-125.

O'Grady-LeShane, Regina. 1995. *Women and Aging: An Agenda for Action.* Waltham, MA: Brandeis University, National Policy and Resource Center on Women and Aging, Heller School.

Orshansky, Molly. 1965. Counting the Poor: Another Look at the Poverty Profile. *Social Security Bulletin 28*(1): 3-29.

Quinn, Joseph F. 1987. The Economic Status of the Elderly: Beware the Mean. *Review of Income and Wealth 33*(1): 63-82.

Social Security Administration. 1996. *Annual Report of the Board of Trustees of the Federal Old-Age and Survivors Insurance and Disability Insurance Trust Funds.* Washington, DC: U.S. Department of Commerce, OASDI Board of Trustees.

Timiras, Paola S. 1994. Demographic, Comparative, and Differential Aging. In Paola S. Timiras (Ed.), *Physiological Basis of Aging and Geriatrics* (pp. 7-21). Boca Raton, LA: CRC Press.

U.S. Bureau of the Census. 1992. *Current Population Reports.* Washington, DC: U.S. Department of Commerce, U.S. Bureau of the Census.

U.S. Bureau of the Census. 1998a. *Poverty in the United States: 1997. Current Population Reports.* Washington, DC: U.S. Department of Commerce, Bureau of the Census.

U.S. Bureau of the Census. 1998b. *Statistical Abstract of the United States: 1998.* Washington, DC: U.S. Treasury Department, Bureau of Statistics.

U.S. Bureau of the Census. 1999. *Statistical Abstract of the United States: 1999.* Washington, DC: U.S. Treasury Department, Bureau of Statistics.

U.S. Department of Justice. 1999a. *Prisoners in 1998.* Report No. NCJ 175687. Washington, DC: U.S. Department of Justice, Bureau of Justice Statistics.

U.S. Department of Justice. 1999b. *Sourcebook of Criminal Justice Statistics 1998.* Washington, DC: U.S. Department of Justice.

U.S. Department of Justice. 1999c. *Women Offenders.* Report No. NCJ 175688. Washington, DC: U.S. Department of Justice.

Vitiello, Michael. 1997. Three Strikes: Can We Return to Rationality? *The Journal of Criminal Law and Criminology 87*(2): 395-481.

Walsh, C. Eamon. 1990. Needs of Older Inmates in Varying Security Settings. Newark, NJ: Doctoral dissertation, Rutgers State University. University Microfilms International.

White House. 1998. Older Americans Month, 1998, Proclamation. May 4. Los Angeles, CA: Office of the Press Secretary.

Untitled (fragment), Tracy Neal
From the collection of the Institute for Research on Women and Gender (The University of Michigan).

Chapter 10

Teenage Pregnancy:
Mediating Rotten Outcomes
and Improving Opportunities

Judy Walruff

Conceiving and giving birth to a baby during the teenage years and out-side of a marriage is a life-changing event that for many young women in America sets them on a lifelong path of social and economic disadvantage. This is so because this culture expects every mother—regardless of her physical age, level of maturity, or life experiences—to be responsible for the care and well-being of her child. As her pregnancy progresses and she gives birth, her childhood ends and her community, institutions, and even her family expect her to behave as an adult without regard to her readiness, ca-pacity, or understanding of the demands that will be made of her.

This chapter provides an overview of teenager childbearing in the United States, a summary of the social and health concerns associated with teenage pregnancy and births, theoretical explanations for trends in teenage child-bearing, a review of the contradictory social and health policies that compli-cate access to reproductive health, and a rationale for public policies that support specific programs and services to assist young mothers.

TEENAGE MOTHERHOOD IN THE UNITED STATES

Teenage pregnancy and birth rates in the United States have been steadily declining since 1990. Even so, compared with adolescent pregnancy and birth rates of other *developed* countries, those of the United States are among the highest in the world. In a cross-national comparative study, the United States, the Russian Federation, and several Eastern European coun-tries have pregnancy rates at least four times the rates in France, Germany, and Japan (Singh and Darrouch, 2000). In 1997, the latest year for which national pregnancy data are available, about 863,700 teenagers in the United States ages fifteen through nineteen became pregnant, and approximately 483,000 gave birth (Centers for Disease Control, 2000; Ventura et al., 2000). Recent birth rates have never equaled those of the post–World War II and post–Korean War decade of the 1950s, but a key difference is the marital status of the teenagers giving birth. While the majority of fifteen-through nineteen-year-olds giving birth at midcentury were married (85 percent), in 1993 only 28 percent were married at the time of birth (Ventura et al., 1995).

The present downward trend in teenage pregnancy and birth rates is credited to later initiation of intercourse, increased use of and access to contraceptives, and better education and economic prospects for disadvantaged teenage girls (Ventura et al., 1999). While these trends may continue, the National Center for Health Statistics (1998) predicts an increase in the number births to teenagers over the next few years due to increases in the teenage population.

ATTITUDES, VALUES, AND ECONOMICS

Although premarital intercourse has been documented from colonial times to the present, pregnancy among the unmarried is traditionally a cause for considerable distress and shame among families. Through the 1950s and early 1960s, pregnant teenagers and many women who did not seek out illegal sources of abortion and who did not marry retreated from community life or left their community until giving birth and then released the baby for adoption. Keeping and raising a baby out of wedlock was not the norm for middle- and upperclass women; it was associated at worst with a lower-class lifestyle or at best was considered deviant and antisocial. At that time, only about 5 percent of women giving birth were unmarried, and approximately 40 percent of these were teenagers, ages fifteen to nineteen. In sum, little national attention was directed at the issue. By 1970, the proportion of out-of-wedlock births was 10.6 percent and had nearly doubled to 17.8 percent by 1980. By 1990, the percentage of out-of-wedlock births had risen to 28 percent. However, only about 31 percent of these could be credited to teenagers nineteen and younger (National Center for Health Statistics, 1995).

When the average age of marriage for women rose from eighteen in 1960 to twenty-four in the 1990s (National Center for Health Statistics, 1995), and the rate of out-of-wedlock pregnancies rose among adolescents, premarital sexual intercourse was reaffirmed as a marker setting apart the "bad girls" from the "good." Research on delinquency and antisocial behavior seemed to confirm this conclusion. From their research, Jessor and Jessor (1977) suggested that drinking, drug use, delinquent behavior, and sexual intercourse together produced a "syndrome" of problem behavior in adolescence. These problem behaviors were defined as deviating from community norms and eliciting a social control response. More recent research also showed an association between sexual behavior, drug use, or behaviors considered illegal or risky to health among certain populations of youth (Benthin, Slovic, and Severson, 1993; Biglan et al., 1990; Jessor, Donovan, and Costa, 1991).

The 1980s brought improvement in research methods and broader conceptualizations of adolescent behaviors and the multiple factors that were associated with the prevalence of teenage pregnancies. These factors included the occurrence of physical and sexual abuse as well as sexual exploitation by older and/or predatory males (Abma, Driscall, and Moore, 1998; Boyer and Fine, 1992; Lindberg et al., 1997; Males and Chew, 1996).

Although not based on research, national policy on teenage sexual activity was promulgated through the Abstinence Education Provision of the 1996 Welfare Law (PL 104-193, Section 510 [42 U.S.C. 710] of the Title V of the Social Security Act). This provision, backed with $50 million in grants to the states to implement abstinence-only education programs, asserts that "abstinence from sexual activity outside marriage is the expected standard for all school-age children" and "a mutually faithful monogamous relationship in context of marriage is the expected standard of human sexual activity." This legislation may reflect cultural norms of certain population groups, but it certainly does not represent the mores of the post–sexual revolution generation's premarital and adolescent sexual behavior. Even though rates of teens engaging in sexual intercourse had begun to fall by the mid-1990s, a majority of teenagers have engaged in sexual intercourse by the time they are seniors in high school (Singh and Darrouch, 1999). Furthermore, research on parent teen communication regarding teens' sexual activity (Jaccard and Dittlus, 1991) showed that 20 percent of parent respondents believed that sex once or twice with a steady boyfriend or girlfriend would not be objectionable to them.

In the late 1970s and early 1980s, adolescent pregnancy gained attention as a serious health and social problem in the United States (Hayes, 1987). National and state concerns for this problem focused on the increasing numbers of adolescents giving birth out of wedlock and before completing their high school education. Dependent adolescents and their children were depending on welfare in increasing numbers, and national and state expenditures for their support were increasing (Lawson and Rhode, 1993). Public debate was fueled when advocates and researchers cited the increasing cost of teenage childbearing to taxpayers as they pressed for programs and strategies to prevent adolescent out-of-wedlock pregnancy (Armstrong and Waszak, 1990; Burt, 1986; Hayes, 1987; Wertheimer and Moore, 1982).

As the phenomenon of young women bearing children out of wedlock became prevalent among poor and middle-class teenagers, the related problems of interrupted education, poor employment prospects, and difficulties finding affordable child care to facilitate employment resulted in a growing underclass of teenage mothers and their babies. Although the poverty rate for children has fluctuated since the early 1980s (reaching a high of 22 percent in 1993), data from the March Current Population survey show the U.S. child poverty rate at 18 percent (Dalaker and Proctor, 2000). These data also document that children in married-couple families are much less likely to be living in poverty than children living only with their mothers. In 1998, 9 percent of children in married-couple families were living in poverty, compared to 46 percent in female-householder families. This difference in poverty rate further differentiates families of minority, racial, and ethnic groups. For example, in 1998, 12 percent of black children in married-couple families lived in poverty, compared with 55 percent of black children in female-householder families. In addition, 23 percent of Hispanic children in married-couple families lived in poverty compared with 60 percent in female-householder families.

Pregnant teenagers are also disadvantaged by their poor record of prenatal care utilization. Unfortunately, in spite of a persistent public health emphasis on prenatal care, national and state vital statistics on birth outcome show that teenagers are among those with the lowest rates of early and adequate prenatal care (Ventura and Martin, 1998). Health outcome data show that adolescent mothers, especially those under age fifteen, have higher rates of complication, maternal morbidity, and mortality than older women and women who have had more children (Fraser, Brockert, and Ward, 1995). Miscarriages and stillbirths are more frequent among teenagers, and they are more likely to have premature and/or low-birth-weight babies (Ketterlinus, Henderson, and Lamb, 1990; Menken, 1980; Mednick and Baker, 1980; Strobino, 1987; Zuckerman et al., 1984). Low-birth-weight babies (those weighing less than 2,500 grams) are at greater risk of dying in the first twenty-eight days of life and may experience developmental delays during infancy (Zuckerman et al., 1984). The poor birth outcomes of adolescents—except for those who are very young—are not generally thought to be a function of age alone but are more likely related to multiple factors of health status, social support, economic circumstances, health behaviors, emotional state, and access to prenatal health care (Gersten, Teitelbaum, and Chapin, 1985; Kramer, 1987; Mercer, Hackley, and Bostrom, 1983; Zuckerman et al., 1984).

Rates of teenage abortion also contributed to public interest in out-of-wedlock sexual intercourse and pregnancy. Abortions outnumbered births as early as 1974, and concern on the part of antiabortion advocates focused on supporting adolescent parenting while at the same time raising the public debate on the morals of abortion (Lawson and Rhode, 1993). Although the tax burden associated with teenage childbearing (and all childbearing out of wedlock) was viewed with increasing alarm, facilitating increased access to abortion was not considered an appropriate public policy response. In 1976, the U.S. Congress passed the Hyde Amendment prohibiting the expenditure of federal Medicaid funds for abortions for any poor pregnant woman. Furthermore, the right to abortion for minors has been restricted by regulations enacted in at least thirty states that require parental consent and/or notification before an abortion can take place (Wattleton, 1990). Access to abortion may also be limited by other factors. Organized protests against abortion occur regularly at clinics where these procedures are performed. Protestors form picket lines and so-called "sidewalk counselors" attempt to dissuade women from entering the clinics to have an abortion, when many of the women entering these clinics may do so for other reasons, such as an annual exam. Some clinics endure daily pickets; however, most "counseling" and harassment occurs on days when abortions are scheduled. Walking past these protestors is like running a gauntlet and requires conviction and a level of maturity that some teenagers have not yet attained.

Abortion access is also affected by the declining number of physicians willing to provide abortions. Some physicians do not perform abortions for reasons of conscience, while a second factor is the escalation of violence toward abortion providers and clinics. During the 1990s, antiabortion groups increased organized protests at the offices and homes of physicians performing abortions and at clinics where abortions were performed. In response to state-imposed regulations that gave women entering clinics for abortions the right to keep at a distance from shouting pickers and sidewalk counselors, antiabortion protestors focused their efforts more personally toward physicians and clinic personnel. Homes of physician providers were picketed; many received threats of bodily harm to themselves and their families. Internet sites list physicians' names and addresses and claim that they are murderers. An extreme radical faction in the antiabortion movement escalated its protest by committing violent acts against the doctors providing abortions and their clinics. Two physicians were murdered and maiming bombs were planted in and around clinic offices. As a result, fewer physicians are electing to perform abortions.

The abortion debate leaves teenagers in a moral and political catch-22: they are condemned for their disregard of a cultural standard prohibiting sexual intercourse outside of marriage when it leads to pregnancy and dependence on public resources, then they are blocked and demonized when they choose to terminate the pregnancy, thus avoiding dependency.

THEORETICAL INTERPRETATIONS

Over the past fifty years, the changing economic status of women, changes in welfare policy, access to legal abortion, and the influence of popular culture all have had a strong impact on the way single motherhood is viewed by large segments of the population. The feminist movement's focus on equal opportunities in employment contributed to a perception that women could achieve economic security outside of marriage. Furthermore, rates of divorce conveyed clearly the message that the past attribution of security to marriage was foundering and that many women would have to carry their maternal responsibilities single-handedly. Media reports of Hollywood stars having children out of wedlock and enjoying the rewards of parenthood with few social sanctions and economic constraints also helped in shaping a new cultural acceptance of single motherhood.

By 1980, changes in Aid to Families with Dependent Children (AFDC) policy permitted young women who established households separate from their parents to receive welfare benefits (Anderson, 1991). This policy change made marrying solely because of conception and impending childbirth an option, not an ultimatum. Young women in poverty could make a decision to parent alone rather than enter into a marital relationship.

To account for the increase in single teenage mothers, cultural and structural explanations were posited. The cultural argument is that family formation patterns among the poor are a result of deviant values or a "culture of poverty," which reinforces values very different from the dominant culture. A structural explanation argues that greater economic trends fundamentally change family formation patterns. Because these theories relate to descriptive meanings and processes of adaptation, they are better explored through qualitative studies (e.g., Maxwell, 1998; King et al., 1994).

Anderson (1989, 1991) provides strong support for a cultural hypothesis. Based on ethnographic data collected in the 1970s and 1980s in lower-class neighborhoods in Philadelphia and Chicago, Anderson concludes that teenage pregnancy and motherhood is part of the adolescent culture in such neighborhoods.

Exploring the cultural explanation in the mid-1990s among girls residing in the inner city of a major metropolitan area in the Southwest, Figueira-McDonough (1998) found no support for this hypothesis. She ran several focus groups with girls aged fourteen through sixteen and, although participants expressed tolerance for teenage sexual activity, they aspired to continuous and monogamous relationships and saw marriage as a desirable outcome. They expressed, however, doubts that they could find stable companions in their neighborhoods. Contrary to the "baby clubs" described by Anderson (1991), these girls saw precocious motherhood as isolating them from adolescent social life.

Jarrett (1994) found further support for the structural argument with studies of adolescent mothers living in very poor Chicago neighborhoods. She studied the economic status of adolescents' families and the contribution of this factor to the decisions black adolescents make about family formation. Through a series of qualitative interviews, Jarrett presented a description of economic and social variables associated with patterns of adolescent childbearing and family formation among never-married black women in low-income inner-city neighborhoods. Her purpose was to describe the ways in which these young women adapt to poverty and to further expand on a structural explanation of the link between patterns of family formation and economic marginality. The population selected for this qualitative study included low-income African-American women who were never married, AFDC recipients, living in high poverty or transitional neighborhoods in Chicago. These women were in their early twenties and had begun their childbearing as adolescents. Four themes were explored in unstructured interview sessions: marriage, the ideal; marriage, the reality; economic impediments to marriage; and alternatives to conventional marriage. The analysis of the responses showed that all of the women believed that legal marriage was the foundation for family formation and maintenance. Marriage for these young women represented establishing their own households apart from parents, economic independence, and commitment and fidelity between the marital partners. These women were, however, pessimistic about their chances and opportunities to establish a traditional, nuclear family bounded by a legal marriage. Their experience and observation of life in poor communities ran counter to this ideal. As Wilson (1996) chronicles, the number of black men in poor urban neighborhoods who are available to assume the responsibilities of marriage is limited by high rates of unemployment (due to migration of commerce and industry out of the inner city), high rates of incarceration, and high rates of mortality due to violence. If an ideal of marriage and economic security could not be achieved because of the tenuous provider prospects of the baby's father, then these young women reasoned they could manage as well on their own. Conditions of poverty did not lessen their desire for independence or their hopes for a better future for themselves and their children. These young African-American women demonstrated that poverty and limited economic opportunity affected their decision-making processes in very pragmatic ways. While holding to traditional values of family formation, they chose to forgo marriage to assure some economic security for their children through AFDC and Medicaid.

This structural explanation for alternative patterns of family formation allows for a public policy response that is based on the pragmatic realities of the environment rather than one that is decried as negative and inherently destructive to the family formation process. Schram (1995) elaborates on this theme in his description of the welfare benefit as a stigmatizing cultural force because of the negative significance it attaches to single-woman-headed families. Through its emphasis on issues of dependence and disincentives to form the two-parent households (married couples with children), assistance to the single-mother family is denigrated and receives only limited public support.

THE CONFLICT OF DEVELOPMENTAL
ISSUES AND POLICY

The conundrum of adolescent sexual behavior, pregnancy, and parenthood is complicated by conflicting social, legal, and institutional responses when adolescents do not conform to societal expectations. In the United States, adolescence is thought of as the last stage of childhood and, thus, it is accepted as a period of time relatively free from the perceived responsibilities, concerns, and pressures that belong to adulthood. Youths are expected to be in school rather than engaged in full-time work; legally, those under the age of eighteen are considered dependent and for both social and economic reasons rely on parents or other adults for the basic necessities of life, such as shelter, food, and medical care. Completing education, obtaining full-time employment, and reaching the age to enter into legal contracts including marriage are social and legal events that, for the most part, signal adulthood. Childbearing and child rearing prior to achieving adult social and legal status, and while still legally and socially dependent, is not considered an expected or accepted event in the lives of the majority of U.S. adolescents at this time. Of late, this view of adolescents as lacking in the judgment to make informed decisions and a resurgence of a "parents' rights" movement has resulted in differing laws and policies in each state concerning the age that teenagers can consent to sex, the conditions under which they may access family planning and abortion services, where they may receive sex education, the content of and the consent for that education, and their eligibility for public assistance programs should they become parents (Boonstra and Nash, 2000).

In general, in the United States there is wide acceptance of these legal constraints placed on adolescents during the time when they are completing the physical and mental development necessary to prepare them for adult decisions and responsibilities. It is well established that during the extended years of adolescent development, youths become more capable of abstract thinking, foresight, and internal control. A greater awareness of the environment and a greater capacity for empathy and idealism also develop (Erikson, 1968; Friedman, 1993). Erikson (1968, 1980) refers to adolescence as a time when youth need a "psychological moratorium" that allows for role experimentation and integration of identity elements, which leads toward a final definition of self in society. During this period of seeking greater autonomy, questioning parental values, and formulating their own view of the world, adolescents complete the remaining psychosocial tasks necessary to prepare them for adult life (Bandura, 1972; Coleman, 1978; Gilligan, 1987; Haan, 1977; Moriarty and Toussieng, 1975; Offer, Ostrov, and Howard, 1981; Savin-Williams and Demo, 1984; Weiner, 1979). Despite the acceptance of this contemporary view of adolescence, at least two examples of policies ignore the developmental processes of adolescence, thereby giving little latitude for imperfect reasoning, lack of foresight, or actions and behaviors that may result from lack of knowledge or inexperience.

In the 1990s, nearly every state in the United States changed its laws so that youths who commit certain crimes are transferred to adult courts to be tried and sentenced as adults (Building Blocks for Youth, 2000). The levels of adolescent cognitive development, maturity, and decision-making skill are not considered in the determination of culpability, and youths need only fall within the prescribed conditions of the laws to be judged as adults for their actions.

A second example of when maturity and the decision-making capabilities of teenagers are almost automatically overlooked is when they give birth. Once teenagers become parents, they are treated as mature enough to make all the legal decisions regarding their own children. Whether they are thirteen or seventeen, they alone can consent to health care for their child, enroll their children in child care, consent for their child to be adopted, or apply for public assistance and social services on behalf of their child. An irony is that a number of states have also placed legal obstacles in the way of adolescents seeking abortions on the grounds that they are not mature enough to make this decision on their own. A majority of states have laws that require parental notification, parental consent, or judicial bypass to assure that the decision to have an abortion is legally competent (Alan Guttmacher Institute, 2000).

Although experiencing pregnancy and childbirth move an adolescent quickly into adult roles and responsibilities, these conditions may not fundamentally change the pace of her cognitive and social development. Neither social welfare nor health policies has effectively responded with programs and services that differentiate the needs of teenage mothers from those of older, disadvantaged women. A result is a precarious future with poor economic and health consequences for teenage mothers and their children.

TEENAGE MOTHERS AND WELFARE REFORM

By the mid-1990s, unwed teenage mothers became the cause célèbre of the political right and a focal point of welfare reform legislation (Jansson, 2000). Based on the premise that access to welfare payments encouraged out-of-wedlock childbearing, reform legislation—replacing the entitlement program Aid to Families with Dependant Children (AFDC)—was crafted with provisions that prohibited direct cash payments to minor parents.[1] The new federal eligibility rules for Temporary Aid to Needy Families (TANF) also required minor custodial parents to live with a parent or approved relative, or in an adult-supervised setting. Exceptions to the residence requirement are allowed if no parent is available or willing to house the minor parent and child; if the state welfare agency otherwise determines it is in the best interests of the minor child to waive the requirement; or if a complaint of abuse and neglect is substantiated by Child Protective Services or other welfare agency. If such an investigation substantiates abuse or neglect, a waiver may be granted to allow the teen to receive assistance in an alternative "approved" living arrangement. These rules presume that teenagers in sufficiently desperate situations will make an allegation against parents or guardians in order to receive welfare. Furthermore, teenagers must be prepared to risk that the allegation will not be proven and then face the dilemma of trying to remain in the household of a parent they have officially accused of abuse. The policy seems contradictory as it is based on the premise that teenage mothers are not competent to manage the public assistance funds for which they may quality, but must have the maturity and self-confidence to make serious allegations against their parents or the guardian in whose home they must reside in order to qualify for assistance. A teenager's maturity, capacity to make reasoned decisions, and plans for the future are secondary to considerations of her chronological age and status as a minor.

To continue to qualify for assistance, teenage parents must also be enrolled in school, vocational training, or a GED program if they have not already received a high school diploma. These requirements reflect a consensus that a high school diploma is a fundamental gateway to employment, essential for future employability and an exit from welfare. States were given wide discretion in developing the types of programs that might assist teenage parents in meeting the school attendance requirement. Primary options include alliances or contracts with public schools to keep teenage parents enrolled until graduation and/or directly support GED programs. Only a small proportion of schools in the United States offer comprehensive support services and flexible curricula that help pregnant and parenting teenagers remain in a traditional high school program. This is unfortunate because school-based, teenage-parent programs that offer onsite child care, case management, and health and social services have been shown to have a positive association with school retention and completion by pregnant teens (Warrick et al., 1993). Funding to develop and support these essential services is usually a discretionary line item in school district budgets, if it exists at all, and is difficult to sustain.

GED programs, directly funded by states, are a primary way for states to assist minor parents in meeting the school attendance requirement. Offering greater flexibility than public school programs and with the option to include essential support services (such as child care and case management), GED programs are favored for their ease of administration and relative low cost when compared to school-based programs (Wood and Burghardt, 1997). Although GED programs may be attractive to many teenage parents (especially those for whom school is overwhelming or viewed as an unsupportive environment) and to welfare agencies, in the long run this option may not serve teenage parents as well as a traditional high school diploma. A review of research on the labor market costs of obtaining a GED instead of regular high school degree suggest that the GED results in substantially lower earnings in later life (Chaplin, 1999). Creating policies and programs that allow teenage parents to use the GED as a prerequisite to advanced education could mediate this result; however, the "work-first" philosophy of many state welfare programs does not support pursuit of higher education, which would lead to higher-paying employment.

Much remains to be learned about the outcomes of welfare reform policies and programs for minor parents in reducing long-term welfare dependency. The broader questions of whether these policies and programs ideally help teenage mothers complete the developmental tasks of adolescence while coping with the responsibilities of early parenthood is more difficult both to measure and to include as a research agenda of interest to welfare policymakers.

TEENAGERS' PRENATAL CARE ACCESS: AN ARIZONA STUDY

Although public health goals for the United States include early and continuous prenatal care for all pregnant women, teenagers (ages fifteen through nineteen) are among those least likely to enter care in the first trimester and to receive the recommended number and frequency of prenatal care visits (Ventura and Martin, 1998). Multiple factors have been shown to be associated with these lower rates of prenatal care use including: poverty, lack of health insurance, concerns about confidentiality, family's attitudes about when to see a doctor, and teenagers' limited skills and resources to negotiate the complexities of using an adult, prenatal care system (Brown, 1988; Klein et al., 1999). Although the economic and social factors can be formidable barriers to prenatal care for pregnant teenagers, planning and carrying out the multiple steps required to gain entry to and use the health care system challenges those teenagers who are less cognitively mature or who have few social supports as they seek and try to obtain care (Walruff, 2000). One reason is that the prenatal care delivery system does not usually differentiate among the ages of pregnant women that come for care and it makes few accommodations for teenage clients. In a review of literature by the Institute of Medicine (Brown, 1988), factors associated with decreased prenatal care clinic utilization by teenagers included: a clinic atmosphere that is formal, institutional, and primarily used by adults; health care staff that do not communicate acceptance and understanding of adolescent concerns; and absence of support to comply with recommended care and keeping appointments. A few obstetric clinics do operate with an understanding of the developmental and psychosocial needs of pregnant adolescents, but most do not tailor their services to this population.

In 1996, this author undertook a study of Arizona teenagers' prenatal care utilization. All of these young mothers were receiving care through the Arizona Medicaid program and thus had incomes at 180 percent of federal poverty levels or less. Although some studies of teenagers' utilization of prenatal care had examined the economic and institutional barriers to care, I wanted to explore cognitive development (maturity), social support, and family communication regarding sexuality and pregnancy as factors associated with early, first-trimester entry to prenatal care and continuity of care. The sample included 105 teens roughly divided between adolescents who were considered minors (ages fourteen through seventeen) and those considered adults (eighteen through nineteen) at the time they gave birth. Nearly all were unmarried at the time of their child's birth. About 60 percent of the total sample entered prenatal care during the first three months of pregnancy in accordance with standards of care recommended by the American College of Obstetricians and Gynecologists (1992). Among the minor teens, nearly 53 percent entered care in the first trimester, while 69 percent of older teens had their first prenatal care visit in the first three months of pregnancy. These data closely matched prenatal care entry statistics for pregnant teenagers in Arizona during the study period and were consistent with the state and national data (showing a larger proportion of younger teenagers entering care after the first trimester of pregnancy).

This study of teenagers' prenatal care utilization was guided by the conviction that the level of adolescent cognitive development (egocentrism and problem-solving skills) also contributed to the timing of the first prenatal care visit (onset) and the continuity of that care throughout the pregnancy. Other psychosocial variables that were expected to affect prenatal care utilization included sexuality information and knowledge, family support, and the influence of peers. The concept of cognitive egocentrism (self-centeredness in thought) occurs early in adolescence and persists in varying degrees through the transition to mature decision-making capacity (Elkind and Flavell, 1969; Piaget and Inhelder, 1958). Egocentrism was measured by the Personal Fable Questionnaire, a forty-three-item survey instrument developed by Green and colleagues (1992). Reasoning and decision-making skills develop during adolescence and are characterized by an ability to construct possibilities, reflect on options, and to anticipate future results. The Problem-Solving and Decision-Making Inventory (Heppner, 1988)—a thirty-two-item, self-perception scale—was used as the measure of problem-solving skills. The Moos Family Environment Scale (Moos and Moos, 1994) measured family support. I constructed an eighty-four-item questionnaire to collect the data to measure parent-teen communication about sex and pregnancy, and family and friends involvement in prenatal care access and continuity. The data were analyzed by total sample (ages fourteen through nineteen) and by the two age strata (fourteen through seventeen and eighteen through nineteen). Although cognitive development and the transition from concrete to abstract thinking does not occur according to a fixed schedule, as teens mature chronologically they become more capable of abstract thinking, foresight, and internal control. These age strata reflect the legal distinction that separates minor adolescents from those deemed to have achieved adult status.

Results of multivariate analyses supported the premise that factors of cognitive development (maturity) as well as social characteristics (such as family communication about sex and pregnancy) were associated with earlier prenatal care onset and care continuity. For the total sample, characteristics that predict earlier initiation of prenatal care are individual maturity (low egotism and high problem solving), living in a mother-only household, discussions concerning sex and pregnancy with mother, and living in a family with high control over family activities.

For the younger teenagers (fourteen through seventeen), minority ethnicity, living in a single-mother household, being more mature (less egotism), having higher problem-solving capacity, living in a family with more controls, and having a mother who discusses sexuality and pregnancy predicts earlier onset of prenatal care. These results also show that earlier onset is predicted by the presence of a nonfamily member at the initial prenatal care visit. A possible interpretation is that peers or the father of the baby are the first confidants regarding the pregnancy and thus are likely to be present at the first visit.

For older teenagers (ages eighteen through nineteen), earlier onset is predicted by having had discussions with their mothers about sex and pregnancy, more maturity, family life that encourages independence, and family presence at the first prenatal visit. Access to health care through use of prescription birth control also predicts earlier prenatal care onset for this age group. Unexpectedly, teenagers who were already enrolled in the Medicaid program entered care later than teenagers who enrolled after the first prenatal care visit.

An unexpected finding of this research was that teenagers in single-mother households entered care earlier than those living in two-parent households. One possible explanation is that daughters in mother-only households may have more open communication regarding sex and pregnancy with their mothers than in two-parent households. Moore and Peterson (1989) found similar results in their analysis of data from the 1987 National Youth Survey. In this survey, mothers were asked how often they or their children's other parent discussed contraceptive methods with their teenagers. Study results showed that mothers from intact families were considerably less likely to have held such discussions than mothers who had been through a marital disruption. Another possibility is that single mothers take a more realistic approach to the risks of sex and pregnancy for their children than in two-parent families.

Starting prenatal care in the first trimester, more cognitive maturity, and living in a family that encouraged self-sufficiency were predictive of continuous care for the total sample of teenagers in the study. These results are consistent with adolescent development theory that more mature teenagers are better able to plan and complete tasks that require a future orientation. For younger teenagers, starting care in the first trimester and living in a family that promotes self-sufficiency predicted continuous care. Keeping the prenatal care schedule of visits for the older teenage mothers in the study was predicted by starting care in the first trimester and a willingness to accept the advice of others.

After earlier onset, family support is more important for younger teens in achieving continuous care, while individual characteristics contribute to continuity for the older teenagers. As teenagers become older, parents usually play a diminishing role in the day-to-day activities of their children and expect them to be responsible for keeping their own appointments. Regardless of age, parents' responses to pregnancy may be to encourage or expect more independence and less parental involvement in keeping the regimen of prenatal care visits. For less mature teenagers, these expectations may not be realistic and the requirements of the prenatal care regimen may not be met.

SUPPORT SERVICES FOR TEENAGE PARENTS

It is well established that case management services are beneficial to teenage mothers and can assist them in successfully making the transition to the adult responsibilities of parenthood (Brindis, Barth, and Loomis, 1987; Brown, 1988; Furstenberg, Brooks-Gunn, and Morgan, 1987). Some states have contracted for case management services along with life-skills classes for minor parents receiving TANF, depending on the school attended or program of work in which they are enrolled. However, each state decides on the type and content of support services offered or mandated, and thus great variation in the type and level of support available to either teenage or older mothers exists. As elegantly described by Ruth Horowitz (1995), social services, job training, and readiness programs for teenage mothers are more or less successful depending on the personalities and approach of those providing the training, the level of congruence between program intent and implementation, and the insight of program providers regarding the psychosocial needs of teenage mothers. Such programs rarely assess the development of their younger (or older) clients, and most do not adjust curriculum content, presentation format, or pace of instruction to accommodate for differences in life experience or social and psychological maturity.

Do the new regulations for minor parents discourage applications for TANF? Do the requirements result in teens waiting until they are eighteen to apply, when program requirements are not as stringent? Would policies that provide a broader safety net with more social support and health services to teenage mothers and their children reduce the risk for long-term disadvantage in this population? Current planned research in these areas may yet answer these questions. Evidence from previous studies on the long-term consequence of early motherhood has answered this latter question in the affirmative (Brown, 1988; Furstenberg, Brooks-Gunn, and Morgan, 1987).

RECOMMENDATION FOR CHANGE
TO HEALTH AND SOCIAL POLICY

Ideally, the health, social, and future life problems associated with teenage pregnancy and childbearing could be addressed, in part, by coherent social policy that supports access to information, health care, and comprehensive social service programs that have been shown to reduce the rate of these pregnancies in the United States. Lacking such policies, the United States continues to have one of the highest teenage pregnancy rates in the industrialized world, with nearly one million teenagers becoming pregnant and approximately 480,000 of them giving birth in 1997 alone (Ventura et al.,

1999). These figures call for health and welfare policies and programs that recognize the developmental and psychosocial needs of young women having children before they are mature enough to assume the long-term commitment of caring for and supporting a child or children.

The most useful health care and social policy reifies case management and follow-up services for adolescents throughout their pregnancies and after childbirth as outlined in the Society for Adolescent Medicine's (SAM's) "Position Paper on Reproductive Health Care for Adolescents" (1991). The SAM guidelines call for comprehensive, age-appropriate, multidisciplinary, prenatal care. Ideally, the same health care provider assures continuity of care throughout the pregnancy as a member of a multidisciplinary team that include services from nutrition, education, job training, nursing, social work, medicine, and obstetrics. Prenatal and postnatal educational programs optimally include family members, as well as the fathers of the babies, and interventions are targeted with consideration of ethnic diversity. Furthermore, these services should remain in place until it is evident that sufficient ancillary support is in place or the adolescent client has shown a capacity for decision making and action that is in the best interests of herself and her child. Younger adolescents, or those who have not yet acquired more complex and abstract forms of reasoning, may need additional assistance from family, medical providers, or service agency staff to access medical care services and then comply with the health care regimen necessary to result in a healthy birth.

Social service policy must align with health policy to assure ongoing support to teenage mothers, their children, and, when appropriate, their partners. Social welfare policy should be designed to encourage young mothers to remain in high school whenever possible, and TANF funds should be used to provide comprehensive service that will include child care, counseling, academic support, and parenting skills. Funding decisions should come with requirements that services and program content differentiate between mothers who are thirteen and those who are eighteen. Program success should be measured by the extent to which teenage mothers gain skills and capacity to meet the challenges of parenthood successfully as they complete the developmental tasks of adolescence.

For teenagers and adult women, having babies out of wedlock need not result in overwhelming disadvantage. Through research and from women in this predicament, the types and scope of services and programs needed to help them live past the potential disadvantage and form strong families and secure futures have been identified. The opportunity continues to reestablish through public policy a link between public assistance payments, health care services, and comprehensive social support services.

NOTE

1. The Personal Responsibility and Work Opportunity Reconciliation Act (PRWORA) was enacted in August of 1996, replacing AFDC with federal block grants to states for TANF, in which no entitlement exists.

REFERENCES

Abma, Joyce, Ann Driscall, and Kristin A. Moore. 1998. Young Women's Degree of Control over First Intercourse: An Exploratory Analysis. *Family Planning Perspectives 30*(1): 12-18.

Alan Guttmacher Institute. 2000. *The Status of Major Abortion-Related Laws and Policies in the States.* September. Washington, DC: Alan Guttmacher Institute.

American College of Obstetricians and Gynecologists. 1992. *Standards for Obstetric-Gynecologic Services,* Seventh Edition. Washington, DC: American College of Obstetricians and Gynecologists.

Anderson, Elija. 1989. Sex Codes and Family Life Among Poor Inner-City Youths. *Annals of the American Academy of Political and Social Science 501:* 59-73.

Anderson, Elija. 1991. *Streetwise: Race, Class and Change in an Urban Community.* Chicago: University of Chicago Press.

Armstrong, Elizabeth and Cynthia Waszak. 1990. *Teenage Pregnancy and Too-Early Childbearing: Public Costs, Personal Consequences,* Sixth Edition. Washington, DC: Center for Population Options.

Bandura, Albert. 1972. The Stormy Decade: Fact or Fiction? In Dorothy Rogers (Ed.), *Issues in Adolescent Psychology* (pp. 157-205). New York: Appleton-Century-Crofts.

Benthin, Alida, Paul Slovic, and Herbert Severson. 1993. A Psychometric Study of Adolescent Risk Perception. *Journal of Adolescence 16*(2): 153-168.

Biglan, Albert W., Charles W. Metzler, Robert Wirt, Donald Ary, John Noell, L. Ochs, C. French, and D. Hood. 1990. Social and Behavioral Factors Associated with High-Risk Sexual Behavior Among Adolescents. *Journal of Behavioral Medicine 13*(3): 245-261.

Boonstra, Heather and Elizabeth Nash. 2000. *Minors and the Right to Consent to Health Care.* The Guttmacher Report on Public Policy. Washington, DC: Alan Guttmacher Institute.

Boyer, Debra K. and Michelle Fine. 1992. Sexual Abuse As a Factor in Adolescent Pregnancy and Child Maltreatment. *Family Planning Perspectives 24*(4): 4-19.

Brindis, Claire, Richard Barth, and Amy P. Loomis. 1987. Continuous Counseling: Case Management with Teenage Parents. *Social Casework 68*(March): 164-172.

Brown, Sarah (Ed.). 1988. *Prenatal Care: Reaching Mothers, Reaching Infants.* Washington, DC: Institute of Medicine, Division of Health Promotion and Disease Prevention.

Building Blocks for Youth. 2000. *Youth Crime/Adult Time: Is Justice Served?* Washington, DC: Building Blocks for Youth.

Burt, Martha, R. 1986. *Estimates of Public Costs for Teenage Childbearing*. Washington, DC: Center for Population Options.

Centers for Disease Control. 2000. *National and State-Specific Pregnancy Rates Among Adolescents, United States, 1995-1997. Morbidity and Mortality Weekly Report* Vol. 49, No. 27. Hyattsville, MD: U.S. Department of Health and Human Services.

Chaplin, Duncan. 1999. *GEDs for Teenagers: Are There Unintended Consequences?* Washington DC: The Urban Institute.

Coleman, John. C. 1978. Current Contradictions in Adolescent Theory. *Journal of Youth and Adolescence 7*(1): 1-11.

Dalaker, Joseph and Bernadette D. Proctor. 2000. *Poverty in the United States: 1999.* Washington, DC: U.S. Bureau of the Census.

Elkind, David and John H. Flavell (Eds.). 1969. *Studies in Cognitive Development: Essays in Honor of Jean Piaget*. New York: Oxford University Press.

Erickson, Erik H. 1968. *Identity Youth and Crisis*. New York: W. W. Norton.

Erickson, Erik H. 1980. *Identity and the Life Cycle*. New York: W. W. Norton.

Figueira-McDonough, Josefina. 1998. Environment and Interpretations: Voices of Young People in Poor Inner-City Neighborhoods. *Youth and Society 30*(2): 123-163.

Fraser, Alison M., John Brockert, and R. H. Ward. 1995. Association of Young Maternal Age with Adverse Reproductive Outcomes. *New England Journal of Medicine 332*(17): 1113-1117.

Friedman, Herbert L. 1993. Adolescent Social Development: A Global Perspective. *Journal of Adolescent Health 14*(8): 588-594.

Furstenberg, Frank Jr., Jeanne Brooks-Gunn, and S. P. Morgan. 1987. Adolescent Mothers and Their Children in Later Life. *Family Planning Perspectives 19*(4): 142-151.

Gersten, Joanne C., Fred Teitelbaum, and Charles Chapin. 1985. *Risk Factors for Low Birth Weight Babies: The Arizona Experience, 1969 to 1983.* Research Notes. Phoenix: Arizona Department of Health Services, Office of Policy and Planning.

Gilligan, Carol. 1987. Adolescent Development Reconsidered. In Charles E. Irwin (Ed.), *Adolescent Social Behavior and Health* (pp. 33-61). San Francisco: Jossey-Bass.

Green, Vickie, Kathi Morton, Barbara Cornell, Freda Jones, and William E. Jaynes. 1992. The Personal Fable in Adolescence: The Development of an Instrument to Measure the Personal Fable Aspect of Adolescent Cognitive Egocentrism. Unpublished manuscript.

Haan, Norma. 1977. *Coping and Defining: Process of Self-Environment Organization.* Orlando, FL: Academic Press.

Hayes, Cheryl D. (Ed.). 1987. *Risking the Future: Adolescent Sexuality Pregnancy and Childbearing,* Vol. 1. Washington DC: National Research Council.

Heppner, Paul P. 1988. *The Problem-Solving Inventory*. Palo Alto, CA: Consulting Psychologists Press.

Horowitz, Ruth. 1995. *Teen Mothers: Citizens or Dependents?* Chicago: University of Chicago Press.

Jaccard, James and Patricia Dittlus. 1991. *Parent-Teen Communication.* New York: Springer-Verlag.

Jansson, Bruce S. 2000. *The Reluctant Welfare State: A Historical Introduction to American Welfare Policies,* Fourth Edition. Belmont, CA: Wordsworth.

Jarrett, Robin L. 1994. Living Poor: Family Life Among Single Parent, African-American Women. *Social Problems 41*(1): 30-49.

Jessor, Richard, John E. Donovan, and Frances M. Costa. 1991. *Beyond Adolescence: Problem Behavior and Young Adult Development.* New York: Cambridge University Press.

Jessor, Richard and Shirley L. Jessor. 1977. *Problem Behavior and Psychosocial Development: A Longitudinal Study of Youth.* New York: Academic Press.

Ketterlinus, Robert D., M. A. Henderson, and Michael E. Lamb. 1990. Maternal Age, Sociodemographics, Prenatal Health and Behavior: Influences on Neonatal Risk Status. *Journal of Adolescent Health Care 11*(5): 423-431.

King, Gary, Leo Hank, Robert O. Keohane, and Sidney Verba. 1994. *Designing Social Inquiry.* Princeton, NJ: Princeton University Press.

Klein, Jonathan D., Karen M. Wilson, Molly McNulty, Cynthia Kapphahn, and Karen S. Collins. 1999. Access to Medical Care for Adolescents: Results from the 1997 Commonwealth Fund Survey of the Health of Adolescent Girls. *Journal of Adolescent Health 25*(2): 120-130.

Kramer, Michael S. 1987. Intrauterine Growth and Gestational Duration Determinants. *Pediatrics 80*(4): 502-511.

Lawson, Annette and Deborah L. Rhode (Eds.). 1993. *The Politics of Pregnancy: Adolescent Sexuality and Public Policy.* New Haven, CT: Yale University Press.

Lindberg, Laura D., Freya L. Sonenstein, Leighton Ku, and Gladys Martinez. 1997. Age Difference Between Minors Who Give Birth and Their Adult Partners. *Family Planning Perspectives 29*(2): 61-66.

Males, Mike and K. S. Y. Chew. 1996. The Ages of Fathers in California Adolescent Births, 1993. *American Journal of Public Health 86*(4): 565-568.

Maxwell, Joseph. 1998. Designing a Qualitative Study. In Leonard Bickman and Debra Rog (Eds.), *Handbook of Applied Social Research* (pp. 69-100). Thousand Oaks, CA: Sage Publications.

Mednick, Birgitter and Robert L. Baker. 1980. *Social and Medical Predictors of Infant Health.* Final report to National Institute for Child Health and Human Development. Los Angeles: University of Southern California.

Menken, Jane. 1980. The Health and Demographic Consequences of Adolescent Pregnancy and Childbearing. In Catherine S. Chilman (Ed.), *Adolescent Pregnancy and Childbearing: Findings from Research* (pp. 157-205). Washington, DC: U.S. Department of Health and Human Services.

Mercer, Ramona T., K. C. Hackley, and A. G. Bostrom. 1983. Relationship of Psychosocial and Perinatal Variables to Perception of Childbirth. *Nursing Research 32*(4): 202-207.

Moore, Kristin A. and J. Peterson. 1989. *The Consequences of Teenage Pregnancy: Final Report.* Washington, DC: Child Trends, Inc.

Moos, Rudolf H. and Bernice S. Moos. 1994. *Family Environment Scale Manual: Development, Applications, Research,* Third Edition. Palo Alto, CA: Consulting Psychologists Press.

Moriarty, Alice and Povl Toussieng. 1975. Adolescence in a Time of Transition. *Bulletin of the Menninger Clinic 39:* 391-408.

National Center for Health Statistics. 1995. *Report to Congress on Out-of-Wedlock Childbearing.* Department of Health and Human Services publication no. PSH 95-1257. Hyattsville, MD: National Center for Health Statistics.

National Center for Health Statistics. 1998. *Report of Final Natality Statistics, 1996.* Report 46 (11). Hyattsville, MD: National Center for Health Statistics.

Offer, Daniel, Eric Ostrov, and Kenneth I. Howard. 1981. *The Adolescent: A Psychological Self-Portrait.* New York: Basic Books, Inc.

Piaget, Jean and Barbel Inhelder. 1958. *The Growth of Logical Thinking from Childhood to Adolescence: An Essay on the Construction of Formal Operational Structures.* A. Parsons and S. Milgram, Trans. New York: Basic Books.

Savin-Williams, Ritch C., and David H. Demo. 1984. Developmental Change and Stability in Adolescent Self-Concept. *Developmental Psychology 20*(6): 1100-1110.

Schram, Sanford E. 1995. *Words of Welfare: The Poverty of Social Science and the Social Science of Poverty.* Minneapolis: University of Minnesota Press.

Singh, Susheela and Jacqueline E. Darrouch. 1999. Trends in Sexual Activity Among Adolescent American Women: 1982-1995. *Family Planning Perspectives 31*(5): 212-219.

Singh, Susheela and Jacqueline E. Darrouch. 2000. Adolescent Pregnancy and Childbearing: Levels and Trends in Developed Countries. *Family Planning Perspectives 32*(1): 14-23.

Society for Adolescent Medicine. 1991. Position Paper on Reproductive Health Care for Adolescents. *Journal of Adolescent Health 12*(8): 649-661.

Strobino, Donna M. 1987. The Health and Medical Consequences of Adolescent Sexuality and Pregnancy: A Review of the Literature. In S. L. Hofferth and C. D. Hayes (Eds.), *Risking the Future: Adolescent Sexuality, Pregnancy and Childbearing* Vol. 2 (pp. 93-123). Washington DC: National Research Council.

Ventura, Stephanie, Christine A. Bachrach, Laura Hill, Kelleen Kaye, Pamela Holcomb, and Elisa Koff. 1995. The Demography of Out-of-Wedlock Childbearing. Unpublished report to the Secretary of the Department of Health and Human Services. Washington. DC: Department of Health and Human Services, Office of the Assistant Secretary for Planning and Evaluation.

Ventura, Stephanie J. and Joyce A. Martin. 1998. Final Natality Statistics, 1996. *Monthly Vital Statistics Report 46*(11S): 66. Hyattsville, MD: National Vital Statistics.

Ventura, Stephanie J., Joyce A. Martin, Sally C. Curtin, T. J. Mathews, and Melissa M. Park. 2000. Births: Final Data for 1997. *National Vital Statistics Reports 47* (18): 25-28. Hyattsville, MD: National Vital Statistics.

Ventura, Stephanie J., William Mosher, Joyce A. Martin, Sally Curtin, Joyce C. Abma, and Stanley Henshaw. 1999. Highlights of Trends in Pregnancies and Pregnancy Rates by Outcome: Estimates for the United States, 1976-96. *Na-*

tional Vital Statistics Reports 47(29): 1-10. Hyattsville, MD: National Vital Statistics.

Walruff, Judy C. 2000. Teenage Mothers' Prenatal Care Utilization: Influences of Cognitive Development, Family Support, and Health Care Access. Doctoral dissertation, Arizona State University, Tempe.

Warrick, Louise, John B. Christianson, Judy Walruff, and Paul Cook. 1993. Educational Outcomes in Teenage Pregnancy and Parenting Programs: Results from a Demonstration. *Family Planning Perspectives* 25(4): 148-155.

Wattleton, Faye. 1990. Teenage Pregnancies and the Recriminalization of Abortions. *American Journal of Public Health* 80(3): 269-270.

Weiner, Irving B. 1979. *Psychological Disturbance in Adolescence.* New York: Wiley-Interscience.

Wertheimer, Richard F. and Kristin A. Moore. 1982. *Teenage Childbearing: Public Sector Costs.* Final Report on Contract No. N01-HD-92822. Washington, DC: Urban Institute, Center for Population Research, National Institute of Child Health and Human Development.

Wilson, William J. 1996. *When Work Disappears: The World of the New Urban Poor.* New York: Knopf.

Wood, Robert G. and John Burghardt. 1997. *Implementing Welfare Reform Requirements for Teenage Parents: Lessons from Experience in Four States.* Washington DC: Mathematica Policy Research.

Zuckerman, Barry D., D. Frank Walker, C. Chase, and B. Hamburg. 1984. Adolescent Pregnancy: Biobehavioral Determinants of Outcome. *The Journal of Pediatrics* 105(6): 857-863.

SECTION IV:
BAD WOMEN,
UNDESERVING MOTHERS

Karen Brown
Reprinted with permission from Kornfeld, Phyllis, 1997. *Cellblock Visions.*
Princeton, NJ: Princeton University Press.

Chapter 11

Controlled and Excluded:
Reproduction and Motherhood
Among Poor and Imprisoned Women

M. A. Bortner

Poor and imprisoned women are commanded by cultural reproductive imperatives, but they are also excluded from the structures of privilege and support that make "successful" motherhood possible. Despite cultural portrayals of parenting as a universal human right, public policies systematically infringe upon this right, condemn poor and imprisoned women to motherhood under conditions of great deprivation, and demonize and degrade them and their children. Punitive policies contribute greatly to the creation and perpetuation of a caste system in which poor and imprisoned mothers are condemned by the cultural emphasis on family integrity and the preeminence of "family values." These deliberate efforts undermine and destroy families despite a cultural catechism of concern for children and reverence for families.

The complexities of reproduction within contemporary society encompass biological capacity and basic human rights, as well as cultural law where women are the "bearers of the greatest norm," reproduction (Cixous and Clément, 1975, p. 8). Poor and imprisoned women are subjected to and often compelled by the cultural motherhood mandate. Similar to others within a patriarchal society, they have learned the lesson of motherhood as a compulsory and singular avenue to true fulfillment and meaning as women (Ikemoto, 1995). But this is not merely a discussion of an abstract cultural imperative; it is about the flesh-and-blood struggles of women and children, including their anguish and survival. It is especially about the suffering of

I would like to express my appreciation to Jolan Hsieh, Susan Trower, and Karla Cohen, my colleagues and co-teachers, and to our students whose minds and spirits are very much alive despite imprisonment.

countless human beings in a culture of cruelty where over 70 percent of all welfare recipients are children (Giroux, 1996) and two-thirds of all imprisoned women are separated from their children under eighteen years of age (Watterson, 1996).

Even as, materially and emotionally, poor and imprisoned women are denied access to privileged forms of motherhood, their lives provide the essential backdrop on which cultural imperatives are writ large. They are the excluded Other in reproductive rhetoric and pageantry, but in a "paradox of otherness . . . [e]ven the exclusion is not an exclusion," for their imagery and lives are appropriated, degraded, and often destroyed in service to cultural illusions (Cixous and Clément, 1975, p. 71). Poor mothers, especially single welfare recipients and mothers behind bars, provide villainous visions against which all others are measured and exonerated. Ideological images of "stable, prosperous families" and "good mothers" are constructed as polar opposites of "dysfunctional, troubled families" and "bad mothers" (Ikemoto, 1995; Farrell, 1998).

Reproduction and motherhood among poor and imprisoned women is very much about the cultural matrix of gender, class, and race, and the pervasive web of sexism, classism, and racism. Both poverty and prison are gendered and racialized spaces deeply embued with class prejudice and discrimination. Women and children are most systematically affected by poverty and increasing rates of women's imprisonment—almost 400 percent since 1980 (Shaylor, 1998, 386)—signaling the "surplus punishment" that characterizes disenfranchised women's lives within contemporary society (Davis, 1998, p. 344).

Socioeconomic structures and dominant ideologies play crucial roles in rendering devastating poverty acceptable and massive imprisonment palatable and profitable within a society ostensibly committed to democracy and social justice (Davis, 1998). Widespread images of poor women and imprisoned women are intermeshed and mutually reinforcing, reflecting deep-seated assumptions that poor women, especially welfare mothers and mothers of color, and imprisoned mothers are deviants who lack economic initiative, rely unnecessarily on public assistance, and will reproduce economic dependence and/or criminality in their children (Gordon, 1998/1999).

The imputed inadequacy and failure of individual poor women, including those who labor daily for impoverished wages, are blamed for the dismantling of social programs to assist them and their children (Shaylor, 1998). As contemporary media culture reinscribes stereotypic images (Sklar, 1995; Giroux, 1996), the official statistics buoy discriminatory practices toward poor women. These responses share in the sexist and racist foundations of U.S. society, with scant acknowledgment that statistics are generated by conditions resulting from structural inequities, punitive policies, and selective enforcement practices. For although white women constitute the largest group on welfare, women of color are disproportionately likely to need public aid to dependent children and incarcerated women are predominantly and disproportionately poor, minority women—especially African Americans and Latinas (Belknap, 1996; Watterson, 1996; Amnesty International, 1999b).

Within the past decade, the numbers of incarcerated women have quadrupled, with over 84,000 women in prisons and 62,000 women in jails (Beck, 1999; Watterson, 1996). Despite persuasive evidence that the tremendous increase in women's incarceration reflects punitive policy changes rather than increased criminality, no end is foreseeable to large-scale incarceration (Donziger, 1996). As Currie suggests, "At the current rates of increase, there will be more women in America's prisons in the year 2010 than there were inmates of both sexes in 1970" (1998, p. 14).

THE LINKS: NO SAFE PLACE

The ravages of daily struggles in poverty, violence against women, and imprisonment are interrelated forms of punishment, and they are all dimensions of the social control and exclusion that are integrally related to women's reproductive capacity and roles. Historically, the most poignant, entrenched, and pervasive forms of punishment for women have been within the institutions of the family and the economy in terms of gendered violence, poverty, and marginalization. Today imprisonment is becoming increasingly central to this matrix of domination and the "web of social conditions over which [women] have no control" (Davis, 1998, p. 343). Indeed, the long-standing historical and philosophical connections between these modes of gendered punishment defy dichotomization into public versus private realms, for both are inextricably bound with reproduction and motherhood.

The parallels between the life situations of poor and imprisoned women are myriad, including economic exclusion, subjection to multiple forms of gender-based punishment, targeting by policies that minimize support services and enhance surveillance, and vulnerability to efforts to remove their children from them and to terminate their parental rights. These responses to poor and imprisoned women, both in public policy and sentiment, are progressively punitive and mean-spirited, as evidenced in miserly regulations for means-tested welfare benefits (Dressel, 1994) and in policies that eventuate the long-term imprisonment of women for nonviolent, primarily drug and property offenses (Donziger, 1996).

A series of deliberate, self-conscious policies have been enacted, with demonstrated impacts on poor and imprisoned mothers and their children. The deleterious consequences are predictable and calculated; they constitute parallel attacks on and curtailment of women's civil and human rights within and outside of prison. Dominant images of incarcerated women pave the way for such action, for "[g]iven the common national disdain for prisoners, such an assault on civil rights can begin there" (Shaylor, 1998, pp. 389-390).

The Personal Responsibility and Work Opportunity Reconciliation Act of 1996 made the retention of even meager aid for poor women questionable; this "welfare reform act" translated into increased misery and insecurity for millions of families. As an important effect, this legislation led many states to discourage or end welfare recipients' educational pursuits by disallowing education as a "workfare" option. The punitive approach that guides federal legislation has also eliminated prisoner eligibility for federal educational loans. Curtailment of educational opportunities is legitimated in the name of organizational expediency and the security needs of prisons, but it has also become an explicit tactic in the political demonization of prisoners as "undeserving of privilege."

Tremendous increases in public funding are used primarily for the construction of more jails and prisons; far less is allocated to hiring and training staff, and drastic cuts in funding for academic or vocational education characterize prison budgets (Donziger, 1996). The resulting lack of educational services is especially grave for the futures of poor and imprisoned women and their children (Rafter, 1990). In turn, these women's inability to provide for their children is used to justify efforts to expedite the termination of their parental rights (Farrell, 1998).

The Prison Litigation Reform Act (PLRA) of 1997 also made it increasingly difficult for prisoners to file lawsuits to assert and retain their rights, including those related to reproduction and motherhood. Even prisoners' basic access to the outside world has been limited by state bans on media coverage of prison life or interviews with prisoners (Shaylor, 1998).

These parallel trends reflect the striking similarities and overlap between the lives of incarcerated and impoverished women. Without diminishing the potential horrors of physical imprisonment, it is clear that poor women lead lives of cultural imprisonment, even on the outside of the brick-and-mortar prisons. Examination of their lives prior to imprisonment suggests that there are multiple kinds of "prisons" in society and some incarcerated women have left one form for another. For example, the pervasiveness of previous sexual abuse is evident in the prison population—as many as nine out of ten women prisoners have been victims of domestic violence and sexual or physical abuse prior to incarceration (Human Rights Watch [HRW], 1996).

Many poor women and their children spend their lives in a no-security "prison," surrounded by danger and deprivation. It is clear that the void in "front-end" services—such as substance-abuse rehabilitation programs, community-based programs, and homemaker services—contributes significantly to women's illegal acts (Golden, 1997). Prisons become warehouses for poor women for whom services were not available within society (Shaylor, 1998). The economic plight and psychological despair generated by poverty make many poor women likely candidates for drug use, prostitution, and property crime. Changes in sentencing laws and practices, rather than increased criminality among women, account for the increases in women's imprisonment.

Nationwide, 70 percent of women in jails and prisons are there for drug, property, or public-order offenses (HRW, 1996). Drug-related offenses alone accounted for 55 percent of the increase in female prisoners between 1986 and 1991 (HRW, 1996). The doubling of the female prison population during the 1980s occurred during a period when the rate at which arrests—including those for petty offenses—that resulted in jailing and imprisonment increased 68 percent (Golden, 1997; Dressel, 1994). Few women are incarcerated for violence (depending on the definition, estimates range from 5 to 20 percent being viewed as a danger to society), and the acts of those few are deeply gendered, reflecting as they often do the desperate acts of violated women. Nearly two-thirds of the women imprisoned for violent crimes assaulted or killed male partners who had a history of abusing them (Watterson, 1996).

Policies portray the plight of poor and imprisoned women as their own making; they emphasize the responsibility of individual women and diminish the accountability of decision makers, public indifference, and societal structures. Policies focus on and extend the role of the state as enforcer, rather than the guardian, of citizens' well-being (Eisenstein, 1994). Poor and imprisoned women are simultaneously provided far less support and subjected to greater surveillance in an unforgiving society.

In specific, the increased surveillance of contemporary prisons is accompanied by gender-specific dangers for women prisoners. The constant surveillance and denial of privileges, particularly in maximum-control units, heighten women's vulnerability to sexual harassment and abuse. These are the extreme of everyday experiences of many imprisoned women; prison architecture and policies purposefully deny women privacy and subject them to surveillance during even their most personal moments, such as when showering and using toilets (Shaylor, 1998). These vulnerabilities are enhanced by the attitudes and behaviors of staff, which range from respectful male staff who announce their arrival in housing units to those who invade housing units unannounced, openly gawk at the women, harass or abuse them psychologically and/or physically. Psychological and sexual harassment by prison staff also plagues imprisoned women at their work assignments, and they have few realistic avenues for protesting and curbing such abuse.

Strip searches are common practice conducted in the name of security or in search of contraband, but also as routine preparation for visitation. An example is one woman's haunting depiction of the indelible violation of constant strip searches—in this instance nine searches per day regardless of prisoners' behavior or "misbehavior":

> They [prison guards] wouldn't be able to admit it themselves, but their search, of course, is for something else [other than contraband], and is efficient; their search is for our pride. And I think, with a sinking heart, again and again it must be, they find it and take it. (Girshick, 1999, pp. 95-96)

Even as poor women are the victims of sexualized mistreatment, imprisoned women are subjected to harassment, abuse, and rape by guards. The societal indifference to crimes against poor women, in the home and on the street, is mirrored in the disregard for the violation of imprisoned women. This is most evident in the minimalization of guards' accountability or punishment for abusing women prisoners. Despite their tremendous power over the day-to-day well-being of prisoners, guards' sexual abuse of women is commonly viewed as "consensual" and official policies favor internal disciplinary action, however minor, over criminal prosecution (Amnesty International, 1999a; Davis, 1998).

The entire prison organization and power structure pressures women not to report sexual harassment and abuse; when grievances are filed there may be a virtual nonresponse from prison officials. Offending personnel may be reassigned to all-male prisons or allowed to retire early. It is also possible that no disciplinary action may be taken and, instead, the female prisoner or prisoners may be transferred to other facilities or disciplined for rule infractions. Similar to their sisters in society, and reminiscent of the pervasive response to domestic violence, the violation of imprisoned women is rarely treated as true crime.

EXCESSIVE PUNISHMENT:
THE SEX AND GENDER TAX

Poor and imprisoned women are highly sexualized within public discourse while simultaneously being rendered asexual by public policies as well as denied sexual identities and relationships. Welfare mothers—particularly single women of color—are portrayed as hypersexed and excessively reproductive (Shaylor, 1998), while imprisoned women are systematically stripped of their identities not only as contributing members of society but as women and mothers. They are branded not only as "bad women," but as "unworthy mothers."

The consequences are monumental because, for many imprisoned women, motherhood is an essential aspect and the core of being a woman. The punitive measures leveled against both poor and imprisoned women take specifically gendered forms, subjecting them to intensified punishment especially virulent for women. It is gender-specific punishment because, although men suffer to varying degrees due to loss of family and separation from children, the magnitude and nature of women's losses are exceptional. Women's reproductive capacities and cultural roles as primary, often single, caregivers render them especially and extremely vulnerable to suffering and grief due to the violation of their relationships with their children. There is an added punishment, the gender tax, inflicted upon poor and imprisoned women, and the abridgment of their reproductive rights and their exclusion from mainstream society continue unabated.

Many women form families within prisons, for family is the associative form that compels their allegiance and passions. In light of the unisex nature of incarceration and the lesbian orientation of some inmates prior to imprisonment, female prisoners' sexual partnering is likely. Not unlike public and political obsessions with the "sexual improprieties" of single welfare mothers, stereotypic and mediated images of prison realities (the "pseudo families" and "sexual intrigues" of imprisoned women) are frequently more titillating for outsiders than serious consideration of the long-term consequences of the disruption and destruction of countless families in society. This is especially irrational in light of the nonviolent crimes for which most women are incarcerated and the devastating impact their incarceration likely has upon their children (Bloom and Steinhart, 1993; Owen, 1998).

Nowhere are the gendered penalties of poverty and prison more evident than in the general unavailability and poor quality of health services. The gravely inadequate care afforded poor women in society is epitomized by the neglect of imprisoned women's reproductive needs, including general gynecological services, prenatal and postpartum care, safe and unharassed childbirth, and medical counsel during menopause. Even the provision of supplies for basic menstrual hygiene more closely approximates privilege than need or right, as evidenced by the doling out of sanitary napkins and toilet paper, the unavailability of tampons except when purchased, and the rare provision of estrogen or alternative therapy for menopause.

The availability and quality of gynecological care varies greatly, including access to regular exams, pap smears, and mammograms, as well as reproductive emergency care and competent services for those women living with physical disabilities, those living with HIV and AIDS, and those who are terminally ill (Flanagan, 1995). In a society in which advanced technologies—such as fetal genetic testing and surgical intervention—have become integral to the reproductive rights of the affluent, it is abundantly clear that these reproductive technologies are not intended for poor women in general, in particular, prisoner requests for such consideration would be viewed as ludicrous (Bortner, 1990).

Reproduction-related issues are relevant to all imprisoned women, not only the approximately 80 percent who have children. Exclusion from family life is very tangible for women without children, the vast majority of whom are imprisoned during their twenties and thirties. For almost all prisoners, but especially for those serving long or life sentences (e.g., mandatory sentences for drug convictions; life sentences for killing abusive partners), the psychological pain and conflict of being denied the opportunity to begin families and have children are unavoidable aspects of their sentences. Imprisoned heterosexual women are denied access to sexual relations with men for biological procreation, and imprisoned lesbian women are denied access to familial and child-rearing relationships with women lovers. The universal right to parenthood is greatly delayed or totally denied to increasing numbers of imprisoned women who have no children at the onset of imprisonment.

This added punishment for both mothers and women without children, their long-term removal from society, has a disturbing eugenic aura when practiced on the tremendous scale of current imprisonment policies. As Zedner has suggested, especially in light of the disproportionate imprisonment of women of color, this is reminiscent of efforts "to have genetically inferior women removed from social circulation for as many of their childbearing years as possible" (quoted in Davis, 1998, p. 347). The experience of a twenty-eight-year-old Latina convicted of conspiracy to possess and distribute methamphetamine and ephedrine speaks to this issue:

> I received a 20-year mandatory sentence. Like many other women here, several people testified against my husband and me so they could receive a lower sentence. Due to the length of my sentence, I will probably not be blessed with having children. (The November Coalition, 2000, p. 2)

There are also unacknowledged surplus penalties for pregnant and postpartum prisoners, despite the fact that an estimated 8 to 10 percent of women are pregnant when they enter prison and an additional 15 percent have given birth in the past year (Watterson, 1996; Bloom and Steinhart, 1993; Wooldredge and Masters, 1993). In 1997-1998, more than 2,200 pregnant women were in U.S. prisons and 1,300 babies were born in prison (Amnesty International, 1999b). For women who become pregnant while in prison, either through ostensibly consensual or forced involvement with male prisoners or guards, possible penalties include severe disciplinary actions at the time that a woman discloses her illicit sexual activity when requesting an abortion (since all sexual activity within prison is forbidden) or, on the other extreme, strong pressure to abort if a prisoner insists on continuing her pregnancy (Shaylor, 1998).

Few prisons address the specific needs of pregnant women, such as appropriate diets, prenatal care, or lighter work assignments. Nor do most prisons have the resources to deal with miscarriages, premature births, or more routine deliveries (Wooldredge and Masters, 1993, p. 195). In most cases, prisoners' pregnancy and childbirth experiences are far removed from public view and scrutiny, but available reports depict degrading and inhumane conditions. Because most prisons have no facilities for childbirth, women are transferred to local hospitals; after giving birth, most are immediately separated from their child and returned to prison (Watterson, 1996). Prison guards are stationed near hospital rooms, prisoners' newborns are taken almost immediately or commonly within two days, and most frequently women give birth without support from friends and family (Amnesty International, 1999b).

The widespread use of shackles and handcuffs to transport even extremely pregnant women provides a graphic example of the exclusion of women prisoners from society's espoused reverence for motherhood. Journalist Rachel Leventhal's recent commentary on women's lives in jail includes a telling example: "One day down in the . . . receiving room I watched a woman who was eight and a half months' pregnant waddle by me with her wrists cuffed and her feet shackled together. 'Where am I gonna run to?' she cried to me later. 'I can hardly walk'" (2000, p. 44).

A vivid symbol of the prioritization of punishment over mothers and children is women who are shackled during childbirth:

> My feet were still shackled together, and I couldn't get my legs apart. The doctor called for the officer. . . . No one else could unlock the shackles, and my baby was coming. . . . Finally the officer came and unlocked the shackles from my ankles. My baby was born then. (Amnesty International, 1999b, p. 1)

Only one-tenth of state prison systems provide specific services for women and newborns, and only three have programs for newborns to stay with their mothers for eighteen months or more (Pollock, 1999). The California Community Prison Mother Program permits infants to remain with their mothers until the end of the incarceration term, but the program can accommodate a maximum of only ninety-four women. Illinois' residential program keeps mothers and infants together for up to twenty-four months, but has space for only fifteen women. In New York, prisoners may keep their newborns up to twelve months; in Nebraska, up to eighteen months; and in South Dakota, up to thirty days (Trower, 2000).

The federal prison system's MINT program (Mother and Infants Together) permits pregnant prisoners in their third trimester of pregnancy to move to community corrections or halfway houses to prepare for childbirth. They are permitted three months with their newborns before family members must take the child or the mothers must relinquish their newborns to foster care before returning to regular prison life. To qualify for this program, prisoners must be pregnant when sentenced, have an unproblematic disciplinary record, and be considered a low flight risk. Women convicted of nonviolent offenses and those serving shorter sentences are given preference.

Although this aspect of the increased incarceration of women—pregnancy and childbirth—is an obvious site for feminist involvement, few volunteer efforts provide support. Two major exceptions are Project REACH (Reunite Each Child) and Atlanta's Project AIM (Aid to Imprisoned Mothers) (Wooldredge and Masters, 1993; Dressel, 1994; Trower, 2000).

PUNISHING THE FUTURE:
WOMEN AND THEIR CHILDREN

Poor and imprisoned women's relationships with their children run a wide gamut, not unlike all such relationships in contemporary society. Enormous hazards, however, accompany these women's parenting, and their structural positions magnify risks and fears. Impoverished mothers often fear that the state will separate them from their children; that nightmare has materialized for women in jails and prisons. Although poor and imprisoned men share these possibilities, the pain of separation and punishment of loss are inflicted far more keenly on women (the vast majority of whom are single mothers).

An article by twenty-six minimum-security federal prisoners provides a poignant example of family devastation due to the incarceration of nonviolent, often first-time, offenders. These twenty-six women have been sentenced to a total of 227 years for nonviolent drug convictions at an estimated taxpayer cost of $5.5 million, plus the cost of welfare and foster care for many of their sixty-eight children who "have become orphans" due to sentencing policies. Although their brief narratives do not disclose uniform information about all the women, many are first-time offenders and the majority were convicted of drug conspiracy charges on the testimony of government informers or codefendants testifying in exchange for reduced sentences (The November Coalition, 2000).

For complex and diverse reasons, some poor and some imprisoned mothers are indifferent to or unconcerned about their children, but the vast majority are ruled by commitment to and constant concern for them. In the case of imprisoned women, serious depression is common early in imprisonment and reemerges during times of crisis. Symptomatic of the helplessness that engenders depression is the fact that, official procedures for delivering emergency news to inmates notwithstanding, families may experience difficulty or be unable to contact prisoners when their children are in trouble. The abyss separating a woman from her loved ones is overwhelming, as epitomized by times when she learns of the serious illness or death of a family member, perhaps her own child, at mail call or in a delayed message from a chaplain or guard.

The despair is especially pronounced for those who do not have a supportive family and must leave their children with unreliable persons, or for those whose children are placed in foster care or adopted. One forty-three-year-old Latina pled guilty to conspiracy after her appointed attorney and U.S. marshals said she would be imprisoned for twenty years and her children would be taken away if she failed to do so. She explains, "I had no information to give them and was sentenced to 46 months. My children have been separated, abused, and moved three times" in the first two years of her three-year, nine-month sentence (The November Coalition, 2000, p. 3).

In the best circumstances, imprisoned women feel powerless to provide the nurturance and support their children need; in the worst situations they may not even know where their children are or the levels of neglect or abuse to which they are being subjected. Prozac and other mind-numbing drugs may be the prison response to these depressions; they may deaden the immediate anguish but they do not address the root problem of women's helplessness and longing for their children.

Children are frequently the focal point of much prison life: they fill conversations and dreams. Many women are committed to regular involvement in their children's lives through letters and phone calls, but this requires resources and, at best, is a modest avenue to parenting. Visitation is also problematic and the responses of women, their families, and children vary tremendously. Imprisoned women commonly rely on mothers, grandmothers, and sisters to care for their children, and it is they who will make the treks to prison. This contrasts with the experiences of imprisoned men in which their children's mothers are the most likely to bring them to visit. Most important, although visitation may appear as a straightforward, positive opportunity for families, it may become a difficult and contested aspect of prison life. Visitation is relatively rare, with as few as 10 percent of women receiving regular visits (Owen, 1998) and less than half the mothers of minor children ever being visited by the children (Golden, 1997).

One thirty-four-year-old Latina serving twelve years for distributing methamphetamine after being convicted "on the word of a paid informant with a long criminal record," tells her story:

> I was badgered into accepting a sentence of 151 months [twelve years, seven months] after threats by the prosecutor to give me life. My two daughters had to be separated from each other. I finally got to see my youngest daughter after two years, both girls live 1200 miles away from the prison where I am being held. (The November Coalition, 2000, p. 7)

Even when family, friends, or foster parents are willing and able to bring children for visits, some women do not want their children to be in the prison environment, to experience the wretched end of visits, or to witness their mother's humiliation behind bars. For example, while many prisons require uniforms that, outside of their institutional sameness, are not pointedly demeaning of prisoners, others require uniforms intended to accentuate the wearers' stigmatized and deviant status. Arizona's Maricopa County Jail epitomizes this trend by issuing uniforms with wide black-and-white stripes, permitting prisoners only slippers or shower thongs rather than shoes, and providing only one change of underwear per week.

The official policy of some prison systems, most notably the federal system, declares that imprisonment itself is the punishment; conditions inside are not to exacerbate this fundamental loss of freedom of movement and decision making. Even under these conditions visitation may seem unnecessarily punitive and demeaning, but it is much more so in those prisons whose every dimension is designed to inflict continuous degradation and punishment upon prisoners. When the official or unofficial philosophy is that prisoners are subhumans who "deserve whatever they get" (Shaylor, 1998, p. 396), visitation routines extend punitive, disrespectful, and undignified treatment to visitors as well as prisoners. Regardless of whether official policies condone such conduct, individual prison guards or administrators may treat visitors in a degrading and punitive way. Thus, policies may support or subvert women's relationships with their children, and individual prison personnel may be kind and compassionate or they may become devious wielders of petty power who humiliate mothers in front of their children.

Visiting conditions impact the desirability and quality of this experience. When women are first arrested, they await trial or plea bargaining in county jails—three-fourths of which allow only noncontact visits in which women and visitors meet separated by plexiglass or glass (Watterson, 1996). Children must talk to their mothers over a phone, and even the youngest are not permitted to touch or kiss their mothers or to sit on their laps. Contact visits are more common after women are sentenced to prison, as are more extended visits or visits in residential settings, but the latter are extremely rare.

As in all aspects of prison life, in the name of institutional security, officials have enormous control over the conditions under which children visit their mothers. Some enforce a demeaning ritual with endless rules about interactions, while regulations for prisoners, such as full strip searches before and after visitation, diminish the quality of the experience. Much more disturbing to most prisoners is the fact that their families and children may also be treated in a suspicious, demeaning, and threatening manner. Likewise, prison officials have near absolute power over when visits will be terminated or denied altogether. Judee Norton tells of her experience when not only were her son's visitation rights suspended because he questioned the dress code, but his "crime" was attributed to her unacceptable attitude toward authority (Chevigny, 1999).

Imprisoned women suffer anguish over their children but they also often live in fear that they will not regain custody when released from prison. Reuniting with children is more likely when they are cared for by the incarcerated woman's parents, sisters, or other relatives (as is true for an estimated 45 percent), or if they live with their fathers (22 percent, compared to 90 percent of imprisoned men's children who live with their mothers) (Watterson, 1996). But the loss of children becomes more imminent when no relatives are acceptable to authorities or available to care for the children, and they become wards of the state and are placed in foster homes, often separated from brothers and sisters (Golden, 1997).

The extent to which foster homes provide effective, sensitive care for children of incarcerated women ranges greatly. When foster homes are "disastrous," the reports of imprisoned mothers and their children may have little to no credibility (Golden, 1997). Equally consequential is the frequent lack of cooperation of foster parents with biological parents, with children caught in a loyalty conflict between their mother and foster parents, and the reality that imprisoned mothers are often treated as if they had died (1997).

When imprisoned mothers return to society, some do not regain immediate custody of their children because they are unable to procure housing and employment, both extremely difficult tasks for most ex-prisoners. These obstacles are enhanced in those states where explicit, punitive legislation and policies deny former prisoners access to public assistance. Often, even when women feel prepared to care for them, their children are not returned. As one advocate remarks, "While sentences for nonviolent offenses are getting longer, the system is moving to terminate parental rights much faster" (Golden, 1997, p. 189). This may be the only possible course at times, but there is also a strong possibility of premature, unnecessary termination of mother's rights. Likewise, there is often considerable pressure for women to "voluntarily" place their children in foster homes or to give them up for adoption (Sametz, 1980; Shaylor, 1998).

Tremendous disruption and sometimes permanent dissolution of their relationships with their children is a well-documented aspect of women's imprisonment—the hidden and unacknowledged exacerbation of women's punishment (Owen, 1998; Golden, 1997; Rafter, 1990). Perhaps the ultimate, most overwhelming penalty for imprisoned women is the enormous guilt that accompanies their frequent or perpetual sense of powerlessness to control their children's lives. Feminist analysts have suggested that for all women in a patriarchal society, "Keeping oneself in a state of permanent guilt is to constitute oneself as a subject" (Cixous and Clément, 1975, p. 46); but the guilt and self-condemnation prevalent among imprisoned women is the height of such realities. These feelings are highlighted by the contradiction of being responsible mothers while subjected to the infantalization of prison life, where women are routinely treated like children devoid of decision-making ability. Self-recrimination and disgust are especially prevalent when one's child is in trouble and, similar to her counterparts among her many poor sisters, an imprisoned woman wears "the look of people who are totally responsible for lives they have no power to save" (Barker, 1992, p. 107).

CONCLUSION

Although the failures of welfare and imprisoned women are heralded, little attention is given to their accomplishments as women and mothers. Denied the structural and personal resources necessary to sustain "successful mothering," many welfare and imprisoned mothers still survive and enable the well-being of their children. In an unsupportive and unforgiving society, they make ways to provide materially for their children and to demonstrate their love and commitment to them. Despite great deprivation, poor mothers are often exceptionally nurturing of their children—emotionally, psychologically, and spiritually.

In the face of monumental obstacles, many imprisoned women also create and continue loving, supportive relationships with their children. Although their physical contact is extremely limited, they maintain a presence in their children's lives through letters and phone calls, and make meaningful gestures of protection and care through advice, handmade gifts, and holiday photographs. Prisoners' efforts to prepare for the future, through education or gaining job skills, are often pursued in the hopes of creating a better life for their children. It is a hard-won victory for an imprisoned woman to maintain vibrant links with her children. Even while they pay greatly for their lack of privilege, poor and imprisoned women's children often evidence depths of gratitude, understanding, and devotion to their mothers. It is often through their children that women assert their complex personhood and resist being reduced to the labels "welfare mom" or "prisoner." For most women, the destruction of the bonds with their children constitutes the most insidious and cruel punishment of all.

Poor and incarcerated women are the invisible, silenced women about whom little is known yet much is presumed. Common, distorted images portray the former as "unfit mothers" and the latter as "unwomanly" and "unnatural criminals" (Watterson, 1996, p. 34). Their fate is circumscribed by gender, race, and social class, and their lives are characterized by discrimination, physical and sexual abuse, and lives out of control—lives filled with the "anguish, catastrophe, fear and humiliation faced by women without economic or social power" (Golden, 1997, p. 184).

The lives of many poor and imprisoned women seem virtually untouched by the gains of the women's liberation movement. Change will be possible only when a vision of their complex personhood is embraced, including their potential as human beings who are capable and—given structural encouragement—desirous of changing their own and their children's life chances within society. Fundamental economic and ideological change is essential to alter the fate of poor and imprisoned women. Only within that context will the transformative powers of being treated with dignity and respect, as one whose potential is honored and nurtured, be of enormous consequences—so, too, will the curative and life-restoring possibilities of feminism and the collective support of women.

REFERENCES

Amnesty International. 1999a. *"Not Part of My Sentence": Violations of the Human Rights of Women in Custody*. United States Rights for All Campaign. Zug, Switzerland: Amnesty International.

Amnesty International. 1999b. Rough Justice for Women Behind Bars. March 4, News Release. News Service: 037/99, AI Index: AMR 51/32/99.

Barker, Pat. 1992. *Regeneration.* New York: Dutton.

Beck, Allen. 1999. *Inmates in State and Federal Prisons.* Washington, DC: U.S. Department of Justice Programs.

Belknap, Joanne. 1996. *The Invisible Woman: Gender, Crime, and Justice.* Belmont, CA: Wadsworth Publishing Co.

Bloom, Barbara and David Steinhart. 1993. *Why Punish the Children? A Reappraisal of the Children of Incarcerated Mothers in America.* San Francisco: National Council on Crime and Delinquency.

Bortner, M. A. 1990. The Necessity and Inadequacy of the Reproductive Rights Discourse. *Social Justice 17*(3): 99-110.

Chevigny, Bell Gale (Ed.). 1999. *Doing Time: 25 Years of Prison Writing.* New York: Arcade Publishing.

Cixous, Hélène and Catherine Clément. 1975. *The Newly Born Woman.* Translated by Betsy Wing. Minneapolis: University of Minnesota Press.

Currie, Elliott. 1998. *Crime and Punishment in America.* New York: Holt and Company.

Davis, Angela Y. 1998. Public Imprisonment and Private Violence: Reflections on the Hidden Punishment of Women. *Criminal and Civil Confinement 24:* 339-351.

Donziger, Steven R. 1996. *The Real War on Crime: The Report of the National Criminal Justice Commission.* New York: HarperCollins.

Dressel, Paula L. 1994. . . . And We Keep on Building Prisons: Racism, Poverty, and Challenges to the Welfare State. *Journal of Sociology and Social Welfare 21* (3-4): 7-30.

Eisenstein, Zillah R. 1994. *The Color of Gender: Reimaging Democracy.* Berkeley: University of California Press.

Farrell, Ann. 1998. Mothers Offending Against Their Role: An Australian Experience. *Women and Criminal Justice 9*(4): 47-67.

Flanagan, LaMont W. 1995. Meeting the Special Needs of Females in Custody: Maryland's Unique Approach. *Federal Probation 59*(2): 49-53.

Giroux, Henry. 1996. *Fugitive Cultures: Race, Violence and Youth.* New York: Routledge.

Girshick, Lori B. 1999. *No Safe Haven: Stories of Women in Prison.* Boston: Northeastern University Press.

Golden, Renny. 1997. Advocates for the Unworthiest of the Unworthy. In R. Golden (Ed.), *Disposable Children: America's Welfare System* (pp. 181-192). Belmont, CA: Wadsworth Publication.

Gordon, Avery. 1998/99. Globalism and the Prison Industrial Complex: An Interview with Angela Davis. *Race and Class 40*(2/3): 145-157.

Human Rights Watch (HRW). 1996. *All Too Familiar: Sexual Abuse of Women in U.S. State Prisons.* New York: Human Rights Watch, Women's Rights Projects.

Ikemoto, Lisa C. 1995. The Code of Perfect Pregnancy: At the Intersection of the Ideology of Motherhood, the Practice of Defaulting to Science, and the Interventionist Mindset of Law. In Richard Delgado (Ed.), *Critical Race Theory: The Cutting Edge* (pp. 478-497). Philadelphia: Tempe University Press.

Leventhal, Rachel. 2000. Lost in the Shuffle: An Inside Look at Women in Prison. *Doubletake* (Winter): 42-59.

The November Coalition. 2000. Over 27 Combined Years in Federal Prison. *The Razor Wire 40*(7): 1-7.

Owen, Barbara. 1998. *In the Mix: Struggle and Survival in a Women's Prison.* Albany: State University of New York Press.

Pollock, Jocelyn. 1999. Parenting Programs in Women's Prisons. Report to the Open Society Institute's Center on Crime, Communities, and Culture. New York: Center on Crime, Communities, and Culture.

Rafter, Nicole Hahn. 1990. *Partial Justice: Women, Prisons, and Social Control,* Second Edition. New Brunswick, NJ: Transaction Publishers.

Sametz, Lynn. 1980. Children of Incarcerated Women. *Social Work* (July): 298-302.

Shaylor, Cassandra. 1998. It's Like Living in a Black Hole: Women of Color and Solitary Confinement in the Prison Industrial Complex. *Criminal and Civil Confinement 24*: 385-416.

Sklar, Holly. 1995. *Chaos or Community? Seeking Solutions, Not Scapegoats for Bad Economics.* Boston: South End Press.

Trower, Susan. 2000. Pregnant Inmates: Neglected, Controlled, Disrespected. Master's thesis, Arizona State University, Tempe.

Watterson, Kathryn. 1996. *Women in Prison: Inside the Concrete Womb,* Revised Edition. Boston: Northeastern University Press.

Wooldredge, John D. and Kimberly Masters. 1993. Confronting Problems Faced by Pregnant Inmates in State Prisons. *Crime and Delinquency 39*(2): 195-203.

Prison Grief, Tina Clay
Exhibited at the Fourth Annual Exhibition of Art by Michigan Prisoners, February 9-25, 1999, University of Michigan, Rackham Galleries.

Chapter 12

Children and Their Incarcerated Mothers

Wendy C. Ascione
Joyce Dixson

Kids of the incarcerated need for people to understand them, and take time with them; and listen to what we have to say. People on the outside don't know what we go through.

Tony Richard, child of an incarcerated mother
(SADOI, 1996)

Society traditionally has stereotyped incarcerated men and women as villains: calculating, evil, immoral, and inhuman beings. These images are evident in popular media but are wholly inaccurate, especially for women who are incarcerated. When one learns more about them, it is apparent that they are a population with needs and concerns similar to those of women in the rest of society. Unfortunately, the general public has little opportunity or time available to discover what is true about incarcerated women, relying instead on the stereotypes and supporting their banishment.

Children of incarcerated mothers needing community support and services are often overlooked. Not only does the justice system not respond to the problems and needs of incarcerated women who are also mothers, but child welfare systems also neglect the needs of their children. They simply do not interpret their mandate to protect children as including this population. Communities also currently offer little support.

As a mother of two and a formerly incarcerated woman, I, Joyce Dixson, never truly understood how badly my children had been hurt by my incarceration until I sat down and had a serious talk with them after my release. I have two sons. They were six and eight years old when I entered prison. The stories they told me were worse than I could have imagined or believed. They talked about how hard it was for them to go to school; how the other children teased and taunted them. They spoke about the many times they

271

would be the last ones to be picked for the baseball game, and how badly they felt whenever a teacher spoke in class about the "bad people" who lived in prison. They spoke about the many times they were told that they were not welcome in the homes of some of their friends; and when they did visit, they would always be reminded (whenever they did something mischievous) that they would end up in prison just like their mother. Their feelings were hurt a lot, and they often wondered what they had done to cause people to treat them so badly.

As they grew up, feelings of grief/loss, abandonment, anger, guilt, and shame grew with them. Each of my sons handled these feelings differently. My youngest son learned at an early age to detach himself from people who would hurt or leave him. He spent much of his time with academics and sports. He loved spelling bees and baseball. As he got older, he found his own positive male role model. He graduated from high school and moved on to college. My oldest son's feelings were often displayed through acts of aggression and delinquent behavior. The older he got, the angrier he became. My children traveled different roads. While the younger was on his way to college, the older was on his way to prison. Although they both grew up in the same house—with the same hurts, pains, disappointments, and angers—and had the same mother who went to prison, they were very different. Each believes that my incarceration played a major role in shaping his life. It would be very easy to conclude from this that one simply turned out "good" and the other "bad." However, that is not the case. Significant trade-offs must be considered. My younger son went to college not with higher education as his primary objective but rather as a means of escape from the family that he was a part of and all the negative baggage that came along with it. He loved his family; nevertheless, to be separated from his family (in its continual state of dysfunctional mayhem) was crucial for his survival physically, psychologically, emotionally, and socially. He was away at school, but he was also detached from the family he knew and loved, alone, and depressed. These factors contributed largely to periods of poor academic performance in school and actual physical illness.

My older son was very outgoing and received most of the attention. He was also the son that my mother depended upon to supplement the family's public assistance income by any means necessary. He was coerced into believing that was his responsibility. To please my mother and to live up to his obligation to her, he took to the streets. He attached himself to other kids like himself (societal discards) and learned how to "hustle" (getting money any way they could). He said to me that he and his brother were alone and people never understood how they felt. He said having no one to talk to or help them sort out their feelings and confusions really hurt them. So they just lived with it the best way they knew how.

It has been seven years since we had that first conversation, and every so often another sad or painful memory rises to the surface. Each one hurts just as much as the first one I heard seven years ago. However, processing these events with my children is very important, no matter how painful. I need to know what happened to them and they need to know what happened to me. They need to be able to speak to me about their hurts and disappointments. Hopefully, in doing so, it will help free them of any suppressed anger toward me and free me from any self-imposed guilt as a result of what happened to me. Only then will I and my children be able to heal and rebuild the normal trust that should exist between mother and son, and brother and brother.

Healing has been difficult for my sons as well as for me. I am now a social worker by profession. I offer advice to clients who are struggling with these same issues. However, it must be understood that it is very difficult for an incarcerated mother, or formerly incarcerated mother, to discuss these issues with her children for many reasons. People should be aware that incarcerated mothers and their children suffer from the same unresolved issues: grief/loss, separation, anger, abandonment, confusion, poverty, shame, and humiliation, just to name a few. Although in totally different settings and under completely different circumstances, the physical, mental, and social trauma being suffered by the incarcerated mother is paralleled by the traumas being suffered by her children.

WOMEN AND MOTHERS IN PRISON

The number of women in prison has been rapidly increasing since 1990. An estimated 61,000 out of the total of 87,000 women who are confined in state and federal prisons have children under age eighteen (U.S. Department of Justice, 1999b). About 64 percent of these mothers had lived with their children prior to their incarceration. Gilliard and Beck (1998) estimate that 200,000 children have mothers in prison. Male inmates in state prisons are estimated to be the fathers of 1.1 million children under age eighteen (U.S. Department of Justice, 1999a), but only 44 percent of them lived with their minor children before incarceration. The majority of these children live with their mothers while their fathers are in prison and, therefore, are less likely to have their daily lives disrupted to the extent that children of incarcerated mothers do. There is even less information available about children whose parents are in jails, albeit for a shorter time than inmates in prison, but it is possible that the number of children with a parent in jail during a given year could substantially exceed the number of children with a parent in prison.

There are really no reliable data on the total number of children whose parents are incarcerated. The Department of Justice has estimated that 2 million children under age eighteen had a parent in jail or prison in 1997 (U.S. Department of Justice, 1999a). Correctional institutions and law enforcement agencies are not required by law to gather information on the children, therefore most do not. The data on children of incarcerated parents are typically taken at one point in time and do not include the number of parents who are repeatedly in and out of the correctional system.

There is currently very little empirical research on the impact of a mother's incarceration on her children. The available research is often based on interviews with the parents or the caregivers, rather than directly with the child.

EFFECTS OF MOTHERS' INCARCERATION ON CHILDREN

Much of the very limited research on the impact of parental incarceration is based on small samples in selective areas of the country. No national surveys have been conducted regarding the effects on children, nor are there any longitudinal studies. The literature does indicate that most children experience emotional and behavioral problems from lack of contact with parents. They often experience multiple and disrupted placements, especially if they are not placed with a close relative. Johnston (1995b) found that one in ten children have two or more changes in caregivers during their mother's incarceration and that siblings are often separated. When assessing the impact of a mother's incarceration on her children, it is important to note that most women in prison are of color and of low socioeconomic status, as are the family members who care for the children while their mother is in prison. It is possible that the impact could differ by race, class, or gender— or a combination of these factors—but such information is not available.

Children of incarcerated mothers have increased vulnerability to emotional problems linked to their mother's incarceration. They may suffer from low self-esteem, anxiety, and depression (Katz, 1998; Jose-Kampfner, 1995). Jose-Kampfner (1995) studied thirty-six children of incarcerated mothers and found that 75 percent of the children reported symptoms that are associated with post-traumatic stress disorder (such as depression, difficulty in sleeping, problems with concentrating, and flashbacks related to witnessing their mother's arrest). School-age children may also display disruptive behavior at home or at school as a result of their mother's incarceration (Myers et al., 1999).

Johnston (1995a) evaluated the effects of a mother's incarceration on children at different ages. Infants under the age of two are likely to suffer negative psychological effects due to separation from their mother. This observation is consistent with psychological attachment theory which suggests that appropriate attachment to parental figures occurs during this formative age and is crucial for normal child development. If the child is placed with an adequate, nurturing caregiver, the likelihood of these problems occurring in the future decreases. However, the child may bond with the caregiver instead of the mother, creating difficulties with mother/child bonding once she is released from prison. When a child is born during the mother's incarceration, satisfactory mother/child bonding is even more problematic, given the policies of immediate separation in most states today.

In early childhood, children aged two through six are most likely to witness the arrest of their mother. Children at this age begin to recognize that their parents have a separate identity from them. They recognize that they could potentially lose their parents, which can cause separation anxiety. In normal development, children overcome this separation anxiety and become autonomous beings. When a mother is removed through arrest and incarceration the sudden separation may result in the child becoming vulnerable to more problems in developing autonomy than children who are not traumatically separated (Johnston, 1995b).

Children ages seven through ten are less likely to witness their mother's arrest, but they still are affected by the resulting incarceration. For single mothers raising children alone, the children have to deal with the arrival of a new caregiver, and they may have to switch homes and schools. At this age, they are likely to have difficulty concentrating and struggle to control emotions (Johnston, 1995b). If their father or a relative cannot take care of them, then the children may end up in foster care.

Adolescents may develop maladaptive coping patterns in response to their mother's incarceration and resulting separation (Johnston, 1995a,b). Early adolescents, ages eleven through fourteen, begin to take on adult responsibilities. They feel that they have lost control because their mother is gone, and they may channel their need for control into antisocial behavior as an adaptive response to the adolescent environment. Older adolescents between the ages of fifteen and eighteen also may develop maladaptive coping responses to the incarceration (Johnston, 1995b). It is less likely at this stage that the mother will be released from prison before the adolescent becomes a legal adult. Many in this age group have become homeless, abuse alcohol or drugs, and engage in acting out sexually. All of this is conducive to delinquent behavior which can eventually result in the children's own incarceration.

Although the probability of children of incarcerated mothers becoming imprisoned themselves is unknown, researchers frequently report that these children are five to six times more likely than their peers to enter the criminal justice system. However, Myers et al. (1999), who extensively reviewed this literature, could not find the original source for this statistic.

A variety of factors may contribute to the impact of a mother's incarceration, including the length of separation between mother and children, the nature of the mother's crime, the children's familiarity with their new caregiver, and the strength of the relationship between the mother and children (Gaudin and Sutphen, 1993; Seymour, 1998). Sometimes children are encouraged not to talk about their mother's incarceration because of the stigma often associated with incarceration. The children may also keep their mother's incarceration a secret out of shame. Emotional problems associated with maternal incarceration increase when children cannot openly discuss their feelings about it (Snyder-Joy and Carlo, 1998; Myers et al., 1999).

BARRIERS IN THE CRIMINAL JUSTICE SYSTEM

When a mother enters the criminal justice system, the child also becomes exposed to that system; however, the criminal justice system traditionally overlooks the children. Sentencing a mother to prison creates a state-enforced and often unnecessary separation of the mother from her children. About 75 percent of the women in prison were convicted of nonviolent crimes. Placing nonviolent offenders in a community-based alternative would allow these mothers the chance to remain with their children while serving their sentences.

Regular contact with the mothers in prison, especially regular visits, can alleviate some problems associated with parental incarceration (Myers et al., 1999). However, correctional regulations often create barriers for children who wish to visit their mothers in prison. Simon and Loundis (1991) surveyed five federal institutions and thirty-seven state institutions that house female inmates only. All of the federal institutions and twenty-three of the state institutions allowed visits. According to the Bureau of Justice Statistics for the 1991 prison population, however, more than half (52.2 percent) of the female inmates with minor children are not visited by them (U.S. Department of Justice, 1994).

Although most institutions do allow children to visit their mothers, they do not provide assistance to facilitate visits. It is often difficult for children to visit their mothers in prison. Often a state has only one prison for women and it is located in a rural area with no public transportation. Thus, children who do not have access to private transportation find it nearly impossible to visit their mothers. The visiting conditions in the prisons are not designed to foster a strong mother/child relationship. Myers et al. (1999) found that prison and jail visits are often without contact as the inmate and visitor are separated by a plexiglass window. Few areas have playrooms or permit toys or books to be brought in for the children. In addition, very few states[1] permit overnight visits by children.

In 1995, a survey was distributed to each state's department of corrections (Sarri and Doctora, 1995) to gather information on visiting programs and services for children of incarcerated parents. Only twenty-three states responded. Once again, most states had little information on the number of inmates with children. Only twelve states reported on prisoner's children; all reported for female prisoners; and half reported for all prisoners, male and female. All but one of the states allowed minor children to visit their parents in prison, but only twelve states reported that they had special programs for the children.

Snyder-Joy and Carlo (1998) studied a visitation program located in a women's correctional facility in a Midwestern state. Thirty-one program participants, along with twenty-seven who were on the waiting list for the program, were interviewed to determine its effectiveness. Snyder-Joy and Carlo found that women in the visitation program noted more contact with their children in addition to more visits. They also spent more time discussing issues important to their children at the visits. Compared to the control group, more women in the visitation program reported having a positive relationship with their children. The womens' worries as mothers varied within the groups, but the visitation group had fewer concerns about their roles as mothers. The possibilities to expand similar programs depend on convincing demonstrations, but such programs are so small that the weight of positive evaluations is limited. On the other hand, visitation is required by child welfare policies. There is a clear contradiction in these two requirements, underscoring the exclusionary treatment of children of prisoners.

Recent studies have shown that imprisoned mothers have some of the same concerns as mothers who are not incarcerated. LeFlore and Holston (1989) interviewed 120 incarcerated mothers regarding their attitudes about parenting behaviors. They compared the results to a sample of 120 non-incarcerated mothers who were matched by age, education, income, and marital status. They found no significant differences between the samples regarding attitudes about parenting behaviors. The majority of incarcerated mothers in this sample (72 percent) felt that the most important thing a mother could do for her children was to love them. They also placed importance on providing guidance (21 percent), teaching them to be honest and respect others (12 percent), and to be a good example for them (11 percent).

One of the dominant concerns of incarcerated mothers is the need for more contact with their children. Block and Potthast (1998) studied a small sample of incarcerated mothers participating in a Girl Scouts program with their daughters. They found that the mothers appeared to be confident in their relationships with their daughters but worried about the emotional harm caused by the incarceration. They were also concerned about their daughters' schooling and friends, as well as their ability to support their daughters after prison.

INCARCERATED WOMEN
AND THE CHILD WELFARE SYSTEM

Research has shown that mothers in prison have a strong interest in their children and are concerned about their welfare. Despite this concern, they are often considered by the courts to be unfit parents. Legally the courts in most states cannot terminate parental rights due to incarceration alone, but it often does play a role in the termination of rights. As a parent, the inmate has a legal responsibility to support her child. Incarceration can be considered an impediment to this responsibility and the parent is often seen as "abandoning" the child. When parental rights are terminated, all legal bonds between the parent and child are severed. The parent has no right to custody, visitation, or even communication.

Women in prison must overcome many obstacles to maintain their parental rights to their children. More than twenty-five states have laws providing for the termination of parental rights or adoption statutes that explicitly pertain to incarcerated parents. Genty (1995) argues that state laws are not designed with incarcerated parents in mind: "State laws were historically aimed at parents who voluntarily abandoned the child. . . . The laws are therefore ill-equipped to deal with the problem of parents who are involuntarily separated from their children through incarceration but who actively strive to continue to be parents" (p. 168). Recent federal legislation, such as the Adoption and Safe Families Act of 1997, has created even more obstacles for parents in prison.

The federal Adoption and Safe Families Act of 1997 (ASFA) was created as a response to the large number of children who were living in foster care. The intent of ASFA appeared to be to expedite adoptions for children in foster care. However, the time limits set by this law made it more difficult for women in prison to maintain their parental rights. The law requires the state to move to terminate parental rights if the child has been in foster care for fifteen of the most recent twenty-two months. Women spend an average of twenty-four to thirty-six months in prison (U.S. Department of Justice, 1995, quoted in Genty, 1998). Women could thus lose custodial rights to their children simply because they are incarcerated.

The federal Adoption and Safe Families Act of 1997 does not require states to terminate parental rights if a relative is caring for the child. Thus to preserve the mother's rights while she is prison, many children are placed with relatives. More than half the women in prison in 1991 had minor children who were living with their own parents, and about 20 percent of women had minor children who were living with other relatives (U.S. Department of Justice, 1994).[2] Hispanic (78 percent) and African-American (80 percent) female inmates were more likely to have children living with relatives than Caucasian (55 percent) female inmates (U.S. Department of Justice, 1994).

Enos (1997) interviewed thirteen women at a correctional facility to examine why women of color were more likely to have their children in the care of relatives. Seven of the women were Caucasian, four were African American, and two were Hispanic. The Caucasian women reported that they were estranged from their relatives and could not go to them for help. They felt they had more control in foster care. Once they left prison, they felt confident they could get their children back, although this requires that the mother secure legal help. African-American women reported that they did not trust the child welfare system and feared racial discrimination by the system. Many had an extended family, as did the Hispanic mothers, and felt they could rely on its members. This difference in family structure was important in explaining placement differences.

Some child welfare laws encourage children to be placed with relatives instead of in foster care. For example, the Child Welfare and Adoption Assistance Act of 1980 requires child welfare agencies to demonstrate "reasonable efforts" to place children with relatives (quoted in Gaudin and Sutphen, 1993). The Personal Responsibility and Work Opportunity Reconciliation Act of 1996 also requires that the state give preference to placing children with relatives over strangers (Phillips and Bloom, 1998). On the one hand, "relative" caregivers in poor families who do not work are likely to be elderly or in poor health. On the other hand, younger and healthier relatives, if on welfare, are required to work. If they are not on welfare, they also need to work for financial reasons. However, the state is only required to provide financial support if the child is placed in formal, foster care. As they stand, these policies are intrinsically contradictory: expressing preference for "relative" care, while putting that option out of the reach of poor families. Relative caregivers often informally assume responsibility for the child without going through the courts (Phillips and Bloom, 1998). As a result, few financial resources are available to the children.

Under the ASFA, the state can claim that terminating parental rights would not be in the best interest of the child. However, there is little interaction between caseworkers and their clients in prison. Beckerman (1994) found that mothers in prison do not receive adequate notice of family court hearings, at which they could address their interest in maintaining parental rights. Mothers are often not notified in enough time to procure transportation to the court hearing and usually cannot attend. Legal services for female prisoners are very limited, having been reduced substantially during the 1990s. Unfortunately, this has occurred in the same period when the population of mothers in prison has increased significantly. The most frequent request of women is for legal services pertaining to their children, but court decisions have not supported such services.

The special needs of children whose mothers are in prison have not yet been recognized. Seymour (1998) says that "it is tempting to characterize these children as no more or less vulnerable than other children receiving child welfare services, but they are different in ways that make them and their families a challenging population to serve" (p. 474). Recent research on the child welfare system indicates that few services deal directly with children of incarcerated parents. The Child Welfare League of America (CWLA) surveyed the states and found that most were unable to provide any substantial demographic information about these children (Harnill, Petit, and Woodruff, 1998). Thirty-five of the states could not provide an estimated number of children with incarcerated parents who are in the child welfare system. Four states estimated percentages of children of incarcerated parents by age group and race/ethnicity, and three of these states provided estimates by gender.

It is apparent from the survey that the child welfare system has not developed adequate methods to gather information on children of incarcerated parents. Only when a parent is in prison for child abuse or neglect does the record usually reflect that information. In other cases, the children of prisoners are not included in the child welfare information system, making it more difficult to provide needed resources. Fortunately, several states that responded to the survey indicated that they are developing systems that can collect information on children of incarcerated parents.

Another purpose of this survey was to gather information on child welfare programs and services that are available to these children. The authors of the 1998 CWLA report noted that it was difficult to determine whether some states listed programs specific to children whose parents were incarcerated or if the programs were available to all children and parents (Harnill, Petit, and Woodruff, 1998). However, the responses were treated as specifically dealing with children of incarcerated parents.

The majority of states in the survey indicated that they involved the incarcerated parents in their children's placement and helped to maintain contact with the child. However, few states provided support services for the children. Twenty-seven of the states included incarcerated parents in permanency planning. Twenty-five states provided transportation for children to visit the incarcerated parent. Only four states provided support groups for the children of incarcerated parents and their caregivers.

Some states indicated that they perceive children of incarcerated parents as having needs that are the same as other children (fourteen states) or greater than other children (eleven states). However, only two states have special training for state agency staff on the needs of children with incarcerated parents.

PROGRAMS AND SERVICES FOR CHILDREN OF INCARCERATED MOTHERS

Table 12.1 gives information about a selected set of programs and services for children of incarcerated mothers.

Child Welfare League of America (CWLA)

The Child Welfare League of America is a nonpartisan, nonprofit organization based in Washington, DC. This national organization is comprised of more than 1,000 public and nonprofit agencies that serve abused and neglected children. The CWLA provides services to a variety of children, including children of incarcerated parents. In 1996, the Children with Incarcerated Parents Initiative was launched at the National Institute on Children of Incarcerated Parents in Washington, DC.

The CWLA encourages child welfare agencies to identify systematically children whose parents are incarcerated and to provide special training for agency staff. Also, child welfare agencies are encouraged to accommodate the needs of incarcerated parents and their children in permanency planning.

Chicago Legal Aid to Incarcerated Mothers (CLAIM)

Chicago Legal Aid to Incarcerated Mothers provides legal services and educational programs to women prisoners in Cook County as well as support groups for women and their families. Although the organization occasionally works with incarcerated fathers, CLAIM focuses mainly on women in prison and their families. CLAIM works with child welfare agencies in the child's placement and encourages mother/child visitation. Staff also provide referrals for services such as substance abuse treatment and parenting classes. CLAIM runs a peer-support and advocacy group called Visible Voices. This all-female group is comprised of former prisoners and work-release residents. The group is facilitated by former prisoners and focuses on both personal and policy changes.

TABLE 12.1. Programs and Services for Children of Incarcerated Mothers

Name of Program	Location	Services
Child Welfare League of America	Washington, DC	Advocacy for children with incarcerated parents Support for children in the child-welfare system (in general)
Chicago Legal Aid to Incarcerated Mothers	Chicago, Illinois	Legal aid and advocacy for women prisoners and families
Parenting from a Distance	Bedford Hills Correctional Facility, New York	Support group for women in prison, run by inmates
Children's Visitation Program	Huron Valley Correctional Facility, Ypsilanti, Michigan	Special contact visits between mother and child
Minnesota Correctional Facility-Shakopee	Shakopee Correctional Facility, Minnesota	Parenting programs for inmates Overnight visits for children of inmates Teen support groups Camp Special program for adolescents
Girl Scouts Beyond Bars	Maryland Correctional Institution for Women, Baltimore	Girl Scout activities for daughters and mothers in prison
Project SEEK	Operating Agency: Mott's Children Center, Flint, Michigan	Home visits Advocacy/referrals Support groups for children, caregivers, and mothers Assistance with inmate communication
Sons and Daughters of the Incarcerated (SADOI, Inc.)	Ann Arbor, Michigan	Group therapy Individual therapy Case management/referrals Community outreach/training
Legal Services for Prisoners with Children	San Francisco, California	Legal advocacy for women prisoners and their children

CLAIM has recently presented a report on the effectiveness of community-based programs (Devine, 1997). The organization argues that the majority of women in prison are serving sentences for nonviolent crimes and would not pose a risk to the community if they were placed in low-security programs. CLAIM's study of community-based programs demonstrated that the programs better preserved family cohesion, reduced recidivism, and were cost effective. Currently, it is estimated that it costs $32,000 to keep a woman in prison for one year (Sarri and Doctora, 1995). It also costs approximately $20,000 to keep one child in foster care for one year (Devine, 1997). The average cost for a mother and up to three children in a community-based program is $26,196 per year. If 500 women with up to two children were in these programs, CLAIM estimates that $23,725,000 would be saved in tax dollars per year (CLAIM, 1997).

Parenting from a Distance

The Parenting from a Distance program serves a small number of the mothers incarcerated in the Bedford Hills Correctional Facility, New York's maximum-security prison for women. Kathy Boudin and Rozann Greco, both inmates at Bedford Hills, cofacilitate this support group for mothers in prison. Ten women meet for three months at a time, five days a week, two and a half hours per day. The group's main focus is on strengthening the mother/child relationship during the mother's incarceration by strengthening the women's roles as mothers (Boudin, 1998).

Members are encouraged to talk about traumatic experiences as children and young adults. The women in this group share these experiences with one another and attempt to comprehend the impact of these experiences on their ability to mother. They deal with the guilt and shame they may feel about how the crime they committed affects their child. They also deal with the women's anger toward their inability to be an active and visible mother.

Parenting from a Distance is unique in that the facilitators are also inmates. The facilitators consult weekly with a social worker and rely on their own backgrounds (both have master's degrees). The support group encourages autonomy and independence but recognizes that the inmates do not have much control in the prison environment.

Children's Visitation Program (CVP)—Ypsilanti, MI

The Children's Visitation Program was located at the Huron Valley Correctional Facility in Ypsilanti. It began in 1988 and served more than 100 children and fifty mothers. The purpose of this program was to strengthen the mother-child relationship through special visits.

Community volunteers provided transportation for these visits, which lasted three hours. The visiting room was temporarily converted to a playroom for the children. Children could spend private time with their mothers without the presence of another adult. The mothers and children were free to move around the room without being chastised. A nonuniformed officer is the only corrections supervisor present.

Inmates who participated in this program believed it was a good program (Jose-Kampfner, 1991). Women in the program were less likely to be written up for misconduct because their visits with the children ended. Also, the inmates felt that the program helps to reestablish their relationships with their children.

Minnesota Correctional Facility—Shakopee

Shakopee, the state prison for women, opened in 1986 and is located in a suburb of Minneapolis. This correctional facility serves women who have been convicted of a felony by the State of Minnesota. The average stay at Shakopee is little more than three years. It is an open prison with no fences around the facility. Thus, to the public it does not have the appearance of a state prison. Outside doors, cell doors, and other access areas are inconspicuously electronically monitored.

Shakopee emphasizes the importance of maintaining family relations for the inmates. The facility has a parenting and family program, which is intended to help women preserve the family unit while incarcerated. On Friday nights children whose mothers reside in the parenting unit may stay with their mothers overnight in her room (a trundle bed is provided). Toys and colorful surroundings are provided in the lounge areas. Mothers are responsible for the feeding and care of the child during each visit. There is also an independent-living center, where older children are allowed to stay with their mothers in small apartments for the weekend.

Girl Scouts Beyond Bars (GSBB)

The Maryland Correctional Institution for Women was the initial site for the Girl Scouts Beyond Bars program, which began in 1992. It was designed to accommodate a maximum of thirty mothers and forty daughters at an annual cost of $30,000. Membership is open to inmates with daughters ages seven to seventeen who live in Baltimore. The inmates must have twelve months remaining on their sentence, have no infractions from the previous thirty days, remain infraction free, and not have a conviction for an offense against children (Block and Potthast, 1998).

Mothers and daughters in GSBB meet twice a month for two hours. The first fifteen minutes are devoted to private mother/daughter conversation, while the rest of the time consists of structured troop activities. Twice a month, the mothers meet to focus on parenting issues and GSBB-related activities. An experienced social worker, a GSBB staff member, or a volunteer leads these sessions. The daughters also meet outside the facility to work on projects started at the institution. Transportation to and from the correctional facility is provided for the daughters. Upon release, the mothers' Girl Scouts memberships end, but the daughters have the option of remaining in a troop.

Over a period of two years, Block and Potthast (1998) interviewed thirty-five mothers and thirty-two daughters who had participated or were currently participating in the Girl Scouts Beyond Bars program at the Maryland correctional institution. They also interviewed twenty-two caregivers of daughter members. The mothers in this sample were slightly younger than the general prison population. They were more likely to have been married and living with their children previous to their incarceration. Ninety percent of the mothers in this sample were African American, compared to 45 percent of the general prison population. Every mother interviewed planned to reunite with her children upon release.

Block and Potthast also studied how GSBB affected the daughters. Members of GSBB received more visits from their daughters than inmates who did not participate in the program. However, 53 percent of the mothers interviewed in the study did not believe that the program had any effect on the number of visits they received from their daughters. It is possible that the daughters in this sample were more likely to visit than others even if the program did not exist.

Both the caregivers and the daughters reported positive outcomes from GSBB. Caregivers noted increased communication and understanding between mothers and daughters. The daughters found it beneficial to interact with other girls. Almost all of the daughters reported that they had made new friends. Half of the girls had contacted other girls outside of the meeting. Overall, GSBB appeared to be beneficial for the members. It has been extended into several states with continued positive results.

Project SEEK (Services to Enable and Empower Kids)

Project SEEK serves children in Genesee County, Michigan, who have a parent in state prison <http://www.strengtheningfamilies.org/html/model_

programs_1997/mfp_pg28.html>, regardless of whether the parent lived with the child prior to the incarceration. Children must be under the age of eleven at intake. Most of the families had annual household incomes below $10,000.

Project SEEK performs four major services: home visits, support groups, advocacy and referral, and facilitation of child/inmate communication. Each family is assigned to a project specialist, who remains their contact for the duration of the program. Project specialists work with twenty to twenty-five families and meet with the caregivers and children in their homes. During these visits, family conflict management and parenting skills are discussed with the caregiver. The specialist also meets with the child individually to talk about the child's concerns regarding family and school. Specialists also assist families in obtaining other services not offered by the project. If the parent is in Genesee County Regional Prison, the specialist makes arrangements for special visits with the children. Otherwise, written and telephone communication is encouraged and facilitated.

Project SEEK also facilitates support groups for children and caregivers. Three weekly support groups target children between ages five and ten. There is one adolescent group for ages eleven through sixteen that also meets weekly. These groups focus on problem-solving skills, cultural-diversity issues, and violence prevention. The caregiver support groups meet annually and focus on stress-management training.

Sons and Daughters of the Incarcerated (SADOI, Inc.)

Sons and Daughters of the Incarcerated (SADOI, Inc., 1996) has been operating since 1995 in Washtenaw and Wayne Counties, in Southeastern Michigan. SADOI is a group counseling program for youths who have (or have had) an incarcerated parent or other close family member. SADOI provides a safe and nurturing setting in which young people can discuss their feelings with groups of their peers. It gives youths an opportunity to process the events that took place before, during, and after their parents' incarceration.

Each SADOI group has a maximum of twelve participants. The groups meet once a week for twelve weeks. Group members are encouraged to talk openly about their parents' incarceration and the impact it has had on their lives. The youths also complete writing assignments as a means of further expressing what they are unable to communicate verbally.

The subject matter covered in the support groups is determined by the ages of the participants. The age-seven-through-twelve groups focus on building and maintaining strong relationships, developing effective communication and coping skills, raising self-esteem, studying the causes and effects of incarceration, and learning how to steer clear of dangerous and unlawful activities. SADOI also provides these youths with skills that enable them to communicate more openly and effectively with family members. For youths ages thirteen through seventeen, the groups cover issues of grief, loss, separation, drug abuse, anger, family relationships, problem solving, racism, sexually transmitted diseases, gangs, self-esteem, the stigma attached to incarceration, and the return of the incarcerated parents to the home. SADOI also offers training for educators and human service professionals, teaching them how to identify children of incarcerated parents and helping them understand the effects of parental incarceration on those children.

Legal Services for Prisoners with Children (LSPC)

Legal Services for Prisoners with Children has taken a very active role in defining legal issues regarding incarceration in political terms. While focusing on the individual needs of the LSPC's clients, they attempt to provide a broader structure for combating the growth of the prison industry.

Throughout LSPC's history, they have provided support to newly formed and grassroots community organizations. Presently, LSPC serves as fiscal sponsor to Families with a Future, California Coalition for Women Prisoners, Women's Positive Legal Action Network, Victory Gardens, and the Critical Resistance Campaign. They also work very closely with the California Coalition for Battered Women in Prison, California Prison Focus, and Jericho.

In their most recent newsletter, LSPC stated that their constituents are some of the most maligned and forgotten citizens in the state. California is the home of the two largest women's prisons in the world: Central California Women's Facility (CCWP) and Valley State Prison for Women (VSPW). LSPC currently has a staff of seven full-time employees, with its founding director, Ellen Barry, working closely with the staff, but no longer at LSPC on a full-time basis (Barry, 1995).

LSPC coordinates a quarterly educational program at the Federal Correctional Facility in Dublin, California, one of only three federal women's prisons in the country. The program provides legal education to female prisoners in the areas of family, immigration, housing and social security law, as well as the Indian Child Welfare Act. LSPC has trained many attorneys and legal advocates on the intricacies of prisoners' rights and family law. While much of this training has been legal in scope, it is always combined with a political analysis of the growth of the prison industrial complex and, in particular, the so-called "War on Drugs" and three-strikes legislation. In addition, their work is primarily with female prisoners, so they have developed a feminist analysis of the work they do.

LSPC also provides internships to law students as well as undergraduates, graduate students, community activists, and advocates.

DISCUSSION

The programs that have been highlighted are representative of the available services for children of incarcerated mothers. These programs have been well received by these children and their mothers. However, some programs are funded through private sources and find it difficult to obtain continuing funds. More public financial assistance would broaden the services that these programs provide.

Children of incarcerated mothers are an overlooked population with special needs. In order to serve this population, changes in the child welfare, criminal justice and public media systems need to occur. Children of incarcerated mothers would be better served if the following solutions were implemented.

Knowledge Gathering

The state agency responsible for children's welfare must gather systematic information about the numbers and location of incarcerated parents.

Currently, no reliable source provides valid demographic information on children whose parents are incarcerated. Such information is essential to begin to address the problems of this group. The U.S. Department of Justice, when gathering statistical information on prisoners, should include questions for prisoners with children and provide that information to the protective services units of child welfare agencies. The child welfare system should also gather data even if the child has been referred for reasons other than a parent's incarceration. There should be interdepartmental responsibility for these children.

Research should be conducted on children of incarcerated parents.

The available research on children of incarcerated mothers suggests that a mother's incarceration can have a dramatic impact on her children. However, many of these empirical studies have methodological limitations that affect their results. For more useful information to be available, future research should have larger representative samples of children of incarcerated mothers. The impact of a mother's incarceration should be examined over time in longitudinal studies. Interviews with children, if possible, should be collected along with information from mothers and caregivers.[3] More research needs to focus on factors that alleviate the impact of a mother's incarceration. The impact of the incarceration should be examined within the contexts of the child's race, gender, and class. More research also needs to focus on children of incarcerated fathers.

The role of the justice and child welfare systems in responding to the special needs of women in prison should be examined.

Currently, most correctional facilities provide at most visitation privileges for children and families. Many children cannot visit, however, due to the inaccessibility of prisons and the lack of transportation. The Adoption and Safe Families Act of 1997 further attests to the importance of visitation between the child(ren) and the incarcerated parent. Permanency plans for said children cannot be determined until the state can show: (1) how much access to the child is afforded to the parent from whom the child has been removed; and (2) what services were provided to the parent from whom the child has been removed (H.R.867-15, SEC. 303(2)(A)(iv)). It also states, for the purposes of successful family reunification, that specific services and activities must be provided toward reunification: individual, group, and family counseling; inpatient, residential, or outpatient substance abuse treatment services; mental health services; assistance to address domestic violence; services designed to provide temporary child care and therapeutic services for families—including crisis nurseries; transportation to or from any of these services and others (H.R. 867-17, SEC. 304(7)(B)(I-v)). The law is clear on this matter, yet the justice and child welfare systems have not adhered to it. Correctional facilities need to provide more assistance with visitation for children, such as transportation at little or no cost. The conditions of the visiting rooms should be better suited for children, such as having toys or wall decorations to make the room more friendly.

The justice system can play a crucial role in preventing prolonged separation between the mother and the child. More parenting programs need to be implemented so that inmates are given the opportunity to strengthen their relationship with their children. More treatment and rehabilitation programs need to be available for inmates so that they are less likely to reenter the prison system. Women are most likely to be in prison for drug offenses and have histories of substance abuse. If they are given adequate treatment for their addiction, they may be less likely to return to prison.

Overcrowded conditions lead to fewer treatment and rehabilitation programs. To alleviate these conditions, more community-based alternatives, such as work-release programs, should be implemented. As the Chicago Legal Aid to Incarcerated Mothers report has demonstrated, community-based alternatives to incarceration assist in preserving the family structure and are more cost effective. Most women in prison are serving for nonviolent crimes and would not pose a risk in these programs; therefore, it would be advantageous for the inmates, taxpayers, and, most important, the children.

Child Welfare Services

Child welfare services for children of incarcerated mothers should be improved.

The child welfare system is intended to serve children in need of protection. Children of incarcerated mothers need protection and should not be neglected, as is presently the situation. The child welfare system needs to recognize that a mother's incarceration does not necessarily mean that the mother has abandoned the child. Child welfare laws, such as the Adoption and Safe Family Act of 1997, allow the state to intervene on behalf of the parent. Child welfare workers need to take advantage of this act and assist parents in maintaining parental rights. The child welfare system has recognized only recently the prominence of children in the care of relatives instead of formalized foster care. More resources and support should be provided for relative caregivers.

Child welfare workers should receive training specific to the needs of children of incarcerated parents. Workers should be trained to assist the children in dealing with the separation from the mother and coping with the stigma associated with the incarceration. Caseworkers should make sure that mothers are aware of their parental rights and assist them in keeping these rights if they wish to do so. Workers should also help maintain contact between the mother and the children.

Child welfare services and the justice system should provide support for programs that aid children whose mothers are incarcerated.

Finally, both systems should unite to expand existing programs (such as those listed in Table 12.1) that help children deal with the trauma of their mothers' incarceration and make them more effective through formative evaluation.

CONCLUSION

> It's difficult for people on the outside, especially those who have been victims of crime, to care for people in prison, or even to accept the fact that many of them are victims of crime, too. But babies have hurt no one. (Harris, 1993, 26)

A society is judged on its protection of its most vulnerable members, and children of incarcerated parents are among our most vulnerable members. Loathing for prisoners tends to supersede the recognition that their children need our support. Perhaps if more people were made aware of the special needs of the children of incarcerated mothers, they would intervene on their behalf. In any case, incarcerated mothers and their children are an important and often-overlooked population. Ignoring their needs now may cost us more in the future if this neglect results in a future generation of maladjusted adults.

NOTES

1. The state of Minnesota has developed a parenting program for women in their state prison. Special units are designated for women with young children who may visit their mother and stay in her private room on weekends. Special provisions are also made for overnight visits by adolescent children.
2. The statistics for relative caregivers do not include children who were living with their fathers.
3. We recognize that some children may be reluctant to be interviewed about their mother's incarceration. It may require highly skilled interviewers to obtain interviews with children in this line of research.

REFERENCES

Barry, Ellen. 1995. Legal Issues for Prisoners and Their Children. In Katharine Gabel and Denise Johnston (Eds.), *Children of Incarcerated Parents,* (pp. 147-166). New York: Lexington Books.

Beckerman, Adela. 1994. Mothers in Prison: Meeting the Prerequisite Conditions for Permanency Planning. *Social Work 39*(1): 9-14.

Block, Kathleen J. and Margaret J. Potthast. 1998. Girl Scouts Beyond Bars: Facilitating Parent-Child Contact in Correctional Settings. *Child Welfare 77*(5): 561-578.

Boudin, Kathy. 1998. Lessons from a Mother's Program in Prison: A Psychosocial Approach Supports Women and Their Children. *Women and Therapy—Special Issue. Breaking the Rules: Women in Prison and Feminist Therapy: II 21*(1): 103-125.

Chicago Legal Aid to Incarcerated Mothers (CLAIM). 1997. Checking Out Alternatives to Jail: Programs Save Kids and Tax Dollars. Press release, May 9. Chicago: Chicago Legal Aid to Incarcerated Mothers.

Devine, K. 1997. *Family Unity: The Benefits and Costs of Community-Based Sentencing Programs for Women and Their Children in Illinois.* Chicago: Chicago Legal Aid to Incarcerated Mothers.

Enos, Sandra. 1997. Managing Motherhood in Prison: The Impact of Race and Ethnicity on Child Placement. *Women and Therapy—Special Issue. Breaking the Rules: Women in Prison and Feminist Therapy: 1* 20(4): 57-73.

Gaudin, James M. Jr. and Richard Sutphen. 1993. Foster Care vs. Extended Family Care for Children of Incarcerated Mothers. *Journal of Offender Rehabilitation* 19(3-4): 129-147.

Genty, Phillip. 1995. Termination of Parental Rights Among Prisoners. In Katharine Gabel and Denise Johnston (Eds.), *Children of Incarcerated Parents* (pp. 167-182). New York: Lexington Books.

Genty, Philip M. 1998. Permanency Planning in the Context of Parental Incarceration: Legal Issues and Recommendations. *Child Welfare* 77(5): 543-560.

Gilliard, Darrell K. and Allen J. Beck. 1998. *Prison and Jail Inmates at Midyear, 1997.* Washington, DC: U.S. Department of Justice, Bureau of Justice Statistics.

Harnill, Sandra, Michael Petit, and Kristen Woodruff. 1998. *State Agency Survey on Children with Incarcerated Parents.* Washington, DC: Child Welfare League of America.

Harris, Jean. 1993. The Babies of Bedford. *New York Times Magazine,* March 28, Sec. 6, p. 26.

Johnston, Denise. 1995a. Effects of Parental Incarceration. In Katharine Gabel and Denise Johnston (Eds.), *Children of Incarcerated Parents* (pp. 59-87). New York: Lexington Books.

Johnston, Denise. 1995b. Incarcerated Parents. In Katharine Gabel and Denise Johnston (Eds.), *Children of Incarcerated Parents* (pp. 3-20). New York: Lexington Books.

Jose-Kampfner, Christina. 1991. Mother and Child Reunion. Two Women's Programs Show That Relaxed Visitation Can Improve Inmate Behavior. *Corrections Today 53*(7): 130-34.

Jose-Kampfner, Christina. 1995. Post-Traumatic Stress Reactions in Children of Imprisoned Mothers. In Katharine Gabel and Denise Johnston (Eds.), *Children of Incarcerated parents* (pp. 89-102). New York: Lexington Books.

Katz, Pamela C. 1998. Supporting Families and Children of Mothers in Jail: An Integrated Child Welfare and Criminal Justice Policy. *Child Welfare* 77(5): 495-512.

LeFlore, Harry and Mary Ann Holston. 1989. Perceived Importance of Parenting Behaviors As Reported by Inmate Mothers: An Exploratory Study. *Journal of Offender Counseling Services and Rehabilitation* 14(1): 5-22.

Myers, Barbara J., Tina M. Smarsh, Kristine Amlund-Hagen, and Suzanne Kennon. 1999. Children of Incarcerated Mothers. *Journal of Child and Family Studies* 8(1): 11-25.

Phillips, Susan and Barbara Bloom. 1998. In Whose Best Interest? The Changing Public Policy on Relatives Caring for Children with Incarcerated Parents. *Child Welfare 77*(5): 531-542.

Sarri, Rosemary and Jocelyn Doctora. 1995. Preliminary Survey. Unpublished data. Ann Arbor: University of Michigan, Institute for Social Research.

Seymour, Cynthia. 1998. Children with Parents in Prison: Child Welfare Policy, Program, and Practice Issues. *Child Welfare 77*(5): 469-493.

Simon, Rita J. and Jean Loundis. 1991. *The Crimes Women Commit, the Punishments They Receive.* Lexington, MA: Lexington Books.

Snyder-Joy, Zoann K. and Teresa A. Carlo. 1998. Parenting Through Prison Walls: Incarcerated Mothers and Children's Visitation Programs. In Susan L. Miller (Ed.), *Crime, Control and Women: Feminist Implications of Criminal Justice Policy* (pp. 130-150). Thousand Oaks, CA: Sage Publications.

Sons and Daughters of the Incarcerated, Inc. 1996. Everything You Need to Know About the Children of the Incarcerated. Ann Arbor, MI: Sons and Daughters of the Incarcerated.

U.S. Department of Justice. 1994. *Bureau of Justice Statistics Special Report: Women in Prison.* Report No. NCJ-145321. Washington, DC: U.S. Department of Justice, Bureau of Justice Statistics.

U.S. Department of Justice. 1999a. *Prisoners in 1998.* Report No. NCJ 175687. Washington, DC: U.S. Department of Justice, Bureau of Justice Statistics.

U.S. Department of Justice. 1999b. *Women Offenders.* Report No. NCJ 175688. Washington, DC: U.S. Department of Justice, Bureau of Justice Statistics.

Chapter 13

Women's Recidivism and Reintegration: Two Sides of the Same Coin

Patricia O'Brien
Nancy J. Harm

How does a woman "make it" when she is released from prison? Given the dramatic rise of women being incarcerated in this country, primarily as a result of the "War on Drugs," this question is gaining increased importance. By midyear 1999, 87,199 women were in state or federal prisons, 6.5 percent of all prison inmates (up from 5.7 percent in 1990). Since 1990, the female proportion of those incarcerated has increased by an average of 8.4 percent per year as compared to the 6.5 percent average annual increase of incarcerated men (Beck, 2000).

Women in prison are disproportionately poor women of color with a number of strikes against them when they entered prison. When they leave prison, they are still poor women of color, carrying the same burdens as when they entered, with the additional label of "ex-con." How, then, do they succeed in the transition back to the "free world"? The overwhelming majority of transition studies have been concerned primarily with the "risk factors" for recidivism of male offenders—those demographic characteristics that predict which ex-prisoners will reoffend after release. Female and male prisoners are similar on many of these factors, such as race, ethnicity, education, and age. However, the differences between male and female offenders may affect the process of reentry. These differences include higher rates of abuse, reported mental illness and physical health challenges, separation from children and/or parenting, types of convictions, and social structural issues.

Forty percent of female federal prison inmates and 57 percent of female state prison inmates reported physical or sexual abuse before their admission (as compared to 7.2 percent of the male federal inmates and 16 percent of the male state inmates) (Harlow, 1999). This self-reported rate of abuse among incarcerated women is higher than the general population estimate of 12 to 17 percent.

Women have much higher rates of mental illness than men—23.6 percent of state inmates and 12.5 percent of federal inmates compared to 15 percent and 7 percent for men (Ditton, 1999). Nationally, the proportion of female inmates who are HIV positive is higher than that of men—about 3.5 percent compared to 2.2 percent (Maruschak, 1999; Greenfeld and Snell, 1999). The high incidence of HIV infection among women in prison can probably be explained by the same factors that place these women at risk for incarceration: poverty, race, and drug use (Smith and Dailard, 1994). Young (1996) found that women enter prison with a poor physical health status related to a combination of societal conditions and personal antecedents.

Forty percent of female inmates, compared to 32 percent of male inmates, reported being under the influence of drugs when the crime was committed. Nearly one-third of female inmates reported they had committed the offense in order to obtain money to support their drug use (Greenfeld and Snell, 1999). These data show that drug use is more prevalent among female inmates, indicating a need for drug treatment programs specifically designed for women both in prison and in the community. Substance abuse may also be an impediment to reunification with children. Fessler (1991) found in her study of both incarcerated women and women on parole that long substance abuse histories had a negative effect on their postrelease reunification with their children. Very few drug treatment programs allow women to have their children with them while in treatment, thus forcing women to choose between continued separation from their children or their own recovery.

Economic conditions also have a more deleterious effect on women than on men. Only 40 percent of women in state prison reported they had been employed full-time prior to their arrest, as compared to 60 percent of incarcerated men. About 37 percent of women and 28 percent of men had monthly incomes of less than $600, with nearly 30 percent of women inmates receiving welfare assistance, compared to 8 percent of the men (Greenfeld and Snell, 1999). These differences, coupled with the commonalities of racial and ethnic disparities consistent across all age groups (Beck, 2000), make the process of reintegration more challenging for women than for men.

FACTORS INFLUENCING SUCCESSFUL VERSUS UNSUCCESSFUL REINTEGRATION

Literature describing how ex-prisoners succeed in reintegration, rather than how they fail, is scarce for both men and women. Research on adult of-

> **Open Arms**
>
> As the audience enters, they hear the Rolling Stones song, "Mother's Little Helper."
> Scene 1. Shree sings "Open Arms." The actors sculpt images that reflect the song.
> Scene 2. Susie's story
> After five years in prison, Susie returns home to her mother, children, and ex-husband. The oldest two children are excited to have her back, but the youngest doesn't know her and holds back. Her ex-husband, Brandy, is distant, and the situation is edgy. The children want her to go to the movies with them, but Brandy says no, not this time, and she doesn't go.
> Scene 3. Wendy's story
> Wendy comes to her mother's home, running from the police. She is pregnant, wants her mother to keep the child, but her mother wants to lead her own life and calls the police; Wendy pushes her mother and escapes the house.
>
> From play, titled *Open Arms,* produced by The Sisters Within Theater Troupe, Florence Crane Correctional Facility, Michigan, in collaboration with Chiara Liberatore and William Alexander (Buzz) of the Prison Creative Arts Project (University of Michigan), May 29, 1999. *Open Arms* is the twelfth play produced by the Troupe since April 1990.

fenders has focused primarily on the predictors and outcomes of recidivism rather than on the negative and positive processes of reentry. Recidivism is the consequence of becoming reinvolved in criminal activity that is reported to and acted upon by law enforcement. While remaining free from involvement with law enforcement is an achievement, it is only one of several criteria for successful reintegration into the community. Other criteria include successful resumption of familial roles, employment, remaining free of drugs, and assuming a role in the community.

Beck and Shipley's (1989) study of adult releases in 1983 identifies a number of variables that correlate with recidivism, most notably gender. Men are slightly more likely than women to be successful after their release from prison (41.9 percent as compared to 33 percent). Other factors found predictive of recidivism were length of time in community (recidivism is higher in the first year), age (older prisoners have lower rates of recidivism), extensive prior arrest record (as the number of previous arrests increases, so too does the chance of recidivism), length of incarceration (those who serve five years or more have lower rates of rearrest), and type of offense (those released for property offenses are most likely to be rearrested) (Beck and Shipley, 1989).

Forty-five percent of all parolees from prison in 1998 successfully met the conditions of their supervision, while 42 percent were returned to prison for new sentences or parole violations. Absconders (9 percent) and death or transfer (4 percent) accounted for the remainder (Bonczar and Glaze, 1999).

Correlates of women's postincarceration success or reintegration include employment (Lambert and Madden, 1976; Schulke, 1993), financial support (Jurik, 1983), family stability (Bloom, 1987; Flanagan, 1995; Hairston, 1991; Lambert and Madden, 1976), relationships (Schulke, 1993), and self-efficacy (Fletcher, Shaver, and Moon, 1993). Factors related to failure for women include involvement in spouse abuse (Bonta, Pang, and Wallace-Capretta, 1995; Danner et al., 1995), coming from a "broken" home (Danner et al., 1995), and race (lower rates of recidivism for black women compared to white women) (Robinson, 1971). Retrospective studies found that positive relationships (Schulke, 1993), family support (Lambert and Madden, 1976), and substance abuse treatment (Fletcher, Shaver, and Moon, 1993) reduces recidivism.

One aspect of successful reentry is the presence or absence of programs in the community to support women in the transition period. Far fewer prerelease programs are designed to prepare women, as compared with those for males, for the transition from prison to the community. A nationwide descriptive evaluation of 100 model programs for women offenders in community settings found effective programs assist participants in gaining self-confidence to increase their successful functioning within their communities (Austin, Bloom, and Donahue, 1992). These programs addressed participants' substance addictions, prior physical and sexual abuse, employment skills and aspirations, and familial relationships.

Koons et al. (1997) surveyed correctional administrators who identified substance abuse education and treatment, counseling for trauma related to previous abuse and current familial relationships, parent education, life-skill training, and basic education as related to successful treatment outcomes. Although these administrators could identify successful programs, few outcome evaluations have been conducted. Austin, Bloom, and Donahue (1992) said that the evidence for the "most promising" programs is limited to impressionistic data, because no research was conducted on the long-term effectiveness of the programs. Longitudinal studies are both very difficult and expensive, so few have been completed. Despite the caveat, they determined the most promising programs worked with clients to increase their coping and decision-making skills.

Most female inmates intend to reunite with their children after release from prison, highlighting the importance of programs that teach parenting skills, support the ongoing relationship between the incarcerated mother and her children, and address issues of housing and employment in the plan for reunification. Young and Smith (2000) report that they were able to locate six evaluation studies of programs in which strengthening families was a primary focus. Four of these were of parent education classes for incarcerated mothers (Browne, 1989; Harm and Thompson, 1997; Moore and

Clement, 1998; Showers, 1993), one of a prison visitation program (Snyder-Joy and Carlo, 1998), and one of a live-in nursery program (Carlson, 1998). All of these institution-based programs demonstrated positive findings and could support reunification efforts at the point of exit to the community when many problems surface (Harm and Phillips, 2001). Young and Smith (2000) stress that reintegration is integrally related to family matters, culturally responsive family programs being essential in the successful adjustment for mothers, children, and the children's caregivers.

A missing element in the literature is the examination of oppression and economic impoverishment. Focusing on a direct practice intervention and the effect of that intervention with the individual ignores the reality that many women in correctional custody spend their lives dealing with racist and sexist attitudes, beliefs, and policies. Young and Smith (2000) emphasize the ecological perspective that takes into account systematic oppression and its impact on women's entry into the prison system. From this perspective, they suggest creating interventions aimed at changing the environment as well as the individual.

Another missing element is a description of the *process* of successfully reintegrating into the community. Zamble and Quinsey (1997) developed a model of recidivism as an ongoing psychological process that examines the interaction between internal dispositions and external events. Their theoretical model includes an examination of a precipitating situation, the situational reaction, individual influences (such as cognitive and learning abilities), the availability of choices in making the response, and the actual response to the situation. The relapse prevention field focuses on helping individuals identify situations, people, and places associated with relapse and teaches skills for responding to these relapse "triggers"(Carroll, 1998). Defining reintegration as a dynamic process in which multiple outcomes reflect the variety of unmarked paths that a woman may negotiate in returning to her family and community is likely more facilitative than recognizing only "no arrest" as success after release from prison.

Two studies of reentry capture this dynamic process. Although the focus of the two studies is different, they complement and support each other. O'Brien (2001) interviewed women in Kansas who self-identified as successful after incarceration. Harm and Phillips (2001) interviewed women in Arkansas who had returned to prison after release. Because she was looking at success, O'Brien described the components necessary for reintegration, as illustrated in Figure 13.1. The critical elements include: (1) living arrangements, (2) supportive relationships, (3) employment, (4) community membership, and (5) internally derived efficacy.

Harm and Phillips (2001), on the other hand, identified comparable variables missing from the women's postprison experience that led to their sub-

FIGURE 13.1. An Empowerment Framework for Assessing Women's Reintegration

sequent return to prison. This framework is used to provide a structure for reporting the findings.

STUDY PARTICIPANTS

The studies used in-depth interviewing procedures to describe the experiences of women who were living in the community after release from prison or who, at the time of the interviews, had been returned to prison. Both studies were conducted in 1996. Table 13.1 provides a summary of selected participant demographics from the two studies.

In addition to these characteristics, O'Brien found that thirteen of the women she interviewed were employed and that, while three of the participants had less than a twelfth-grade education, more than half of the group (56 percent) had completed some college. Harm and Phillips found 66 percent of their respondents were living in rural counties prior to being sent to prison for the first time.

Table 13.2 provides a summary of the institutional history of the participants in these two studies. Participants in O'Brien's study had served sen-

TABLE 13.1. Study Participant Demographics

	Number of participants	Mean age (range)	Race	Mother/children	Marital status
Kansas (O'Brien, 2001)	18	34.6 (20-67)	56% Caucasian 22% African American 11% Hispanic 11% Other	72% mothers for 30 minor children	39% not married 28% divorced/separated 28% married 6% widowed
Arkansas (Harm and Phillips, 2001)	38	30 (16-50)	66% Caucasian; 35% African American	84% mothers of 71 children 11% pregnant	37% not married 37% divorced/separated 18% married 8% widowed

TABLE 13.2. Participant Institutional History

	Type of convictions	Number of incarcerations[1]	Jurisdiction
Kansas (*n* = 18)	39% property 39% drug charges 22% violent	61% - 1 11% - 2 6% - 3 6% - 4 6% - 5 11% - 10	State 61% Federal 39%
Arkansas (*n* = 38)	50% property 13% drug charges 11% violent[2]	50% - 2 24% - 3 13% - 4 10% - 5 7% - 6	State 100%

[1]Completed prior to interview
[2]Percentages do not add up due to missing data

tences that ranged from six months to eight years and had been released from prison three months to twelve years. Ten of the participants were either on parole or on supervised release.

METHOD AND ANALYSIS

Both qualitative studies relied on data collected by trained interviewers using a semistructured interview guide. O'Brien's study also used a focus group (Lincoln and Guba, 1985) of about half of the participants to test and deepen findings. The investigators analyzed the interview transcripts by using the constant comparative method (Glaser and Strauss, 1967; Lincoln and Guba, 1985). This method, in which continuous and simultaneous data collection and processing occurs, provides the basis for the integration of similarities and differences to produce the findings.

FINDINGS

Living Arrangements—Safe and Sufficient Housing

The women in the Kansas study had two distinct ways of dealing with housing depending on whether they were federal or state inmates. Federal inmates were released from the prison to a community placement facility. The facility provided room, board, and supportive services for the remainder of each woman's sentence, in most cases 90 to 120 days. Residents at the facility were expected to obtain employment within their first month and thereafter pay a percentage of their income for "subsistence" while residing at the facility. They were also expected to save the bulk of their earnings to enable them to manage initial living expenses upon leaving the facility.

The other Kansas women came directly from the state prison to the community with little more than hope in their pockets. These women were much more dependent upon family members or friends for temporary and often unstable housing. For example, Mandi initially stayed on the couch at her brother's home, then moved in with friends from work, and eventually (when she was working two jobs) rented her own home. Ashley stayed with her parents; when that became conflictual, she moved in with a boyfriend before finally moving into her own residence. At the time of the interviews, two of the women were still living with a family member and trying to save enough money so they could move into independent housing. Participants who moved to the community via the community placement facility made an average of 1.3 moves, while women who came to the community directly from prison made an average of 2.25 moves. Thus, the halfway house concept facilitated at least one aspect of reentry: the ability to secure housing.

In the Arkansas study, most women lived with their mothers and their children after release. This living arrangement was very conflictual for the majority of the women. Only 35 percent of the women reported expenses for rent, suggesting that the majority were dependent on others for housing. Although some of the women realized these living arrangements were not conducive to their reintegration, they saw no alternatives. Some even stated that their parole officers described the arrangements as "free rent."

Supportive Relationships

Relatives

The experiences of the Kansas women were similar to those of the Arkansas group. In fact, both groups of women could identify relapses and reoccurring problems that they associated with family conflicts, primarily problems with their mothers. The differences in their abilities to succeed depend upon relational competence learned while incarcerated or in the context of their transition. For Sadie, for example, it was a matter of getting connected to a support group offered by a local domestic violence group inside the prison facility that not only provided her education but also a sense of efficacy when she completed the training and was enabled to cofacilitate the group.

A characteristic of relational competence is the concept of drawing boundaries. Several women in the group referred to this concept when they indicated they no longer tolerated certain behaviors from others, including abusive or criminal conduct. Ashley's ability to assert herself to her mother opened the door to having a more bounded relationship. She explained,

> My mom and I were never really close . . . because she did abuse me. I would never open up to her and talk to her. So, about a year ago, I just sat her down one day, and I said, "Look, Mom, this is me and this is the way I am. You either deal with it or you don't, because you don't have another daughter. But I'm not gonna let you downgrade me and talk bad about me. You have to accept me the way I am."

Susan took responsibility for the behaviors that resulted in her two incarcerations, but recounted that she has also gained insight by examining some of the abuse in the family history that she feels attributed to her criminal behavior. The examination began for Susan during her last incarceration and continued when she was referred for mental health sessions during her parole. Meanwhile, her mother also obtained counseling and began to address some of what she had done to her daughter in previous years before her incarceration.

Families were both the best and most difficult part of returning to the community in Arkansas. One woman states: "The best part was being with my family and getting away from people telling me what to do and when to do it." Another: "The best part [of being released] was being able to spend time with family and getting to know my daughter." However, most saw their relationships with their families as the most difficult part of the reintegration process. After each prison sentence, the majority of women were paroled to the home of a relative—usually their mothers'. Women identified multiple sources of stress associated with these arrangements. One source of stress stemmed from negotiating the resumption of the parenting role while living with the person who had cared for their children while they were incarcerated. In other cases, the sources of stress were the family members' distrust of the former inmate or criminal behavior by family members, such as dealing drugs and prostitution. For many women, the relationship with their families was a source of anxiety, poor self-esteem, and isolation rather than one of support. Most notably, women described their mothers as controlling, mistrusting, and a source of embarrassment to them.

Children

Sixteen of the eighteen Kansas participants had children, including children who had been born to four of the participants since their release. At the time of the interviews, eight of the participants had alternative physical or legal custody arrangements for their children—meaning their children were not residing with the mother or she had voluntarily relinquished custody. These parents had chosen a graduated process of regaining eventual custody because they recognized they were not yet materially able to support their children. The children were being cared for by family members so the women were able to see them regularly and continue working toward establishing their own economic stability.

All the parents discussed the pain they had experienced in being separated from their children while incarcerated. For those who had decided not yet to resume their residential parenting role, they described relationships with their children that were both supportive and challenging—supportive in that the women felt they had been given a chance to address some of the trauma that the children had experienced prior to and during their incarceration; challenging due to the ambivalence the women felt in not being able to resume their parenting role immediately upon release.

Nan (a single mother of five children, including one that was born while she was incarcerated in a federal prison facility) actively continued her parenting role while in prison only because her younger sister and Nan's children moved to the town where she was incarcerated to ensure that she had regular visits with them. Nan felt that resuming care for her children after release was a major source of efficacy and satisfaction. She explained how she was able to overcome the need she previously had for "good living"—which had resulted in her conviction—by creating a home for her children:

> Havin' to go to prison, livin' in a matchbox room and only havin' X amount of dollars and havin' nowhere to go and nobody to turn to. I don't ever want that again. All them fine fancy clothes and good livin' . . . I wasn't even happy. Now, I'm so happy bein' right here with my kids with little money and nothin' because it's real, true love right here in the home with me and my kids.

The majority (65 percent) of the Arkansas women who were mothers were living with their children before serving their first prison sentence. An even larger proportion (80 percent) lived with their children after their first sentence. As the number of incarcerations increased, the percentage of women who lived with their children declined. During the first incarceration, the children were most often left in the care of either a maternal or paternal grandmother (71 percent)—an arrangement that was largely stable from incarceration to incarceration. Only three sibling groups changed caregivers over the course of their mothers' incarcerations. Eighteen percent of the mothers reported that their children had been separated from their siblings. In these cases, sibling groups were most often split between a father and a grandmother.

When asked what was positive about living with their children while in the community, the women discussed the sense of companionship their children provided (e.g., doing things together, having fun with them). They also identified the fact that the children were protective of them and took care of them. The women used phrases such as: "They kept me going," "They lifted my spirits," "He would fight other kids if they talked about me," "I wouldn't do drugs if he was there," or "They helped me stay focused."

The women gave a variety of responses regarding what was difficult about living with their children. Some feared not being able to support their children, while others felt pressured to make up for being away. Some stated that the anxiety of being with their children led to their using drugs or that they wanted to use drugs but could not because the children were present. Others discussed their inability to parent and their difficulties in getting reacquainted with their children. Still others felt they were not able to discipline their children because their own mothers, who had been caring for their children, had assumed the role of disciplinarian. During the time the women were in the community, some of them did not live with their children. Although these women stated that this separation was painful, they realized their children were in a more stable environment than they themselves could provide.

Parole Officers

"I am so grateful for her [parole officer] today," says Mandi, a former crack addict and one of the Kansas participants. For this group of women, facilitative relationships with correctional staff provided another element to their successful postrelease reentry. Some of the women described how they gained a sense of self-efficacy by earning respect from correctional officers for how they did their time. Demi recalled that a correctional officer told her, "You don't belong here," which reinforced her motivation to use the drug treatment program while she was incarcerated.

At the time of the study in Kansas, ten of the eighteen women were still accountable to the system under some form of supervision by state or federal officers. Many of the women described the parole or postrelease supervision process as "doing what I have to do." However, the ways women negotiated meeting their conditions of supervision and their relationship with their supervisory officer were instrumental for success in their reentry. Four of the participants in the study shared the same parole officer, who was cited for her willingness to extend herself to meet a parolee's needs (for example, meeting Mandi at her home when she did not have transportation to the parole office) and her flexibility in modifying parole conditions when it seemed appropriate to do so.

Other officers were recognized for the respect they showed the women. As Suzy said, "He treated me like a person instead of a number." Jeanette said she would send a thank-you card to her officers when she was released because the officer respected her enough to "leave her alone."

In Arkansas, reports of relationships with parole officers were mixed. Some women described parole officers as helpful, while others saw parole officers as not responsive to their situations. Some women attributed their return to prison to parole officers who did not get them into drug treatment programs when their drug screens tested positive but let them continue their drug use while other officers had no tolerance for dirty drug screens.

Employment

Participants in the Kansas study discussed the difficulties of securing and retaining employment (including the challenge of having a realistic understanding of how they would assume job responsibilities upon release) when they had not been enabled to assume decision-making responsibilities during incarceration. Elena expressed this concern when she said, "In there [prison], it's like vacation time. Here [in the community], if you got children or [are] goin' to work and getting' back on your feet, tryin' to get on the right track, it's stressful." The women that were most successful at managing the vagaries of a job search, disclosure of felony status, and the everyday work world were those who had been consistently employed while in prison. Women reported that they had to self-advocate to ensure they were involved in something productive, because they perceived that prison culture and policies reinforced a lack of planning for legitimate opportunities after release.

The women who were released to the federal community placement center had more support and referrals for job placement, especially with potential employers who would not discriminate on the basis of their criminal history. The state-released women gave a range of responses to how they managed disclosure of their legal status. Elizabeth did not reveal her ex-inmate status, but when it was discovered she was fired from two different jobs. Mandi used the data entry job training and experience that she had gained while in prison and personal contacts at a company to secure her first job. Later, she "sold herself" by her friendly demeanor and became a manager at the McDonald's she frequented. Sadie's first job was at the domestic violence shelter that had sponsored the support group she attended while in prison. Thirteen of the eighteen women reported that they had been subjected to discrimination on the basis of their criminal record which prevented them from getting the jobs they wanted. One woman was denied admission to a proprietary business school because the school could not guarantee her employment after she completed the program due to her record.

Most of the women in the Kansas sample struggled with finances. One woman received Supplemental Security Income (SSI) due to a disability; another received a limited amount of public assistance for her newborn child. The overwhelming concern among all the working women was that they could not gain employment that paid them a sufficient income to support themselves and their children. Rather, they were scraping by, often working more than one job, and drawing upon other family and social resources to supplement their wages.

Prior to their current incarceration, in Arkansas only 16 percent of the women interviewed had a job waiting for them when they were released from prison. An additional 57 percent of the women found work after they returned to the community. The median income from wages for this group of women was $560 per month. Nearly half (47 percent) of all the women in the study received some form of legal income other than, or in addition to, wages such as Aid to Families with Dependent Children,[1] social security benefits, food stamps, child support, and financial support from relatives. Approximately one-quarter of the women (27 percent) were unemployed throughout their entire time in the community. Of the unemployed group, 62 percent received income from public assistance programs, 13 percent supported themselves by illegal activities, and the remaining unemployed women reported no source of income.

For some women, employment was a positive experience, giving them a sense of self-worth. However, for a number of women, employment was another stressful element in their return to community. Low wages, lack of child care, discrimination based on being a felon, and co-worker conflict were frequent employment-related problems. A return to using drugs was the most often cited reason for leaving a job.

Community Attitudes and Resources

The ex-inmates in the Kansas study reported a number of professionals from various private and public agencies provided concrete assistance to them especially during the early stage of their transition. Aftercare was a challenge more often identified by the women released directly to the community from the state prison. One woman, Mandi, acknowledged relapsing with crack cocaine but, with the support and assistance of her work supervisor, she was able to get the treatment she needed. Some women expressed a concern about using community resources to acquire assistance because it put them in a recipient position in which they had to disclose their record of incarceration. Nan, for example, likened the intrusion to an extension of control she already felt in her postrelease supervision. She exploded,

> The federal government was all in my business and turned it upside down and told me what to do, when to do, not three-hundred sixty-five days a year, but four times three-hundred sixty-five days a year. And I live with my [probation] officer that does the same thing. I don't want to go nowhere else and nobody ask me nothin' about my business. Can I have some privacy? Can I be a citizen? Can I have rights? Can I be human?

Nan's questions reflect what many of the women said or implied about how they felt the community contributed to their success, not so much for the formal and informal resources it provided them, but for the sense that they were able to contribute to others. Bernie shared her experiences with churches and civic organizations to raise funds and collect clothing to give to other ex-inmates. Denni was able to make available a fitness regime that she provided at her place of employment to the residents of the federal community residence. Elena discussed her urge to work with adolescents so they would not get involved in drugs. This notion of "giving back" enabled the women to feel they belonged to their communities. As Sadie articulated, and other participants in the study confirmed, it is crucial that people in the "free world" recognize that former inmates are often living and working in the same community as they are:

> Almost everybody who goes to prison gets out [and] they are teaching in your school or shopping in the same stores . . . they are helpin' you out and doin' this and that and the other and in many ways are part of the community. I fix your kids' bicycles now. That's who ex-cons are, you know.

Throughout the interviews, the women in Arkansas talked about the stigma and shame of having been in prison. Women from small towns particularly felt the stigma of everyone in the town knowing they had been to prison and, consequently, not trusting them sufficiently to give them an opportunity for a job. The women were asked the question: "What would have helped you stay out of prison?" Thirty-four percent responded counseling and another 34 percent answered drug treatment. Other responses included concrete resources such as a car and a job (18 percent), a halfway house (5 percent), a different town (8 percent), and a better parole officer (11 percent). The lack of drug treatment programs in their communities was a problem for some of the women. Of the thirty-three women who stated they had a substance abuse problem, only 30 percent entered treatment programs when they left prison, primarily because few programs were available.

Building Self-Efficacy

The women in the Kansas sample described a phenomenon of growing from the "inside out" that often began when they learned how to manage their incarceration. The women themselves have claimed that prison saved them from death or worse. Prison certainly allows a "time out" from outside pressures and drug availability. It provides them with resources they might not otherwise have, including some programming, drug treatment, and vocational training. Numerous prisoners make use of the opportunities offered in prison and other correctional facilities and make positive changes despite soul-deadening limitations imposed on them by the prison structure. Many women in this study have survived circumstances far more perilous than a prison term, and most will continue to survive, and even thrive, in the new lives they are constructing.

Similar to the Arkansas women, the Kansas women described major struggles in gaining housing and employment. However, they reflected an ability to bounce back from adversity, as well as other personal attributes that supported their postincarceration success. Some of the internal strengths they identified included tenacity, stubbornness, problem-solving skills, willingness to take responsibility for one's behavior and choices, and a sense of competence for handling challenges.

The Arkansas women described emotional states such as depression, frustration, self-pity, guilt, anger, bitterness, and self-hatred associated with their return to using drugs. Within a matter of days after release, some of them gave up trying to be sober and/or drug free. They reported an inability to say "no" and relapses were often associated with old friends and the same neighborhood, as well as an inability to cope with certain stressors. For example, one woman relapsed after five years of being clean when her father died.

The women's discussions of both prison and community drug treatment programs centered on their own inadequacies rather than the limitations of the programs. Two of the women left community programs before they had completed them; two others stated that they did not have transportation to get there; the others stated they simply were not ready to "work the program." Although the programs in which they participated may not have included relapse prevention or addressed the issues with which they were faced, the women believed the lack of effectiveness of the programs lay solely within them. Only 55 percent participated in drug treatment while they were in prison the first time. Women identified an important internal component of the process as being "ready" to make use of drug treatment. For most of the women in this study, the process of recidivism was the process of relapse. They recognized the cues in their environment that led to relapse but did not have the coping skills to handle the situations differently; alternative resources were not available in the community; or they were locked into negative situations because of parole conditions.

In addition to having some insight about the elements that contributed to their efficacy in making a successful reentry, these women expressed aspirations that also reflected their sense of hope for transforming their lives. These aspirations included returning to college, better paying employment, and doing meaningful work. Table 13.3 summarizes the findings of the two studies along these five dimensions.

DISCUSSION

Knowledge

It is apparent from both studies that the process of successful reintegration is dependent upon the woman's development of a sense of self-efficacy and resiliency *and* the availability of external resources. Empowerment practice has at its foundation a dual focus on person and environment that evolves from a historical understanding of a concomitant need for simultaneously aiding people in need and attacking the social ills that relate to individual behaviors (Pinderhughes, 1994; Rose and Black, 1985). In this paradigm, the welfare of individuals and their families is linked inextricably with the life-promoting qualities of their social contexts. Figure 13.1, an empowerment framework, described the external resources and internal resiliencies that women who succeeded in the transition from prison drew upon for coping with obstacles, both during the incarceration and since their release. The framework reflects the overlapping nature of sources of support

TABLE 13.3. Dimensions of Reintegration for Women Returning to the Community After Incarceration

	Living Arrangements	Relationships	Employment	Community	Self-efficacy
Arkansas	No community placement available—dependent on family	Family issues not addressed, reunification difficult Children used as support and protection Parole officers not seen as relevant to process	Low-wage jobs and no child care prevented women from supporting themselves and their children	No sense of belonging to community—lack of appropriate services	Lack of coping strategies Blamed themselves for lack of access to treatment
Kansas	Community placement facilitated housing	Reconstructed relationships with relatives and more gradually with children Parole officers identified as supportive	Low-wage jobs coupled with family and/or employer support enabled women to support themselves and eventually their children	Received concrete assistance from social services and individuals; some sense of belonging as time from incarceration increased	Identified sources of internal and external efficacy

in the environment, as well as the permeability between and among the categories identified as most salient to the transition.

The studies contribute to a greater understanding of the women's process of exiting prison by demonstrating that, for those who successfully exited prison, there was not one sequential or temporal order to the process of transition. Rather, success begins when the woman herself is an active participant in the social world rather than a passive object, acted upon by the forces in and around her. Once determining that stance, resources become critical. Most of the women in the Kansas study described how they took responsibility for the decisions they made, and chose to make use of the incarceration both to bolster their internal strengths and resilience, and to amass other external resources they could use after their release. It was apparent that the women in the Arkansas study blamed themselves for their reincarceration but were not able to identify other options they may have chosen.

As the women noted, when they exited prison they had to adjust to new responsibilities and a loss of routine. They were almost immediately faced with the need for housing and a way to support themselves. It is in this interaction between the self and the environment that the transition is situated. How an ex-inmate makes daily choices, the types of relationships she engages in, the ways in which she is bounded, and, finally, the management of the multiple expectations she faces determines her capacity to begin a cycle of efficacy (Bandura, 1992) that is self-perpetuating and reinforces her desire to assert a noncriminal identity.

Better coping skills combined with the availability of some resources or support were both necessary to prevent reincarceration. As Denni so eloquently stated, "It has to be a combination. It's just like bakin' a cake. You can't leave out the flour. You need all the ingredients to make it come out right."

Policies

Although the process of transition from prison begins with the woman herself, it is located within an environment that either facilitates or inhibits the process. Current policies directly impede the ability of women to reintegrate in the same way that these policies led to their original imprisonment. For example, even those women who realized they were facing the possibility of relapse and sought drug treatment were often blocked in that attempt. Yet the current emphasis on punitive sanctions for illegal drug use by the "War on Drugs" has created a propensity for communities to incarcerate rather than treat. A lack of drug treatment programs in their communities, transportation problems, and parenting their children were obstacles that many women believed they could not overcome.

These studies indicate the need to examine policies and advocate for change in those policies that contradict the goals of reintegration. For example, the Arkansas General Assembly recently approved legislation that precludes women with criminal records from employment in a number of low-skill, entry level jobs (such as driving school buses or providing health care). Thirty-seven states have passed legislation, following the provisions of the Personal Responsibility and Work Opportunity Reconciliation Act of 1996, that disallows women convicted of a drug felony from eligibility for Temporary Assistance to Needy Families (TANF). Both of these policies clearly reduce women's avenues for support as they attempt to resume parenting after release from prison.

Affordable and safe housing is a crucial first step in reintegration. In Kansas, individuals with criminal records were not eligible for public housing. The lack of halfway houses for state offenders in both Arkansas and Kansas illustrates another aspect of the punitive approach in criminal justice programming.

On the positive side, the Family Unity Demonstration Project Act, enacted as part of the Violent Crime Control and Law Enforcement Act of 1994, supported the development of demonstration projects that assist eligible prisoners who are parents to live in structured, community-based centers with their young children. Although never federally funded, this act did stimulate states to allocate funds to residential alternatives to incarceration at which women can receive services focused on many of the issues that led them to prison (with a special emphasis on parenting concerns). As of 1997, fourteen states had created Family Unity projects (Joanne Archibald, Chicago Legal Advocate for Incarcerated Mothers, personal communication, April 24, 2001).

Practice

Conceptualizing reintegration and recidivism as processes and focusing on the modifiable elements rather than static variables can assist parole officers and other practitioners with specific targets for intervention. These studies identify the situations in which women released from prison will need support—not only for meeting concrete needs, but also for learning coping and relational skills. Practices that emphasize community reconnection can promote the reintegration of women to the community. Social workers can facilitate these connections to community members through mentoring programs, spiritual/religious ministries, and involvement in community-based aftercare and advocacy projects.

Clearly, social workers—concerned about the welfare of children separated by their mother's incarceration—can assist newly released women in developing strategies for resuming relationships with their children and eventually regaining custody. Programs must deal effectively with the interests of all parties concerned including the children, the mothers, and the caregivers.

Finally, social workers could work with correctional staff to promote the inculcation of a "free-world" attitude within prison facilities. This shift in attitude would challenge correctional institutions to examine their policies and practices that shape the day-to-day experience of incarcerated inmates and look for ways to widen the array of reparative services to address the multiple needs of incarcerated women during a time when there is potential for transformative change. As Sadie stated, "We [ex-inmates] are your neighbors, your co-workers, your friends, and your family members." Programs must be developed with an appreciation of women's relational capacity to learn from each other and from us about how they can manage the challenges of returning to the free world.

CONCLUSION

These studies are an initial attempt to describe and understand women's obstacles and supports for reentry after incarceration. It is a small representation of the thousands of women who enter and exit prison every year in this country. Imprisonment affects a disproportionate number of women of color and those marginalized by circumstances of oppression and economic deprivation, family background, personal abuse, and destructive individual choices. Women in prison represent not only individual mistakes but also the damage done to women through such shortsighted and detrimental policies as the War on Drugs and the overreliance on incarceration for social control. Recidivism and reintegration are indeed "two sides of the same coin."

Former Supreme Court Chief Justice Warren Burger stated in the 1970s that one way to tell the character of a society was in how it treated those who had transgressed against it. It is time to begin a constructive dialogue in our schools of social work, in our neighborhoods, and in our media that reflects a belief in solutions that challenge women's criminality and their disposability. These narratives of the lives of women as they strive to "make it" after release from incarceration offers a starting point for this dialogue and the consequent public policy changes concerning the experiences of women on their own terms.

NOTE

1. Now known as Temporary Assistance for Needy Families (TANF) under the auspices of the Personal Responsibility and Work Opportunity Reconciliation Act of 1996.

REFERENCES

Austin, James, Barbara Bloom, and Trish Donahue. 1992. *Female Offenders in the Community: An Analysis of Innovative Strategies and Programs*. Washington, DC: U.S. Department of Justice, National Institute of Corrections.

Bandura, Albert. 1992. Exercise of Personal Agency Through the Self-Efficacy Mechanism. In Robert Schwarzer (Ed.), *Self-Efficacy: Thought Control of Action* (pp. 3-38). Washington, DC: Hemisphere Publishing Corporation.

Beck, Allen J. 2000. *Prison and Jail Inmates at Midyear 1999*. Washington, DC: U.S. Department of Justice.

Beck, Allen J. and Bernard E. Shipley. 1989. *Recidivism of Prisoners Released in 1983*. Washington, DC: U.S. Department of Justice.

Bloom, Barbara. 1987. Families of Prisoners: A Valuable Resource. Paper presented at the annual meeting of the Academy of Criminal Justice Sciences, St. Louis, Missouri.

Bonczar, Thomas P. and Lauren E. Glaze. 1999. *Probation and Parole in the United States, 1998*. Washington, DC: U.S. Department of Justice.

Bonta, James, Bessie Pang, and Suzanne Wallace-Capretta. 1995. Predictors of Recidivism Among Incarcerated Female Offenders. *The Prison Journal* 75(3): 277-294.

Browne, Dorothy C. 1989. Incarcerated Mothers and Parenting. *Journal of Family Violence* 4(2): 211-221.

Carlson, Joseph R. 1998. Evaluating the Effectiveness of a Live-In Nursery Within a Women's Prison. *Journal of Offender Rehabilitation* 27(1/2): 73-85.

Carroll, Kathleen M. 1998. *A Cognitive-Behavioral Approach: Treating Cocaine Addiction*. Rockville, MD: National Institute of Drug Abuse.

Danner, Terry A., William R. Blount, Ira J. Silverman, and Manuel Vega. 1995. The Female Chronic Offender: Exploring Life Contingency and Offense History Dimensions for Incarcerated Female Offenders. *Women and Criminal Justice* 6(2): 45-66.

Ditton, Paula M. 1999. *Mental Health and Treatment of Inmates and Probationers*. Washington, DC: U.S. Department of Justice, Office of Justice Programs, Bureau of Justice Statistics.

Fessler, Susan R. 1991. Mothers in the Correctional System: Separation from Children and Reunification After Incarceration. Doctoral dissertation, State University of New York at Albany.

Flanagan, LaMont W. 1995. Meeting the Special Needs of Females in Custody: Maryland's Unique Approach. *Federal Probation 59*(2): 49-53.

Fletcher, Beverly R., Lynda D. Shaver, and Dreama G. Moon. 1993. *Women Prisoners: A Forgotten Population.* Westport, CT: Praeger.

Glaser, Barney G. and Anselm L. Strauss. 1967. *The Discovery of Grounded Theory.* Chicago: Aldine.

Greenfeld, Lawrence A. and Tracy L. Snell. 1999. *Women Offenders.* Special Report. Washington, DC: U.S. Department of Justice, Office of Justice Programs, Bureau of Justice Statistics.

Hairston, Creasie F. 1991. Mothers in Jail: Parent-Child Separation and Jail Visitation. *Affilia 6*(2): 9-27.

Harlow, Caroline W. 1999. *Prior Abuse Reported by Inmates and Probationers.* Washington, DC: U.S. Department of Justice, Office of Justice Programs, Bureau of Justice Statistics.

Harm, Nancy J. and Susan D. Phillips. 2001. You Can't Go Home Again: Women and Criminal Recidivism. *Journal of Offender Rehabilitation 32*(3): 3-21.

Harm, Nancy J. and Patricia J. Thompson. 1997. Evaluating the Effectiveness of Parent Education for Incarcerated Mothers. *Journal of Offender Rehabilitation 24*(3/4): 135-152.

Jurik, Nancy C. 1983. The Economics of Female Recidivism. *Criminology 21*(4): 603-622.

Koons, Barbara A., John D. Burrow, Merry Morash, and Tim Bynum. 1997. Expert and Offender Perceptions of Program Elements Linked to Successful Outcomes for Incarcerated Women. *Crime and Delinquency 43*(4): 512-532.

Lambert, Leah R. and Patrick G. Madden. 1976. The Adult Female Offender: The Road from Institution to Community Life. *Canadian Journal of Criminology and Corrections 18*(4): 319-331.

Lincoln, Yvonna S. and Egon G. Guba. 1985. *Naturalistic Inquiry.* Beverly Hills, CA: Sage Publications.

Maruschak, Laura M. 1999. *HIV in Prisons 1997.* Washington, DC: U. S. Department of Justice.

Moore, Alvin R. and Mary J. Clement. 1998. Effects of Parenting Training for Incarcerated Mothers. *Journal of Offender Rehabilitation 27*(1/2): 57-72.

O'Brien, Patricia. 2001. *Making It in the "Free World": Women in Transition from Prison.* Albany: State University of New York Press.

Pinderhughes, Elaine. 1994. Empowerment as an Intervention Goal. In Lorraine Gutiérrez and Paula Nurius (Eds.), *Education and Research for Empowerment Practice* (pp. 17-30). Seattle, WA: Center for Policy and Practice Research.

Robinson, Elaine B. 1971. Women on Parole: Reintegration of the Female Offender. Doctoral dissertation, Ohio State University.

Rose, Stephen M. and Bruce L. Black. 1985. *Advocacy and Empowerment: Mental Health Care in the Community.* Boston: Routledge and Kegan Paul.

Schulke, Beverly B. 1993. Women and Criminal Recidivism: A Study of Social Constraints. Doctoral dissertation, The George Washington University.

Showers, Jacy. 1993. Assessing and Remedying Parenting Knowledge Among Women Inmates. *Journal of Offender Rehabilitation* 20(1/2): 35-46.

Smith, Brenda V. and Cynthia Dailard. 1994. Female Prisoners and AIDS: On the Margins of Public Health and Social Justice. *AIDS and Public Policy Journal* 9(2): 78-85.

Snyder-Joy, Zoann K. and Teresa A. Carlo. 1998. Parenting Through Prison Walls: Incarcerated Mothers and Children's Visitation Programs. In Susan L. Miller (Eds.), *Crime Control and Women: Feminist Implications of Criminal Justice Policy* (pp. 130-150). Thousand Oaks, CA: Sage Publications.

Young, Diane S. 1996. Contributing Factors to Poor Health Among Incarcerated Women: A Conceptual Model. *Affilia* 11(4): 40-46.

Young, Diane S. and Carrie J. Smith. 2000. When Moms Are Incarcerated: The Needs of Children, Mothers, and Caregivers. *Families in Society* 81(2): 130-141.

Zamble, Edward and Vernon L. Quinsey. 1997. *The Criminal Recidivism Process.* New York: Cambridge University Press.

SECTION V:
PRAGMATIC KNOWLEDGE,
LEGAL REDRESSING,
AND WOMEN'S SOLIDARITY

Chapter 14

Charity, Ideology, and Exclusion: Continuities and Resistance in U.S. Welfare Reform

Yvonne Luna
Josefina Figueira-McDonough

The welfare state will probably always be a contested terrain to the extent that it decommodifies social needs and redistributes costs of risks in a market economy. Yet opinion polls show that across countries most people disagree that social security benefits are too expensive and should be reduced (Ferrera, 1997). As Marshall (1985) foresaw, once a social right is granted, citizens will strongly resist its withdrawal. At the same time, it is clear that not all elements of the welfare state are equally popular. Targeted (categorical) programs are considerably less popular (Taylor-Gooby, 1996). Furthermore, signs suggest generational polarization between those supporting pensions, health care, and aging benefits versus those supporting youth programs, family benefits, employment benefits, and education (Anderson, 1990). Evidence from welfare programs shows that the elderly group tends to be favored, largely because their voting participation is the highest of all age groups.

According to Heclo (1981, 1986), welfare crises should be expected not only because of the inherent tension between individualism and group interests but also because the means to pursue this balance is contingent on changes in the socioeconomic environment. Different types of crises have been identified over the previous five decades.

Calls for welfare reform are, therefore, intrinsic to the nature of welfare states. It is the responses to these crises that matter: to salvage welfare as it is, to transform it, or to do away with it. The United States stands alone in pursuing the third option, although the effects of the economic strains (deindustrialization) are similarly distributed across all Western welfare states (Esping-Andersen, 1999).

Signing the 1996 welfare bill, the Personal Responsibility and Work Opportunity Reconciliation Act (PRWORA), President Clinton did away with the sixty-year-old welfare state instituted by Franklin Roosevelt. Studies of national welfare systems consistently comment on the exceptionalism of the United States (e.g., Rimlinger, 1971; Quadagno, 1994; Klass, 1985). Not only was the United States lagging by about two or three decades in becoming a welfare state, it never adopted universal programs such as health and family benefits. With the 1996 reform, the American system clearly became an extreme outlier among other welfare states.

It is not, however, entirely accurate to equate this reform with the end of the welfare state. Its main target is public assistance and within it is Aid to Families with Dependent Children (AFDC), a program that in 1992 consumed less than 4 percent of welfare expenses (as compared to 43 percent of Old-Age and Survivors Insurance and Disability) (House Committee on Ways and Means, 1992) and in 1999 less than 2 percent of the federal budget (Executive Office of the President, 1999). The delegation of this program to the states meant that American mothers in poverty could not depend on it as a citizen right; response to their needs was no longer an entitlement. With this entitlement severed, single mothers in poverty lost the civil power rights given to them, however weakly implemented, by the Social Security Act of 1935.

Institutionalizing Temporary Assistance to Needy Families (TANF) to take the place of AFDC is consistent with the roots of public assistance and its history. The present reform was made possible by twenty years of discourse emphasizing the priority of the market over social policy. Both institutional path dependency and communicative neoconservative discourse made possible the "end welfare as we know it" mind-set, further disempowering single mothers in poverty.

Because the target population was excluded from hearings and consultation in the construction of the policy (Naples, 1997), particular attention will be paid to groups of mothers contesting the assumptions of the circumstances of family poverty and their insights about the supports needed to lift them out of poverty. Finally, the road taken by the United States as compared to other developed nations will be analyzed and, within the Anglo-Saxon liberal frame, contributions made by members of the target population toward a system consistent with American democratic values will be evaluated.

CHARITY AS INSTITUTIONAL PATH DEPENDENCY

The preference for private care has a long history in the United States. As a country that was a refuge for many Christian sects, it embraced charity as a way of dealing with the social problems in the colonies and later in the new republic.

Charity from early Christendom to the enlightenment served as a means to help the poor, disabled, and sick. The intent was not to do away with poverty, for that was part of God's natural order. Great inequities were permitted because compensation would occur in the afterlife: the poor would be guaranteed joy in the presence of God, while access of the rich to heaven would be much harder. Wagner (2000) claims that charity developed mostly to the benefit of the latter. Helping the poor and the sick was a means for the rich to obtain credits for the afterlife.

Protestant reforms and, in this country, the Puritan influence in particular left a strong imprint on charity by making it contingent on the moral reform of the poor. Poverty was not just part of the social order created by God but a secular expression of lack of virtue. Since poverty was the result of bad habits, the role of charitable organizations was to resocialize the poor in Christian virtues. Once the poor were defined as deviants, resocialization easily favored punishment rather than incentives as means of rehabilitation (Wagner, 2000; Rothman, 1971).

The poor were seen not only as sinners; they were also designated to be inferior. Even William Penn, leader of the most progressive of the Protestants sects—the Quakers—urged an attitude of submission on the poor. "God had not placed men on the level, but has arranged a descending order of subordination and dependency: due respect for those God ordained required Obedience to Superiors, Love to Equals . . . Help and Countenance to Inferiors" (Bremmer, 1960, pp. 8-10). Depicting the poor as the "other" meant defining them in terms of deviance and inferior status.

By the nineteenth century poverty, hunger, and unemployment were seen not as issues of economics and politics but of morality. Help become contingent on the willingness of the poor to submit to the moral codes of the philanthropies. This approach separated those deserving help and those undeserving of charity.

Benefactors, including the Charity Organization Society (COS), opposed government relief—especially outdoor relief—in part because it detracted from their power as a separate sphere addressing the moral ills of society; in part because it would decrease the contingency of help on deservedness and therefore lead to irresponsibility; and, finally, because they favored counseling advice and role modeling as a means of rehabilitation. Their motto "Not alms but a friend" expressed the belief that the chief need of the poor was not material assistance but moral support (Katz, 1986; Wagner, 2000).

It took the depression of the 1890s, the growing awareness of the costs of housing children in orphanages, and the emerging progressive movement for most states to develop mothers' pensions. However, confirming Esping-Andersen's (1990) thesis that welfare reforms are framed by prior institutions (what he and his followers call institutional pattern dependency), material benefits were not only very skimpy, they were also contingent on moral worthiness (proper work habits, temperance, character, hygiene, and acquiescence) (Abramovitz, 1988).

The emerging profession of social work, in its search for respectability, reformulated the friendly approach into therapy. Although in principle the new approach attempted to erase the differentiation in terms of social status between donor and recipient, it reinforced the focus on the conversion of clients to the ways of the middle class (Polsky, 1991; Richmond, 1969).

The Social Security Act of 1935 was an attempt to respond to the structural disaster of the depression, but it was designed as a two-tier system, in which public assistance as opposed to social insurance programs, inherited the pre–welfare state charity dimensions (Cates, 1983; Loseke, 1997). Guaranteed by the federal government as an entitlement, public assistance was implemented by the states, which determined levels and benefit criteria. Again, benefits were contingent on moral acquiescence; means testing facilitated the introduction of moral criteria separating deserving from undeserving poor families. Abramovitz (1988), Quadagno (1994), and Gordon (1994)—among others—have documented how gender- and race-dominant norms conditioned the access of poor mothers to benefits.

Over time, especially in the 1960s and 1970s, AFDC benefits were amplified by work incentives, medical care, food stamps, and housing allowances, resulting in improved support of mothers in poverty and their children. Public assistance nonetheless retained the stigma of deviance and inferior status, and cash benefits kept recipients below the poverty level. Furthermore, the policy of means tests and the continuous preoccupation with undeserving recipients allowed for violations of individual rights that would have provoked political and legal clamor had they been perpetrated by the police.

With the present punitive policies of TANF, some argue that the poorhouse of old has been replaced by homeless shelters, group homes, and correctional institutions. In this view, the forced labor of the workhouse is now remanded workfare and the opposition to outdoor relief is now parallel to the war against the poor (Piven and Cloward, 1997, pp. 3-14; Gans, 1992).

Examination of political communicative discourses in the past two decades helps to understand how a program such AFDC, which had been constrained since its inception by pattern dependency on institutional charity, could come almost full circle with TANF legislation.

IDEOLOGICAL REINFORCEMENT THROUGH COMMUNICATIVE DISCOURSE

Charitable institutions prior to the emergence of welfare were common in all Western nations, so historical roots cannot by themselves explain the selective infiltration of charitable principles into public assistance in the United States—much less the present legislation. The view of poverty as a personal deficit, the ideal of moral reform, the distinction between deserving and undeserving poor, the preference for enforced resocialization, and the superiority attributed to private and nonmaterial help could not have been maintained in the face of countering evidence if it had not been reinforced by convergent discourses that found resonance with the public (Schmidt, 2000).

Although Heclo (1986) argues that notions of social welfare have divided social sources sustaining both national values of individualism as well as communitarianism, he acknowledges that the first is dominant. Ellwood (1988) agrees on the dominance of national individualist ideals and how this ethos reinforces the interpretation of poverty as self-made. Individualism in the land of the free means that citizens can choose their destiny and therefore are responsible for their choices. Such choices include the access to work and belief in economic rewards as reinforcers of work. The harder you work, the better off you will be. This same principle of individualism expands to the nuclear family ethic: family privacy is protected as long as the adult members accept full responsibility for its members.

Finally, included in this ideology according to Ellwood (1988), a community ethic persists—one that attributes to the community the autonomy and responsibility for local decisions regarding their own. Ellwood does not propose that this ideology is seamless and fully accepted by all citizens, but that it is a strong part of national identity. To the extent that this is so, there will be a tendency to accept that poverty is self-made, likely to be the result of lack of effort and of irresponsible family decisions, and that whatever problems come from bad choices should be the concern of local charities and local government.

Surveys of public opinion consistently confirm this view of poverty as a personal or cultural deficiency, associated with negative views regarding public assistance as a means to help the poor (Free and Cantril, 1967; Huber and Form, 1973; Feagin, 1975; Nilson, 1981; Kluegel and Smith, 1986; Smith and Stone, 1989). Responses to the 2000 Census show that 85 percent of Americans believe that it is possible in America to be what you want to be (Powers, 2000).

Although many of the negative perceptions that are associated with receiving welfare have been proven to be empirically invalid (e.g., Blank, 1997; Berrick, 1995; Bane and Ellwood, 1994; Handler and Hasenfeld, 1997; Jencks, 1996; Edin, 2000) and a variety of structural explanations have proven much more credible (e.g., Block, 1986, 1996; Massey and Denton, 1993; Kasarda, 1989), these facts appear to have no influence in the ideological construction of recent welfare reform.

Ideologies, as Swidler (1986) argues, are not integrated or coherent. They more commonly embrace contradictory values. Individuals will selectively use the values that make sense or serve their interests better in different situations. Such contradiction is present in any liberal democracy that embraces both a market vision of free competition, most consistent with the diverse forms of individualism, and a commitment to social justice as translated into equal opportunity and participation for all citizens. Social philosophers such as Rawls (1971) have tried to develop a logical link between the two sets of principles, but the evidence in the United States shows instead that each set of principles is dominant at different periods of national history. So in the 1960s and 1970s, public assistance rights were asserted, equal opportunity was the rallying cry of the civil rights movement, and maximum feasible participation was the motto of the War on Poverty.

The election of Ronald Reagan signaled a change in the mood of the country and with it the start of what Gans (1992) called the "war on the poor" and what Piven and Cloward (1971) called "the mean society." The communicative discourse of Reagan emphasized proud national chauvinism to a country afraid of losing world dominance.[1] An optimistic future was promised by projecting a golden past of laissez-faire that never was and attaching to it virtues of American individualism (Reagan, 1983). The project had both economic and symbolic purposes. It favored the rich and created a scapegoat for the economic insecurities of the middle class: welfare. The political popularity of this maneuver was embraced not only by two Republican administrations, but also by a "third-way" democratic president (Green-Petersen, van Kersbergen, and Hemerijk, 2000).

Out of twenty years of ideological discursive reinforcement, "homo liberalismus"—barely distinguishable from "homo economicus"—gained ascendancy. This prototype is guided by a personal welfare calculus. The well-being of others is their own affair; self-reliance, the maximum virtue. Kindness toward others is a personal affair not to be imposed by the government. The state function is to protect freedoms. Those who can, play the market; the others receive charity (Esping-Andersen, 1999).

Welfare, not poverty, is the target of welfare reform. Legitimizing this target took a variety of routes from the Big Brother theory introduced by Murray (1984), which proposed that public assistance created poverty by eroding the capabilities of initiative, work, entrepreneurship, and family responsibility of recipients; to claims that poverty did not exist in the country (Gilder, 1981) to Mead's emphasis on poor citizens' obligations (1986). Neoliberal political imagery converged with neoconservative imagery (Fraser, 1989). Liberals and conservatives agreed that dependence was demeaning to poor families and that the solution was to put single mothers to work. That the discourse of one group centered on "obligations" and the other on "capacity" to participate in mainstream institutions made no difference. The common purpose was to develop a set of managerial practices designed to rehabilitate poor persons by forcing them to work (Polsky, 1991; Fraser and Gordon, 1994; Haveman, 1996; Fraser, 1989).

Before That I Rested

so i am a woman
in poverty
with three beautiful kids
and an investment
in hope
that it won't always
be this
hard
because it used to be harder
believe it or not
when he lived with us
or before that even
but i can't talk
about that
if i want
to rest tonight
and i want
to
rest
to
night
(And i rested tonight).

Angela Thompson

Disregarded were any plans for restructuring the low-skill labor market for better pay at the bottom, job training for decent work, and reinvesting in communities and schools. It was as if all policymakers had never heard about the pervasiveness of structural dislocation, or were unable to calculate what it takes to keep a family together (Edin and Lein, 1997). A reversal of logic seemed to occur so that symptoms become causes and coping practices were translated as a culture of poverty.

The list of punishing regulations that formed the heart of TANF—from time limits, to denial of benefits to teen mothers, to compulsory work for benefits, to denial of help to mothers having another child while receiving assistance, and the like—branded recipients the "deficient others" failing to conform to the norms of good citizenship. Disentitlement guaranteed that their rights could be infringed. Contrary to other citizens, who were expected to work in response to incentives, assistance recipients had to be compelled to work. The rationale was the same that created the workhouses of the nineteenth century.

The reinforcement of recipients as "other" has a lot to do with institutional path dependence. The "charity" components of public assistance sustained by neoconservative discourse emphasized the values of individualism as *the* national virtue. Schram (1995) stresses the symbolic value of denial, offering a simple nonstructural response to the insecurities raised by postindustrialism (see also Esping-Andersen, 1999). Issues of growing inequality and displacement are to be handled by rehabilitating the work and family habits of public assistance recipients. Since this "solution" has been embraced in spite of clear evidence of structural dysfunctions brought about by postindustrialization, Schram (1995) interprets this outcome as a clear example of hegemony at work—ideological control over evidence (Hoare, 1978).

Of central importance in the process of establishing a policy is the power of the group that is being targeted and the social worth attributed to them. Schneider and Ingram (1993) have developed a complex model of predicting policy outcomes, considering the characteristics of the target group. The greater the power and the more favorable the public construction of the target group, the more favorable the policy decision is expected to be. Such outcomes usually involve communication and consultation between policymakers and target groups about the latter's preferences.[2]

The reverse would happen for powerless target groups perceived negatively by the public. To the extent that public assistance recipients have been defined as "other," making them the target of controlling and punishing policies raised few problems. Furthermore, poverty, disentitlement, and the bureaucratic structure of public assistance (Piven and Cloward, 1971, 1997) coalesce to further disempower such groups. In sum, attributed deviance and powerlessness have facilitated the hegemonic process identified by Schram (1995) and relieved policymakers of the need to consult with public assistance recipients in the process of formulating TANF (Naples, 1997).

Even if subordinate groups are not given the opportunity, they can articulate their needs in ways intended to challenge, displace, or modify dominant responses. Because their knowledge is experiential, their views are essential for politics of interrogation and structural critique. Foucault (Kritzman, 1989), among others, argues that these views from the margins are extremely useful for a critical evaluation of political economy and the process of economic marginalization. In fact, what is at the bottom is arguably what needs to be understood: the process through which the political economy creates hierarchies of power and privilege.

Talk about poverty, working poor, and the public assistance system, examination of numbing statistics, and competing arguments can be validated only by understanding how these abstract notions play out in the lives of marginalized Americans (Schwarz and Volgy, 1992).

LISTENING TO VOICES FROM BELOW

To fill the void created by the absence of dialogue between TANF policymakers and the target population, the first author conducted a series of focus groups with single mothers living in poverty in Phoenix. The site was selected in part for convenience, but also because Arizona is one of the states that, under a waiver, started the implementation of a pre-TANF consistent with the reform. So the experiences of the mothers with restrictive regulations and work requirements started earlier (in 1995) than in some other states. In addition, the state has a history of both strong antiwelfare sentiment and a high level of poverty, offering an extreme context for the exploration of voices from below.

The evidence that the rich are getting richer and the poor poorer is irrefutable. Over the past twenty years in Arizona, the average income of middleclass families fell by 22 percent, the largest drop of any state in the nation. Conversely, the wealthiest fifth of Arizona's population holds nearly 50 percent of the state's income. In fact, Arizona ranks fourth in the nation in terms of income inequality (Perez-Pena, 1997).

Although Arizona's economy has been booming, the problems of poverty and homelessness keep growing. From 1978 to 1989, the number of people living in poverty increased by 61 percent as compared to a national increase of 16 percent (Hall, 1993/1994). According to the 1990 census, 15.7 percent of Arizona's population lived below the federal poverty level as compared to 13.1 percent nationally. Of those, 22 percent were children and

17.5 percent were families with children under eighteen. According to the Bureau of the Census data for 1996, the Arizona poverty rates continue to rise; the average poverty rate for 1994-1995 was 16 percent while in 1995-1996 it was 18.3 percent (Lamison-White, 1997).

Increasing poverty in a period of economic growth suggests that it may be due in part to the restrictive policies adopted by the state in 1995. The name Arizona chose for its welfare program was "Employment and Moving People Off Welfare and Encouraging Responsibility" (EMPOWER). The sense of uplift projected by this acronym hides the reality of poverty. During April 1995, 67,913 Arizona families received welfare benefits averaging $298 per month, compared to a national average of $381. In April 1997, Arizona's welfare caseload dropped to 52,624 with the average family receiving $287 per month (Sissons, 1997). By October of the same year, the caseload was further reduced to 49,000 (Kelley, 1998). EMPOWER might have "moved people off welfare," but it has not improved the poverty rates.

The purpose of the study reported here is to hear the voices of poor single mothers most likely to be impacted by the changes in public assistance in Arizona. We selected neighborhoods in Phoenix with at least 15 percent of the population receiving public assistance and organized focus groups in those areas. Seven focus groups were held with a total of forty-four participants. All were single mothers living in poverty, their ages ranging from nineteen to sixty, with diverse ethnic backgrounds

The women were asked to discuss a series of topics related to their lives as single mothers living in poverty. The first sets of questions were general and descriptive: about their assessment of welfare reform, the circumstances that led them to public assistance, and their feelings about work.

To a large extent, the purpose was to investigate whether there was support or resistance to the new policy. Their answers show quite a striking normative consistency between the policymakers and the target population. The women consider work superior to assistance; they share to some extent the notion that some recipients of welfare are undeserving; and they support the ideas behind TANF. Nonetheless, they are concerned about negative generalizations about recipients.

Participants chose to be identified by the initials of their first names rather than by pseudonyms. The following interchange was representative of how they viewed the changes:

P.: You know how I feel about those changes? I knew it was coming, and I don't feel—in a way, I am glad for JOBS, the welfare reform. Out of five years, you get two years of cash assistance. And if you use your two years—and if you use the two years, you cannot get it for another three years. You only get two years out of five years. I think—I don't feel . . . I don't have any kind of—I am not upset about it . . . because it's about time that we do start doing what we got to do. And I'm glad for the resources that they have, like JOBS; the clothing voucher once you get a job; they pay thirty dollars—up to thirty dollars a week for your bus transportation, for your gas, for whatever; they pay your child care. I'm thankful for the resources they have. And I'm glad. It is about time that we do something.

N.: Cause you get those lazy women that don't want to work.

P.: They keep having babies. Like there is a lot of women that do.

M. B.: People that are on it all the time, that don't want to do nothing and just constantly have babies to get bigger checks, I say it's good for them. But for people who really have had jobs and want to get themselves out of it? When you need the help, they treat you as you were sitting on welfare for about fifteen years.

As the discussion becomes centered on their personal experiences with poverty and public assistance, it becomes clear that when a family crisis arises (father abandonment, the birth of a baby, the loss of a job), providing for their children is the major factor in asking for assistance. Also, the women experience a real conflict between mothering and work. Life in poverty entails living in dangerous neighborhoods, lacking health and school services, isolation from relatives, and so forth. Mothering in such conditions is very time consuming.

The apparently compelling argument, first made in the introduction of the Family Support Act of 1988—that since most middle-class mothers work so should poor mothers—loses its credibility in these reports. It is not that mothering and paid work are incompatible, but that mothering in conditions of poverty is much more demanding.

Most women explained that they turned to welfare to provide for their children's basic needs. This is a sample of their responses:

A.: Just the children, to give them a roof over their heads, to give them the clothing they wear, the shoes they wear, the food they eat. Sometimes that's all you have is welfare. It helps to pay the rent; it helps to pay the bills. The food stamps help to provide food, and that's the only reason I did it. And I don't want to be on it forever. I want to be able to do it on my own.

B.: Because I couldn't find no jobs; they wouldn't hire. Like I'm young and I don't have all the education I need to get a good job—no . . . no education. That's it, no education.

S.: My husband left me and he wouldn't help me, so I had no other alternative but go to welfare.

W.: What happens if you go to bed thinking and you start worrying and all you do is think, so you have to decide, "What can I do? I feel like I'm going crazy. I got to do something." How would you feel if you're laying down in your room, you're staring at the ceiling, you're looking at the four walls, you can't sleep, you are thinking, "Tomorrow my kids are going to wake up, they are going to want breakfast, and what am I going to do then?"

Z.: My situation was me and my kids were hungry. I had my baby—my baby was three and a half months old when I went to welfare. So I had to turn to welfare because I couldn't afford to go to work with four young kids. I had no one to watch the kids. My kids were sick. I had to go to welfare.

Furthermore, the women described often living in situations that endangered the lives of their children and lacked access to services. We have sampled some of these remarks:

C.: Where I live it's hard because if one person gets sick, we all get it. I mean, we've had hepatitis on our floor and everybody's like—you know, I have a little baby. I mean, she got her shots, but you know can't be vaccinated for it. I mean, it's really scary. I mean, there's—little kids get . . . but I mean, it's really living in that kind of setting, you know your child could get sick like that.

C.: AHCCCS [Arizona's Medicaid program] is doing such a big cutback, they're not even providing transportation for their carriers. I have Health Choice and I've had it for five years now. And they used to provide us transportation back and forth for the doctor. They are not doing it anymore.

L.: I'm only making $5.15 an hour, that's maybe four hundred to five hundred dollars a month and it isn't enough to raise two children and yourself. It's just not easy, and living in the projects. You know people say, "Where do you live?" And it's like, you just stop. "Well, I don't really want to tell you where I live," 'cause you're living in a house where it looks like everybody else's house. It's a cement block, you know? I mean, you can't let your kids go outside and play. I can't.

N.: It's just not easy. It is hard on her (my daughter). You get twenty groups of this kind of kids and twenty gangs, like gang members. And you know it's not easy, because we are not from here and it's that you don't want your kids being in the projects. It's really easy for them to get into gang violence.

C.: My son got his hair burned, my daughter got shot in the head in the two months I lived there.

J.: My kids, you know, I have a son who's fourteen and he has been going to school since kindergarten and I'm still having trouble with him. A lack of the teachers, the principal not giving me directions or referring us where to go. 'Cause, it took like four to five years to get him tested for special ed, and he finally got tested. Just the education.

In spite of the aspirations of all these women to work, in part to free them-selves of the stigma and control of welfare, their experiences are over-whelmed by frustration with the rules of the system. Bureaucratic control, the stinginess of the cash benefits, the unreasonable punishments, and the lack of a safety net are interpreted by some of them as simply a strategy to get rid of recipients, not to support them or give them a chance to make it on their own. Many turned to charities to make ends meet.

T.: My feelings about being on welfare? Some times I feel depressed, some-times shamed. I do; I feel ashamed sometimes to say that I am on AFDC. I don't—I guess there's anger as well. Anger about the time that they take, 'cause I already know what's going to happen when I got to apply for welfare, for my food stamps, the way they make you wait, all the red tape that they give you when you try to ask them what's going on. We have all these other cases. I understand, but I complied.

E.: Because they told me my twenty-four months was up. I could not believe that was true, but—so they cut me off. So then they turned around—I was trying, I was just trying to get it to my two kids. They already know I was employed and everything. They told me income was okay. I was getting like $275 for my kids. They told me I could get a part-time job and I would still be okay. But I went and got a part-time job. A week later, my kids check was cut to $33.

R.: Oh yeah, I have been [on welfare] before and it sucks. So you get a job and you get away from the system. You know they try to control you. They give you $200 and try to control your life! And then when you get a job and report your income, they still want to control your life! And I don't have no time for it. You cannot control my life!

These mothers complain about the stinginess of the assistance program and the lack of understanding of how the regulations do not take into consid-eration other aspect of their lives, especially their responsibilities to their children:

P.: You get punished for not being able to be on time due to child care not getting through, having to miss work due to child care or due to your child being sick. Or sometimes getting verbal warnings and getting maybe suspended or something. It's just when you are a single parent and you have children and you're at work and they call you and say, well, your child is running a fever, you got to leave right then and there. Or if you can't come in because they are sick, or if you can't come in because you don't have child care for that day, or something didn't go through. That's one of the disadvantages of welfare.

E. What is this all for? What is this for? Who is the people? And who is serving who really? The welfare is to help us. If you got people who want to work, and you [are] holding them back telling them you got to come to this meeting, but you got an interview. And if you cancel, you're off AFDC. What kind of mess is that, man? You holding us there. You holding us here. You holding us there. It's a trap. Welfare is a trap. It's a trap. I don't care what nobody says. It's a trap.

The groups' participants uniformly felt that they would prefer work to being on assistance. The following excerpts summarize their reasons:

N.: [Work means] more income, self-esteem. Your kids look at you different. I mean, when I was working, my daughter—she didn't like the fact that I worked so much but the fact that I had more money.

P.: I also [would rather be] working. Right now my self-esteem is very low. Usually, I wear makeup and I fix my hair and I get dressed up. And right now I just feel down right now because of the situation that I'm in. But working, it would bring my self-esteem up. It would take a lot of stress off me because of the bills, getting my rent paid. I want to get a car. So that's one of my dreams is to have a car. And another thing is having a little freedom from my kids. Because I'm with my kids twenty-four hours a day, and sometimes I go nuts 'cause they fight, they want this, they want that, and there's times when I just need to be alone. So working would give me that time . . . it's a little bit of freedom.

L.: When I go to work, I know my check better be there. Ain't nobody can tell me that you didn't comply with this paper. Now give me my check; give me my money.

Speaking about their experiences with work, these women comment on the incongruity, even exploitation, between what is offered to them and the minimum they would need to get out of poverty.

N.: One disadvantage I found out with working is this last job that I had to quit because they didn't have reliable employers, or employment people. So, I would be working anywhere from twelve to fourteen hours a day. They give me a day off, and they come to my door, ask me to come to work. So I wasn't spending any time with my daughter, no time. I mean, it got to where on my days off, my daughter would sit on the front porch and when they would pull up she wouldn't even tell them I was home. She'd be like, "No, she is not coming to work." I worked one month straight without a day off, and it makes it hard when you don't get to spend any time with your kids. They get to where it's like you're not spending any time with me, this job isn't worth it. You know, I will live without money. I'll live without the things I want. You know, she told me to take Mother's Day off, is when it was, and I told them I was going to take Mother's Day off. He goes, don't bother to come back in. And I was like, I'm not coming back in then.

O. The time that I was working in the fields for two weeks, I would go walking and come back. I used to work eight to ten hours a day without lunch, cause I couldn't afford it. The money I got for two weeks would be seventy dollars. That's being taken advantage of.

S.: If you have an established job, say a minimum-paying job, like the kind of work we most likely to get is hotel jobs, cleaning, in the winter, and that even ends. When summer comes, the job ends because people go back north. When winter comes, the people come again, and we have a job again. Even when we are working, we just work three to four hours a day. I feel that, say we are working eight hours a day, and with wages $6 or $7 an hour that we would make, it probably would be okay. But if we go work at $4.25 an hour and only work for three or four hours a day, well then no.

E.: They want you to work at Taco Bell and they only want to give you $4. You know what I'm saying? You would be working and sweating for fifteen years. What kind of mess is that?

S.: I feel trapped. I have nowhere to go, no way to find help, cause the resources that they provide, they have so many stipulations. And I mean what good is a resource if they have all these stipulations that you can't meet? It's not your fault, you know.

C.: Yeah, being a single mother with few resources is very, very hard. I have a two-month-old, and before that I struggled a lot to get where I am, and without resources it's really, really hard. And I don't know how to find resources. The place I stay at now is the YWCA; they help with a lot of resources.

Asked further to propose what changes would be essential to help them out of poverty, the groups' participants were pretty unanimous: good public child care and skills training. Their arguments were straightforward. Without safe and predictable child care, mothers cannot get stable work. Given the minimum-wage salary that most available jobs pay, it is impossible to pay rent, transportation, food, and child care. Conversely, the women pointed out, if they did not receive training, there was no hope of raising their income and working at minimum wage trapped them in poverty. This argument was echoed by Jencks (1996), Edin and Lein (1997), and Wilson (1996). Fraser (1989) succinctly describes the situation: "The welfare system creates a double bind for women raising children (alone). It decrees simultaneously that these women must be and yet cannot be normative mothers" (p. 153).

Issues of child care touched a strong cord in all the women. They spoke at length about their concerns with the care of the children, the unpredictability of using friends and family, the limitations of the Department of Economic Security (DES) vouchers while on welfare, the high costs when they started their low-pay jobs, and the general lack of affordable care. The following statement is representative of what they see as a solution to these limitations.

O.: If we could get government assistance to help pay for a baby-sitter, then at least we could say we are working to better ourselves. But if we have to work, the baby-sitter is going to cost at least half of what we make.

Support for training as a condition to improve their lives was strong, as the following excerpts show.

N.: Schooling for me would be the top priority 'cause I don't have, you know, like I said, the college or . . . I don't have any of that experience that I wanted to get cause I spent most of my time, you know, raising children. I want to drive a truck, big rigs. So, I mean, with the state, the only thing with JOBS program, is they don't accept schooling. You know, if you're trying to better yourself and get off welfare, they should say, "Well, hey, take part-time and get a part-time job." But no, you got to have at least thirty-five hours a week. You know, thirty-five hours is a lot of time. Where are you going to fit schooling in?

C.: I don't understand them cutting the check and not giving you a regular job. Instead of putting you to work, training you . . . you could get off welfare and get a better life.

R.: [What would help to be more self-sufficient] Skills maybe. Job skills training.

Finally, the discontent of the women grew as they reflected on their experiences. They concluded that the policymakers could make those rules because they were ignorant about what was involved in raising children in poverty.

K.: I think that the people who voted for this welfare reform, or the person— I believe welfare reform was formed for the people in mind. But the people who got this welfare reform going need to live on welfare for a year and see what it is really like. I mean, come out of homes, come out of your cars, come out where you are at.

R.: See what it is like before you start telling us what we supposed to do and what we supposed to be able to do. Get down here with us and see what it's really like before you starting telling us what its supposed to be like. And stop giving the money away.[3]

CONVERGENCE OF PROPOSALS

Thus far we have pursued three interpretive lines for the emergence of TANF: institutional path dependency (charity), communicative political discourse emphasizing individualism, and distancing from policy targets. But interpreting a policy does not address its consistency with national principles. Why does an affluent welfare state committed both to capitalism and equal citizen participation cut the rights of the poor and engage in punitive control of noncriminals? The argument that the state is responding to imperatives of globalization has been discredited. No evidence suggests that the United States is any more integrated in the global economy than other advanced capitalist nations (Piven and Cloward, 1997; Block, 1996) At the beginning of the 1990s, the level of internationalization of trade, finance, and capital was not greater than at the beginning of the century (Bairoch, 1996). Fully 95 percent of investments by Americans are in domestic stocks and bonds, so the notion that we need to keep the wages of the unskilled below the poverty level for fear of competition from third-world countries does not have much credibility (Samuelson, 1995; Kuttner, 1984). Employment lost to trade competition is rather trivial in comparison with the volume of job loss due to structural change. The powerful impulse of deindustrialization is rapid technological change which affected unfavorably the industrial labor market of the unskilled. The net growth of jobs has been in the service sector. However, such growth followed a hierarchy of compensation with business services (e.g., accounting, engineers) at the top, followed by distributive services (e.g., communication experts) and professional social services (e.g., doctors, nurses, teachers). At the bottom of the hierarchy are personal/consumer services, for the most part receiving wages at or near the poverty level (Elfring, 1988; Esping-Andersen, 1993).

All developed countries have been affected by postindustrialism and its demand for flexible labor and technological know-how. But responses have been quite different. For example, the social-democratic nations of northern Europe restructured their welfare state without increasing inequality or poverty; however, they report a very high level of unemployment. In the United States inequality keeps growing. The rate of growth in inequality accelerated at the period of greatest economic expansion (1995-2000) when the unemployment rate was at its lowest since 1960. Differences in institutional path dependency, ideology, and distance between policymakers and target populations explain these discrepancies.

The United States represents the most extreme case of the type of welfare state that Esping-Andersen (1990) defines as liberal. Liberal welfare states rely primarily on the market for redistribution. The belief is that a near-faultless economic system is at work and that those who contribute most to society will be compensated accordingly (a modified version of social Darwinism)—that is, everyone according to his or her contribution. This system will work best the more the market is deregulated, thus promoting labor flexibility, entrepreneurship, and the creation of jobs. From this perspective, the American model has been successful: it decreased assistance and increased employment (Goodin et al., 1999).

While the evaluation of TANF across the states is still incomplete, other trends are clear and can be analyzed relative to the outcomes of other welfare reforms. We are experiencing in this nation the sharpest rates of income inequality since the turn of the twentieth century. Wealth has reached historic extremes, with 1 percent of families controlling close to half of the country's wealth. In no other first-world country have wages fallen so steadily, nor has poverty reached our national levels, nor are so many citizens held behind bars (Piven and Cloward, 1997).

In Europe, by contrast, income inequality and poverty have changed little despite high levels of unemployment. Although 30 percent of the population resides in an economic environment less favorable than in the United States, they have been able to maintain generous welfare with little poverty and low inequality (Nickell, 1997). Esping-Andersen (1999) even questions the comparative advantage of the liberal model regarding employment. While Europe counts about 15 million unemployed, the United States counts 15 million of its citizens who are in poverty while working full-time year-round (Newman, 1999). If we add to the unemployed rate the 2 million people imprisoned at any given time (ten times the average rate of Europe), the claimed superiority of the model can be further questioned (Davis, 1998). By this accounting, the most problematic outcome of TANF is to add poor mothers to the already staggering number of working poor.

Another consequence of the American model is that the disentitlement of public assistance has weakened the boundaries between government benefits and charity. Programs are contracted out to nonprofit and profit organizations, not only fragmenting access to needed resources for the poor but also blurring accountability. Declines in real value of wages as well as cuts in benefits have led to an increase of emergency programs (providing shelter and food) to a level unknown since the Great Depression (Wagner, 2000).

In sum, it is important to point out that the American model is not predetermined by economic conditions and to show that other developed countries, under similar pressures, have managed to maintain a capitalist system that not only survives but flourishes, while striving to protect the economic rights of their most vulnerable citizens.

However, we must acknowledge that our history and beliefs differ from those of other countries. You cannot remake history, and transforming national beliefs seems unrealistic. We might instead take seriously the proposals from the welfare mothers to improve the system and consider the consequences for all of us if we do not do so.

The women interviewed indicated that the major changes necessary for TANF to live up to its promises (lifting families from poverty and making them active participants in the life of the nation, as told by Clinton in 1996) were reliable, trustworthy, and cheap child care and training so that they could get jobs that paid a nonpoverty wage.

In fact, Esping-Andersen (1999) considers that those are the most important challenges facing welfare states in the postindustrial era, since they relate to the central structural changes in the labor market and in the family. For the unskilled, chances for upward mobility in a postindustrial society depends primarily on acquiring skills. According to Bjorn (1995), the probability of exiting from economic marginality jumps by 30 points with vocational training and 50 points with professional training, both extremely important in closing the skill gap.

Commodification of women's work, both in double-earner families and single-mother households, constitutes the most dramatic change of the second half of the twentieth century (Fox and Hesse-Biber, 1984). This has meant a great increase in national productive output, but also a need for child care. In the United States, the market responded quickly to this new demand, addressing the needs of middle-class mothers. The efficiency of this response depended in part on cheap female labor. For poor women, this usually represents three problems. First, as a job market, child care offers poverty wages. Second, while on public assistance, the child care subsidies are inadequate (Meyers and Heintze, 1999). Third, when off public assistance, the women have to pay for it out of very low wages.

Esping-Andersen's (1999) proposal to solve these problems would be to increase public child care. This would mean an expensive enterprise that needed to be supported through general revenue and, therefore, would imply some type of progressive taxation.

Jencks (1996), Blank (1997), and Bane and Ellwood (1994) argue that such an alternative would be very costly and there would be little or no political support to sustain it. They all favor the use of tax credits for families below a certain economic level as the most politically viable. Esping-Andersen (1999) disagrees. He views those credits as subsidizing employer's paying low wages and, in fact, reinforcing low-wage jobs. Unless they are coupled with programs of active skills and educational formation, these measures will maintain the status quo of the working poor.

His advice for gaining support for these programs (training and child care) sounds rather wishful. He recommends that political leaders break the deadlock of median voter support for anachronistic modes of welfare production. Heclo (1986), on the other hand, recommends a strategy of highlighting group self-interest. This has less to do with solidarity than with long-term interests. The programs might be "sold" to the general public in terms of cost benefits for the nonpoor. For example, it is irrational to spend millions on incarceration of nondangerous criminals rather than on rehabilitation and education for a more productive and competitive labor force (Tonry, 1995). It is unthinkable to punish mothers who are standing by their children in the most dire conditions instead of helping them to improve their own and their children's lives, and to avoid the high price of institutionalization and foster care with their extensive record of failure (Figueira-McDonough, 1994).

Considering Swidler's (1986) arguments that ideologies have diverse, not necessarily integrated, norms, we believe that a political discourse focused on the American belief in equal opportunity might resonate with the general public. Its appeal is likely to be especially powerful in relation to children.

The decline of value of real wages, the deterioration of poor communities and schools (given the inequities of public education financing), and the dangers of environments of despair (as reported by the mothers interviewed) have to be brought forward in a composite that frames the commulative[4] and systematic disadvantages that affect the entire life course of growing up poor (Figueira-McDonough, 1995). Lack of opportunities for children puts in question even passive-liberal claims of equal opportunity. If such disadvantages are carried from generation to generation, we are in fact creating a caste of outsiders (untouchables) and cannot claim to be a democracy.

NOTES

1. The welfare state itself is a sociopolitical construct that could not exist without the support of normative arguments and moral convictions. To succeed with reforms, the government actively constructs a legitimizing discourse with the intent of selective activation of values. In countries such as the United States, this process is taken up by political elites and is called communicative discourse. Coordinative discourse, an integrative process of policy construction, is prevalent in multiauthor systems with more diffuse governmental power and social representation such as in Germany, Austria, and the Netherlands (Schmidt, 2000).

2. Schneider and Ingram (1993) do not assume that the two dimensions (power and favorable public constructions) vary together; they give examples of groups with power and unfavorable public constructions. In such instances, communication between decision makers and the target group tends to persist but is more hidden from the public. This discussion is interested in instances of low power and unfavorable public construction of the target group and the resulting distance between them and policymakers.

3. It is of interest to mention that at this time in Arizona a sizable amount of money from the reduction of TANF rolls has been earmarked for a program on character formation, perpetuating the belief that the cause of poverty is individual character weakness.

4. At the end of 2000, even in a "flourishing" economy about 20 percent of American children lived in poverty. The percentages of minority children in poverty were much higher: 36 percent of African Americans and 34 percent of Hispanics. Thirty-five percent of these children lived in extreme poverty, in families with incomes 50 percent lower than the poverty line. Finally, 26 percent African-American children lived in poverty six or more years between 1982 and 1991 (Child Trends, 1999).

REFERENCES

Abramovitz, Mimi. 1988. *Regulating the Lives of Women: Social Welfare Policy from Colonial Times to the Present.* Boston: South End Press.

Anderson, Walter T. 1990. *Reality Isn't What It Used to Be.* San Francisco: Harper.

Bairoch, Paul. 1996. Globalization, Myths and Realities: One Century of External Trade and Foreign Investment. In Robert Boyer and Daniel Drache (Eds.), *State Against Markets* (pp. 173-193). London: Routledge.

Bane, Mary Jo and David T. Ellwood. 1994. *Welfare Realities: From Rhetoric to Reform.* Cambridge, MA: Harvard University Press.

Berrick, Jill D. 1995. *Faces of Poverty.* New York: Oxford University Press.

Bjorn, Niels H. 1995. Causes and Consequences of Persistent Unemployment. Doctoral dissertation, Copenhagen University, Department of Economics.

Blank, Rebecca M. 1997. *It Takes a Nation: A New Agenda for Fighting Poverty.* Princeton, NJ: Princeton University Press.

Block, Fred. 1986. Political Choices and the Multiple Logics of Capital. *Theory and Society* 15(1-2): 175-192.

Block, Fred. 1996. *The Vampire State and Other Myths and Fallacies about the U.S. Economy*. New York: The New Press.

Bremmer, Robert. 1960. *American Philanthropy*. Chicago: The University of Chicago Press.

Cates, Jerry R. 1983. *Insuring Inequality: Administrative Leadership in Social Security, 1935-1954*. Ann Arbor: The University of Michigan Press.

Child Trends. 1999. *Trends on the Well-Being of American Children*. Washington, DC: U.S. Department of Health and Human Services.

Davis, Angela. 1998. What Is the Prison Industrial Complex? What Does It Matter? *Colorlines* (Fall): 13-17.

Edin, Kathryn. 2000. What Do Low-income Single Mothers Say About Marriage? *Social Problems* 47(1): 112-33.

Edin, Kathryn and Laura Lein. 1997. *Making Ends Meet: How Single Mothers Survive Welfare and Low-Wage Work*. New York: Russell Sage Foundation.

Elfring, Tom. 1988. Service Employment in Advanced Economies. Doctoral dissertation, University of Groningen, Department of Economics.

Ellwood, David T. 1988. *Poor Support: Poverty in the American Family*. New York: Basic Books.

Esping-Andersen, Gøsta. 1990. *The Three Worlds of Welfare Capitalism*. Cambridge, England: Polity Press.

Esping-Andersen, Gøsta. 1993. *Changing Classes: Stratification and Mobility in Post-Industrial Societies*. London: Sage Publications.

Esping-Andersen, Gøsta. 1999. *Social Foundations of Postindustrial Economies*. New York: Oxford University Press.

Executive Office of the President. 1999. *Budget of the United States Government, Fiscal Year 1999*. Washington, DC: U.S. Government Printing Office.

Feagin, Joe R. 1975. *Subordinating the Poor: Welfare and American Beliefs*. Englewood Cliffs, NJ: Prentice Hall.

Ferrera, Maurizio. 1997. The Uncertain Future of the Italian Welfare State. *Western European Politics* 29(1): 231-249.

Figueira-McDonough, Josefina. 1994. Family Policies: The Failure of Solidarity and the Costs of Motherhood. *Journal of Applied Social Sciences* 18(1): 42-54.

Figueira-McDonough, Josefina. 1995. Expendable Children. *Journal of Progressive Human Rights* 6(2): 21-44.

Fox, Mary and Sharlene Hesse-Biber. 1984. *Women at Work*. Palo Alto, CA: Mayfield.

Fraser, Nancy. 1989. *Unruly Practices: Power, Discourse and Gender in Contemporary Social Theory*. Minneapolis: University of Minnesota Press.

Fraser, Nancy and Linda Gordon. 1994. A Genealogy of Dependency: Tracing a Key Word of the U.S. Welfare State. *Signs* 19(3): 309-336.

Free, Lloyd and Hadley Cantril. 1967. *The Political Belief of Americans: A Study of Public Opinion*. New Brunswick, NJ: Rutgers University Press.

Gans, Herbert. 1992. Fighting the Biases Embedded in Social Concepts of the Poor. *The Chronicle of Higher Education* 38(18): A57.

Gilder, George. 1981. *Wealth and Poverty.* New York: Basic Books.

Goodin, Robert E., Bruce Headey, Ruud Muffels, and Henk-Jan Dirven. 1999. *The Real Worlds of Welfare Capitalism.* Cambridge, England: Cambridge University Press.

Gordon, Linda. 1994. *Pitied but not Entitled: Single Mothers and the History of Welfare.* New York: Free Press.

Green-Petersen, Christopher, Kees van Kersbergen, and Anton Hemerijk. 2000. Neoliberalism: Third Way or What? Paper presented at the International Conference of Europeanists, Chicago, IL, March 30-April 1.

Hall, Duane (Report Coordinator). 1993/1994. *Poverty in Arizona: A Shared Responsibility: Addressing the Needs of Arizona Poor.* Phoenix, AZ: Arizona Community Action Association, Inc.

Handler, Joel and Yeheskel Hasenfeld. 1997. *We the Poor People: Work, Poverty and Welfare.* New Haven, CT: Yale University Press.

Haveman, Robert H. 1996. *Earnings Inequality: The Influence of Changing Opportunities and Choices.* Washington, DC: AEI Press.

Heclo, Hugh. 1981. Towards a New Welfare State? In Peter Flora and Arnold Heidenheimer (Ed.), *The Development of Welfare States in Europe and America* (pp. 383-406). New Brunswick, NJ: Transaction Books.

Heclo, Hugh. 1986. General Welfare and Two Political Traditions. *Political Science Quarterly 10*(2): 179-195.

Hoare, Quintin (Ed.). 1978. *Antonio Gramsci: Selections from His Political Writings.* Trans. by Quintin Hoare. New York: International Publishers.

House Committee on Ways and Means. 1992. Overview of Entitlement Programs. *1992 Green Book.* Washington, DC: U.S. House of Representatives, Committee on Ways and Means.

Huber, Joan and William H. Form. 1973. *Income and Ideology: An Analysis of the American Political Formula.* New York: The Free Press.

Jencks, Christopher. 1996. Can We Replace Welfare with Work? In Michael R. Dardy (Ed.), *Reducing Poverty in America: Views and Approaches* (pp. 69-81). Thousand Oaks, CA: Sage Publications.

Kasarda, John. 1989. Urban Industrial Transition and the Underclass. *Annals of the American Academy of Political Science 501*(January): 26-47.

Katz, Michael B. 1986. *In the Shadow of the Poorhouse: A Social History of Welfare in America.* New York: Basic Books.

Kelley, Matt. 1998. Officials Report State's Welfare Reforms Working. *Casa Grande Dispatch,* January 15, p. 2.

Klass, Gary M. 1985. Explaining America and the Welfare State. *British Journal of Political Science 15*(4): 472-490.

Kluegel, James R. and Eliot R. Smith. 1986. *Beliefs about Inequality: Americans' Views of What Is and What Ought to Be.* New York: Aldine de Gruyter.

Kritzman, Lawrence D. (Ed.). 1989. *Michael Foucault: Politics, Philosophy, Culture: Interviews and Other Writings, 1977-1984.* Trans. by Alan Sheridan et al. New York: Routledge.

Kuttner, Robert. 1984. *The Economic Illusion: False Choices Between Prosperity and Social Justice.* Boston: Houghton Mifflin Co.

Lamison-White, Leatha. 1997. *Poverty in the United States: 1996.* Current Population Reports, Series P60-198. Washington, DC: U.S. Bureau of the Census.

Loseke, Donileen R. 1997. The Whole Spirit of Modern Philanthropy: The Construction of the Idea of Charity. *Social Problems 44*(4): 425-444.

Marshall, Thomas H. 1985. *Class, Citizenship and Social Development.* New York: Doubleday.

Massey, Douglas S. and Nancy A. Denton. 1993. *The American Apartheid.* Cambridge, MA: Harvard University Press.

Mead, Lawrence. 1986. *Beyond Entitlement: The Social Obligations of Citizenship.* New York: The Free Press.

Meyers, Marcia and Theresa Heintze. 1999. The Performance of the Child Subsidy System. *Social Service Review 73*(1): 37-64.

Murray, Charles. 1984. *Losing Ground: American Social Policy, 1950-1980.* New York: Basic Books.

Naples, Nancy. 1997. The New "Consensus" on the Gendered "Social Contract": The 1987-1988 U.S. Congressional Hearings on Welfare Reform. *Journal of Women in Culture and Society 22*(4): 907-945.

Newman, Katherine. 1999. *No Shame in My Game: The Working Poor in the Inner City.* New York: Russell Sage Foundation.

Nickell, Stephen. 1997. Unemployment and Labor Rigidities: Europe versus North America. *Journal of Economic Perspectives 11*(3): 55-74.

Nilson, Linda Burzotta. 1981. Reconsidering Ideological Lines: Beliefs About Poverty in America. *Sociological Quarterly 22*(4): 531-548.

Perez-Pena, Richard. 1997. Study Shows That New York Has Greatest Income Gap. *The New York Times,* December 17, p. A14.

Piven, Frances F. and Richard Cloward. 1971. *Regulating the Poor: The Functions of Public Welfare.* New York: Pantheon.

Piven, Frances F. and Richard Cloward. 1997. *The Breaking of the American Social Compact.* New York: New Press.

Polsky, Andrew. 1991. *The Rise of the Therapeutic State.* Princeton, NJ: Princeton University Press.

Powers, Richard. 2000. American Dreaming: The Limitless Absurdity of Our Belief in an Infinitely Transformable Future. *New York Times Magazine,* May 8, pp. 66-67.

Quadagno, Jill. 1994. *The Color of Welfare: How Racism Undermined the War on Poverty.* New York: Oxford University Press.

Rawls, John. 1971. *A Theory of Justice.* Cambridge, MA: Bellnap Press of Harvard University Press.

Reagan, Ronald. 1983. *Ronald Reagan Talks to America.* Old Greenwich, CT: The Devin Adair Company.

Richmond, Mary. 1969. *Friendly Visiting Among the Poor.* Montclair, NJ: Patterson Smith.

Rimlinger, Gaston. 1971. *Welfare Policy and Industrialization in Europe, America and Russia.* New York: Wiley and Sons.

Rothman, David. 1971. *The Discovery of the Asylum.* Boston: Little Brown and Co.

Samuelson, Robert. 1995. Global Myth-Making. *Newsweek 125*(19): 55.

Schmidt, Vivien A. 2000. The Role of Values and Discourse in Welfare State Reform: The Politics of Successful Adjustment. Paper presented at the Council for European Studies Conference, Chicago, IL, March 30-April 2.

Schneider, Ann and Helen Ingram. 1993. The Social Construct of Target Populations: Implications for Politics and Policy. *American Political Science Review* *87*(2): 334-347.

Schram, Sanford F. 1995. *Words of Welfare: The Poverty of Social Science and the Social Science of Poverty.* Minneapolis: University of Minnesota Press.

Schwarz, John and Thomas J. Volgy. 1992. *The Forgotten Americans: Thirty Million Working Poor in the Land of Opportunity.* New York: Norton.

Sissons, Edin. 1997. Welfare Moms Defy Stereotypes: Average Applicant, White, 28 Years Old, 1 Young Child. *Arizona Republic,* November 2, p. A2.

Smith, Kevin B. and Lorene H. Stone. 1989. Rags, Riches and Bootstraps: Beliefs about the Causes of Wealth and Poverty. *Sociological Quarterly 30*(1): 93-107.

Swidler, Ann. 1986. Culture and Action. *American Sociological Review 51*(2): 273-286.

Taylor-Gooby, Peter. 1996. The United Kingdom: Radical Departures and Political Consensus. In Vic George and Peter Taylor-Gooby (Eds.), *European Welfare Policy: Squaring the Welfare Circle* (pp. 95-116). London: MacMillan.

Tonry, Michael. 1995. *Malign Neglect, Race, Crime and Punishment in America.* New York: Oxford University Press.

Wagner, David. 2000. *What's Love Got to Do with It? A Critical Look at American Charity.* New York: The New Press.

Wilson, William J. 1996. *When Work Disappears: The World of the New Urban Poor.* New York: Knopf.

Sole Asylum, Nancy Jean King
Exhibited at the Fourth Annual Exhibition of Art by Michigan Prisoners, February 9-25, 1999, University of Michigan, Rackham Galleries.

Chapter 15

Women, the Law, and the Justice System: Neglect, Violence, and Resistance

Deborah LaBelle

[T]he notions of institutions of oppression, rejection, exclusion, marginalization, are not adequate to describe, at the very center of the carceral city, the formation of the insidious leniencies, unavowable petty cruelties, small acts of cunning, calculated methods, techniques, "sciences" that permit the fabrication of the disciplinary individual. In this central and centralized humanity, the effect and instrument of complex power relations, bodies and forces subjected by multiple mechanisms of "incarceration," objects for discourse that are in themselves elements for the strategy, we must hear the distant roar of battle. (Foucault, 1979, p. 308)

It is oft quoted that, "[T]he degree of civilization in a society can be judged by entering its prisons" (Dostoevsky, 1956, p. 76). American prisons are particularly closed and isolated institutions. They are inaccessible to public viewing and are closed to the media, making it exceedingly difficult to gauge the state of civilization in our society as viewed through the lens of our treatment of lawbreakers. Until recently, conditions in American prisons were viewable mainly through the lens of judicial rulings on challenges to conditions and treatment of prisoners. This chapter reviews significant legal trends involving the incarceration of female prisoners in the United States and analyzes the impact gender has had on the treatment of women prisoners throughout the justice system.

With the United States incarcerating 455 out of every 100,000 citizens and holding the record for the highest rate of female prisoners, a look into the conditions of incarceration for female prisoners in the United States provides more than a microcosm for viewing American social ills. It offers a picture of an application of justice based on race, class, and gender. Socially constructed notions of gender and power conflate to create a system of punishment for women at the margins (which has an increasing ripple effect into our communities at large). The result is a prison system that defeats the very purpose of its creation.

The American prison system had, at its core, a notion that, "The prison must be a microcosm of a perfect society in which individuals are isolated in their moral existence, but come together in a strict hierarchical framework with no lateral relation, communication being possible only in a vertical direction" (Foucault, 1979, p. 238). In order to restore the "habits of sociability," prisons were charged with teaching the value of adherence to the rule of law as a mechanism for transformative behavior. Irrespective of a belief in the efficacy of this behavioral model, there can be little dispute that a system of criminal justice that is itself discriminatory in application would undermine any model of rehabilitation. The following addresses the manner in which gender and race are used to disparately punish and undermine rehabilitative opportunity for women in U.S. prisons.

The profile of incarcerated women in the United States, as detailed in Chapter 3, identifies race and class disparity which has received little official recognition and less effort at redress.[1] In the first international inquiry on the treatment of female prisoners in state and federal prisons in the United States, the report of the Special Rapporteur, appointed in accordance with the United Nations Commission on Human Rights Resolution 1997/44, highlighted the absence of official concern:

> The disparities experienced by the African American community in the United States and their large numbers within the criminal justice system does not appear to have resulted in any comprehensive policy discussion of racial discrimination in the United States either at the state or federal level. The Special Rapporteur did not receive any indication that any federal body was concerned with the issue of why African Americans are in prisons in such large numbers and what could be done to alleviate the situation. Although there is a national dialogue on race, no federal agency has been entrusted with the task of studying the intersections between race, poverty and criminalization in greater detail and providing recommendations for possible avenues of redress. (Coomaraswamy, 1999, p. 9)

Similarly, little official effort has been directed at the growing numbers of women in prison and the impact their incarceration, for largely non-assaultive crimes, has on successive generations. This chapter addresses how judicial neglect and gender bias combine to create conditions of incarceration that violate our basic precepts of fairness and humane treatment.

THE CYCLE OF NEGLECT BEGINS

Arrest and Conviction

The rate of female incarceration in the United States continues to rise at a faster pace than the male incarceration rate.[2] With nearly two-thirds of all women prisoners reporting children under the age of eighteen, and the majority of those being single mothers, the incarceration of women in the United States dramatically impacts the lives of minor children (U.S. Department of Justice, 2000). In 1999 alone over 125,000 minor children had mothers incarcerated in state or federal prisons. This figure does not include children of women in jails, on parole, or on probation. Despite the obvious impact arrest and incarceration of single mothers has on the legal status and placement of minor children, the justice system neither addresses this reality nor provides indigent parents access to counsel to protect parental rights or legal status of their children.

The U.S. Supreme Court first recognized the right to counsel for indigents charged with crime in 1932. *Powell v. Alabama*, 287 U.S. 45 (1932)[3] However, it took until 1956 for the Supreme Court to extend the rationale of the Powell case to all criminal defendants in state or federal trials, with the recognition that, "[t]here can be no equal justice where the kind of trial a man gets depends on the amount of money he has." *Griffin v. Illinois*, 351 U.S. 12 (1956) In 1963, the Court held in *Gideon v. Wainwright*, 372 U.S. 335, 344 (1963), that "in our adversary system of criminal justice, any person haled into court, who is too poor to hire a lawyer, cannot be assured a fair trial unless counsel is provided for him."

The vast majority of female prisoners are unable to afford the services of a private attorney at the time of their arrest and are represented by assigned criminal defense counsel. The disparity between assigned counsel and private counsel is reflected in the conviction rates of people charged with crimes who rely solely on often overworked and underskilled appointed counsel.[4] While poor defendants are victims of the inadequacy of the assigned-counsel system, women defendants and their children are additionally victimized by a justice system that does not recognize their needs, including access to attorneys for purposes of maintaining family integrity.

The typical conditions of confinement impede most women from effectuating decisions regarding the placement and alternative care of their children during their incarceration. Indeed, many alternative-care arrangements require some legal proceeding or transfer of custodial authority, a difficult process without the aid of counsel—even when not incarcerated. This, added to the fact that most prisoners are indigent at the time of the arrest and cannot afford to hire private counsel, subjects incarcerated mothers to increased risks of loss of custody of their children and the eventual termination of their parental rights due to their inability to exercise parental rights and responsibilities.

The right to establish and maintain family relationships has long been recognized as a fundamental right protected by the U.S. Constitution. *Griswold v. Connecticut,* 381 U.S. 479 (1965); *Loving v. Virginia,* 388 U.S. 1 (1967); *Zablocki v. Redhail,* 434 U.S. 374 (1978) "[F]reedom of personal choice in matters of marriage and family life is one of the liberties protected by the Due Process Clause of the Fourteenth Amendment." *Cleveland Board of Education v. LaFleur,* 414 U.S. 632, 639-640 (1974) Natural parents have a fundamental liberty interest "in the care, custody, and management of their child." *Santosky v. Kramer,* 455 U.S. 745, 753 (1982) The parents of minor children have a fundamental right to control the upbringing of their children, which includes deciding with whom the children can associate and how best to maintain familial relationships. *Meyer v. Nebraska,* 262 U.S. 390 (1923); *Pierce v. Society of Sisters,* 268 U.S. 510 (1925)

Prisoners do not lose their parental entitlements nor forfeit their status as a parent simply by virtue of a criminal conviction. *M.L.B. v. S.L.J.,* 519 U.S. 120 (1996); *Lewis v. Casey,* 518 U.S. 343 (1966)—Justice Souter concurring and dissenting; *Prince v. Massachusetts,* 321 U.S. 158, 166 (1944)—"It is cardinal with us that the custody, care and nurture of the child reside first in the parents, whose primary function and freedom include preparation for obligations the state can neither supply nor hinder"; *Troxel v. Granville,* 530 U.S. 57 (2000)[5]

However, a right to counsel to protect these rights is yet to be recognized. The general rule is that indigent people in the United States have a right to appointed counsel when a litigant may lose his or her physical liberty. It is the interest in personal freedom that triggers a right to appointed counsel. As the threat of loss of personal freedom diminishes, so does the right to appointed counsel. *In re: Gault,* 387 U.S. 1 (1967) Although the Supreme Court has recognized a limited right to appointed counsel where there is a threat to the loss of parental rights, this right has not yet been extended to address the needs of incarcerated parents. *Lassiter v. Dept. of Social Services of Durham County,* 452 U.S. 18 (1981); *Mathews v. Eldridge,* 424 U.S. 319 (1976) In light of the significant impact to families and communities resulting from the incarceration of mothers, it is time to recognize the fundamental rights at stake for incarcerated parents and apply the entitlement of counsel for indigents in this area to preserve the family bonds.

Preservation of Families

Protecting Parental Rights

In an aspect of the *Glover v. Johnson* case[6] the district court recognized that 90 percent of the female prisoners were unmarried—with the majority having dependent children and whose parental rights were threatened by incarceration. The court held that:

> [A]s a result of their confinement, incarcerated women are unable to exercise their parental rights and legal responsibilities in making decisions regarding the care and placement of their children over whom they have legal custody. The inability to structure alternative care arrangements during their incarceration subjects incarcerated mothers to increased risk of loss of legal custody of their children and subsequent termination of parental rights.[7] *Glover v. Johnson,* 850 F. Supp. 592, 594 (1994)

The appeals court rejected the lower court's finding that indigent female prisoners should be entitled to legal assistance to preserve their parental rights, stating:

> [T]he ordinary law-abiding Michigander has no constitutional right of access to the public purse for legal assistance on [such] claims, [and] it does not seem to us that such a constitutional right springs into existence by virtue of the needy person's having been convicted of a crime and sentenced to prison. *Glover v. Johnson,* 75 F. 3d 264, 269 (6th Cir. 1996)

Of course, the appeals court missed the fact that ordinary single mothers do not have to make the long-term legal custodial arrangements for their children required of incarcerated mothers, because they are not physically separated from their children by virtue of imprisonment. Nor, of course, are they prohibited from appearing in court, making direct phone calls, or obtaining legal assistance through county or federally funded programs.[8] Through ignoring the realities facing incarcerated parents and their children, the court missed the opportunity to provide a mechanism to ensure the physical and emotional well-being of children during their parents' incarceration, at significant cost to our communities.

Visitation

The ability of prisoners to visit with and maintain ties to their family and community is the single most important factor in determining their successful reintegration into society upon their release. Visitation between an incarcerated parent and child is also crucial to ameliorate the trauma to the child occasioned by the separation due to incarceration (Hairston, 1991, p. 87; Kupers, 1999). Yet visitation is made extremely difficult for female prisoners due to arbitrary restrictions by prison administrators, their indigent status, and the absence of a clear legal entitlement to visitation.[9]

The Supreme Court, in *Olim v. Wakinekona*, 461 U.S. 238, 248 (1983), ruled upon a prisoner's challenge to his transfer from Hawaii to the mainland and held that "[t]he inaccessibility of a prisoner to his family does not deprive an inmate of a liberty interest protected by the Due Process Clause in and of itself." This case has affected the Supreme Court's subsequent rulings on both prisoners' and their families' rights to visitation. Although the Supreme Court has not yet recognized a right to visitation per se, the underlying right to establish and maintain intimate associations is protected by the First Amendment. The Supreme Court has long recognized that "it must afford the formation and preservation of certain kinds of highly personal relationships a substantial measure of sanctuary from unjustified interference from the state." *Pierce v. Society Sisters*, 268 U.S. 510, 534-535 (1925) Although prisoners admittedly retain First Amendment rights not incompatible with incarceration, and the Supreme Court has expressed concern with the prohibition of all visits, a strong affirmation of prisoners' and their families' rights to preserve their relationships through visitation is long overdue. *Block v. Rutherford*, 468 U.S. 576 (1983); *Thornburgh v. Abbott*, 490 U.S. 401 (1989); *Kentucky Dept. of Corrections v. Thompson*, 490 U.S. 454 (1989)[10] The first step toward this affirmation was taken in 2001 by a federal district judge in Michigan who recognized visitation as the single most important factor in stabilizing a prisoner's mental health, aiding in rehabilitation, preserving the family unit, reintegrating prisoners into society upon release, and decreasing recidivism. Striking down restrictive visitation policies, as violative of the First, Eighth, and Fourteenth Amendments, the Court refused to deny the humanity of prisoners and their families, nor to ignore the impact that needlessly harsh prison policies have on our communities. *Bazzetta v. McGinnis*, 148 F. Supp. 2d 813 (E.D. Mich. 2001)

In addition to time, place, and manner restrictions, some prisons have strictly defined what constitutes a family for purposes of visitation privileges, placed limits on who accompanies a minor child to the prison, and have used visits as part of an internal punishment/reward system.[11] Unlike the children of male prisoners, who often continue to reside with their mothers and can accompany her on visits with their father, the children of female prisoners most likely reside with an extended family member or within the foster care system. The lack of resources for transportation and unavailability of child care for other children residing in the home, together with limits on visitation by minor children, combine to isolate female prisoners from their families and communities.

The failure of the Supreme Court to recognize an affirmative right to visit has resulted in prisons continuing to place extensive barriers to visitation on top of the nearly insurmountable barriers posed by economics, lack of transportation, and child care. Although the Supreme Court has recognized the existence of diversity in families and the importance of maintaining family ties, together with the right of parents to make decisions for children, they have not yet extended these concepts and rules of law to women in prison.

Justice Powell observed in a nonprison setting in the case of *Moore v. City of East Cleveland, Ohio,* 431 U.S. 494, 505-506 (1977) that:

> Ours is by no means a tradition limited to respect for the bonds uniting the members of the nuclear family. The tradition of uncles, aunts, cousins, and especially grandparents sharing a household along with parents and children has roots equally venerable and equally deserving of constitutional recognition. Over the years millions of our citizens have grown up in just such an environment, and most, surely, have profited from it. Even if conditions of modern society have brought about a decline in extended family households, they have not erased the accumulated wisdom of civilization, gained over the centuries and honored throughout our history, that supports a larger conception of the family.

Testifying in the *Bazzetta* case on the impact of visitation restrictions, a child of a female prisoner stated:

> I think that's when I really started rebelling. . . . [Until then] I was doing very well. [After I lost visitation with my mother] my grades dropped. . . . I started running away, I started being more disrespectful to my adoptive parents. *Bazzetta v. McGinnis,* 148 F. Supp. 2d 813 (E.D. Mich. 2001)

The United States can ill afford the implications of further fractioning families, communities, and next generations as a result of the destructive policies of prison administrations. These policies are not a necessary result of incarceration but rather demonstrate simple neglect rising to the level of deliberate indifference and sometimes intentional punitiveness. The increasing numbers of female prisoners have resulted in new prisons being built at distances further from family which, combined with poverty and prison restrictions, prevent visits between incarcerated mothers and their minor children and family. This lack of contact consequently endangers both their parental rights and the well-being of the children. It also necessitates a strong ruling on entitlement to visits by the courts.

Equal Protection: Equal Treatment or Gender Specific

The Fourteenth Amendment of the United States Constitution provides:

> All persons born or naturalized in the United States, and subject to the jurisdiction thereof, are citizens of the United States and of the State wherein they reside. No State shall make or enforce any law which shall abridge the privileges or immunities of citizens of the United States; nor shall any State deprive any person of life, liberty, or property, without due process of law; nor deny to any person within its jurisdiction the equal protection of the laws. (U.S.C.A. Constitutional Amendment, Article XIV, section 1, ratified 1868)

The Supreme Court has recognized that "prison walls do not form a barrier separating prison inmates from the protections of the Constitution." *Turner v. Safley,* 482 U.S. 78, 84 (1987) However, increasingly courts are refusing to apply the Equal Protection Clause appropriately to protect the constitutional rights of female prisoners.

Original concepts of criminal justice incorporated the courts' reliance on prisons to actualize rehabilitation during the period of confinement. At the current time, little connective theory exists between the judicial system and prisons. Courts send women to prison, often for a legislatively mandated period of years with little discretion for alternative sentencing, length of sentence, or specifications of conditions of confinement—such as the dire need for substance abuse treatment (despite the majority of offenses involving drugs), mental health treatment (despite the typical female prisoner having a history of sexual abuse resulting in trauma and depression), and education and job skills (despite female prisoners' average seventh-grade education level and lack of employable skills). Courts fail to address these issues and simply impose a length of sentence of incarceration, leaving all corrective action or rehabilitative treatment, if any is available, to the prison system. The prisons' subsequent failure to address differences in the social and offense characteristics of female prisoners, in favor of relegating all prisoners to one treatment model designed for the "violent male offender," perpetuates the discriminatory treatment afforded female prisoners through the neglect of the system.

While lip service is universal that prisoners should be returned to society in no worse condition than when they arrived at prison, the prison and judicial system has failed to implement this concept. They have abandoned in large part the rehabilitation model, which motivated the first equal protection cases filed for female prisoners. Nearly two decades after *Craig v. Boren* 429 U.S. 190 (1976) established the model for analysis of equal protection in a gender context and required a heightened scrutiny standard for "all gender-based classifications," courts have begun to carve out exceptions to this standard for female prisoners.

One of the first class actions on behalf of female prisoners that raised an equal protection claim was the case of *Glover v. Johnson,* 478 F. Supp. 1075 (E.D. Mich. 1979) This case was filed in 1977 and challenged the lack of equal programming for female prisoners, as compared to male prisoners who were being provided highly skilled vocational and apprenticeship training, as well as opportunities to participate in college degree programs and to work off grounds to obtain skilled training and enhance rehabilitation opportunities. Ruling in favor of the class of women, the Court firmly rejected the defendants' argument that the provision of equal educational and vocational programs to women was impracticable due to the economies of scale.[12] This was one of the first, but not the last, of the arguments which asserted that, because women were such a small segment of the criminal population, they could not be provided with the range of programs and education offered to the larger male population.[13]

Throughout the 1980s, education and training for female prisoners remained inferior to that provided to male prisoners. Second only to visitation in its rehabilitative value, educational programs were so limited that female prisoners had little opportunity to further skills or education during their incarceration. They would reenter society with a felony record as their major accomplishment. The Glover case challenged these circumstances for women in Michigan's prisons who were receiving little more than home economics classes, while male prisoners' programs included skilled apprenticeship training and college courses.

The district court rejected defendants' analysis, holding that prison officials were required to provide women prisoners with treatment and facilities "substantially equivalent" to those provided to male prisoners. The prison officials' decision to separate the sexes had resulted in the women being placed in a facility without access to the range of educational and vocational programs provided to men. The court, therefore, created an equal protection analysis that allowed for gender differences, while also creating a model of rehabilitation for all prisoners in which female prisoners were deemed to be entitled to their fair share of opportunity.[14]

The Supreme Court has made it increasingly clear that "all gender-based classifications today warrant heightened scrutiny," requiring states to demonstrate "an exceedingly persuasive justification for any classification based on gender." *United States v. Virginia,* 518 U.S. 515, 531-533 (1996) This level of scrutiny, however, has not been applied to analyze gender-based discrimination against female prisoners. In Nebraska, female prisoners successfully challenged their lack of equal programming. However, on appeal, the Eighth Circuit Court of Appeals reversed the ruling and sanctioned the existence of separate and unequal prison facilities for male and female prisoners. The court reasoned that female prisoners—whose programs were found to be inferior in both quantity and quality—were not similarly situated to male prisoners due to the different profile of female prisoners. *Klinger v. Department of Corrections,* 31 F. 3d 727 (8th Cir. 1994) The court noted that women generally served shorter sentences for less violent crimes than men and were a much smaller portion of the overall prison population. The court noted their status as single mothers, along with substance abuse histories, and used these gender differences to deny female prisoners equal educational and programming opportunities (rather than create a model of rehabilitative opportunity that took into consideration differences that could be addressed to enhance rehabilitative program choices). After finding male and female prisoners to be different, the court rejected the female prisoners' equal protection claim, stating, "Dissimilar treatment of dissimilarly situated persons does not violate equal protection." *Klinger v. Department of Corrections,* 31 F. 3d 727, 731 (8th Cir. 1994)

Such an approach eviscerates equal protection, which has never meant identical treatment but rather equal treatment, and has never assumed identity of circumstances. Rather than recognize differences that simply must be taken into account to provide equal opportunity for rehabilitation and successful reintegration into the community, the Klinger decision—and its progeny—rejected the possibility of a common goal that could be applied equally (taking into consideration differences in gender), in favor of asserting that the differences render any comparative analysis of equality impossible.

The Klinger court's analysis also turn the concept of equal protection on its head by relying, in part, upon the very dissimilarity prison officials created in order to justify discrimination in the provision of benefits. As noted by the dissent in one of Klinger's progeny:

> Two people commit the same crime. Each is similarly convicted by a [court]. In all respects . . . criminal history, family circumstances, edu-

cation, drug use, favorite baseball team—they are identical. All save one, that is: they are of different sexes. Solely because of that difference they are sent to different facilities at which the man enjoys superior programming options. . . . The Court relies on the different characteristics of the facilities to conclude that the otherwise identical men and women incarcerated therein are not similarly situated, and on that basis holds that there can be no judicial comparison of the differences in treatment. *Women Prisoners v. District of Columbia,* 93 F. 3d 910, 951 [Rogers, J., dissenting] (D.C. Cir. 1996)[15]

If the Klinger analysis is extended, women would not be entitled to equal treatment with males in most contexts, there being recognizable differences between the groups that may not relate to the discriminatory treatment at issue.[16]

The Klinger case and progeny combine paternalism toward women (resulting in women being classified to separate facilities to protect them from male inmates) and the differences between the genders (whether socially constructed or not, women constitute only 5 percent of the prison population and are generally incarcerated for nonviolent property or drug crimes) to justify denial of equal rehabilitative programs and education necessary for successful reintegration into the community based solely on their sex and the differences attributable to that sex.[17]

Although some correctional departments have continued to excuse inequality based on differences, others have attempted to simply ignore the differences between male and female prisoners and treat them all identically based upon a male prisoner model. An example of how this approach discriminates against women is the area of classification. Classification is a crucial dimension of any correctional system. It is the process by which prisoners are assessed and grouped with other prisoners for purposes of security and custody designation. It affects all aspects of prison life, including conditions of housing, access to programs, privileges, visitation, and parole dates. Classification systems, developed mostly in the early 1980s, were based on a model of male prisoners with the central assumption being that prisoners' crimes could predict their assaultive behavior in prison. Prison officials have asserted that they have validated this prediction model, which allows them to separate out the most violent prisoners for placement in higher security levels. Despite the lack of validation for female prisoners, and the relatively low risk of violence inside women's prisons, the male model of classification was adopted for women.

Although most women serving sentences for assaultive crimes were not the perpetrators of the violence but rather accessories to crimes committed by males, or involved in domestic abuse situations, the actual crime they are sentenced for does not reflect their underlying lack of involvement.[18] The crime offers little prediction of future violence, and the overlay of classification tools developed for men on female prisoners results in female prisoners being arbitrarily classified to high custody levels with attendant loss of privileges and increased solitary confinement. Indeed, in many systems, higher percentages of women are classified to maximum security than are men, despite the widely acknowledged fact that very little violence among prisoners occurs in women's prisons.[19]

In this manner, prison officials continue to fail to address concerns about unequal treatment adequately by applying identical treatment in some areas—such as security and custody—where it results in a disparate negative impact on female prisoners and using gender differences to justify unequal opportunity and treatment of women in the area of programming and education.

VIOLENCE INSIDE

Gender Used As a Basis for Punishment

Motherhood and sexuality are two characteristics that differentiate female prisoners from their male counterparts. Both aspects have been used to create conditions of incarceration for women that rise to the level of cruel and unusual punishment. Nowhere is this more evident than in prison officials' decision to assign men to guard female prisoners.

Sexual Abuse and Sexual Harassment

One of the issues that has arisen most prominently in litigation in the past ten years has involved sexual abuse of female prisoners by their male guards. Starting in the early to mid-1980s, many correctional facilities in the United States began to deviate from the practice of same-sex supervision of prisoners.

The consequences of placing a vulnerable group of women, whose typical history includes sexual abuse, under the complete authority of ill-trained male guards was entirely predictable. Without mechanisms for safe reporting, and with nonparticipating staff looking the other way, many of the women's prisons in the United States began to resemble the following description of Michigan's women's prisons as described by the U.S. Department of Justice:

Nearly every inmate we interviewed reported various sexually aggressive acts of guards. A number of women reported that officers routinely "corner" women in their cells or on their work details . . . and press their bodies against them, mocking sexual intercourse. Women described incidents where guards exposed their genitals while making sexually suggestive remarks and routinely abused women by "fondling and squeezing their breasts, buttocks and genital areas." The verbal reports ranged from verbal sexually and degrading harassment, to prurient viewing to groping to rape.[20]

In March of 1994, the international human rights group, Human Rights Watch, undertook a research project to conduct interviews in eleven state prisons regarding the issue of sexual misconduct by male officers in authority over female prisoners. The interviews took two and a half years and resulted in Human Rights Watch issuing a report entitled *All Too Familiar, Sexual Abuse of Women Prisoners in U.S. State Prisons* (Human Rights Watch, 1996).

Human Rights Watch found extensive sexual abuses being perpetrated against women prisoners in U.S. state prisons. The sexual abuse itself was compounded by the fact that a woman who was sexually abused could not escape her abuser and was, in many instances, dependent upon her abuser to fulfill basic needs; that the grievance and investigatory procedures, where they existed, were ineffectual; and that a female prisoner was more likely to suffer retaliation for reporting than to have any real resolution occur. One of the difficulties the report found was that:

> In the course of committing such gross misconduct, male officers have not only used actual or threatened physical force, but have also used their near-total authority to provide or deny goods and privileges to female prisoners to compel them to have sex or, in other cases, to reward them for having done so. . . . In addition to engaging in sex with prisoners, male officers have used mandatory pat frisks or room searches to grope women's breasts, buttocks and vaginal areas and to view them inappropriately while in a state of undress in the housing or bathroom areas. Male correctional officers and staff have also engaged in regular verbal degradation and harassment of female prisoners, thus contributing to a custodial environment in the state prisons for women which is often highly sexualized and excessively hostile. (Human Rights Watch, 1996, pp. 1-2)

The constraints on female prisoners in reporting the sexual misconduct of those who were guarding them, combined with clear messages that were sent to women that they would not be believed over staff people on this issue, resulted in class-action litigation being the only mechanism for addressing widespread sexual abuse. Individual cases often fell prey to a credibility challenge, while class-action litigation allowed women who were subjected to sexual misconduct both to ban together within the prison for necessary support to continue their litigation and to lend support for the credibility of each of the women's accounts in the courts.[21] The issues of credibility were not limited to whether the sexual asaults occurred, but included disputes on the alleged consensual nature of the act. Recognizing the power differentials, states have responded by passing criminal statutes that eliminate consent as a defense for prison staff charged with sexual contact with a prisoner (Smith, 2002).

Although in the past men did work in women's prisons as officers, in deference to concerns with privacy and potential for sexual misconduct they were generally restricted to noncontact positions and/or positions outside of the living areas. Typically, however, female officers were not assigned to male facilities, more out of a concern for the female guards' safety than any expressed concern with the privacy of male prisoners. With the passage of Title VII of the Civil Rights Act of 1964, and the subsequent introduction and litigation for the equal employment rights of women, female correctional officers made challenges to their restriction from working in the majority of prisons in the country, which were male.[22] Reacting, in some instances, to challenges from female employees to their exclusion from supervision opportunities in male prisons, *Griffin v. Michigan Department of Corrections,* 654 F. Supp. 690 (E.D. Mich. 1982), and in other circumstances to staffing needs for the increasing numbers of female prisoners, cross-gender supervision became the norm in the United States.[23]

Male staff were introduced into facilities that were structured with very little opportunity for privacy and allowed male staff, indeed required male staff, to view women nude in close proximity and watch women performing basic bodily hygiene functions on a routine day-to-day basis. Although only some institutions allowed male officers to perform the strip searches of women prisoners, the majority of institutions required male officers to perform routine clothed body searches of women, resulting in female prisoners being subjected on a day-to-day, hour-to-hour basis to male authority figures touching their breasts and genitalia.

The placement of male officers, often in overwhelming numbers, into women's institutions without adequate training and without any recognition for the potential for abuse resulted in widespread and pervasive sexual abuse of female prisoners in many states. Based on the resulting problems, some courts have been willing to restrict male officers' presence in the living areas and in contact positions in women's prisons.

Courts have utilized a number of different bases for allowing same-sex supervision and prohibiting male officers from contact positions with female prisoners. *Torres v. Wisconsin Department of Health and Social Services,* 859 F. 2d 1523 (7th Cir. 1988) cert. denied 482 U.S. 1017 (1989); *Robino v. Iranon,* 145 F. 3d 1109 (9th Cir. 1998); *Reid v. County of Casey,* 184 F. 3d 597 (6th Cir. 1999) One of the rationales that is important for the maintenance of basic human rights of all prisoners is the recognition of privacy rights. Courts have been more impressed with the privacy rights of female prisoners perhaps in light of the socially constructed concerns regarding bodily integrity, which are heightened for women. It is important in all litigation to impress courts and juries continually with the fact that the sentence for prisoners in the United States is the exclusion from free society for a period of years. The incarceration of a person for violating the country's laws is in and of itself sufficient punishment. The remaining rights of citizens, including privacy, should be maintained to the fullest extent allowable in light of the conditions of incarceration.

Class-Action Litigation

Class-action litigation in this area has begun to make significant inroads on this issue. At last count, over twenty prison systems were involved in litigation challenging some form of sexual misconduct against female prisoners (Amnesty International, 1999; U.S. General Accounting Office, 1999). In Georgia, a combination of class-action litigation and extensive media coverage resulted in a settlement that precluded male officers from working in housing units or subjecting women to cross-gender searches. In addition, the state was required to provide psychological counseling to women affected by the abuse and to institute new reporting and investigating procedures. *Cason v. Seckinger,* CV (No. 84-313-1-MAC) In Washington, a group of female prisoners brought suit when, after a period of prohibition of male officers performing body searches on female prisoners, the practice was resumed, resulting in trauma to women who were still suffering from a history of sexual abuse by males. *Jordan v. Gardner,* 986 F. 2d 1521 (9th Cir. 1993) (*en banc*)

In *Jordan v. Gardner,* the issue was whether female prisoners have a legitimate expectation of bodily privacy that was violated by the touching of male officers even when performing "proper" cross-gender body searches. *Jordan v. Gardner,* 986 F.2d 152[24] The court, in ordering an end to the practice, relied upon the Eighth Amendment prohibition of "any punishment which violates civilized standards and concepts of humanity and decency" to stop the cross-gender body searches. The ruling was based on evidence that (1) women experienced unwanted intimate touching by men which was different from men subjected to comparable touching by women; (2) there was a high probability of severe psychological injury to some inmates, including those with personal histories of rape or sexual abuse;[25] and (3) the searches were not justified in light of the pain they would cause.[26]

Privacy Violations and Sexual Abuse Consequences

The privacy violations and sexual abuse of women in custody is one of the most significant issues that must be addressed concerning conditions of incarceration. The victimization and, indeed, in many cases, the revictimization, of women in prison violates every notion underlying the purpose for incarceration. It eliminates the possibility of rehabilitation, undermines any model of citizenship by allowing jailors to commit criminal acts without consequence while continuing to punish the female lawbreaker, and permits a punishment that no civilized nation would allow. The long-term consequences of this type of abuse cannot be understated. A female prisoner's cycle of sexual abuse, trauma, self-medication through substance abuse, and incarceration is perpetuated not only upon herself but the cost of the depression, loss of self-worth, and trauma ripples through her family and community.

The identification and elimination of abuse together with the provision of adequate mental health treatment during and after incarceration should be as prominent a goal as addressing alternatives to incarceration and reentry programs, in order for the latter goals to succeed.[27]

RESISTANCE THROUGH LITIGATION

Class Actions

The majority of class-action litigation filed on behalf of prisoners has sought primarily injunctive relief. Public interest lawyers' and legal services' historical reliance on the law as a mechanism for change, as well as a history of extremely low damage awards for prisoners, resulted in the vast majority of cases involving treatment of prisoners being filed as class actions to alter conditions, not to obtain compensatory damages. Litigation also serves the crucial function of providing the public insight into what is happening in state and federal prisons. Prisoners have little access to the public or the media, and litigation requires reticent prison officials to provide documents, videos, and tours that allow the media, and ultimately the public, access to pleadings and information on conditions inside. Generally, the public, if made aware, has little stomach for abuses of human rights.

Expanded definitions of the class of litigants is also an important mechanism for education and change. Conditions and issues involving prisoners are rarely isolated from community impact. Who can visit affects families, friends, and activists. The lack of rehabilitation programs impacts communities and taxpayers. Where possible, the reality of the impact prisons, and the conditions under which prisoners are confined, have on communities should be reflected in the class of individuals challenging treatment and conditions.[28]

The class-action suit can have a value beyond its substantive issues. The active involvement of prisoners in the legal process, with the opportunity to organize and support one another's challenge to unconstitutional treatment, has an empowering effect. Without discounting the often severe retaliation at the hands of prison officials and employees, the overall benefit of stepping forward to change the public's perception and the conditions under which they are held is an important accomplishment that can result from a litigation.

The damage and harm caused to incarcerated people and their families by violations of statutes and the Constitution should also be compensated, in addition to seeking injunctive relief. An injunction against future harm does not compensate the prisoners who have already been assaulted or harmed by prison officials' inhumane treatment. Courts have recognized that "damages have been regarded as the ordinary remedy for an invasion of personal interests in liberty," and this applies to prisoners as well. *Bivens v. Six Unknown Agents,* 403 U.S. 388, 395 (1971)

Insisting on damages for prisoners resituates them as members of our community entitled to constitutional protection, places the conditions in our prisons before a public jury, and, through damages, encourages officials to correct their behavior. Although litigation has been important in preserving prisoners' rights, the growing movement critical of the prison buildup is crucial to redefining concepts of crime and punishment. It is especially important at a time when federal legislation has impacted the ability of prisoners to seek remedies for constitutional violations in federal court.

The recently enacted Prison Litigation Reform Act provided that:

> No civil action may be brought by a prisoner confined in a jail, prison, or other correctional facility, for mental or emotional injuries suffered while in custody without a prior showing of physical injury. (42 U.S.C. § 1997e[e])

This provision provided that although free people may seek compensation for violations of their constitutional rights which resulted in severe emotional and psychological injury, prisoners who suffer severe psychological damage from sexual harassment or assault that does not rise to the level of physical injury are without any recourse. Prisoners subjected to racial epithets, threats, and psychological torture—including lengthy solitary confinement and retaliation—could under this provision be precluded from any relief (Human Rights Watch, 1996, 1998; Amnesty International, 1998; Geer, 2000).

The Prison Litigation Reform Act also sets up other preconditions for suit by prisoners through prohibition of any action "with respect to prison conditions . . . until such administrative remedies as are available are exhausted." Independent of whether the administrative procedures available in a prison or jail did not provide the kind of relief sought in litigation, were futile, or required a lengthy process to exhaust remedies prior to seeking relief for violation of a constitutional right, this provision prohibits a prisoner from seeking any relief in the federal courts absent exhausting of these procedures (42 U.S.C. § 1997e[a]).

Significantly, the Prison Litigation Reform Act also amended the Civil Rights Act of 1964 to preclude prisoners who have demonstrated a violation of their constitutional rights from recovering costs and attorney fees. The Civil Rights Act provided that parties who prevail in civil rights actions are entitled to recover reasonable attorney fees. The purpose of the Civil Rights Act is clearly and forcefully expressed in the Senate Report on the Bill, which stated:

> The purpose and effect of [42 U.S.C. § 1988] are simple. . . . It is designed to allow courts to provide the familiar remedy of reasonable counsel fees to prevailing parties who sue to enforce the Civil Rights Act which Congress has passed since 1966. . . . All of these civil rights laws depend heavily upon private enforcement, and fee awards have proven an essential remedy if private citizens are to have a meaningful opportunity to vindicate the important congressional policies which these laws contain.
>
> In many cases arising under our civil rights laws, the citizen who must sue to enforce the law has little or no money with which to hire a lawyer. If private citizens are to be able to assert their civil rights, and if those who violated the nation's fundamental laws are not to proceed with impunity, then citizens must have the opportunity to recover what it costs for them to vindicate these rights in court. (U.S. Senate, 1976)

In particular with prisoners, the majority of whom are indigent and who have difficulty obtaining any attorney, this provision was crucial to the ability to raise constitutional challenges to inhumane treatment in our nation's prisons. As noted by the Supreme Court in the context of ensuring fair treatment of workers:

> Not to award counsel fees in cases such as this, is tantamount to repealing the [Civil Rights Act] itself by frustrating its basic purpose. . . . Without counsel fees the grant of federal jurisdiction is but an empty gesture. *Hall v. Cole,* 412 U. S. 1 (1973)

It was the hope of recouping costs and recovering fees that sustained legal service groups, not-for-profit groups, and legal organizations in their pursuit to obtain constitutional conditions in prisons and to allow private counsel to represent prisoners in attempts to vindicate the violation of their constitutional rights.[29]

Cases limiting the ability for counsel to recover costs, federal legislation prohibiting legal services groups from representing prisoners, and the Prison Litigation Reform Act's exclusion of prisoners from the provisions of the Civil Rights Act's allowance of reasonable attorney fees (in successful suits demonstrating constitutional violations) will make challenges to inhumane conditions in prisons increasingly difficult to bring to the courts.

Looking to International Norms

Although the federal laws of this country limit the rights of female prisoners,[30] international laws and standards provide a standard to adhere to:

> Women are entitled to the equal enjoyment and protection of . . . (b) the right not to be subjected to torture, or other cruel, inhuman, or degrading treatment or punishment. For purposes of this Declaration, the term "violence against women" means any act of gender-based violence that results in, or is likely to result in physical, sexual or psychological harm or suffering to women, including threats of such acts, coercion or arbitrary deprivation of liberty whether occurring in public or private life. (Declaration on the Elimination of Violence Against Women G.A. Res. 48/104 U.N. GAOR, 48th Sess. Annex., Supp. No. 49, at 217 Art. 3, 4, U.N. Doc A/48/49 [1993])[31]

A number of reports specifically highlighting human rights abuses in U.S. women's prisons have recently been issued that encourage the United States' adherence to international norms in the treatment of female prisoners. The

United Nations Standard Minimum Rules for Treatment of Prisoners adopted by the First United Nations Congress on the Prevention of Crime and Treatment of Prisoners in 1955, and the Basic Principles of the Treatment of Prisoners adopted in 1990, set out the following international standards for the treatment of prisoners based on consensus and practice:

- Women shall be as far away as possible, detained in separate institutions.
- Where facilities house both men and women, the whole of the premises allocated to women shall be entirely separate.
- No male member of the staff shall enter the part of the institution set aside for women unless accompanied by a female officer.
- Female prisoners shall be attended and supervised only by female *officers*.
- Sleeping accommodations should be in separate cells.
- There shall be special accommodation for all necessary prenatal and postnatal care and treatment.
- Where practicable, children shall be born in a hospital outside of the institution.
- If a child is born in prison, this fact shall not be mentioned on its birth certificate.
- Where nursing infants are allowed to remain in the institution with their mothers, provision shall be made for a nursery staffed by qualified persons.
- Chains or irons shall not be used as restraints.
- The treatment of prisoners should emphasize not their exclusion from the community but their continuing part in it. There should be, in connection with every institution, social workers charged with the duty of maintaining and improving relations of prisoners with families and with social agencies. Steps should be taken to safeguard the rights relating to civil interests, Social Security rights, and other social benefits of prisoners.
- Special attention shall be paid to the maintenance and improvement of relations between prisoner and family as are in the best interests of both.
- All prisoners shall be treated with respect due to their inherent dignity and value as human beings.
- All prisoners retain their fundamental rights under the Universal Declaration of Human Rights as well as all other rights as spelled out in other international conventions and declarations. (United Nations General Assembly, 1990)

There is increasingly a need to apply the international standards and insist on customary international norms in this area where inhumane treatment can be maintained under existing interpretation of federal constitutional law. These norms of customary international law should be recognized as part of our federal common law.[32] In *The Nereide,* 9 U.S. (9 Cranch) 388, 423 (1815), the U.S. Supreme Court asserted that it was "bound by the law of nations which is part of the law of the land." The opinion in the *Paquete Habana,* 175 U.S. 677, 700-701 (1900), further stated that "[i]nternational law is part of our law, and must be ascertained and administered by the courts of justice of appropriate jurisdiction as often as questions of right depending on it are duly presented for their determination."

The status of customary international law has also been acknowledged by federal courts deciding cases under the *Alien Tort Claims Act* (ATCA).[33] In *Filartiga v. Pena-Irala,* 630 F. 2d 876, 885 (2nd Cir. 1980), the court recognized that "the law of nations . . . has always been a part of federal common law."[34] Norms of customary international law are therefore "secured by the Constitution and laws" of the United States.

The U.S. Supreme Court has recognized that the law of nations "may be ascertained by consulting the works of jurists, writing professedly on public law; or by the general usage and practice of nations; or by judicial decisions recognizing and enforcing that law" *United States v. Smith,* 18 U.S. [5 Wheat] 153, 160-161 (1820), quoted in *Filartiga,* 630 F. 2d at 880 In *Filartiga,* a panel of the Second Circuit enunciated that norms of international law must enjoy the "general assent of civilized nations." 630 F. 2d at 881 Courts in the 9th Circuit have described norms of customary international law as "universal, definable, and obligatory."[35] Universality, however, has been described as requiring "general recognition among states that a specific practice is prohibited" rather than "unanimity among nations" (*Forti v. Suarez-Mason,* 694 F. Supp. 707, 709 [N.D. Cal. 1988] [Forti II]). Recognition of a norm as obligatory is not undermined by even widespread violation of the norm in practice (see, e.g., *Filartiga,* 630 F. 2d at 880).

These judicial descriptions of the means of ascertaining the norms of customary international law are in accord with Article 38 of the Statute of International Court of Justice (ICJ).[36] Along similar lines, the Restatement (Third) of Foreign Relations Law of the United States sets out specific criteria for determining whether a human rights norm is customary or "accepted as law" as required by Article 38:

[1] [V]irtually universal participation of states in the preparation and adoption of international agreements recognizing human rights principles generally, or particular rights;

[2] the adoption of human rights principles by states and in regional or-
     ganizations in Europe, Latin America, and Africa;
[3] general support by states for United Nations resolutions declaring,
     recognizing, invoking, and applying international human rights
     principles as international law;
[4] action by States to conform their national law or practice to stan-
     dards or principles declared by international bodies . . . [and]
[5] invocation of human rights principles in national policy, in diplo-
     matic practice, in international organization activities and actions,
     and other diplomatic communications.[37]

Treaties are key indicators of whether human rights principles have become
customary international law.[38] In addition to indicating the present state
of customary international law, widespread participation in treaties or other
international instruments may lead to the further development of international norms.[39]

Corrections policymakers in the United States have consistently failed to
resolve conflicts on how to humanely incarcerate mothers, wives, sisters,
daughters, aunts, and grandmothers. It is time for community members (including the international community), lawyers, social workers, doctors,
psychologists, activists, and service organizations to assert their concerns
with the treatment of these members of our communities and to insist upon
humane treatment inside prisons and mechanisms for successful reentry to
the outside world upon release.

NOTES

1. The judicial system has failed to address the racial disparities in the criminal
justice system despite significant statistical studies and strong evidence of bias per-
meating arrests, prosecutions, convictions, sentencing, treatment, and parole. See,
for example, the Supreme Court's rejection of the Constitutional challenge to the
death penalty despite evidence of discriminatory application. *McCleskey v. Kemp,*
481 U.S. 279, 327 (1987); see also Cole (1999).

2. Female prisoners accounted for 3.8 percent of the prison population in 1975
and 6.3 percent in 1995. Between 1985 and 1995, the female population tripled
while the number of incarcerated men doubled.

3. Known as the "Scotsborough Case," nine young African-American men
were charged with raping two white women and tried and sentenced to death within
a matter of days. The U.S. Supreme Court reversed their convictions on the grounds
that the defendants had been denied assistance of counsel. Although the judge had
appointed counsel, the manner in which the counsel had been appointed and the limited time for preparation rendered the representation inadequate.

4. More than half of women in prison were unemployed at the time of their arrest and account for mostly nonviolent property crimes. Nearly half of the rest of female prisoners are behind bars for drug offenses. However, approximately one-third are guilty of possession or drug use. The remainder are typically couriers who receive relatively small fees and, unlike many male drug offenders, lack sufficient involvement in the drug trade to have information to barter for reduced sentences.

5. Eight of nine justices agreed that the interests of parents in the care, custody, and control of their children is a fundamental constitutional right as the child is not "a mere creature of the state." *Troxel v. Granville,* 530 U.S. 57, 65 2061 (2000)

6. 478 F. Supp. 1095 (1979); 850 F. Supp. 592 (1994), *rev.* 75 F. 3d 264 (6th Cir. 1996) A class action on behalf of female prisoners in Michigan challenging equal treatment in programming and access to the courts.

7. The children of poor women were at heightened risk where phone calls from prisoners are limited to expensive collect calls and visiting prisoners often requires traveling great distances to areas where public transportation is unavailable.

8. Indigent civilians have the option of obtaining assistance from federal-, state-, and county-funded legal services, an option that is not available to prisoners. *Glover,* 850 F. Supp. at 601. See also H.R. 3019, § 504(a)(15) (April 26, 1996). The Supreme Court in *Lewis v. Casey,* 518 U.S. 343 (1966) undermined the ability of prisoners to obtain legal assistance to challenge inhumane treatment by defining adequate access to the courts for prisoners to consist of an ability to file a complaint document in the limited area of criminal appeals and conditions of confinement.

9. Enlightened prison systems providing for family overnight visitation and/or residential programs for mothers and infant children are in the distinct minority. Separation of the mother and child immediately after birth and the lack of adequate visitation programs to maintain the parent/child bond are more the norm.

10. Lower court decisions have found that denial of all visits would constitute cruel and unusual punishment in violation of the Constitution's Eighth Amendment protections. *Laaman v. Helgemoe,* 437 F. Supp. 269 (D.N.H. 1977); *Valentine v. Englehardt,* 474 F. Supp. 294 (D.N.J. 1979) Some early cases also recognized a First Amendment right to visits, although the trend has been decidedly against interfering with visitation restrictions. See *Valentine v. Englehardt,* 474 F. Supp. 294 (D. N.J. 1979); *Navin v. Iowa,* 843 F. Supp. 500, 502 (N.D. Iowa 1994) (both inmate-parent and child have First Amendment associational/family rights); *Stewart v. Gates,* 450 F. Supp. 583, 586 (C.D. Cal. 1978); *Boudin v. Thomas,* 533 F. Supp. 786 (S.D.N.Y. 1982); *Bazzetta v. McGinnis,* 902 F. Supp. 765 (E.D. Mich. 1998); 124 F. 3d 777 (6th Cir. 1998); 148 F. Supp. 2d 813 (E.D. Mich. 2001) *(on remand).*

11. The definition of family most often reflects a Eurocentric model as opposed to the extended family which is more prevalent in the affected population.

12. The subtext of many defendants' arguments in 1979 were outgrowths of outmoded gender perceptions and biases. Relying upon women as moral arbitrators, defendants viewed female criminals as failures at femininity. The offering of what amounted to homemaker training was a direct response to the defendants' implicit belief that providing these "feminine skills" were all the rehabilitation women needed. Further, the low women's population appeared to heighten in the defendants' mind the aberrant nature of that population.

13. That female prisoners remained the "forgotten offender" for so long was not only attributable to their smaller numbers, but also prison officials' lack of concern about violent riots in women's prisons—which on occasion served as an impetus for providing out-of-cell programs and benefits to male prisoners.

14. Explicitly, this did not require that female prisoners have identical programs as male prisoners had. Rather it required prison officials to take into consideration women's needs, abilities, and the realities of social constraints while providing female prisoners the opportunity to leave prison with rehabilitative skills on par with male prisoners. The court, recognizing that female prisoners had an added burden in returning to society as single mothers and taking judicial notice of the wage disparity based on gender in society at large, declined to require additional training for female prisoners in order to compensate for the outside discrimination. Thus, female prisoners were entitled to not the same opportunity as male prisoners but parity as defined within the context of the existing discrimination in the outside free world. Following the Glover case, women prisoners throughout the country successfully challenged their lack of equal programming resulting in increased rehabilitation opportunities for female prisoners in the 1980s. The 1980s' positive trend dissipated in the 1990s due to a loss of support for rehabilitative programming for prisoners overall and a change in the equal protection law as applied to female prisoners. *Batton v. North Carolina*, 501 F. Supp. 1173 (E.D.N.C. 1980); *Vukhari v. Hutto*, 487 F. Supp. 1162 (E.D. Va. 1980); *Cantarino v. Wilson*, 546 F. Supp. 174 (W.D. Ky. 1982)

15. The original Glover analysis is the proper analysis for equal protection:

> [A] female in the State of Michigan will be sent to Huron Valley by reason of her gender alone and will necessarily have access only to those programs currently available at that location. A male prisoner, on the other hand, can be classified and later transferred to a wide variety of prison facilities in the State or have access to more program opportunities than his female counterpart. I conclude, therefore, that because of these limitations, women as a group are treated differently than men as a group, and that these differences in treatment are directly related to their gender. *Glover,* 478 F. Supp. 1075, 1078 (E.D. Mich. 1979)

16. See *Keevan v. Smith,* 100 F. 3d 644 (8th Cir. 1996) following Klinger.

17. As addressed later, the development of a male model of incarceration has resulted in either applying this male model to female prisoners without regard to the differences (creating often cruel and unusual punishment and disparate treatment) or, in cases where the male model provides some benefits, denying the benefits to female prisoners (justified upon the differences of women).

18. For example, a woman who drives the getaway car for a man who committed a robbery and associated murder will receive the same felony murder sentence as the man who actually committed the violent acts.

19. Violence against women by male guards is addressed in a separate section.

20. March 27, 1995, findings letter from the United States Department of Justice to Michigan Governor John Engler reporting on their investigation into Michigan women's prisons, p. 2.

21. See, for example, *Fisher v. Goord,* 981 F. Supp 140 (W.D.N.Y. 1997) where the court found that if the acts occurred, they were consensual; see also Human Rights Watch follow-up report to *All Too Familiar,* entitled *Nowhere to Hide: Retaliation Against Women in Michigan State Prisons* (1998), which detailed the retaliation female prisoners suffered for speaking out on the sexual abuse by male guards. The retaliation included having their access to visits with their children cut off, physical punishment, placement in solitary confinement, increased sexualized body searches, and denials of basic needs.

22. Pursuant to Title VII, an employer may not discriminate on the basis of sex absent the sex being determined to be bona fide occupational qualification (BFOQ), necessary to perform the specific job. In general, courts have been unwilling to recognize sex as a BFOQ with regard to female correctional officers in male facilities. *Griffin v. Michigan Dept. of Corrections,* 654 F. Supp. 690 (E.D. Mich. 1982); *Gunther v. Iowa State Men's Reformatory,* 462 F. Supp. 952 (N.D. Iowa, 1979) aff'd 612 F. 2d 1079 (6th Cir. 1980), cert. denied 446 U.S. 966 (1980); *Dothard v. Rawlinson,* 433 U.S. 321 (1977); *Forts v. Ward,* 621 F. 2d 1210 (2nd Cir. 1980)

23. The practice, however, is contrary to Customary International Law. The recognized international standards of fair treatment of prisoners are set forth in the United Nations Minimum Rules for the Treatment of Prisoners, which prohibit guards from serving in positions where they are in constant physical proximity to prisoners of the opposite sex. Standard Minimum Rules for the Treatment of Prisoners, adopted by the First United Nations Congress on the Prevention of Crime and the Treatment of Offenders, reprinted in United Nations (1993) E. 93. XIV. 1, pp. 243-262.

24. At the present, the majority of women's prisons have retreated from the practice of allowing male officers to perform body searches of female prisoners.

25. The personal histories relied upon by the court included the following commonalities: A childhood history of sexual or physical abuse by an adult male in authority; severe physical and sexual abuse by adult partners followed by related criminal acts that resulted in incarceration, such as violent resistance to the abuse, self-medication through drug use, and cooperating in illegal acts with a partner to avoid additional, threatened abuse to self or children.

26. The Jordan appeals court did not reach the issue of whether the searches were also unconstitutional based upon a violation of the female prisoners' rights to bodily integrity and privacy upon which the district court based its decision in addition to the Eighth Amendment. See also *Women Prisoners of the District of Columbia v. District of Columbia,* 877 F. Supp. 634 (D.D.C. 1994).

27. In a recent case involving twenty-nine women prisoners, a $4 million damage award was obtained in the settlement of claims of sexual misconduct ranging from verbal harassment to rape and retaliation for reporting of the same. *Nunn v. MDOC,* 96-CV-71416-DT (E.D. Mich.)

28. *Bazzetta v. MDOC,* 902 F. Supp. 765 (1998); 124 F. 3d 777 (6th Cir. 1998); 148 F. Supp. 2d 813 (E.D. Mich. 2001) was comprised of a class of prisoners and members of the community whose rights were affected by prison regulations.

29. Without counsel, it is extremely difficult for any layperson, much less an inmate, to overcome the hurdles in establishing a constitutional violation. The ab-

sence of an attorney is likely to be a fatal error even to meritorious claims, especially when prisoners are unable to actually appear in court and extensive barriers exist to their ability to present their claims even beyond indigence (see Turner, 1979).

30. The Violence Against Women Act (42 U.S.C. sec. 13981 et seq), which provided a right of action for female prisoners, has recently been declared violative of our concepts of federalism. *United States v. Morrison,* 529 U.S. 598 (2000)

31. Female prisoners shall be attended and supervised only by female officers. *United Nations Standard Minimum Rules for Treatment of Prisoners,* Rule 53(B)(2) adopted August 30, 1955, U.N. Doc/A/CONF/6/1annex I A (1956), amended May 13, 1977, E.S.C. Res. 2076, 62 U.N. ESCOR Supp. No. 1 at 35 U.N. Doc. E/5988 (1977). [Ch 1996 revision to include in prison, public, or private].

32. At least one court has also stated that U.S. treaty obligations are part of the rights protected by U.S. law and therefore by section 1983. See *Wyatt v. Ruck Construction, Inc.,* 117 Ariz. 186, 191 (Ariz. Ct. App. 1977), noting that "the only rights protected by 42 U.S.C. § 1983 are rights owing their existence to the federal government, its laws, and *its treaties*" (emphasis added).

33. 28 U.S.C. § 1350 (1988), "The district courts shall have original jurisdiction of any civil action by an alien for a tort only, committed in violation of the law of nations or a treaty of the United States."

34. The Court in *Filartiga* also rejected the argument that international law constitutes federal common law "only to the extent that Congress has acted to define it." *Id.* at 886. *See also In re Estate of Ferdinand E. Marcos Human Rights Litigation,* 978 F. 2d 493, 502 (9th Cir. 1993) ("Estate I"); *Hawa Abdi Jama v. United States Immigration and Naturalization Service,* 22 F. Supp. 353, 362 (S.D.N.J. 1998); *Xuncax v. Gramajo,* 886 F. Supp. 162, 179 (D. Mass. 1995).

35. *Forti v. Suarez-Mason,* 672 F. Supp. 1531, 1540 (N.D. Cal. 1987) (*Forti I*). This standard was accepted by the Ninth Circuit in *In re Estate of Ferdinand E. Marcos Human Rights Litigation,* 25 F. 3d 1467, 1475 (9th Cir. 1994) ("Estate II").

36. Article 38 states that the Court will determine international law by applying:

(a) international conventions, whether general or particular, establishing rules expressly recognized by the contesting states;

(b) international custom, as evidence of a general practice accepted as law;

(c) the general principles of law recognized by civilized nations;

(d) judicial decisions and the teachings of the most highly qualified publicists of the various nations, as subsidiary means for the determination of the rules of law.

Quoted in *Fiartiga,* 630 F.2d at 881 n. 8.

37. Restatement of the Law (Third), Foreign Relations Law of the United States (1986), § 701, Reporters' Notes 2.

38. See, e.g., *Jama v. U.S. I.N.S.,* 22 F. Supp. 2d 353, 362 (D.N.J. 1998): "Highly relevant to the inquiry whether international law confers a fundamental right on all people are treaties . . . internationally or regionally adopted covenants or declarations of human rights and foreign policy goals of the United States and other countries in the field of human rights."

39. Id., § 324, comment (e).

REFERENCES

Amnesty International. 1999. *United States of America: Rights for All.* New York: Amnesty International.

Cole, David. 1999. *No Equal Justice: Race and Class in the American Criminal Justice System.* New York: The New Press.

Coomaraswarmy, Radhika. 1999. *Report of the Special Rapporteur on Violence Against Women, Its Causes and Consequences, Addendum Report of the Mission to the U.S.A. on the Issue of Violence Against Women in State and Federal Prisons.* United Nations Commission on Human Rights, 55th Session, E/CN.4/1999/68/Add. 2, Jauary 4, 1999.

Dostoevsky, Fyodor. 1956. *Memoirs from the House of the Dead.* Trans. Jessie Coulson. New York: Oxford University Press.

Foucault, Michel. 1979. *Discipline and Punish: The Birth of the Prison.* Trans. Alan Sheridan. New York: Vintage Books.

Geer, Martin A. 2000. Human Rights and Wrongs in Our Own Backyard: Incorporating International Human Rights Protections Under Domestic Civil Rights Law—A Case Study of Women in United States Prisons. *Harvard Human Rights Journal 13*(spring): 71-140.

Hairston, Creasie F. 1991. Family Ties During Imprisonment: Important to Whom and for What? *Journal of Sociology and Social Welfare18*(1): 85-102.

Human Rights Watch. 1996. *All Too Familiar, Sexual Abuse of Women Prisoners in U.S. State Prisons.* New York: Human Rights Watch, Women's Rights Project.

Human Rights Watch. 1998. Nowhere to Hide: Retaliation Against Women in Michigan State Prisons. 10 *Human Rights Watch Reports 2*(G): 5.

Kupers, Terry. 1999. *Prison Madness: The Mental Health Crisis Behind Bars and What We Must Do About It.* San Francisco: Jossey-Bass Publishers.

Smith, Brenda. 2002. *End to Silence: Prisoners' Guide to Address Staff Sexual Misconduct,* Second Edition. Washington: Washington College of Law.

Turner, William Bennett. 1979. When Prisoners Sue: A Study of 1983 Suits in the Federal Courts. 92 *Harvard Law Review:* 610-24.

United Nations General Assembly. 1990. *Basic Principles for the Treatment of Prisoners* [adopted by the General Assembly in its resolution 45/111 of December 14, 1990]. New York: United Nations General Assembly.

U.S. Department of Justice. 2000. *Special Report, Incarcerated Parents and Their Children.* Report No. NCJ 182335. Washington, DC: U.S. Department of Justice, Bureau of Justice Statistics.

U.S. General Accounting Office. 1999. *Women in Prison, Sexual Misconduct by Correctional Staff: Report to the Honorable Eleanor Holms Norton, House of Representatives/U.S. GAO.* Washington, DC: U.S. General Accounting Office.

U.S. Senate. 1976. Rep. 94-1011 at p. 2, reprinted in 1976 U.S.C.C.A.N. 5908, 5909-10.

A few years ago in New Haven, I tried to relate to feminism through a local women's center (located in a Yale basement). I was politely informed that I should "organize" with Black wimmin. In other words, get out. I wanted to start several projects that would include more third world wimmin, but I was told to talk to black wimmin about that. In short, white only. (davenport, 1981, p. 85)

Chapter 16

Borders and Bridges:
Building New Directions
for the Women's Movement

Janet L. Finn

Cherrie, you asked me to write about internationalization, and at first
it made sense. . . . I am a Latin woman in the United States, closely involved with Latin American movements in the rest of the continent. I
should write about connection. But when I tried, all I could think was:
No, write about the separation. (Levins Morales, 1981, p. 53)

INTRODUCTION

I was asked to contribute some thoughts toward a new agenda for the
women's movement, one which placed community building and empowerment of our marginalized sisters as central to the feminist struggle. The language of community, empowerment, and sisterhood is evocative and hope-
ful and, at first, it made sense. As I began gathering my thoughts and
revisiting accounts of women's struggles and action, I found myself returning to the words of Aurora Levins Morales. I cannot start from a place of
community and sisterhood. I must start from separation, from difference.
First, I argue that a women's movement committed to community building
and empowerment must start by recognizing and honoring difference. Surface claims of sisterhood crafted in images of connectedness and belonging
often serve both to mask and to reinforce the many boundaries of difference
that separate women and the relations of power and inequality which justify
and naturalize these divisions. Second, I contend that the current *discourse*
of blame and shame targeting poor women, especially poor women of color,
is *not* marginal but central to the continued divisiveness among women and
to the oppression of all women. Finally, those committed to taking the

knowledge, experiences, and concerns of "women at the margins" seriously need to grapple honestly with the power relations at work among women as part of a vibrant women's movement.

That commitment calls for ongoing critical reflection on key questions: Who constitutes the "we" placing "their" concerns at the center of a feminist agenda? Whose politics, histories, and memories inform that agenda? Is it an agenda in which "women at the margins" wish to participate as protagonists at the center? What sorts of values, commitments, and practices should inform a movement of women committed to respecting and bridging separation in the process of social transformation? How do women who enjoy the privileges of more powerful positionings remain cognizant of those power differences even as they try to transform them? How might we disrupt the very distinction of center and margin by starting from the knowledge and practice of women who live and challenge poverty, violence, and oppression every day? In thinking through these questions, I contend that transformative change is possible only if the knowledge, practices, and concerns of poor and working-class women activists are central to defining and directing our efforts.

The possibilities for women's community building depend on a critical understanding of community as a dynamic arena of struggle and support (Finn, 1998). Community, whether grounded in place or common concern, entails the ongoing negotiation of belonging and difference. The practice of community building must go hand in hand with what I have come to call the practice of "bordering," the acknowledgment of and engagement with the meaning and power of difference. As we engage with the forces at work in structuring difference and exclusion, we also encounter patterns that connect women's concerns and actions across diverse boundaries. The boundaries separating "us" from "them" take many forms—from customs checkpoints, prison walls, welfare office windows, and the gates of suburbia to the more nuanced distinctions of color, language, labor, and mobility. The notion of bordering provides a means for addressing shifting boundaries of "we-ness" among women and for imagining and strategically building the bridges of solidarity for effective action. When we start from the position that community among women is never given but always contingent, we gain a deeper appreciation for the strength and vulnerability of connections through which women build support and mobilize action. As we attend to borders, we are forced to examine what separates us, how separation is articulated, where borders are disrupted and transgressed, and where their acknowledgment may signal a place to initiate dialogues and build coalitions. In this chapter, both accomplishments and challenges of the women's movement are highlighted; the lessons learned from women's community practice "at the margins" are considered; and some possibilities for creating knowledge, solidarity, and change across borders are posed. Although this chapter focuses largely on the United States, I draw examples from my experiences with women's groups in Chile and from creative transnational efforts in looking at women's movements beyond U.S. borders. Hopefully, readers will bring their own experiences to bear in thinking through the intersections of local struggles and global processes that shape women's lives.

LEARNING FROM HISTORY:
A SHORT STORY OF THE ACCOMPLISHMENTS
AND CHALLENGES OF THE WOMEN'S MOVEMENT

As addressed in the introduction to this book, the feminist movement in the United States has been critiqued for its white, middle-class bias, failure to engage with the experiences and knowledge of women of color, and lack of commitment to the daily struggles that shape the lives of less privileged women. Particularly glaring has been the lack of attention by the mainstream feminist movement to concerns of women in prison, whose lives embody the disciplinary practices of the patriarchal state in its most blatant forms. Reflections on the history of the women's movement should not, however, be reduced to a litany of critique. The rich legacy of accomplishments has been strengthened through challenges to exclusionary thought and practice. Ongoing debates among feminists and with our critics continue to shape new directions in scholarship and activism. For the purposes of this discussion, three interrelated accomplishments and the challenges contained within them are addressed: recovering the history of women's activism; recognizing gender politics as infused with those of race, class, sexuality, citizenship, and religion; and attending to the intersection of local, state, and transnational forces in women's lives.

The accomplishments of the women's movement are far-reaching. Feminists have made gender an issue and exposed interlocking forms of power, prestige, and hierarchy that have historically naturalized and devalued women's social positions (Ortner and Whitehead, 1981; Jaggar, 1983; Rosaldo and Lamphere, 1974; Smith, 1987). They have explored ways in which gender shapes theoretical interpretation, public discourse and policy, organizational processes, and social movements (Hyde, 1992; Ferree and Martin, 1995; Alvarez, Dagnino, and Escobar, 1998; Franco, 1998; Sidel, 1986; Skocpol, 1992; Gordon, 1990). They have redefined what counts as "political" and have made a commitment to social justice and social change (Valdés and Weinstein, 1993). Feminists have located the question of women's rights in the context of human rights writ large (Jelin and Hershberg, 1996; Yeager, 1994; Nash, 1994; Schild, 1998). In addition, they have disrupted assumed dichotomies (e.g., objective versus subjective knowledge; public versus private spheres) which maintain certain axes of difference while obscuring others. In so doing, they have also challenged the politics of knowledge development and have posed alternative ways and means of knowing the world (Butler and Scott, 1992; DiLeonardo, 1991; Smith, 1987; Harding, 1986; Haraway, 1988).

In the process of disrupting received truths about the order of things, feminists have recognized that the telling of a historical narrative is a political act (Gluck et al., 1998; Gordon, 1990). It is through ongoing critical dialogue with history that we not only confront the partiality of our knowledge but also address the systemic patterns of privilege that shape certain exclusions and sanction certain "ignorances." In this spirit, a number of feminist scholars have engaged in critical projects to reclaim silenced voices and complicate the picture of women's history both in the United States and beyond. These efforts are broadening and deepening knowledge of women's community building, grounded in the experiences of poor and working-class women whose stories had been neglected historically. For example, the contributors to Bookman and Morgen's classic collection *Women and the Politics of Empowerment* (1988) chronicled diverse examples of community, labor, and civil rights activism on the part of poor and working-class African-American, Latina, and Anglo women. They explored the "reverberations" of women's activism among family, community, and work spheres; documented the development of women's political consciousness through collective action; and attended to the structural constraints on women's activism. Reflecting on these diverse examples of women's activism, Ackelsberg concluded that "women's coming to political consciousness [and I suspect that this applies to men as well] . . . may be more a phenomenon of *relationship* and *connection,* than one of recognizing *interests* in the traditional, individualist sense" (1988, pp. 305, 308). She argued that any new paradigm must have the politics of *relationship* as a central focus.

A number of feminist scholars (cf. Milkman, 1985; Baron, 1991; Faue, 1991; Frank, 1985; Jones, 1985; Kessler-Harris, 1982) have located women in labor history and have provided us with a more complex understanding of gender, labor, and social protest. Others have recognized women as makers of history, explored the strategies through which women have mobilized collective action, and pointed to women's concerns for basic survival and consumption—food, housing, health, infrastructure—as motive forces in the development of critical consciousness and action (Kaplan, 1982; Frank, 1985, 1991; Moser, 1987; Kingsolver, 1989; Nash, 1994). Some have examined the motivations, histories, and practices of collective community building by poor and working-class Latina, African-American, Native American, and white women—many of whom recognize themselves as part of a "movement of women" but hold themselves apart from a "women's movement" (Paul, 1993, p. 47; Naples, 1998a,b; Kaplan, 1982; Young and Padilla, 1990; Gunn Allen, 1995; Castello, 1986; Naples, 1991; Pardo, 1998). Others have expanded our knowledge of ways in which women have mobilized "traditional" concerns for family and community survival into radical forms of social action, revolutionizing the meaning of motherhood, the power of gendered social relations, and the practice of community organizing the process (Alcoff, 1988; Guzman Bouvard, 1994; Stephen, 1997; Nash, 1979). This work has inspired continued critical attention to the question of gender and social movements (Alvarez, Dagnino, and Escobar, 1998; Taylor and Whittier, 1998).

Feminist scholars have challenged the erasure of women of color from the historical record and have critiqued both the politics of feminism and academic knowledge production that have perpetuated these absences (Davis, 1981; Thornton Dill, 1994; hooks, 1984; Moraga, 1986; Hill Collins, 1990; Hull, Bell Scott, and Smith, 1982; Mohanty, 1991; Hurtado, 1996). For example, Jones (1985), Thornton Dill (1994), and Lerner (1972), among others, have provided important, detailed accounts of the diversity of experience and common struggles in African-American women's histories. Carol Stack's (1974) classic study of social kinship networks as the bases for collective support among low-income African-American women demonstrated the strength of loose ties and challenged the "poverty-as-pathology" discourse that virulently targets black women. Zavella (1987) and Baca Zinn (1990) have contested static and limited representations of Latina women in the United States. They have advanced theoretical understandings of gender and kinship, community, and women's social participation through documentation of Latina women's experiences. These projects have challenged us to see gender, class, race, and ethnicity not as discrete social categories but as complex and interlocking systems of meaning and power through which difference is produced. A number of these contributions have examined the complexity and creativity of women's lives beyond the problem-focused lens of "reaction," which constructs women solely as victims or resisters of oppression. In so doing they have enriched appreciation of women as social actors, crafting lives and creating change.

Feminists have made critical contributions to understanding women's relation to the state (Gordon, 1990; Piven, 1990; Skocpol, 1992; Jelin and Hershberg, 1996). Some feminist activists have addressed the relationship between violence against women and the sanctioned violence of the state. For example, the battered women's movement began as an underground effort by and for survivors of "domestic" abuse who found themselves ignored or further violated by the interventions of the state. Similarly, Beth Richie and Sue Osthoff (1999) invoke this powerful connection in describing the lives of women prisoners. They write: "Being in prison is like being in an abusive relationship, only with the state. It is an arbitrary detail that you have got to be silent, you have got to figure out ways to negotiate for what you want that do not insult the potential abuser. . . . Prison is about the arbitrary use of authority: you never know why" (p. 158). Their work on the margins is part of a critical effort to challenge the invisibility of women in prison, give voice to battered women and women of color trapped in the criminal justice system, and break the silence in mainstream feminism regarding their concerns (Richie, 1996).

Women have illustrated the importance of linking questions of gender to explorations of the nexus of race, representation, and citizenship and exposing—as Williams and Peterson have done—"citizenship as a construct that has been and continues to be racialized and gendered even as those who invoke it promote it as a 'natural' category" (1998, p. 7). These contributions have been particularly important in addressing the politics of gender, welfare, and punishment. A number of women who have lived the experience of welfare in the United States have gone on to challenge the gender oppression of the welfare system through their words and actions (cf. Kramer, 1996; Dujon and Withorn, 1996; Tillmon, 1976). They have been joined by feminists engaged in activist scholarship in support of a just social welfare system. Their provocative contributions have advanced our understanding of the disciplinary practices of the welfare state, their intimate linkage to race and class politics, and the possibilities for their transformation (Abramovitz, 1988; Fraser, 1990; Fraser and Gordon, 1994; Gordon, 1988, 1990, 1991, 1994; Piven, 1990; Mink, 1995; Boris, 1995; Brewer, 1994; Quadagno, 1994).

For example, Mimi Abramovitz's important historical analysis of gender and welfare in the United States, *Regulating the Lives of Women* (1988), provided a model for seriously engaging with race and class in feminist historical projects. Diane Dujon and Ann Withorn's provocative, experimental text, *For Crying Out Loud: Women's Poverty in the United States* (1996), not only confronts race and class politics in the text, but it also provides a model for "talking across tables" by bringing poor women and working-class women, activists, academics, and committed men together for collective knowledge production. Others have explored more broadly the ways in which the meaning of citizenship is deeply gendered, thus raising fundamental questions about what "democracy" means to women. Important work in the area of gender, citizenship, and democracy is under way in Chile and other countries reconstructing democracy in the wake of brutal dictatorships (Jelin and Hershberg, 1996; Schild, 1998; Franco, 1998). Feminists are addressing ways in which forms of gender oppression are reinscribed in the process of recuperating democracy. In critical analyses reminiscent of the work of Frances Fox Piven (1990), these authors consider the state as an ambiguous terrain that women can exploit in diverse ways even as it constrains them.

The questions they raise regarding women's rights and human rights resonate with current concerns about welfare rights and social justice activists in the United States. For example, Angela Davis (1999) has called for a "new civil rights movement" that critically examines the situation of growing numbers of people who cannot exercise their civil rights because they are in prison. She argues the importance of drawing on a body of human rights principles writ large in order to defend the rights of women in prison and critically question the relationship between punishment and democracy in the United States. Davis reminds us that our fundamental sense of personhood and human dignity lies in the right to have rights, which is being denied to the escalating number of incarcerated persons. Amnesty International's (1999) report on women in prison in the United States bears out Davis's concerns. One need only consider the facts that the incarceration rate of women in the United States is ten times that of Western European countries—and that the incarceration rate of African-American women is eight times that of white women—to see that the practice of democracy and promise of human rights in the United States are heavily compromised at best (Amnesty International, 1999; Casa, 1999).

In a similar vein, feminist scholars in Latin America are questioning the celebration of civil society as the "new way" to democratic participation, critiquing the class and gender politics that characterize many nongovernmental organizations (NGOs), and questioning assumptions of the "autonomy" of civil society from either the state or larger systemic forces of gendered power (Franco, 1998; Jelin and Hershberg, 1996; Schild, 1995, 1998). Important opportunities for dialogue across diverse borders exist here, which can help us expose the patterns that connect "welfare reform" in the United States and "structural adjustment" programs abroad. Similarly, critical reflection on the reconstitution of a "civil" state in the wake of violent military regimes exposes the blurriness of the boundary between democracy and dictatorship, especially for those "on the margins" who are often the center targets of state violence. Attention to the question of citizenship begs that of social, political, and economic exclusions shackling women to the violence, poverty, and oppression which transcend borders.

Common themes resonate across diverse examples of women's struggles and collective action: the centrality of supportive social relations to activism; concern for family and community survival as motive force for action; the contested nature of what counts as political space and practice; the contradictions in women's relations to the state; the insidious presence and tolerance of violence against women in its many guises; the challenges of grappling simultaneously with local struggles and global processes; and the transformative possibilities that are obtained through engagement with those contradictions. These themes speak to the importance of *praxis*—the intimate linkage of critical thought and practice—to the understandings of social reality that can be built from the perspective of women's differing subject positions; and to the possibilities for linking the patterns that connect the women's "traditional" concerns regarding family, labor, health, environment, peace, and social equity with radical politics. Ongoing dialogue with our histories enables us to challenge particular inventions of "tradition," which distort more than inform, inspire collective memory with historic possibility, and acknowledge the reclamation of our histories as a political act.

CONFRONTING THE CHALLENGES

*"The Women's Movement and the Movement of Women"**

These accomplishments contain within them challenges that need to be addressed in order to build a movement with relevance and resonance for historically marginalized women. One of those challenges has been framed by Eileen Paul as the "movement of women" versus the women's movement (1993). Paul argues that community change efforts of poor and working-class women, particularly women of color, focus first on their commitment to community and struggles against oppression and social injustice as lived and felt therein. According to Paul, many poor and working-class women who are activists see themselves as doing "women's work" but not as being feminists. They identify with a localized sense of community, with neighbors facing common struggles of poverty, racism, and the hidden injuries of class. Historically, their work has been undervalued both by feminist activists and by the male-dominated realm of community organization. These women's personal, grounded experiences with the injuries of oppression have often been the motivating force for their activism. Many have forged their critical consciousness of gender and power and their commitment to radical practice through their community activism. However, they have been left feeling frustrated and disappointed in their encounters with feminism and have advocated not for inclusion in the "women's movement" but for recognition of the movement of women.

---

*This phrase is drawn from the title of Eileen Paul's article. See Paul, 1993, for an examination of the tensions that exist between these two concepts.

Nancy Naples (1998b), in her important study of grassroots warriors, as she terms women community action workers fighting the war on poverty, offers a similar account. Drawing on oral histories of female community workers, Naples speaks to their long-term commitment to community. She develops the concept of "activist mothering" to articulate the intimate linkage between women's "traditional" responsibilities and roles and the ways in which they draw on these identities to inform and justify transformational social action. Echoing Eileen Paul, Naples shows how one's personal political history shapes one's framework for understanding and action. Many community organizers in the war on poverty were women of color living in poverty. They drew on their previous organizing experiences and daily confrontations with racism and classism to inform their politics and practice of community building. Previous faith-based action also often served as a pathway to women's community work.

I found similar patterns in my comparative study of women's social participation in two copper-mining communities, one in the United States and the other in Chile (Finn, 1998). I put forth the notion of "crafting the everyday" to describe the process through which working-class women maintained vigilance of everyday life during times of (men's) employment in the mines and mobilized networks of kin and friends during strikes and other times of community crisis. They made claims as women and mothers that politicized questions of family and community survival, developed critical consciousness of power relations, and engaged in transformational social action. They spoke from their perspectives as women, criticized labor unions for mirroring company power, and redefined political boundaries in the process. Few of these women identified as feminist, yet all saw gender as an issue and themselves as social actors capable of critiquing the conditions of their lives; they were committed to changing those conditions.

Similar accounts of women's transformational action toward urgent concerns for family and community survival have been documented in diverse historical, cultural, and political contexts. From bread riots and cost-of-living protests among U.S. women in the early 1900s to solidarity strikes in mining towns from Bolivia to Arizona, women have politicized their family and community concerns. They "revolutionized motherhood" as a means of confronting state violence and demanding recognition of the "disappeared" during Argentina's brutal dictatorship known as the "Dirty War." They have disrupted the distinction between "private" and "public" matters in the process (Frank, 1991; Kingsolver, 1989; Nash, 1979; Guzman Bouvard, 1994). These examples of women's activism reflect Paul's concept of a "movement of women" informed by what Temma Kaplan terms "female consciousness" rather than a women's movement inspired by feminist consciousness (Kaplan, 1982). A key challenge for the future of the women's movement, then, is crafting possibilities of common cause with movements of women while exploring the meaning and power of borders between female and feminist consciousness. It calls for a gendered-border diplomacy in which women can come together, learn from one another, build alliances, and respect differences in the meaning and power of being (and not being) feminist. It creates an opportunity to further articulate to one another and to a larger public both the diversity and commonality of what it means to be feminist.

The Projects of Whiteness and Classlessness

The women's movement must also confront and disrupt the "racial project of whiteness" (Gasparin, 1998) and its partner in oppression, the project of classlessness. Through these mutually constituting projects, white, middle-class understandings of the order of things are implicitly assumed and naturalized, while the "difference" of other realities and understandings becomes marked as deviant, dubious, or dangerous. A key practice of the women's movement thus entails recognizing and dislodging these discourses and practices, especially as they are entangled in the movement itself (Hurtado, 1996). It is not a matter of "adding" poor white women and women of color and welcoming "them" to "our" movement; the approach must be transformative, not additive. It calls for deep soul-searching about the power of privilege and the risks involved in letting go. These projects of whiteness and classlessness are manifest in assumptions and practices of professionalism through which women of privilege "reach out" to "other" women. The very notion of "outreach" assumes a center that reaches out to the margin. However, as Naples and others have demonstrated, activists in movements of women are very centered, grounded in neighborhoods in which they live, responsible to friendship and kinship networks, and sympathetic to the concerns of those who confront similar circumstances. Rather than reaching out, women concerned with—yet removed from—these daily struggles need to seek permission from grounded women, learn from and with them, share resources, and respect the terms of their invitation to participate.

Challenging the projects of whiteness and classlessness demands careful attention to interpersonal relations and institutional practices. Even the best-intentioned, collaborative efforts can reinscribe the differences that separate women. This is well illustrated in Cumming and Mandel's (1996) insightful discussion of the publication of *Survival News*—a Roxbury, Massachusetts-based activist welfare rights newspaper that brings low- and middle-income women together in a collaborative effort. Cumming and Mandel present a careful, honest look at what it takes to maintain day-to-day workings of *Survival News,* develop relationships among equals, and challenge privilege in the process.

Participants begin with the recognition of women on welfare as experts. They pay close attention to organizational structure and call one another on the ways in which middle-class "certainty, confidence, and condescension" is manifest—from the assumption that all women have bank accounts and access to cash, checks, and transportation, to the belief that all are able to wait for the reimbursement of expenses associated with their participation. Welfare dollars do not stretch to accommodate such niceties. Organizational practices need to assure access to basic resources needed for full participation of all. They must mitigate against a two-tier system or one of "noblesse oblige" that leaves low-income women indebted to the "generosity" of middle-income women for offering a ride, buying lunch, and so forth. As those who have written about the challenges of organizing across class and racial borders teach us, the devil is in the details. Building trust must be part of everyday practice; it cannot be taken for granted. From organizational issues such as board representation and decision-making processes to provision of material and social support needed for full participation to day-to-day interactions, we must be willing to take risks, challenge privilege, and be open to transformation of our certainties and selves in the process.

The insidious impact of the projects of whiteness and classlessness is perhaps most clearly seen in mainstream feminism's historic lack of engagement with the concerns of women in prison. The troubling irony here is that the site at which the racism, violence, sexism, and patriarchal power of the state is most keenly practiced in the discipline and punishment of poor women is largely excluded from the terrain of feminist struggle. Prison walls continue to define borders between "us" and "them," demarcating spaces of sanctioned ignorance from which many feminists are insulated by race and class privilege. Richie and Osthoff (1999) bring this point home in their critique of the battered women's/antiviolence movement. They argue that twenty years ago the movement posed a radical challenge to the order of things, but it has increasingly become more about the needs of individual women rather than a movement for social change. The projects of whiteness and classlessness are implicit in the message that rape can happen to anyone and that police intervention and recourse through the criminal legal system is the best response.

In contrast, as Richie and Osthoff point out, the prisoners' rights movement is solidly located in race and class dynamics, recognizing the vulnerability of poor people of color to many forms of violence, including the violence of policing. They describe the split within the antiviolence movement that occurred when decision-making power was taken over by white, middle-class, professional women who advocated police intervention:

> [Calling the police] only works if you have a telephone first, right? And then if you have police who respond to you when you call, if you have community members who think calling the police is a good solution to problems, and if you do not feel fearful for yourself or for the people that you care about, in some cases the person who is abusing you. Then calling the police was a very good solution, but it was a solution that was defined for a very narrow group of women who could potentially be battered or raped. (Richie and Osthoff, 1999, p. 159)

In writing this chapter, I have had to confront my own insularity from these struggles and question the everyday practices through which the seduction of choice dulls the urgency of action. My own coming to feminist consciousness was profoundly shaped by my first postcollege job in a state institution for "delinquent" girls. There I witnessed young women's vulnerability and strength, encountered the masculine power of the state, and got caught in the institutionalized contradictions of care and control. After two years, I sought other spaces to work within and against the state. Although much of my work has addressed the possibilities and constraints of women's social action, it is largely silent on the concerns of women in prison. I must ask myself how much my own participation in the projects of whiteness and classlessness has shaped and sanctioned that silence.

Closely linked to the border politics of class and race that challenge the women's movement is the challenge of heterosexism. Activists in the women's movement have long been accused of "lesbianism" by their reactionary critics. The accusation is used with the evocative force of the label of "communism" during the McCarthy era. Some heterosexually identified women express reluctance to embrace feminism for fear of being so labeled, even as they embrace some key feminist values and principles. Yet to respond with the message that feminism does not equal lesbianism is to reinforce the distance between a heterosexual "we" and a lesbian "other" implicitly, thus fortifying another border of difference and devaluation. Dividing women along lines of sexual identity serves to reinforce sexual dichotomies while leaving the underlying power of heterosexism unquestioned. This poses an important challenge to the women's movement. How do we articulate and embrace an inclusive respect and advocacy for gendered identities and relations that challenges dichotomies and disrupts the underlying assumptions of heterosexism and power of homophobia?

A return to the work of Raymond Williams (1977), a pioneer in cultural studies, is instructive here in grasping the differential structuring of women's struggles. Williams writes of the "structure of feeling" to describe the felt and lived experiences through which we engage with, internalize, and resist the institutional rules, cultural schema, and scripts that shape our lives. Our differing daily encounters with and practices of privilege, oppression, negation, and inclusion powerfully shape our aspirations and longings, life projects, and sense of limits and possibilities. Our personhood is thus a "living commemoration of the actions which produced it" (Strathern, 1988, in Harvey, 2000, p. 100). A woman whose life is structured by the fear, violence, and humiliation of the welfare and justice systems may find little common ground with women whose worlds are differently structured. The thought of trying to educate well-intentioned "sisters" may be overwhelming. The patronizing gaze of surface understanding that masks the doubt of a woman whose life is well-insulated by privilege can be simply too much to bear. For all her good intentions, the woman of privilege may find herself incapable of suspending disbelief and transgressing the boundaries of her certainties to truly hear and honor another's experience. An open and honest women's movement cannot afford to perpetuate these injuries.

Engaging the Local, the State, and the Transnational

As previously discussed, much of women's creative and critical action has been grounded in local communities and informed by local knowledge. We have also seen how questions of gender are intimately bound to the state and the meaning and power of citizenship. Further complicating the terrain of thought and action are the cultural and political disruptions of transnational movements of capital that challenge spatialized notions of culture, the autonomy of states and their political boundaries, and state- and place-based notions of "us" and "them" (Alvarez, Dagnino, and Escobar, 1998, p. 4). A central challenge to and opportunity for women's movements involves critical attention to and action in the ambiguous spaces of power and possibility shaped by these intersecting forces.

Differing cultural constructions of gender and selfhood, rights of citizenship, relations to the state, and historical experiences among women suggest the tremendous difficulty we face in trying to build a border-crossing women's movement in its many senses. We need to address the logic of the neoconservative market economy and its accompanying patterns of structural adjustment at home and abroad that leave women multiply burdened and further divided. We need to critically examine the constructions of gender and power encoded in the ideology and political strategy of globalization that have consequences for all women (Piven and Cloward, 1997). We need to be mindful of ways in which policies and practices designed to benefit some women in some places may come at a price to other women in other places.

First, the class and race politics that shape women's relations to states demands ongoing confrontation. A number of critics writing about the state in U.S. and Latin American contexts have addressed the class bias of state ministries concerned with "women's issues" and the class- and often party-based connections between the state and NGOs. They challenge both the notion of the democratic state as neutral arbiter and that of civil society, so celebrated at present, as a third sector that is "autonomous" from the state. For example, Schild (1998), addressing the Chilean case, examines the ways in which women's political struggles to define new political identities and expand notions of citizenship have been absorbed into the very neoconservative state project they were seeking to transform. The result, she argues, is that "this Chilean modernizing project has come to *depend* on the many activities of professionals and activists working for NGOs, universities and independent research institutes, a majority of whom are women" (p. 99). As my colleagues in grassroots community organizations of Santiago attest, the women whose voices count in state and NGO circles are well-educated, middle class, positioned in party politics, and invested in the dominant order of things. Meanwhile, women's grassroots groups addressing survival and social justice issues relevant to the 40 percent of the country that lives in poverty find their knowledge dismissed and labor devalued.

These struggles against classist ideologies and structural adjustment policies addressed by Schild resonate with the contradictions of "welfare reform" in the United States. The project of "ending welfare as we know it" is grounded in and promulgates antiwoman, antipoor beliefs, and, at the same time, it is a system that relies upon a predominantly female workforce. U.S. welfare bureaucracies are structured in ways that pit women against women. Frontline welfare workers, many of whom have received public assistance themselves, are thrust into the role of disciplinarians of poor(er) women. The contradictions of grappling with the uncertainty of their own economic and social positions while serving as gatekeepers for the welfare system work against the possibility of finding common cause with their "clients" (Finn and Underwood, 2000). As recent evaluations of welfare reform under TANF indicate, the plight of poor women—especially women of color and their children—is growing more serious.

An important area for crafting common ground, then, is among welfare clients, workers, and advocates through living-wage campaigns, welfare worker unionizing campaigns, and community-based demands for housing, health, education, and child care that benefit all residents. Such campaigns must go beyond a self-help, community development model and challenge the ethics and logic of commodifying the body and its basic needs and privatizing the foundations of social life, but we cannot stop there. We must also trace the patterns that connect projects of global capitalism in their many guises—privatization, structural adjustment, modernization, downsizing, outsourcing the prison industrial complex, welfare reform, workfare, managed care—to their human consequences. Transformative power lies in first recognizing the *necessary* connections among these practices for maintaining the inequities of wealth and poverty. We can then mobilize resistance from site to site, moving capillary-like among the connections and exposing the underlying patterns of power and inequality. For example, how might we articulate connections among growing income disparity, increasingly punitive welfare policies, shrinking social safety nets, and expanding prison populations so that we can craft interlocking chains of site-based advocacy and resistance?

Second, the question of reproductive choice merits consideration in thinking about the complexities of women's relations to states and to transnational feminist movements. Within the women's movement in the United States, choice has become the proverbial line in the sand demarcating who is with us and who is against us; questioning the line is something of a taboo. However, we face a fundamental dilemma here. The pro-choice position assumes a Western conception of the autonomous self, a liberal democratic state, and a notion of citizenship premised on individual rather than collective rights. In short, it assumes the universality of a particular worldview and political order. Sensitive ethnographic inquiry along the choice divide has pointed to the complex and often contradictory beliefs and emotions that many women hold regarding the meaning and power of choice (Ginsberg, 1989). These complexities are obscured by either/or thinking, and the underlying binary logic itself runs contrary to feminist efforts to question and disrupt dichotomies. Furthermore, much of the discussion regarding choice ignores historic and contemporary racist and classist reproductive politics that have shaped the lives of poor women, especially poor women of color both in the United States and abroad. For example, a discourse that reduces reproductive politics to a question of individual choice neglects the patterned practices through which African-American women were forced into reproduction and denied the right of motherhood. It ignores experiences of Native American and Puerto Rican women subjected to state-based sterilization policies, and of poor young women currently subjected to mandated contraception and denied assistance to support a child born to them while receiving welfare. It is a sanitized discourse that neglects the larger context through which personhood is denied to incarcerated women forced to give birth in shackles.

The politics of pro-choice also mask more muted class-based assumptions on the limits of "good" choice. Advocates have strongly supported choice regarding contraception, single motherhood, and pregnancy termination. Yet one also encounters a discourse among some pro-choice advocates of "too young, too poor, too many," indicating that advocacy goes only so far. Its limits coincide with the "correctness" of contemporary Western middle-class notions of proper motherhood. The professional and popular preoccupation with teen pregnancy is a case in point, as is the widespread concern with providing third-world women with access to contraception. Some Latin American feminists have critiqued the representation of choice within the U.S. women's movement. They have advocated reframing the debate around a more inclusive concept of "voluntary motherhood," indicating a subtle but significant shift in the politics of choice. Although the language harkens to historic reproductive rights debates in the United States, it is informed by struggles for women's rights under particular historical, cultural, and political conditions.

The question of choice also places a problematic wedge between the women's movement and many women who are inspired by faith to justice-oriented action. Although some faith-based activists may share a common concern for social justice with feminist activists, their deeply held religious convictions may bring them to a very different place regarding the meaning and power of abortion within the realm of choice. Perhaps this is a place to highlight a border, built on the dignity of difference, that becomes a place for respecting that which is not negotiable and crafting the cross-border possibilities for collective action. It is through the ongoing recognition and respect of such borders that we can practice feminist values and build alliances with others who share many, though not all, of our commitments and concerns.

A third challenge we face is the power difference among women of differing social, economic, and institutional positions joining together in cross-border projects. In the cross-national context, Wilson and Whitmore (1995) use their experiences as Canadian academic/activists working in partnership with Nicaraguan women to speak to the dilemmas that must be personally and programmatically addressed in cross-national work among women's groups who have differing access to resources, sources of funding, and so on. Wilson and Whitmore sensitively address the politics of time and space in cross-national research and action projects. Too often, such projects are characterized by women in privileged positions moving in and out of poor communities. They set the agenda and they assume not only the availability of other women's time, but also, more fundamentally, a shared understanding of time, interests, and goals. They return to their positions of privilege with esoteric knowledge of the "other" in tow. Wilson and Whitmore also speak of the need to address the politics of language, not only in the literal sense, but also in terms of the languages of class and professionalism that can block meaningful communication. Further, they criticize the inequalities of power that such practices reinforce, even though the goals of the project may be women's empowerment or gender-conscious development. Wilson and Whitmore call instead for a practice of "accompaniment": a joining over time across borders to build mutual trust, to explore possibilities for cooperative work and division of labor, and to create a two-way movement of people, knowledge, and power. Their insights are instructive in engaging in the many forms of "border work" that women's movements face. As we question both assumed and imposed borders, we are positioned to respond with affirmative action to the question posed by anthropologist June Nash (1994):

> Once we reject the false opposition of First and Third worlds, can we grasp the commonalities in the welfare problems faced by women trying to feed their families and keep their children alive, whether they live in drug-infested inner cities of industrialized countries or in militarized countries where conflicts are exacerbated by U.S. arms shipments? (p. 9)

The issues outlined previously reflect the contradictory nature of the challenges facing the women's movement at philosophical, strategic, and personal levels. For example, as we resist essentialist views of women and point to the ways in which gender and difference are socially constructed, we destabilize the political ground from which to speak and make claims as women. The history of action and claims made by women as mothers illustrates this dilemma. On the one hand, we have witnessed the transformational power in activist mothering. On the other, motherhood as a central organizing theme reduces women to a single social identity, excludes "nonmothers," and reinscribes essentialist views of gender. We face political dilemmas as we challenge what counts as "expert knowledge" and at the same time try to voice an alternative expertise countering woman-blaming political debate. We face the challenges of responding to urgent concerns and engaging in critical reflection, of speaking against stereotypes without reinscribing those very stereotypes in the process, of building alternative organizational models and practices while trying to survive in a top-down world of policy and practice, and of respecting difference while building a cohesive base of power. We must make ethical and political decisions regarding which borders we honor, cross, disrupt, and transform. We are constantly challenged by the intimate linkage of local struggles and global processes, and by the conundrum between the partiality of our knowledge and the ripple effects of our actions. We must embrace these contradictions and appropriate the spaces of ambiguity and uncertainty they afford. We must take on the paradox of power and engage in "deep play," entering into the games we seemingly cannot win but can*not* play (Finn, 1998). Perhaps we can transform the rules, players, relations, and outcomes in the process.

FOOD FOR THOUGHT AND ACTION

The work ahead is daunting. Women in the center of the struggles for personal, family, and community survival are tackling these challenges and crafting new possibilities for thought and action. They start from a place of local knowledge, value the wisdom gained through their positions in and perspectives on the world, and recognize the partiality of their knowledge. They face exhaustion, hostility, and reprisals for their efforts. And they celebrate successes large and small along the way.

Some use a new *language* of activism, reminding us of the power of naming and the intimate relationship between our words and our actions. For example, prison rights activist Ellen Barry uses the language of *critical resistance* to describe the stance from which to build a proactive and progressive justice movement (1999). Angela Davis (1999, p. 34) calls on us to "give the words 'prison industrial complex' a new currency that would extricate people from fear and enable them to talk" about the real issues at stake. Concern with the power of language to shape possibilities for action has broad implications for feminist activism. For example, how might we question the "liberal" in "neoliberal" economic policies? Denounce the exploitation and disenfranchisement inherent in and masked by the language of welfare reform? Expose the private profits behind anxious political discourses regarding the social costs of human health and welfare? Replace the language of blame with a language of honor for those who have found ways to survive the indignities of the antiwelfare state? Reclaim the linkage between justice and compassion?

Others use a language of connection, speaking not so much of social movements, but of *webs* and *networks* of solidarity, support, and action. Through this language, activists recognize the fragile and dynamic nature of social ties, rather than assuming their strength or stability. They pay attention to the work that must go into building and maintaining healthy networks of support. Also important, they recognize social relations as ends in themselves, not as means to an end. The value of friendship and support that blurs the boundaries of women's "public" and "private" concerns is central to the stories of many female community activists. They have learned that social movements cannot be built on organizing strategies and tactics alone. As Susan Stall and Randy Stoecker (1998) have argued, women's collective actions challenge the masculine logic of San Alinksy-style organizing. Rather than "community organizing," women-centered movements are about "organizing community"; that is, valuing community building as an outcome of organizing. In my own recent work with women building an infrastructure in a poor sector of Santiago, I was struck with how often women used a language of beauty to describe the process and products of their collective labors. They taught me the importance of the *aesthetics* as well as the politics and ethics of women's social action (Finn, n.d.).

The language of "activist mothering," "revolutionizing motherhood," and "nurturing activism" speaks to the inseparability of caring and activism—challenging the gendered divide that has historically split the "feminine" world of social support from the masculine world of community organizing. Similarly, my use of "crafting the everyday" in speaking of the ways in which women worked from the materials at hand to create new possibilities intentionally challenges notions that community work is something women simply do by virtue of their sex. This language does not essentialize womanhood but serves instead to politicize the social roles associated with women. It simultaneously draws on traditional representations of womanhood and transforms them from naturalized roles to radical forms of social practice. It moves us from either/or to both/and thinking where compassion and justice, vulnerability and power, *cariño y coraje* (caring/affection and courage) are inseparable—the basic blocks of community building.

Once we break out of a binary logic, we open ourselves to fresh ways of thinking. In conversations with women building community, I have encountered what Anthony Kelly and Sandra Sewell (1988) have described as a "trialectic" logic. This is a logic of openness that asks us to "think in threes" and open ourselves to the possibilities that emerge from understanding three or more independent concepts in relationship, such as "I-you-we" or "being-doing-becoming." A trialectic logic encourages us to break with our center margin and self/other splits. As Kelly and Sewell argue, this logic is exemplified in the practices of community building grounded in the fundamental relatedness of head, heart, and hand. It is a logic central point to women's community-based efforts considered here.

Social geographer David Harvey's (2000) recent work, *Spaces of Hope,* offers bold new thinking about physical, social, and political spaces and possibilities for social transformation. Harvey examines the patterns that connect oppression across disparate arenas. He calls for dialectical thinking and practice that critically engages "militant particularism" and universal rights claims. He uses the metaphor of "theaters" of thought and action as a

way of envisioning possibilities on "some long frontier of insurgent political practice" (p. 233). How might we map out our diverse "particularisms,"
strategize possibilities for variably respecting and bridging the differences
that separate us, and occupy the space in between with the knowledge, passion, and support that fuels insurgent practice? Perhaps Harvey's image
could be expanded to a "trialectical" one in which we envision and enact the
possibilities of transforming spaces of oppression into places of hope and
bases of action. Perhaps we transform the language of militarism into that of
passion and justice in the process.

There are exciting examples of new movements of women, linking local
struggles and global processes, redefining women's political space and participation, and challenging the projects of whiteness and classelessness. The
resurgence of grassroots welfare rights organizations across the United
States is an important case in point. Local groups are strengthening their
webs of local and regional alliances with faith-based groups, economic-jus-
tice organizations, disability rights advocates, and gay and lesbian groups
(Finn et al., 2000). At the same time, they are joining with regional education and advocacy centers, building a common set of political goals and
strategies at the national level, and taking the violation of rights under welfare reform to the world court as a human rights issue. The National Welfare
Rights Union, in conjunction with advocacy groups across the United
States, is documenting violations of the United Nations Declaration of Human Rights Charter, which includes the right to work, earn a living wage,
and have access to health care and education as basic human rights. The
movement links poor women to a broad-based coalition of advocates for social and economic justice, engages grassroots groups, and speaks to the
need to think and act across borders in building alliances. The efforts for incorporating Canadian and South American participation are fledgling.
However, they signal the importance of forging cross-national ties in the
face of NAFTA and other multilateral trade agreements which serve corporate interests while leaving poor women ever more vulnerable to exploitation.

A number of woman-centered organizations are putting national border
politics at the center of their activism. For example, *La Mujer Obrera* (The
woman worker), an El Paso-based advocacy group, takes a popular education approach to raise women's consciousness of their rights and prepare
women for leadership in their communities (*La Mujer Obrera,* 1999). They
recognize the demands of women's paid and unpaid labor, and pay particular attention to the multiple jeopardies facing immigrant women regarding
protection of their civil, labor, and human rights. *La Mujer Obrera* women
locate their organizing in the workplace and community, responding to the
particular concerns of women in the local textile factories. *La Mujer Obrera*

has started small and spread out to Spanish-speaking female workers and their families through local, person-to-person contacts. Their goals include the promotion of women's leadership, worker-run organizations, and community empowerment through insistence on meeting basic needs including jobs, housing, health care, education, food, and peace. The holistic approach that links work place and community, food, and peace as common demands of the movement reflects the values and strategies of many movements of women in diverse cultural, political, and historical contexts.

We are witnessing exciting moments in the arena of organized labor as women join with progressive unions to craft new possibilities for community-based social movement unionism. The work of the Service Employees International Union (SEIU) in helping to organize Latino/Latina janitors in Los Angeles is especially noteworthy. As Crawford describes (1998), the business services industry—drawing on inequalities of gender, race, class, and citizenship—shifted to nonunion janitors in the early 1980s to exploit and guarantee a low-wage, unorganized workforce. Women workers were deliberately brought into the industry in an attempt to "deskill" previously unionized jobs. Latina immigrants, in particular, were concentrated in the lowest-paying service sector and factory jobs. By 1990, however, these women—brought in to maintain the low-wage unorganized structure of janitorial work—began to organize with the support of SEIU's "Justice for Janitors" campaign. By 1995, 81 percent of Los Angeles' janitors had gained union representation and higher wages. SEIU has also been instrumental in organizing thousands of domestic and health care workers. Crawford argues that the success of these efforts is due to the combination of SEIU's commitment to organizing women and immigrants; radical, community-based organizing tactics; sophisticated market research; and the past experiences of Latin American immigrants. The "Justice for Janitors" campaign also points to the possibilities that emerge when we make a commitment for the long haul and grapple with the inequalities of gender, race, class, and citizenship as they play out in our daily lives.

Dujon and Withorn and their collaborators set forth a vision of a movement to abolish poverty based on the model of the abolitionist movement. Their argument is compelling: "We love the Abolitionist Movement because it was big and brave, funky and disorganized, and accomplished a lot. For probably the widest range of people in the history of this country there was a period of time when, if you felt 'radical'—whatever that word meant to you—there was a connection" (1996, pp. 309-310). The themes and activities of the abolitionist movement have inspired them to think creatively about a multidimensional movement to abolish poverty based on popular education, direct response to material needs, and militant action. Echoing the message of the prisoners' rights movement, they address the need to build a broad-based group of allies

---

Building Community

It was so important. It was really a beautiful thing, women coming together to work together. We started small and we learned everything. We learned we were capable, we could do this. We talked and laughed and it was so special. It was a road to a new life of learning. It was a beautiful experience, working and learning together, block by block, helping each other.

Pobladora, Villa Paula Jaraquemada (Finn, n.d.)

---

with the message that when some people's basic rights are violated in a society, everyone's rights are in jeopardy. They advocate teach-ins, campus and community partnership, Survival Sanctuaries (which, like the Underground Railroad, will serve as refuges for "runaways from poverty"), and centers for community outreach and organizing. They stress the importance of the "You're next" message: we are all vulnerable. It is a vision of possibility for women's movements writ large: one that starts from the most fundamental yet unarticulated human right—the right to have rights—that recognizes the right to and potential in difference, and that looks boldly and humbly to history and to the future not with certainty but with hope.

The challenge ahead, then, lies in thinking not in terms of a single "women's movement" but in the movements of women tackling broad-based and community-connected concerns. Feminist activists can play key roles in facilitating the bridging of cross-border dialogue and solidarity among these efforts and promoting the fundamental right to have rights and the right to difference in the process. As feminists we can continue to articulate the politics of inequality central to these struggles, to critically examine the patterns that connect local struggles across cultural, national, and geographic boundaries, and to participate in direct action. A concrete commitment to participation is key here. Women on welfare face ever-increasing and exploitative demands on their time in order to "earn" their benefits. Women on the bottom of the flexible labor force work longer and longer hours under precarious conditions in their struggle to meet basic needs. Incarcerated women are increasingly dependent on aggressive advocates on the outside to give voice and visibility to their concerns in the face of the privatization of punishment and denial of basic human rights. The time and space for activism by women who live in poverty and oppression is constricted and the stakes are high. Those of us with relative freedom of movement and access to resources need to confront the complacency of privilege and lend our energies to necessary struggles, to the mundane tasks, and to the details that make a movement.

Women with access to institutional power need to appropriate the spaces afforded them to demand parity of participation and challenge the projects of whiteness and classlessness that goes without saying. Perhaps discussions of "empowerment," so popular these days, need to be tempered with a challenge to women in privileged positions: What are we willing to give up? What are we willing to risk? What borders are we willing to transgress in order to build new alliances across other borders?

Drawing on the lessons of female community builders, we need to start where we live, make a commitment for the long haul, and risk personal and political transformation. The practice of participatory teaching and learning is key. But we must go beyond a language of participation to a practice of deep play, of "guerrilla tactics" through which we stretch the boundaries, break the rules, and reconfigure the playing fields in the process. We can bring multiple technologies to bear in crafting border-crossing alliances. Advanced information technology has opened a range of possibilities for linking local struggles to global solidarity movements. At the same time, given deep systemic inequality, there is a tremendous risk for exacerbating inequities among women along the "digital divide." We can bring a practice of vigilance to bear through work for technological equity. We can engage with and document the personal and political importance of woman-to-woman, face-to-face relations and "low-tech" human action.

I close with a story of the courage and action of two women friends in northern Chile. Their husbands were executed in the early days of the Pinochet dictatorship in a systematic, state-sponsored massacre known as the "Caravan of Death." The bodies of their loved ones were believed to have been dynamited and the remains buried in the Atacama Desert. One recalled their decision to begin to search in the desert for the bodies, an open challenge to the dictatorship:

> There was a small group of us that went to the edge of town. Others were too afraid. I was so filled with fear, I could hardly move. I thought, "What if they kill me? What if my children lose their mother, too?" But I couldn't not go. In spite of our fears, I took my friend's hand and the two of us set out for the desert. We had to act. We had to say we are here and we will be here. (Finn, 1998, p. 172)

These women risked everything to position themselves directly in the face of brutality, because the power and meaning of survival dictated that they could not do otherwise. As my friend summed up her actions in the face of fear, "We women have changed the course of history in this country." It is time to join hands and follow their lead.

REFERENCES

Abramovitz, Mimi. 1988. *Regulating the Lives of Women: Social Welfare Policy from Colonial Times to the Present.* Boston: South End Press.

Ackelsberg, Martha. 1988. Communities, Resistance and Women's Activism: Some Implications for a Democratic Polity. In Ann Bookman and Sandra Morgan (Eds.), *Women and the Politics of Empowerment* (pp. 297-313). Philadelphia, PA: Temple University Press.

Alcoff, Linda. 1988. Cultural Feminism versus Post-Structuralism: The Identity Crisis in Feminist Theory. *Signs 13*(3): 405-436.

Alvarez, Sonia, Evelina Dagnino, and Arturo Escobar (Eds.). 1998. *Cultures of Politics and Politics of Cultures: Re-Visioning Latin American Social Movements.* Boulder, CO: Westview Press.

Amnesty International. 1999. *Not Part of My Sentence: Violations of the Human Rights of Women in Custody.* New York: Amnesty International USA.

Baca Zinn, Maxine. 1990. Family, Feminism and Race in America. *Gender and Society 4*(1): 68-82.

Baron, Eva (Ed.). 1991. *Work Engendered: Toward a New History of American Labor.* Ithaca, NY: Cornell University Press.

Barry, Ellen. 1999. Keynote Panel Presentation. In Christina Jose Kampfner and Jean M. Borger (Eds.), *Breaking Down the Walls: Communities in the New Millennium* (pp. 25-29). Proceedings of the Ninth National Roundtable for Women in Prison. Ann Arbor: University of Michigan Press.

Bookman, Ann and Sandra Morgen (Eds.). 1988. *Women and the Politics of Empowerment.* Philadelphia, PA: Temple University Press.

Boris, Eileen. 1995. The Racialized Gendered State: Constructions of Citizenship in the United States. *Social Politics 2*(2): 160-180.

Brewer, Rose. 1994. Race, Class, Gender and U.S. State Welfare Policy: The Nexus of Inequality of African-American Families. In Gay Young and Bette J. Dickerson (Eds.), *Color, Class and Country: Experiences of Gender* (pp. 115-127). London: Zed Books.

Butler, Judith and Joan Wallach Scott (Eds.). 1992. *Feminists Theorize the Political.* New York: Routledge.

Casa, Kathryn. 1999. Prisons: The New Growth Industry. *National Catholic Reporter 35*(33): 15-18.

Castello, Ana. 1986. The Watsonville Women's Strike: A Case of Mexicana Activism. In Ana Castello (Ed.), *Massacre of the Dreamers: Essays on Xicanisma* (pp. 43-62). Albuquerque: University of New Mexico Press.

Crawford, Cynthia. 1998. Gender and Citizenship in the Restructuring of Janitorial Work in Los Angeles. *Gender Issues 16*(4): 25-51.

Cumming, Claire and Betty Reid Mandel. 1996. Finding Voice: Building Beyond Community at Survival News. In Diane Dujon and Ann Withorn (Eds.), *For Crying Out Loud: Women's Poverty in the United States* (pp. 163-182). Boston: South End Press.

davenport, doris. 1981. The Pathology of Racism: A Conversation with Third World Wimmin. In Cherríe Moraga and Gloria Anzaldúa (Eds.), *This Bridge Called My Back: Writings by Radical Women of Color* (p. 85). Watertown, MA: Persephone Press.

Davis, Angela. 1981. *Women, Race and Class*. New York: Random House.

Davis, Angela. 1999. Keynote Panel Presentation. In Christina Jose Kampfner and Jean M. Borger (Eds.), *Breaking Down the Walls: Communities in the New Millennium* (pp. 32-38). Proceedings of the Ninth National Roundtable for Women in Prison. Ann Arbor: University of Michigan Press.

DiLeonardo, Micaela. 1991. *Gender at the Crossroads of Knowledge*. Berkeley: University of California Press.

Dujon, Diane and Ann Withorn (Eds.). 1996. *For Crying Out Loud: Women's Poverty in the United States*. Boston: South End Press.

Faue, Elizabeth. 1991. *Community of Suffering and Struggle*. Chapel Hill: University of North Carolina Press.

Ferree, Myra Marx and Patricia Yancey Martin. 1995. Doing the Work of the Movement: Feminist Organizations. In Myra Marx Ferree and Patricia Yancey Martin (Eds.), *Feminist Organizations: Harvest of the New Women's Movement* (pp. 3-23). Philadelphia: Temple University Press.

Finn, Janet. n.d. The Women of Villa Paula Jaraquemada: Building Community in Chile's Transition to Democracy. Unpublished manuscript.

Finn, Janet. 1998. *Tracing the Veins: Of Culture, Copper, and Community from Butte to Chuquicamata*. Berkeley: University of California Press.

Finn, Janet, Raquel Castellanos, Toni McOmber, and Kate Kahan. 2000. Working for Equality and Economic Opportunity: Education and Advocacy for Welfare Reform in Montana. *Affilia 15*(2): 292-308.

Finn, Janet and Lyne Underwood. 2000. The State, the Clock and the Struggle: An Inquiry into the Discipline for Welfare Reform in Montana. *Social Text 62 18*(1): 109-134.

Franco, Jean. 1998. Defrocking the Vatican: Feminism's Secular Project. In Sonia Alvarez, Evelina Dagnino, and Arturo Escobar (Eds.), *Cultures of Politics and Politics of Cultures: Re-Visioning Latin American Social Movements* (pp. 278-289). Boulder, CO: Westview Press.

Frank, Dana. 1985. Housewives, Socialists, and the Politics of Food: The 1917 Cost of Living Protests. *Feminist Studies 11*(2): 265-285.

Frank, Dana, 1991. Gender, Consumer Organizing, and the Seattle Labor Movement, 1919-1929. In Eva Baron (Ed.), *Work Engendered: Toward a New History of American Labor* (pp. 273-295). Ithaca, NY: Cornell University Press.

Fraser, Nancy. 1990. Struggle Over Needs: Outline of a Socialist-Feminist Critical Theory of Late Capitalist Political Culture. In Linda Gordon (Ed.), *Women, the State and Welfare* (pp. 199-225). Madison: University of Wisconsin Press.

Fraser, Nancy and Linda Gordon. 1994. A Genealogy of Dependency: Tracing a Keyword of the U.S. Welfare State. *Signs 19*(3): 309-336.

Gasparin, Fernando. 1998. Local Union Transformation: Analyzing Issues of Race, Gender, Class, and Democracy. *Social Justice 25*(3): 13-30.

Ginsberg, Faye. 1989. *Contested Lives: The Abortion Debate in an American Community.* Berkeley: University of California Press.

Gluck, Sherna Berger, with Maylei Blackwell, Sharon Cotrell, and Karen Harper. 1998. Whose Feminism, Whose History? Reflection on Excavating the History of (the) U.S. Women's Movement(s). In Nancy Naples (Ed.), *Community Activism and Feminist Politics: Organizing Across Race, Class and Gender* (pp. 31-56). New York: Routledge.

Gordon, Linda. 1988. *Heroes of Their Own Lives: The Politics and History of Family Violence, 1880-1960.* New York: Viking.

Gordon, Linda (Ed.). 1990. *Women, the State and Welfare.* Madison: University of Wisconsin Press.

Gordon, Linda, 1991. Black and White Visions of Welfare: Women's Welfare Activism, 1890-1945. *Journal of American History 78*(2): 559-590.

Gordon, Linda, 1994. *Pitied But Not Entitled: Single Mothers and the History of Welfare.* New York: Free Press.

Gunn Allen, Paula. 1995. Angry Women Are Building: Issues and Struggles Facing American Indian Women Today. In Margaret Anderson and Patricia Hill Collins (Eds.), *Race, Class and Gender: An Anthology* (pp. 32-36). Belmont, CA: Wadsworth Publishing.

Guzman Bouvard, Marguerite. 1994. *Revolutionizing Motherhood: The Mothers of the Plaza de Mayo.* Wilmington, DE: Scholarly Resources.

Haraway, Donna. 1988. Situated Knowledges: The Science Question in Feminism and the Privilege of Partial Perspective. *Feminist Studies 14*(3): 575-599.

Harding, Sandra. 1986. *The Science Question in Feminism.* Ithaca, NY: Cornell University Press.

Harvey, David. 2000. *Spaces of Hope.* Berkeley: University of California Press.

Hill Collins, Patricia. 1990. *Black Feminist Thought: Knowledge, Consciousness, and the Politics of Empowerment.* New York: Unwin Hyman.

hooks, bell. 1984. *Feminist Theory from Margin to Center.* Boston, MA: South End Press.

Hull, Gloria, Patricia Bell Scot, and Barbara Smith (Eds.). 1982. *All the Women Are White, All the Blacks Are Men, But Some of Us Are Brave.* Old Westbury, NY: Feminist Press.

Hurtado, Aida. 1996. *The Color of Privilege: Three Blasphemies on Race and Feminism.* Ann Arbor: University of Michigan Press.

Hyde, Cheryl. 1992. The Ideational System of Social Movement Agencies: An Examination of Feminist Health Centers. In Yeheskel Hasenfeld (Ed.), *Human Services As Complex Organizations* (pp. 121-144). Newbury Park, CA: Sage.

Jaggar, Alison. 1983. *Feminist Politics and Human Nature.* Totowa, NJ: Rowman and Allenheld.

Jelin, Elizabeth and Eric Hershberg (Eds.). 1996. *Constructing Democracy: Human Rights, Citizenship, and Society in Latin America.* Boulder, CO: Westview Press.

Jones, Jacqueline. 1985. *Labor of Love, Labor of Sorrow: Black Women, Work and the Family, from Slavery to the Present.* New York: Vintage Books.

Kaplan, Temma. 1982. Female Consciousness and Collective Action: Barcelona, 1910-1918. *Signs* 7(3): 545-565.

Kelly, Anthony and Sandra Sewell. 1988. *With Head, Heart and Hand: Dimensions of Community Building.* Brisbane, Australia: Boolarong Press.

Kessler-Harris, Alice. 1982. *Out to Work: A History of Wage-Earning Women in the United States.* New York: Oxford University Press.

Kingsolver, Barbara. 1989. *Holding the Line: Women in the Great Arizona Mine Strike of 1983.* Ithaca, NY: ILR Press.

Kramer, Marian. 1996. Speaking for Ourselves: A Lifetime of Welfare Rights Organizing. In Diane Dujon and Ann Withorn (Eds.), *For Crying Out Loud: Women's Poverty in the United States* (pp. 355-366). Boston: South End Press.

La Mujer Obrera (The woman worker). 1999. Available online: <http://www.mujerobrera.org>, continually updated. Date of access: 2001.

Lerner, Gerda. 1972. *Black Women in White America: A Documentary History.* New York: Pantheon.

Levins, Morales, Aurora. 1981. . . . And Even Fidel Can't Change That! In Cherríe Moraga and Gloria Anzaldua (Eds.), *The Bridge Called My Back* (pp. 53-56). New York: Kitchen Table/Women of Color Press.

Milkman, Ruth (Ed.). 1985. *Women, Work, and Protest: A Century of U.S. Women's Labor History.* New York: Routledge and Kegan Paul.

Mink, Gwendolyn. 1995. *The Wages of Motherhood: Inequality in the Welfare State, 1917-1942.* Ithaca, NY: Cornell University Press.

Mohanty, Chandra Talpade. 1991. Under Western Eyes: Feminist Scholarship and Colonial Discourses. In Chandra Talpade Mohanty, Ana Russo, and Lourdes Torres (Eds.), *Third World Women and the Politics of Feminism,* (pp. 51-80). Bloomington: Indiana University Press.

Moraga, Cherríe. 1986. From a Long Line of Vendidas: Chicanas and Feminism. In Teresa de Lauretis *Feminist Studies: Critical Studies* (pp. 173-190). Bloomington: Indiana University Press.

Moser, Caroline. 1987. Mobilization Is Women's Work: Struggles for Infrastructure in Quayaquil, Ecuador. In Caroline Moser and Linda Peake (Eds.), *Women, Human Settlements, and Housing* (pp. 166-194). London: Tavistock.

Naples, Nancy. 1991. Just What Is Needed to Be Done: The Political Practice of Women Community Workers in Low-Income Neighborhoods. *Gender and Society* 5(4): 478-494.

Naples, Nancy. (Ed.). 1998a. *Community Activism and Feminist Politics. Organizing Across Race, Class, and Gender.* New York: Routledge.

Naples, Nancy, 1998b. *Grassroots Warriors: Activist Mothering, Community Work, and the War on Poverty.* New York: Routledge.

Nash, June. 1979. *We Eat the Mines and the Mines Eat Us: Dependency and Exploitation in Bolivian Tin Mines.* New York: Columbia University Press.

Nash, June. 1994. Global Integration and Subsistence Insecurity. *American Anthropologist* 96(1): 7-30.

Ortner, Sherry and Harriett Whitehead (Eds.). 1981. *Sexual Meanings: The Cultural Construction of Gender and Sexuality.* New York: Cambridge University Press.

Pardo, Mary. 1998. Creating Community: Mexican American Women in Eastside Los Angeles. In Nancy Naples (Ed.), *Community Activism and Feminist Politics: Organizing across Race, Class and Gender* (pp. 275-300). New York: Routledge.

Paul, Eileen. 1993. The Women's Movement and the Movement of Women. *Social Policy 23*(4): 44-50.

Piven, Frances Fox. 1990. Ideology and the State: Women, Power and the Welfare State. In Linda Gordon (Ed.), *Women, the State, and Welfare* (pp. 250-264). Madison: University of Wisconsin Press.

Piven, Frances Fox and Richard Cloward. 1997. *The Breaking of the American Social Compact.* New York: New Press.

Quadagno, Jill. 1994. *The Color of Welfare: How Racism Undermined the War on Poverty.* New York: Oxford University Press.

Richie, Beth. 1996. *Compelled to Crime: The Gender Entrapment of Battered Black Women.* New York: Routledge and Kegan Paul.

Richie, Beth and Sue Osthoff. 1999. The Battered Women's Movement and Prisoners' Rights Movements: How to Increase Effective Collaboration. In Christina Jose Kampfner and Jean M. Borger (Eds.), *Breaking Down the Walls: Communities in the New Millennium* (pp. 158-162). Proceedings from the Ninth National Roundtable for Women in Prison. Ann Arbor: University of Michigan Press.

Rosaldo, Michelle and Louise Lamphere (Eds.). 1974. *Women, Culture, and Society.* Stanford, CT: Stanford University Press.

Schild, Veronica. 1995. NGOs, Feminist Politics and Neo-Liberal Latin American State Formations: Some Lessons from Chile. *Canadian Journal of Development Studies* (Special Issue): 123-147.

Schild, Veronica. 1998. New Subjects of Rights? Women's Movements and the Construction of Citizenship in the "New Democracies." In Sonia Alvarez, Evelina Dagnino, and Arturo Escobar (Eds.), *Cultures of Politics and Politics of Cultures: Re-Visioning Latin American Social Movements* (pp. 93-117). Boulder, CO: Westview Press.

Sidel, Ruth. 1986. *Women and Children Last: The Plight of Poor Women in Affluent America.* New York: Viking Penguin.

Skocpol, Theda. 1992. *Protecting Soldiers and Mothers: The Political Origins of Social Policy in the United States.* Cambridge, MA: Belknap Press of Harvard University Press.

Smith, Dorothy. 1987. *The Everyday World As Problematic: A Feminist Sociology.* Toronto: University of Toronto Press.

Stack, Carol. 1974. *All Our Kin: Strategies for Survival in the Black Community.* New York: Harper and Rowe.

Stall, Susan and Randy Stoecker. 1998. Community Organizing or Organizing Community? Gender and the Crafts of Empowerment. *Gender and Society 12* (6): 729-756.

Stephen, Lynn. 1997. *Women and Social Movements in Latin America: Power from Below.* Austin: University of Texas Press.

Strathern, M. 1988. *The Gender of the Gift.* Berkeley: University of California Press.

Taylor, Verta and Nancy Whittier. 1998. Guest Editors' Introduction: Special Issue on Gender and Social Movements. Part 1. *Gender and Society 12*(6): 622-626.

Thornton Dill, Bonnie. 1994. *Across the Boundaries of Race and Class: An Exploration of Work and Family Among Black Female Domestic Servants.* New York: Garland.

Tillmon, Johnnie. 1976. Welfare Is a Women's Issue. *Liberation News Service 415* (February 26, 1972). Reprinted in Rosalyn Baxandall, Linda Gordon, and Susan Reverby (Eds.), *America's Working Women: A Documentary History, 1600 to the Present* (pp. 354-359). New York: Vintage Books.

Valdés, Teresa and Marisa Weinstein. 1993. *Mujeres que Suenan: Las Organizaciones de Pobladoras en Chile: 1973-1989.* Santiago de Chile: Facultad Latino Americana de Ciencias Sociales.

Williams, Raymond. 1977. *Marxism and Literature.* Oxford: Oxford University Press.

Williams, Rhonda and Carla Peterson. 1998. The Color of Memory: Interpreting Twentieth Century U.S. Social Policy from a Nineteenth Century Perspective. *Feminist Studies 24*(1): 7-25.

Wilson, Maureen and Elizabeth Whitmore. 1995. Accompanying the Process: Social Work and International Development Practice. *Canadian Journal of Development Studies* Special Issue (1): 57-74.

Yeager, Gertrude M. 1994. *Confronting Change, Challenging Tradition: Women in Latin American History.* Wilmington, DE: Scholarly Resources.

Young, Eva and Mariwilda Padilla. 1990. *Mujeres Unidas en Accion*: A Popular Education Process. *Harvard Educational Review 60*(1): 1-18.

Zavella, Patricia. 1987. *Women's Work and Chicano Families.* Ithaca, NY: Cornell University Press.

SECTION VI:
ACTION STRATEGIES FOR TODAY

The Beauty Out There, Nancy Jean King
Exhibited at the Fourth Annual Exhibition of Art by Michigan Prisoners, February
9-25, 1999, University of Michigan, Rackham Galleries.

Chapter 17

Whither the Twenty-First Century for Women at the Margins: Resistance and Action

Rosemary C. Sarri
Josefina Figueira-McDonough

When we decided to write *Women at the Margins* and sought the assistance of the authors who have contributed to the several issues addressed in this book, we had several goals in mind. First, we wished to show that the public control of poor and imprisoned women cannot be understood without taking into consideration the effects that policies of the welfare and justice systems have on them. These policies force women to make decisions that are often contrary to their best interests. When faced with caregiving responsibilities, their options for employment are constrained because of the lack of essential supportive services. These policies also do not assure sustainable wages and require that workers organize to secure "living wages."

Second, we wished to describe and analyze how these two systems jeopardize poor women through their ideologies, policies, and practices. The two systems are closely interlinked even though they operate independently of each other, so it is useful to examine their interface. The decline in public assistance support for poor women and children since the 1980s is correlated with the continuing rise in the population of women under the control of the criminal justice system in jail, on probation, or in prison. Beckett and Western (1999) point out that institutional responses to deviance depend upon how deviance is defined in public policy. Policies can attempt to integrate persons into the society or they can serve to exclude them. Since the 1980s the response to the public assistance needs of poor women has been to exclude them and create the conditions whereby many then entered the justice system. As the proportion of the public assistance population was increasingly women of color, incarceration rates for them increased to where they are now eight times those of white women (Beck, 2000).

Third, we wished to expose the contradictions that have developed between policies and practices in a variety of organizational contexts. The so-called welfare reform of 1996 was promoted as policy that would enable women to have successful employment careers and serve as positive role models for their children. In reality, the practices that were implemented in most states made little provision for caregiving, education, and necessary work-related expenses. Moreover, it was generally accepted that minimum wages would be common even when it was clear that such wages would not produce even poverty-level income for a family. In the case of women in prison, drug policies put them in prison where there is usually no treatment programs for substance abuse.

Fourth, and perhaps most important, we wanted to make poor and marginalized women visible through their stories, art, and work. In this way we can gain greater understanding of their perceptions of their experiences and their lives. We hope to expose and contest the "politics of invisibility and silencing" as those in authority reproduce and justify the marginalization. Women on welfare and in prison are both exploited and blamed as we seek to make clear distinctions between "us" and "them." Only by listening to them or seeing their art do we gain understanding and empathy. Lastly, we wanted to bring greater awareness to the public about these women, their needs, and their problems, along with the factors that influence their lives. Both the general public and many in the professional community are uninformed about the needs of these women because they have so little direct contact with them. All too often the public is primarily informed about them through stereotyped stories by the media. Thus, the sanctioned ignorance serves to maintain and justify the gendered systems of inequality.

CONTEMPORARY AND CONFLICTING ROLES

Women fulfill critical roles in society as workers, mothers, daughters, and citizens. Multiple binds are at work as women attempt to meet the demands of these various roles. Yet they are often denigrated and punished for their performance of these roles given the various situations in which many women find themselves. Moreover, criteria for the performance of their roles are arbitrarily imposed by others, and they have no opportunity to express their reaction or obtain clarification. Few if any attempts have been made to measure achievement in terms of criteria that are feasible for the requirements that they must meet (child care, housing, health care, employment, taxes). Some policies governing poor women and women in prison attribute deviance to these women in the ways that they perform their vital roles and place emphasis on family responsibilities. On the other hand, middle-class women may be commended for prioritizing these roles as necessary for stable families and effective child rearing. However, they face difficulties in managing their conflicting roles as recent new accounts report that female executives are often handicapped by child care and other family responsibilities, while male executives seldom experience such problems. Women of color often must negotiate these conflicting demands within racialized and gendered systems of inequality. Women of color face dilemmas in the conflicts they experience in identifying with their group of color versus identification as women. The feminist movement has not aided in resolving these dilemmas, which may be one of the reasons for the rift between white women and women of color. The incoherence of policies dealing with poor women and offenders is overlooked by attributing their failure to the dependent and deviant behavior of the women (Fraser and Gordon, 1994).

Women need a variety of options in order to fulfill family roles, employment roles, and citizen roles. These are not tasks that can be resolved without policies providing child and health care, family leave, pay equity, adequate housing, continuing education, and sufficient time to meet essential citizen role requirements (Ackelsberg, 1988). Many decry the absence of community volunteers to perform tasks that are needed, but working-class women lack the needed time to volunteer. In addition, many must be caregivers to elderly members of their families. To date, the United States has lagged behind many Western countries in the provision of both financial and social supports essential for effective family caregiving. In Sweden, custodial mothers receive incentives to work less than full-time so that they will have sufficient time to care for their children (Rosenthal, 1990). A study of cross-national comparisons with respect to family support, financial assistance, and adequate employment benefits can provide options that will meet needs in the United States (Goldberg and Kremen, 1990). The Scandinavian model of social welfare developed by Alva Myrdal (1941) and others placed the "solo mother" at the center of the policy that was focused on increasing children's well-being and achieving greater equality for women. All indicators suggest that the Scandinavian model has achieved its goals to a substantial extent. Scandinavian children rank among the highest in the world on indicators of well-being, yet both parents have high levels of participation in the workforce. The state shares with the family responsibility for children's well-being. However, in the United States, as a society we express concern and pity about the plight of poor single mothers, but we eliminate the entitlements that could provide for them (Gordon, 1994).

During the 1990s, employment opportunities increased for low-income women, but most of the jobs provided wages well below the poverty level for the family and also lacked the provision of needed benefits. Needed is a national commitment to helping poor women to leave poverty, not just to go to work (Schein, 1995). In the voices of poor women, Schein (1995) poignantly reminds us why poverty reduction is the critical goal for these women and their children, and why welfare reform must be approached from a comprehensive perspective, not just as a strategy to reduce welfare rolls and get women to work regardless of the costs. Federal welfare policies promoting marriage as a solution to the problems of poor children and their mothers are discriminatory and unlikely to succeed when they do not address cause of poverty. Among persons of color, the incarceration of a high percentage of young men of color is another important constraint, as William Julius Wilson has observed (1987). The abolitionist movement by Massachusetts women to eliminate poverty reflects that poor women view poverty as an important detriment to family well-being (Dujon and Withorn, 1996).

RECOMMENDATIONS FOR ACTION

Each of the contributors in this book points to the need for activism for and by marginalized women. Although the feminist movement has often ignored this victimized and shunned population, it is clear that there are many alternative ways in which significant changes can be effected. MacAdoo (Chapter 4) points to the particular needs of arguably the most marginalized women, African-American women and other women of color. She emphasizes the need to address issues of diversity, discrimination, and integration. Handler, Whitley and Dressel, Pearce, and Luna and Figueira-McDonough (Chapters 2, 5, 6, and 14, respectively) all emphasize the need for activism to change the orientation of existing welfare and public assistance policy to focus on poverty alleviation, commitment to the development of women's human capital, education, affirmative action and living wages, and health and child care. The primary emphasis on reducing welfare rolls through requiring women to work without qualification resulted in many unexpected problems for these women and their children, such as substance abuse, petty crime, and so forth, as they struggle to survive with little means to do so. Recently, we have become acutely aware of the risk situation for school-age children because of lack of any after-school supervision. It is estimated that only one in five kindergarten through eighth grade children participate in any after-school program (Capizzano, Tout, and Adams, 2000). It is not surprising, therefore, that 3:00 p.m. to 9:00 p.m. is the peak period for delinquency by this group.

Walruff emphasizes the need for special programming for teen mothers, a population that has been ignored or said to be almost eliminated by pregnancy reduction policies. The simplistic approach of threatening these young women with no assistance unless they live at home or with a supervising adult ignores the fact that these young women are often abused in that home or are told to leave. Research findings document negative outcomes for these women and for their children unless they receive substantial support and assistance during their early years of parenting. Juvenile institutions for female delinquents are populated by many of these pregnant and parenting teens while their children are placed in foster care. Thus, another generation of children grows up with high probabilities of serious problems (Maynard, 1997).

Recommendations to change the criminal justice system for women are the focus of several of our contributors. Flynn (Chapter 9) particularly calls for action to help a group ignored by almost everyone: older women in prison. Many of these older women have had no previous involvement in the criminal justice system, but they have been given long sentences for spouse homicide even though they were usually the victims of domestic violence which resulted in the perpetration of violence. In prison they seldom if ever receive help in addressing their problems regarding domestic violence. Bortner, Ascione, and Dixson (Chapters 11 and 12) call for local and state efforts to provide services and support for incarcerated women and their children, another population largely ignored until recently. The rise in the incarceration of women has meant that their children often go unattended by the child welfare system, perhaps an unintended consequence of the reduction of the public assistance formerly available to their mothers. Without services these children frequently end up in the foster care, mental health, or prison systems, but these latter costs are never publicly acknowledged. Pimlott and Sarri and Burke (Chapters 3 and 8) call for action to change drug policy if the numbers of women in the criminal justice system are to be reduced. O'Brien and Harm (Chapter 13) call attention to what is perhaps the greatest failure of the criminal justice system: the lack of supportive services for reintegration and reunification of offenders with the family and community. Along with Naples (1998), Barry (1999), and Davis (1999), they speak of the need for massive community grassroots and self-help efforts if these policies are going to be changed, given the levels of resistance in the United States. It is probable that the dramatic growth in the incarceration of women will be arrested only with concerted efforts from the larger community. LaBelle's (Chapter 15) analysis of several major issues affecting women in prison (education, legal services, protection from sexual assault by staff, and family visitation) provides us with ways in which defense attorneys can make major inroads in improving the conditions of incarceration. She notes that the United States has almost ignored and refuses to rat-ify UN Conventions on Human Rights as well as international law govern-ing prison conditions, executions, the comingling of juvenile females with adult female offenders, family visitation, and many other provisions (Am-nesty International, 1999; Human Rights Watch, 1999).

Housing is increasingly a basic need, but, as Mulroy (Chapter 7) points out, it is often unattainable because of the absolute lack of low-cost housing and because of the insufficient income of many women to even pay the rent in low-cost housing. She notes that policies that give Section 8 vouchers for women needing housing provide only a "ticket to roam." She calls for action at multiple levels, from grassroots organizations to state and federal agen-cies, if the serious problem of the lack of housing is to be alleviated.

How then can we begin to bring about positive changes in the systems governing the lives of marginalized women?

Janet Finn (Chapter 16) proposes a comprehensive approach to commu-nity building among groups and within the feminist movement as the key strategy for successful change. She shows that the strategy of building bridges between groups can extend beyond U.S. borders to the international community of women. As at other times when major social change is under way, active involvement is required of the public, professionals, local com-munities most affected by current policies, and the women most impacted by these policies. Just as the majority of women seek full equality, mar-ginalized women are entitled to be full citizens of society in all that it im-plies. In promoting such changes, we must be aware of the resistances in so-ciety. What are those elements and how can some be overcome and others built upon?

We must publicize the distorted ideologies that shaped policies and prac-tices which produce situations that are contrary to women's and communi-ties' needs. Because of the unquestioned acceptance of the ideology of indi-vidualism, professionals often attribute to individuals pathologies that are the result of discrimination, inequality, and ignorance about poor women's actual needs (Mink, 1995). Most of the workers in public assistance are paraprofessionals with the primary goal of getting women off welfare and to work. Little understanding exists of the constraints that women face when trying to meet the numerous responsibilities that are thrust upon them. Nei-ther these agencies nor the media attempt to inform the public about results of evaluations that show how ineffective these welfare policy changes have been since 1996 (Morgen, Acker, and Heath, 2001; Loprest, 1999; Sweeney, 2001; U.S. Conference of Mayors, 2001). There are many studies which show that women leaving welfare do not improve their economic, housing, health care, or child care situations, but the findings from these studies need more widespread publicity. The numbers of poor women with children who are homeless and seeking shelter has continued to rise since the passage of the Personal Responsibility and Work Opportunity Reconciliation Act of 1996 (PRWORA) despite the vastly improved economy that supposedly provided "adequate" income for all workers (Bernstein, 2001). The situation of poor women leaving welfare is magnified several times by women in prison, but this is the group most ignored by all of "us." Because prisons severely restrict visitation by relatives, friends, or the public, very few have any idea of what really goes on in prison. When women leave prison, they lack community supports that are essential for their reintegration into appropriate roles so that they can assume their adult responsibilities. Thus, they suffer in both situations and are rejected when they reach out for legitimate support.

ACTION STRATEGIES

Which groups can bring meaning and vitality to the "call for action"?

Strategies from the Grass Roots

First of all, there are marginalized women themselves, as hooks (1984) suggested in another context, but they can be helped to transgress what seems to be inevitable for them. Since the 1960s, welfare rights organizations have been actively fighting for policies and programs to benefit poor women and to establish essential public welfare programs. Such groups include the Kensington Rights Group, University of the Poor, and the Westside Mothers' Club described by activist and welfare mother Marion Kramer (1996). Diane Dujon and Ann Withorn (1996) describe the many interrelated grassroots organizations in Massachusetts that have effectively fought for rights and benefits in that state. As I write, the Westside Mothers' Club in Detroit has sued the director of community health in the federal court in Michigan (*Westside Mothers v. Haveman* No. 99-734442, E.D. Mich.) to secure Medicaid monies for the provision of mental health services to their children. Surgeon General David Sacher's National Action Agenda for Children's Mental Health recommended provision of these services for the Medicaid eligible population, but Michigan refuses to implement fully those recommendations (Sacher, 2000). However, the suit by a welfare mothers' group may be more effective than efforts by the professional and administrative community.

Although their efforts are visible only to a few, there is a growing prisoners' rights movement in many states. For many years female prisoners seldom challenged their treatment or conditions in prison other than on an individual basis. Such individual action resulted only in segregation and punishment. The National Roundtable for Women in Prison brings women prisoners, advocates, and professionals together biennially to discuss strategies for policy changes affecting women in the criminal justice system. It has been an important mechanism for change in corrections policy and programs involving women in several states. Women tolerated great abuse, but since the late 1970s they have been spurred to action by civil liberties defense attorneys such as Deborah LaBelle. These efforts have been partially successful in improving family visitation, health care, education, and sexual assault and harassment. Women's efforts often differ considerably from the male collective resistance that often erupts in violence. Rather, female prisoners have sought action and support from external groups through class-action suits. Since such suits often require courageous action by one or a few prisoners, they must accept the costs that are attendant upon such action. Women petitioners often endure arbitrary authority, denigration and punishment from prison staff, greatly increased length of sentence because of negative parole board action, and isolation within the prison. Nonetheless, they have persisted and increasingly are organizing to effect change.

Characteristic of all of these activities by marginalized women is that they become aware of their rights and are willing to advocate for them (Naples, 1998). As Friere (1978) notes in his advocacy strategies for building critical consciousness by oppressed groups, women must come to recognize their oppression and be willing to struggle if they are to be successful in achieving their goals. Collaborators must respect their knowledge, their description of reality, and their perspectives on causes and correlates of their status. The biennial National Roundtable for Women in Prison provides opportunities for female offenders and community groups of lay and professional women to work together to address concerns of women in prison (Borger, 1999).

Building Collaboration

Solidary action by groups with and on behalf of women to build bridges for effective action continues to grow and has had many positive outcomes for once-marginalized women. William Alexander and a group of University of Michigan colleagues and students have promoted the development of theater groups in both female and male prisons. He and Phyllis Kornfeld have promoted opportunities for artists to be trained and have a place to display their art. Many of the paintings and drawings displayed in this book are the result of their efforts, as described by Deborah Zinn in the Introduction.

Other groups who have worked collaboratively with women in prison to effect changes or provide benefits include the American Friends Service Committee, Unitarian Universalist Service Appeal, Citizens United for the Rehabilitation of Errants (CURE), and many religious organizations. One organization that began locally and is now national is Families Against Mandatory Minimums (FAMM). This group grew rapidly when family members of prisoners and their friends recognized that they had more influence as an organized group. It has become a large organization that has not only been effective in individual cases but also in class actions and legislation, especially with respect to sentence reduction in drug-related cases (FAMMGRAM, 2000).

The Critical Resistance movement initiated by Angela Davis (1999) and Ellen Barry (1999) have stimulated action and interest across the United States to challenge the prison industrial complex, especially the growth in privatization and issues of minority overrepresentation. In the case of women who are or have been welfare recipients or are in need of financial assistance there have been many collaborations with community groups throughout the country to advance programs for education, child care, health care, and housing. Their work has been aided by organizations such as the Service Employees International Union (SEIU), which focuses much of its organizing on immigrants, women of color, and other low-income women working in nursing homes, building maintenance, child care, and as paraprofessionals in health care. They have organized workfare recipients in a joint program with public employers who subsequently assist them in enrolling in community colleges to improve their skills so that they can move beyond entry level positions. SEIU emphasizes the need for broad community action to advance those in the service industries. From their participation in the activities of unions many women have come to occupy leadership positions in their communities. Unions have probably been the most effective group in raising wages and benefits for low-income working women.

Targeting Policies

Increasing numbers of national and local advocacy organizations are effective in social change and policy development on behalf of and/or with marginalized women, but more unified and concerted action is called for. These groups include Amnesty International, Human Rights Watch, Planned Parenthood, Institute for Policy Research on Women, the Urban Institute, the Center for Budget Priorities, and numerous other policy research groups. Organizations that target policies from more of a policy advocacy perspective for women include: Network, Children's Defense Fund, LaRaza, NAACP, the Older Women's League, Kids Count, along with many local and state organizations that are working for policy change. The efforts to secure postsecondary education for poor women and prisoners have operated largely at the state level because of the TANF provisions that provide for state options to find alternative ways in which the work requirement can be fulfilled. Similar efforts to secure access to higher education for female prisoners result primarily from class-action suits and the work of local higher education organizations and students.

Piven (2001) points out that although TANF and other programs have reduced public support for poor women and children, this may be the time to organize group action by the poor and their supporters. She outlines a multilevel strategy that includes women, children, advocates, professionals, and the press to promote dignity and justice for all. We are reminded that in the past half-century major changes have occurred in family structure so that more egalitarian structures and processes exist. Educational opportunities have grown, as have labor-market participation, affirmative action, and family leaves. Engagement in politics characterizes the situation today far more than a couple of decades ago. Government has assumed greater responsibility for the well-being of women with children, although we have had major setbacks in the 1980s and 1990s with the reduction in entitlement programs and increased pressure to be in the labor force but without provision for child care or health care. The present picture of the status of women at the margins appears problematic and negative when compared with that of "mainstream" women. Nonetheless, it is unusual but not impossible for poor women, including women of color, to be elected to local state or national office and thus to be in a position of substantial policy leadership. Many gender-related laws that have been passed were authored by women legislators, so the payoff from their activity is apparent. The efforts of women's organizations such as the National Women's Political Caucus, Emily's List, and the American Association of University Women have paid off in the increased election of women legislators at both the state and national levels.

Voluntary associations and informal community groups must be able to access information readily and have training in how it can be effectively utilized in promoting programs and policies, and in critiquing or opposing harmful policies and programs. The Internet, electronic mail, and other information technologies can be available, but people must be effectively trained if they are to be utilized in the policy advocacy or monitoring processes. Of at least equal importance is access for poor women and prisoners to use electronic media themselves. Women have established online Internet "chat rooms" between states and countries to inform each other about steps that can be taken. These groups can also provide social support for women.

Lastly, the print, television, and radio media all need to be mobilized and utilized effectively if the public is to have information other than the stereotypic negative information that is common today about poor women and female prisoners. Hearing the stories of women's experiences and situations can be compelling for the general public, for legislators and law enforcement officials, and for professional human service workers. Such information has been seriously lacking in the past few decades.

In conclusion, it is our hope that this book will provide women in various careers, statuses, and situations with information and analyses that can be utilized in promoting the well-being of all women. Such an approach could also result in a more inclusive integrationist approach in contrast to our present criminal justice policies which are directed toward excluding poor women and women of color. Welfare policies in the United States, with the exception of Social Security, have been means-tested and limited to the lowest income population. Given the situation today in which many middle-class families cannot meet the costs of health care, child care, education for themselves, and even costs of housing in some communities, it is appropriate to consider the development of welfare programs that provide support to everyone (Myrdal, 1941; Gordon, 1994). Such universal programs are likely to generate much wider public support as they have in many other Western countries.

REFERENCES

Ackelsberg, Martha. 1988. Communities, Resistance and Women's Activism: Some Implications for a Democratic Polity. In Ann Bookman and Sandra Morgan (Eds.), *Women and the Politics of Empowerment* (pp. 297-313). Philadelphia, PA: Temple University Press.

Amnesty International. 1999. *United States of America: Not Part of My Sentence: Violations of the Human Rights of Women in Custody*. New York: Amnesty International.

Barry, Ellen. 1999. Keynote Panel Presentation. In Christina Jose Kampfner and Jean M. Borger (Eds.), *Breaking Down the Walls: Communities in the New Millennium* (pp. 25-29). Proceedings of the Ninth National Roundtable for Women in Prison. Ann Arbor: University of Michigan Press.

Beck, Allen J. 2000. *Prison and Jail Inmates at Midyear 1999*. Washington, DC: U.S. Department of Justice, Office of Justice Programs.

Beckett, Katherine and Bernard Western. 1999. The Institutional Sources of Incarceration: Deviance, Regulation and the Transformation of State Policy. Presented at the American Society of Criminology Annual Meeting, Toronto, Canada.

Bernstein, Nina. 2001. Shelter Population Reaches Highest Level Since 1980s. *The New York Times*, February 8, p. 27.

Borger, J. (Ed.). 1999. *Breaking Down the Walls: Communities in the New Millennium.* Proceedings of the Ninth National Roundtable of Women in Prison. Ann Arbor: University of Michigan.

Capizzano, Jeffrey, Tout, Kathryn, and Adams, Gina. 2000. *Child Care Patterns of School-Age Children with Employed Mothers.* Washington, DC: Urban Institute.

Davis, Angela. 1999. Keynote Panel Presentation. In Christina Jose Kampfner and Jean M. Borger (Eds.), *Breaking Down the Walls: Communities in the New Millennium* (pp. 32-38). Proceedings of the Ninth National Roundtable for Women in Prison. Ann Arbor: University of Michigan Press.

Dujon, Diane and Ann Withorn (Eds.). 1996. *For Crying Out Loud: Women's Poverty in the United States.* Boston: South End Press.

FAMMGRAM. 2000. 1,800 Eligible for Sentence Reductions. *FAMMGRAM 3*(1): 1-9.

Fraser, Nancy and Linda Gordon. 1994. A Genealogy of Dependency: Tracing a Keyword of the U.S. Welfare State. *Signs 19*(3): 309-336.

Friere, Paolo. 1978. *Education for Critical Consciousness.* New York: Seabury Press.

Goldberg, Gertrude S. and Eleanor Kremen. 1990. *The Feminization of Poverty: Only in America?* New York: Praeger.

Gordon, Linda. 1994. *Pitied But Not Entitled: Single Mothers and the History of Welfare.* New York: Free Press.

hooks, bell. 1984. *Feminist Theory from Margin to Center.* Boston: South End Press.

Human Rights Watch. 1999. *No Place to Hide.* New York: Human Rights Watch.

Kramer, Marian. 1996. Speaking for Ourselves: A Lifetime of Welfare Rights Organizing. In Diane Dujon and Ann Withorn (Eds.), *For Crying Out Loud: Women's Poverty in the United States* (pp. 355-366). Boston: South End Press.

Loprest, Pamela. 1999. *Families Who Left Welfare: Who Are They and How Are They Doing?* Discussion Paper 99-02. Washington, DC: The Urban Institute.

Maynard, Rebecca A. 1997. *Kids Having Kids: Economic Costs and Social Consequences of Teen Pregnancy.* Washington, DC: Urban Institute Press.

Mink, Gwendolyn. 1995. *The Wages of Motherhood: Inequality in the Welfare State, 1917-1942.* Ithaca, NY: Cornell University Press.

Morgen, Sandra, Joan Acker, and Tony Heath. 2001. *Welfare Reform Outcomes in Oregon.* Eugene: University of Oregon, Center for the Study of Women in Society.

Myrdal, Alva R. 1941. *Nation and Family—The Swedish Experiment in Democratic Family and Population Policy.* New York: Harper.

Naples, Nancy (Ed.). 1998. *Community Activism and Feminist Politics. Organizing across Race, Class, and Gender.* New York: Routledge.

Piven, Frances F. 2001. Welfare: What Is to Be. *Social Policy 32*(1): 40-44.

Rosenthal, Marilyn. 1990. Sweden: Promise and Paradox. In Gertrude Goldberg and Eleanor Kremen *The Feminization of Poverty: Only in America?* (pp. 129-156). New York: Praeger.

Sacher, David. 2000. *National Action Agenda for Children's Mental Health.* Washington, DC: U.S. Department of Health and Human Services, Office of the Surgeon General.

Schein, Virginia E. 1995. *Working from the Margins: Voice of Mothers in Poverty.* Ithaca, NY: Cornell University Press.

Sweeney, Eileen. 2001. *Windows of Opportunity: Strategies to Support Low-Income Families in the Next Stage of Welfare Reform.* Washington, DC: Center for Budget and Policy Priorities.

U.S. Conference of Mayors. 2001. *Hunger and Homelessness in American Cities.* Washington, DC: U.S. Conference of Mayors.

Wilson, William J. 1987. *The Truly Disadvantaged.* Chicago: University of Chicago Press.

Index

Abortion
    by prisoners, 261
    reproductive choice, 389-390
    by teenagers, 232-233, 237
Abstinence Education Provision, 231
Abuse of female offenders, 71
Action recommendations, 410-413
Activist mothering, 383, 391, 393
"Addiction careers," 181-183
Adolescent development and policy,
    236-237
Adoption and Safe Families Act of 1997
    (ASFA), 278, 279-280, 289, 290
Advocacy groups for policy changes,
    415-416
AFDC. *See* Aid to Families with
    Dependent Children
African-American women
    containment, 107
    cultural legacies, 91
    demographics, 92
    employment, 92, 96-97
    family structure, 93-94
    marginalization of, 21, 87-90, 97
    parenting in Africa, 91
    roles of males, 94-95
    slavery, 91
    urban sprawl, 95-96
Aftercare for released prisoners,
    308-310, 311, 312
After-school supervision, 410
Age. *See* Older women
"Aging-out effect" of older female
    offenders, 222
Aid to Dependent Children (ADC), 11,
    34
Aid to Families with Dependent Children
    (AFDC). *See also* Temporary
    Assistance to Needy Families
    autonomy of women, 13
    contradictions of, 12
    delegation of program to states, 322
    history of, 8-9, 33, 34, 110

Aid to Families with Dependent
    Children *(continued)*
    improved benefits in 1960s-1970s,
    324
    price indexing, 11
    teenage mothers, 234
Alcohol abuse, 67, 178-180. *See also*
    Drug abuse; Substance abuse
    by female offenders
*All Too Familiar, Sexual Abuse of
    Women Prisoners in U.S.
    State Prisons* report, 359
American model of welfare, 337-340
Amnesty International, 76, 77
AOD (alcohol and other drugs), 175.
    See also Alcohol abuse; Drug
    abuse; Substance abuse by
    female offenders
Argentina's "Dirty War," 383
Arizona focus group study, 329-337
Arizona study of teenagers' prenatal
    care utilization, 239-242
Arkansas study of recidivism. *See*
    Reentry study
Arrest and loss of personal freedom,
    349-350
Art
    defined, 1
    prisoner, 2-4
    purchasing of, 3-4
Ascione, Wendy C., 24, 271
Assaults of female offenders, 71
Assessment prison placement, 68-69
Assigned criminal defense counsel, 349
Atlanta waste management hiring
    practices, 103
Attorneys assigned by the court, 349
Auburn New York State Prison model,
    63
Auden, W. H., 5
Autonomy of women and
    AFDC/TANF policies, 13

421

Order a copy of this book with this form or online at:
http://www.haworthpressinc.com/store/product.asp?sku=4622

WOMEN AT THE MARGINS
Neglect, Punishment, and Resistance

_____ in hardbound at $69.95 (ISBN: 1-56023-971-9)

_____ in softbound at $34.95 (ISBN: 1-56023-972-7)

COST OF BOOKS_____

OUTSIDE USA/CANADA/
MEXICO: ADD 20%____

POSTAGE & HANDLING_____
(US: $4.00 for first book & $1.50
for each additional book)
Outside US: $5.00 for first book
& $2.00 for each additional book)

SUBTOTAL_____

in Canada: add 7% GST____

STATE TAX____
(NY, OH & MIN residents, please
add appropriate local sales tax)

FINAL TOTAL____
(If paying in Canadian funds,
convert using the current
exchange rate, UNESCO
coupons welcome.)

❏ **BILL ME LATER:** ($5 service charge will be added)
(Bill-me option is good on US/Canada/Mexico orders only;
not good to jobbers, wholesalers, or subscription agencies.)

❏ Check here if billing address is different from
shipping address and attach purchase order and
billing address information.

Signature_____

❏ **PAYMENT ENCLOSED: $_____**

❏ **PLEASE CHARGE TO MY CREDIT CARD.**

❏ Visa ❏ MasterCard ❏ AmEx ❏ Discover
❏ Diner's Club ❏ Eurocard ❏ JCB

Account # _____

Exp. Date_____

Signature_____

Prices in US dollars and subject to change without notice.

NAME_____

INSTITUTION_____

ADDRESS_____

CITY_____

STATE/ZIP_____

COUNTRY_____ COUNTY (NY residents only)_____

TEL_____ FAX_____

E-MAIL_____

May we use your e-mail address for confirmations and other types of information? ❏ Yes ❏ No
We appreciate receiving your e-mail address and fax number. Haworth would like to e-mail or fax special
discount offers to you, as a preferred customer. **We will never share, rent, or exchange your e-mail address
or fax number.** We regard such actions as an invasion of your privacy.

Order From Your Local Bookstore or Directly From
The Haworth Press, Inc.
10 Alice Street, Binghamton, New York 13904-1580 • USA
TELEPHONE: 1-800-HAWORTH (1-800-429-6784) / Outside US/Canada: (607) 722-5857
FAX: 1-800-895-0582 / Outside US/Canada: (607) 722-6362
E-mail: getinfo@haworthpressinc.com
PLEASE PHOTOCOPY THIS FORM FOR YOUR PERSONAL USE.
www.HaworthPress.com

BOF02